No Peace *for the*
Wicked

No Peace *for the*
Wicked

Northern Protestant Soldiers and the American Civil War

David Rolfs

THE UNIVERSITY OF TENNESSEE PRESS • KNOXVILLE

Copyright © 2009 by The University of Tennessee Press / Knoxville.
All Rights Reserved. Manufactured in the United States of America.
First Edition.

The paper in this book meets the requirements of American National
Standards Institute / National Information Standards Organization
specification Z39.48-1992 (Permanence of Paper). It contains 30 percent
post-consumer waste and is certified by the Forest Stewardship Council.

Library of Congress Cataloging-in-Publication Data

Rolfs, David.
No peace for the wicked: northern Protestant soldiers and the American
Civil War / David Rolfs. — 1st ed.
    p. cm.
Includes bibliographical references and index.
ISBN-13: 978-1-57233-662-9 (hardcover: alk. paper)
ISBN-10: 1-57233-662-5 (hardcover: alk. paper)
1. United States—History—Civil War, 1861–1865—Religious aspects.
2. United States—History—Civil War, 1861–1865—Social aspects.
3. United States. Army—Religious life—History—19th century.
4. Soldiers—Religious life—United States—History—19th century.
5. Protestants—United States—History—19th century.
I. Title.
E635.R645 2009
973.7'1—dc22   2008039665

For Kathleen, Joshua and Anna,
and all the brave soldiers who rallied around the Union Flag

Contents

Acknowledgments

BEHIND EVERY WORK of a man is the great woman who inspired and supported him unconditionally. Thank you, Kathleen. This manuscript could never have been completed without the sacrificial support and encouragement of my extended family. I am particularly indebted to James P. Jones, Steven E. Woodworth, and Mark Noll for their warm friendship and special encouragement with this project, and to the remarkable community of Civil War scholars whose work continues to both inspire and humble me.

Successful projects require many advisers, and several other individuals provided me with invaluable assistance. Sally Hadden offered excellent editorial advice on an early draft of the manuscript and helped me refine some of my initial arguments. I also thank Valerie Conner, Peter Garretson, Graham Kinloch, and John Kelsay for their important insights and gracious editorial feedback. The unsung heroes of this project are the numerous manuscript assistants who helped me with my survey of all those Civil War letters. Special thanks are extended to Cheryl Schnerring, the manuscripts librarian of the Abraham Lincoln Presidential Library; Alan Aimone, the reference librarian at the U.S. Military Academy; and Eric Mundell, the director of reference services at the Indiana Historical Society. I would also like to express my appreciation to the remarkable and hard-working archival staffs at Emory's Robert W. Woodruff Library and the Wisconsin State Historical Society.

One of the guiding lights of this project has been Scot Danforth, the director of the University of Tennessee Press. I will always be grateful to Scot for recognizing the potential value of this project and helping to bring it to fruition. Finally, special thanks to University of Tennessee Press manuscript editor Gene Adair, freelance copyeditor Karin Kaufman, and the rest of the press's production staff for all their helpful advice and suggestions with the finished manuscript. This book is as much a testimony to their labor as to mine, but if there are any remaining flaws, they are solely of my making.

A Note on Permissions

PORTIONS OF CHAPTERS 1 and 9 were previously published in the entry "Chaplains," from *Gale Library of Daily Life—Slavery in America*, copyright 2007 by Gale, a part of Cengage Learning, Inc. Reproduced by permission. www.cengage.com/permissions.

Chapter 9 was published, in somewhat different form, under the title "No Nearer Heaven Now but Rather Farther Off" in *View from the Ground: Experiences of Civil War Soldiers*, edited by Aaron Sheehan-Dean, copyright 2007 by the University Press of Kentucky. Reproduced by permission.

I also gratefully acknowledge permission from the University of South Carolina Press to quote excerpts from various Civil War–era sermons, particularly James D. Liggett's "Our National Reverses," published in *"God Ordained This War": Sermons on the Sectional Crisis, 1830–1865*, edited by David B. Chesebrough (1991). Thanks go as well to the University Press of Kansas for granting permission to quote from soldiers' writings published in *While God Is Marching On: The Religious World of Civil War Soldiers* by Steven E. Woodworth (2001).

Finally, for permission to print excerpts from the archived letters of various soldiers, I wish to credit the Manuscript, Archives, and Rare Book Library at Emory University and the Bentley Historical Library at the University of Michigan.

Introduction

Religion, understood in its broadest context as a culture and community of faith, was found everywhere the war was found—in the armies and the hospitals; on the farms and plantations and in the households; in the minds and souls of men and women, white and black. In short, wherever our contributors chose to look, the findings were substantial. God was truly alive and very much at the center of this nation's defining moment.

> Randall M. Miller, Harry S. Stout, and Charles Reagan Wilson, "Introduction," *Religion and the American Civil War*

There is no peace, saith the LORD, unto the wicked.

> Isaiah 48:22

IN THE SPRING of 1861 tens of thousands of young men in the North and South donned uniforms and marched off to consummate their manhood in the fires of war. For many, this was the first time they would be traveling more than a few miles from their homes or spending extended time away from their families. Few ever dreamt the war would be so terrible, that it would last as long as it did, or that so many of them would fail to come back. In most cultures the late teen years represent a symbolic passage from youth to manhood, but for the young recruits of 1861, this celebration was marred by a sudden and catastrophic loss of innocence that forced many of them to reexamine the core beliefs of their simple, childhood faith.

When confronted with the horrors of a bloody civil war that completely divided their nation, families, and churches, oddly enough, most Northern religious soldiers had little trouble rationalizing the wartime violence. Socialized in a culture that embraced a strict code of absolute values and a literal, commonsense interpretation of the Bible, they sincerely believed the Union had become the latest vehicle for advancing God's kingdom on earth. Well acquainted with the consequences of disobedience spelled out in the Old Testament stories of the prophets and patriarchs, they believed any communal evils corrupting their country's holy experiment had to be immediately and mercilessly uprooted before they provoked a righteous God's terrible judgment.

During the traumatic events of 1860–61, Northern Christians naturally turned to their religious worldview to help them define the meaning of Southern secession and the attack on Fort Sumter. Following the lead of their pastors, most Northern Christians generally associated Southern secession with Satan's original rebellion against God. Just as Satan had once mobilized an army of fallen angels to overthrow God's heavenly kingdom, the forces of evil were now using secession and civil war to attack God's chosen instrument for spreading freedom and Christianity to the rest of the world.

Given this understanding, Northern Christians' duty was clear. They were to enlist in a holy war to save their Christian government from a wicked rebellion. As they enlisted by the thousands in 1861 and 1862, few believers had any doubts about the morality of their cause or the war's ultimate outcome. Since their crusade to save an ordained Union was surely God's fight, he would bless their side with victory and reward the faithful for their sacrifice.

Only a small minority of religious soldiers had difficulty reconciling their wartime experiences with their faith. In most cases, soldiers resolved this wartime contradiction by abandoning or temporarily ignoring the religious principles that proved morally troublesome. Although such "backsliding" was hardly considered orthodox behavior, it was an understandable psychological response to the wartime stresses. One of the most common moral compromises revolved around the Christian doctrine of loving and forgiving one's enemies. Given the terrible passions stirred up by a bloody civil war, it proved extraordinarily difficult for some believers to uphold these Christian virtues.

Other Christians who were morally troubled by their wartime duties, however, chose to retain their prewar beliefs, even as they felt increasingly convicted by them. If anything, this apparent moral contradiction between faith and military duty became more pronounced as the fighting continued and intensified, and both sides increasingly resorted to the harsher measures of total warfare. In some cases, hardened Christian veterans who had never previously wavered in their duties or faith complained that the increasing scale, frequency, and brutality of the fighting in 1863–64 made the killing seem more and more like murder. Tormented by their consciences and the thought that they might be just as guilty of violating God's law as their fallen enemies, a few distraught soldiers wondered if they would ever escape the dreadful wartime judgment.

In the fall of 1864, after losing most of the men in his unit and his favorite brother in the fighting, a veteran Yankee artilleryman named Will tried to articulate his own feelings about God's divine judgments in a letter to Kitty—a young Wisconsin girl with whom he was corresponding. Responding to a recent letter in which Kitty had laid out her own Christian convictions, Will explained that while he too was a Christian, he had a difficult time accepting the concept of an eternal punishment. This may have been because he knew from personal experience just how terrible and inescapable God's temporal punishments could be. Paraphrasing a few lines from an old evangelical tract titled *Come to Jesus. No. 110* by Newman Hall, Will wrote:

> I do believe as God has appointed a heaven of glory for all who
> do right, he has also a punishment for those who do wrong,
> but I do not think that punishment can be eternal. What
> punishment can be worse than a guilty conscience? 'God Saith'
> There is no peace for the wicked, 'a guilty conscience will dart
> its sting.' We may try all the pleasures of the world in turn; but
> we cannot be happy. We may plunge deeper and deeper in to
> the wildest excitements but we cannot drown that conscience.
> I cannot write a cheerful letter today, but I will not cease to
> remember my friends.[1]

Perhaps tormented at having survived when seemingly better men had died, or because he felt as though he had somehow failed his God or friends, Will could not imagine Providence imposing a worse punishment than a guilty conscience. Either ignoring or only partially heeding the subheadings in Hall's tract, "Hell Awaits You, Come to be Saved" and "For Peace of Conscience, Come," Will apparently embraced the prophet Isaiah's admonition that in this life there could be "no peace for the wicked." Even if he somehow managed to survive the war, without Christ's pardon Will would never escape his guilty conscience.[2]

"No peace for the wicked" provides an excellent motif for a book examining how religious soldiers justified their initial enlistment and sustained their commitment to Northern victory in the Civil War. This seemingly unambiguous phrase actually encompassed a multitude of meanings for the religious soldier. In its most elemental sense, it referred to the traditional Christian understanding that fallen human beings could never enjoy true peace until they acknowledged their evil nature and submitted to their Creator's will. No one could ever fully satisfy the requirements of a perfect God's law, but believers could still escape the consequences of sin and death by confessing their sins and embracing Christ's atoning sacrifice for them on the cross.

Beyond the Christian's duty to acknowledge his depraved nature and need of a Savior, "no peace for the wicked" also became the battle cry of the Northern Church as it rallied believers around a "just" war to save the world's greatest Christian republic from destruction at the hands of an evil slave empire.[3] God sometimes used evil men and nations to discipline his flock, but the wicked were predestined for destruction and God was now calling faithful Northern Christians to serve as the instruments of His judgment.

Other Northern believers thought their churches and government were just as guilty as those of the South. The North's government and mainline churches had repeatedly compromised with the slave power to preserve national peace and prosperity. Early Southern victories and horrendous Northern casualties were stark reminders of the North's failure to repent of its own prewar sins. For judgment always began with the family of God.[4] Since there "was no peace for the wicked," victory would continue to elude the North until it sincerely repented and made proper amends for its prewar compromises with slavery.

A minority of Christian soldiers experienced a final, terrible meaning of this phrase when they began to entertain serious doubts about the morality of their military service. A growing realization that their combat duties seemed to contradict the basic tenets of their faith prompted many religious soldiers to abandon beliefs they found morally trouble-some. Some, however, refused to discard either the values that pricked their conscience or the duty they felt they owed their country and comrades. Believers who continued to fight despite a growing conviction they were violating God's law knew, perhaps better than anyone else, that there could be "no peace for the wicked."

In his 1998 afterword to *Religion and the Civil War,* James M. McPherson noted that while there have been many excellent histories focusing on the religious beliefs of gener-als and prominent Northern clergymen, "the ways in which ordinary northerners and southerners, inside and outside the army, managed to rationalize the killing is a subject in search of a historian."[5] McPherson himself had already provided some tentative answers to that question a year earlier in his book *For Cause and Comrades.* After poring through thousands of Northern soldiers' letters, McPherson concluded that while their sense of duty and honor motivated them to enlist, it was their belief in the North's republican cause, strong religious faith, and commitment to their comrades that sustained them on the war's battlefields. In a chapter dedicated to religion's role in motivating Union soldiers, McPherson briefly discussed how Christian concepts such as predestinarianism, Arminianism, heaven, and just warfare comforted religious soldiers and helped them courageously perform their duties. But given the scope of *For Cause and Comrades,* McPherson simply did not have the time or space to examine the rich background and diversity of these soldiers' Reformed Protestant beliefs or all the ways they used their faith to interpret and justify their wartime experiences.

Another great book examining how Civil War soldiers managed to sustain their com-mitment to the cause, even after they realized the enormous sacrifices that would be required to uphold it, is Earl J. Hess's *Union Soldier in Battle.* Hess's primary focus, how-ever, is how Union soldiers mastered the physical challenges and horrors of Civil War combat. Although he does briefly discuss how the soldiers' faith inspired them to enlist and helped them justify the killing, he only discusses their religious justifications in passing.[6]

Perhaps the most important book to be published about religion and the Civil War in the last few years, and one that somewhat overlaps my own study, is Steven E. Woodworth's *While God Is Marching On.* Woodworth's book is the most comprehensive picture of Christian soldiers' religious beliefs, experiences, and ultimate influence in the Civil War. Although Woodworth also discusses some of the motives that inspired religious soldiers to enlist and continue fighting, his primary focus is to provide a general history of the Civil War armies' religious life and demonstrate the vital role religion played in sustaining those armies' war efforts.[7]

Woodworth's book provided a much better understanding of the religious world Civil War soldiers inhabited, but it was more a general compilation of all the common soldiers' religious experiences in the Civil War armies. He discussed the soldiers' religious beliefs and practices, the work of the chaplains, and the major wartime revivals that swept both armies, but he failed to provide a comprehensive analysis of the Northern soldiers' religious worldview or the various ways they used their faith to justify and sustain their military duties. Other scholars have noted that his book oversimplified the antebellum period's complex religious setting. Finally, and perhaps most seriously, Woodworth's portrait of the religious soldier's experiences seems too rosy and monolithic. For example, after reading hundreds of collections of soldiers' letters, I discovered a number of examples where apparently devout Christian soldiers experienced serious spiritual doubts or faith crises after prolonged periods of combat. Although Woodworth examined many of the same sources, he apparently failed to find any examples of religious soldiers experiencing similar moral conflicts during the war. But if they occurred, these more negative religious experiences should certainly be included to provide readers with a more complete picture of Christian soldiers' experience. In spite of these shortcomings, however, Woodworth's book remains to date the best overall history of the Civil War armies' religious life.

No Peace for the Wicked seeks to build on Woodworth's successful framework by providing a more detailed and nuanced picture of the antebellum religious setting and worldview that shaped Northern Christians' beliefs and how they used those beliefs to justify, interpret, and sustain their wartime participation. It highlights the important roles religion played in the Civil War that until recently were overlooked by most historians and examines the unique origins, historic development, and theology of the sectional churches.

The religious background of the Northern churches and clergy excerpts were included because they played such a crucial role in shaping the soldiers' beliefs and subsequent wartime justifications. I thought it would also be difficult, if not impossible, for modern readers to understand the soldiers' profoundly different religious perspectives without thoroughly grounding them in antebellum America's predominantly Protestant religious worldview. The rest of the book is devoted to my principal subject, which is furthering our understanding of the various ways Northern Christians used their religious worldview to justify and provide meaning to their wartime enlistment and experiences. The last chapters examine what happened when those religious justifications sometimes temporarily broke down and what lessons, if any, can be drawn from this study concerning the relationship between religious revivalism and warfare.

The first and most significant historiographic obstacle confronting my project was determining how I would arrive at my sample of "religious soldiers." What, for the purposes of my book, would constitute a "Christian soldier"? I initially considered using church membership lists but later abandoned that formula when I discovered hundreds of thousands of antebellum Christians never formally joined their churches because of the strict membership requirements. Relying solely on church membership lists would have excluded both regular churchgoers who were not members and the thousands of Union soldiers who converted to Christianity during the 1863–65 revivals. Given the United States' dominant nineteenth-century Protestant culture, it was also extremely difficult—if not impossible—to distinguish "cultural Christians" who were merely attending church out of habit or parroting the popular religious expressions of that day from the "true believers" who frequently used Christian beliefs and doctrines to justify and interpret their wartime experiences.

In the end, I gave up any hopes of "scientifically" classifying each soldier's level of religious commitment and instead employed a more subjective formula for identifying the more "religious soldiers" who frequently invoked Christian beliefs and themes when discussing their motives for fighting or interpreting their wartime experiences.[8] In most cases if a soldier used significant religious language, ideas, or symbols to define, justify, or interpret some wartime experience on at least two or more occasions, he qualified as a religious soldier for my purposes.[9] This method proved extremely labor-intensive, as it involved carefully reading through the bulk of each soldier's wartime correspondence in search of such religious statements. While there was probably more subjectivity and potential for error involved in this approach, in the end it netted additional extracts that might otherwise have been missed and increased the likelihood that the compiled excerpts did in fact come from religious or, in some cases, deeply religious soldiers.[10]

An analysis of Protestant membership statistics reveals that Northern Christians constituted a small but significant percentage of the Union armies. According to the 1855 census, out of a total U.S. population of twenty-seven million people, four million, or approximately 15 percent, of the population were Protestant Church *members*.[11] This means that based on conservative estimates, at least 10–15 percent of the Union armies' original volunteers were Protestant church members or seriously committed to their Christian faith.[12]

If one replaces the term "church members" with a more modern definition of "Christian believers," however, the resulting number would almost certainly be higher than the official membership rolls reveal. It might also be more accurate since this was an age when many Christians believed they needed additional spiritual preparation before they could formally commit themselves to a particular church or were simply reluctant to endure the demanding clerical interviews often required to join a particular denomination. For example, several church historians have estimated that 20–30 percent of antebellum Americans attended weekly religious services without formally joining a church for a variety of personal reasons.[13] A more liberal estimate of Christian believers would include an appropriate fraction of these four to six million informal Northern Christians as well as the new members from 1855–61 and the converts of the 1858 "Businessman's Revival." With these additional inputs, the percentage of Christian believers initially serving in the Union armies could conceivably have been as high as 20–25 percent.[14]

To ensure these observations and conclusions reflect the religious understandings of the common soldier and not just the beliefs of high-ranking elites, the vast majority of the primary excerpts used in this study were drawn from Union enlisted men or company officers. The letters and sermons cited in this study represent only a tiny fraction of the available source material, but given their common themes, they are probably fairly representative of popular Northern Protestant religious sentiment during the war. For purposes of simplification, this study mainly addresses the wartime experiences of white Reformed Protestant soldiers. Only a handful of collections from Catholic soldiers were examined, and the book only includes excerpts from one self-identified Catholic soldier, Peter Welsh, to illustrate that in some cases Catholic soldiers' justifications and rationalizations mirrored those of their Protestant comrades.

Readers will note that while most historians traditionally shy away from or deliberately exclude overt religious expressions in their work, given my purposes I decided to pursue an opposite approach with this study. Considering the intensity of most antebellum Protestants' faith and their extensive grounding in the Scriptures, I decided that whenever soldiers seemed to allude, either directly or indirectly, to a particular verse or passage I would reference it in the text or citations.[15] I took this unusual step because antebellum Protestants attached such vital importance to these passages. Reading them in their entirety, in a similar literal, commonsense manner, can help us better understand both the meanings they ascribed to them and the various ways they used them to interpret their wartime experiences.[16] Given their importance to the soldiers, I suspect any religious history that ignored these sources would be as flawed as a history of the founding fathers that ignored the literary influences of the Enlightenment.[17]

The ultimate goal of this project has been to resurrect, as accurately as possible, the forgotten voice of the Christian soldier and the sincere religious ideals that inspired his wartime sacrifices. Lest my own thoughts and beliefs unduly influence what follows, wherever possible I have tried to incorporate the soldiers' own words directly into the text so they can share their own understanding of these momentous wartime events.

Chapter 1

THE ROLE OF RELIGION IN THE AMERICAN CIVIL WAR

> Because the American Civil War was not a war of religion, historians have tended to overlook the degree to which it was a religious war.
>
> James M. McPherson, "Afterword," *Religion and the American Civil War*

> For they would not walk in his ways, neither were they obedient unto his law. Therefore he hath poured upon him the fury of his anger.
>
> Isaiah 42:24–25

NEARLY A MONTH after the Battle of Shiloh, Pvt. Thomas Miller still had not come to terms with the traumatic events he experienced on that bloody Tennessee field. Miller had seen some of his best friends shot down like animals and nearly been killed himself. But as Miller later told a family friend back in Illinois, he realized he could not "murmur or complain at all this for a Soldiers duties and Ententions are to kill or get killed. for he that taketh up the Soward Shall perish by the Sword." As a Reformed Protestant who interpreted the Scriptures literally, Miller apparently concluded Christ's admonition to Peter in the Garden of Gethsemane that all "that take the sword shall perish with the sword" meant that it must somehow be God's will for these soldiers to die in battle. Oddly enough, this passage somehow comforted him because it provided a spiritual justification for his friends' deaths or meaning to what otherwise might have been a senseless wartime tragedy. For the greatest fear confronting many religious soldiers was not so much death or disfigurement on the war's battlefields as a life or death devoid of meaning. They wanted to ensure that the manner in which they lived and died brought honor, not shame, to their God, cause, and families. More than anything else, the religious soldier needed to believe that by fighting he was advancing some higher purpose, and that his family, friends, and community would remember his wartime sacrifices.[1]

In any event, after the war, Christ's admonition to Peter in the garden must have seemed eerily prophetic to the hundreds of Northern families who lost fathers, brothers, or sons in the conflict. Of the estimated 2.1 million soldiers who served in the Union armies, more than 360,000 would die over the course of the conflict, with approximately a third perishing from wounds suffered on the battlefield. Three out of every ten Union soldiers either died or were seriously wounded in the war. As a proportion of its population, the South suffered even more grievously, losing more than a quarter of a million of its soldiers to disease and battlefield wounds, or one out of every four soldiers who fought for the Confederacy.[2] This enormous human sacrifice, offered up for what each side believed was the noblest of causes, made the Civil War America's greatest national tragedy. Given the war's tremendous impact on the nation's cultural, economic, and political institutions, over the years American historians have naturally sought to develop a better understanding of the conflict and its ultimate meaning.

Reexamining the Role of Religion in the American Civil War

Although past historiographic interpretations of the war's causes and consequences have all reflected important truths, with the sectional conflict over slavery the dominant theme, until recently most historians have overlooked the religious life of the Civil War armies and the common Christian soldier. For example, much of what we know about the great Confederate revivals that took place in late 1862 and 1863 still comes from William W. Bennett's *Narrative of the Great Revival Which Prevailed in the Southern Armies During the Late Civil War* and J. William Jones's *Christ in the Camp*, both of which were published shortly after the war. In 1987, Gardiner H. Shattuck Jr. published *A Shield and Hiding Place* and provided his profession with its first serious study of the religious life of the Civil War armies. Primarily concerned with the history of the Northern and Southern chaplaincies, benevolent organizations, and wartime revivals, the book does not provide much insight into the religious world of the common soldier. Nonetheless, it was a ground-breaking book about the Union and Confederate armies' religious life, and inexplicably, most serious Civil War scholars paid little attention to it.

Increasingly concerned with this persistent historical vacuum, in 1994 a small group of distinguished historians organized the Symposium on Religion and the Civil War at Louisville's Presbyterian Theological Seminary to discuss their profession's failure to develop an adequate religious historiography of the war. Instead of castigating historians for their past failures, the participants of the symposium decided it would be more helpful to develop strategies for promoting such study in the future and laid the foundation for such an effort by preparing a series of provocative essays to illustrate the war's diverse religious dimensions. Subsequently published in Randall Miller, Harry Stout, and Charles

Wilson's *Religion and the American Civil War,* these essays focused on a wide variety of religious topics, from broad overviews of the role of religion in the war to the impact a literal nineteenth-century biblical hermeneutics had on the national debate over slavery. The book's most important contribution, however, was its clarion call to the profession that since religious faith was vitally important to the men who fought in the Civil War, historians needed to reconsider the various ways soldiers' religious beliefs may have impacted the war. Recent scholarship in the field suggests their message did not go unheeded.[3]

In discussing the influence of religion in the American Civil War, historian Edward L. Ayers noted, "Religion lay at the heart of who Americans were even as they killed one another in unthinkable numbers."[4] If religious faith occupied such a seminal place in antebellum Americans' lives, why does it receive such marginal treatment in most of the seminal histories of the war? Indeed, when it comes to the religious history of the war, the silence in most history textbooks has been deafening.

Throughout the twentieth century a more secular profession grounded in the physical realities of this world has concentrated on the economic competition between an agrarian South and industrial North, the political miscalculations that precipitated the conflict, or both sides' prewar balance sheets—all of which are crucial to our understanding of the Civil War. But the war also had a vital religious dimension, which must be considered to gain a more balanced perspective of the central ideas, people, and social movements that shaped the war. Modern scholars need to ensure their own modernist, materialist presuppositions do not prevent them from exploring the influence of the antebellum generation's religious values. For example, when considering slavery's role in the war, most twentieth-century historians have tended to focus on either the antebellum political conspiracies that fueled sectional conflict or the prewar economics of the Southern institution—especially when juxtaposed against a rising Northern industrial juggernaut. Few, however, have systematically explored how the religious fervor and moral certainties produced by the Second Great Awakening may have heightened Northern Protestants' awareness of their Southern neighbors' sins and traditional Yankee fears of communal judgment should they continue to "tolerate" such sin in their midst. In short, religious belief and motivation have often been overlooked. But as James M. McPherson explained in the afterword to *Religion and the Civil War,* that is precisely the story which must now be told: "Religion was central to the meaning of the Civil War, as the generation that experienced the war tried to understand it. Religion should also be central to our efforts to recover that meaning."[5] Perhaps the best place to begin our journey is by briefly reviewing some of the critical roles religion played in the Northern war effort.

The God of Battles and the True Christian Republic

Although few modern textbooks mention it, the same Reformed Protestant religion that figured so prominently in antebellum U.S. history also played a vital role in the American Civil War. This powerful, and increasingly evangelical, faith had a major influence on each side's interpretation of the conflict and helped both inspire and sustain their respective war efforts. When war finally broke out in 1861, each side also shared a similar Reformed

Protestant understanding of God's providential role in human history. According to this religious perspective, human beings served a sovereign and immanent God who regularly intervened in the world to ensure the proper enfolding of his will. Nothing could happen apart from his will. Thus when the lower South seceded from the Union, evangelicals in both sections could only conclude that God had ordained the sectional crisis. The only real remaining question was how the Christian peoples of the North and South should best resolve this political impasse? In the United States such national conflicts had traditionally been resolved by Congress or federal courts, but with secession this was no longer possible, and the problem was further compounded by each side's refusal to accept the legitimacy of the opposing government.

Since there was no longer any nationally recognized government that could adjudicate the sectional conflict, both sides decided to invoke the political legacy of their revolutionary forefathers and appeal directly to the God of battles to judge between them. In his *Second Treatise on Government,* John Locke had located the biblical precedent for such martial appeals in the Old Testament story of Jephthah. According to Locke, when no earthly court could resolve the dispute between the Hebrews and the Ammonites, Jephthah appealed to heaven: "'The Lord the Judge,' says he, 'be judge this day between the children of Israel and the children of Ammon' (Judges xi. 27), and then prosecuting and relying on this appeal he leads out his army to battle. . . . Where there is no judge on earth, the appeal lies to God in heaven."[6]

Heavily influenced by Locke's writing, America's founding fathers also had "appealed to the Supreme Judge of the world" when they felt their rights were being violated by the British government and sought "the protection of Divine Providence" in their subsequent military struggle against England. Despite the intervening years, this tradition would have made perfect sense to a generation that believed in a sovereign and just God who actively intervened in human affairs. So when war came, Jefferson Davis proclaimed that Southerners too should recognize their complete "dependence on God . . . [and] supplicate his merciful protection." With the Union dissolved, many on both sides appealed to the God of battles for justice in their sectional dispute, firmly convinced that an immanent God would ensure the more righteous side won.[7]

Implicit in this appeal to heaven, however, was the belief that only one side was the true Christian republic worthy of divine assistance. Earlier in U.S. history, when Americans had waged war against Indians and Catholics, it had been relatively simple for Yankees to assert the moral superiority of their Protestant faith over their enemies' so-called false religions, but the Civil War was different in that it was a familial conflict between two predominantly Reformed Protestant peoples. Each side claimed that it was the true Christian republic advancing God's will and that its sectional opponents were spiritual counterfeits who were compromising both Americans' republican liberties and their sacred millennial mission. But as Abraham Lincoln prudently observed after the second Union defeat at Bull Run, "In great contests each party claims to act in accordance with the will of God. Both *may* be, and one *must* be wrong. God can not be *for,* and *against* the same thing at the same time."[8] In a world governed by moral absolutes, slavery and secession were either right or wrong, and thus only one sectional government could truly represent the cause of Christ. So now, as both sections mobilized their human and material resources for war in 1861, they also entered into a fierce spiritual contest to determine which side was the true Christian nation.

Since both parties shared a similar Reformed Protestant religious background, they often employed the same religious symbols and rituals to prove their alleged spiritual superiority. For example, both governments proclaimed official days of thanksgiving and days of fasting and prayer to demonstrate their side's complete dependence on God and humble acknowledgment that he alone was responsible for their armies' victories and defeats. As Harry S. Stout and Christopher Grasso have explained, since "through[out] all of American history to 1860, public fasts were quintessentially northern and 'Puritan.'" This required a little sleight of hand on the part of the Confederacy. In effect, Davis and the Southern clergy appropriated the Yankee fast and made it their own. After equipping his side with this ecclesiastical weapon, Davis used it with a vengeance. If Lincoln's government proclaimed three national fast days during the war, Davis would trump him by declaring ten, and if the language Southerners "used sounded remarkably like the Puritans of old, that fact was never announced. Confederate clergymen spoke as if theirs were the first truly legitimate, God-honoring political fast and thanksgiving days spoken in America since the Revolution."[9] Other symbolic steps Southerners took to prove the "Christian" nature of their cause included drafting a new Confederate constitution that invoked "the favor and guidance of Almighty God" and adopting a new national motto for the Southern republic: *Deo vindice,* or "God will avenge."

Not to be outdone, in 1864 Northern clergy from nearly every major Protestant denomination proposed an amendment to the Preamble of the U.S. Constitution in which "We the People of the United States" would now acknowledge "Almighty God as the source of all authority and power in civil government, the Lord Jesus Christ as the Ruler among nations, [and] his revealed will as the supreme law of the land, in order to constitute a Christian government." While this quasi-theocratic constitutional amendment failed to gain enough popular support to become law, the Northern government found other ways to express the Christian nature of its cause throughout the war. To remind the nation's citizen-soldiers they were fighting for a Christian republic, the U.S. government began minting coins stamped with the phrase "In God We Trust." After the Union's triumphs at Gettysburg and Vicksburg in the summer of 1863, Lincoln also finally granted official government recognition to the public days of thanksgiving that were already being celebrated in many Northern states. In the fall of 1863, a presidential proclamation appeared in Northern newspapers announcing that the last Thursday of November would be officially designated as a national holiday "of Thanksgiving and praise to our beneficent Father who dwelleth in the Heavens . . . for such singular deliverances and blessings."[10]

Ministry to the Soldiers

Although the Confederate government, and its politicians and soldiers, often engaged in more symbolic, public demonstrations of religious faith than their Yankee counterparts, the Federal government did a far better job of meeting its soldiers' spiritual and physical needs. At the beginning of the war, Northern and Southern churches took an active interest in the spiritual welfare of their soldiers, but the North also organized a new military chaplaincy to support its soldiers in May 1861. President Lincoln took a personal interest in the project, convinced that an effective chaplaincy would not only address Union soldiers' religious needs but also help raise Northern morale by helping volunteers adjust to army life and become better integrated into their units. In General Orders Nos. 15 and 16, the president ordered the colonels of all regular and volunteer regiments to appoint regimental chaplains, whose principal duties would include maintaining troop morale and issuing regular reports on the "moral and religious condition" of their units. In addition to conducting their regular religious duties, Northern chaplains also helped soldiers write letters home, served as regimental postmasters and unit librarians, assisted with work and food details, and cared for wounded soldiers and freedmen. When such work was done well, it had a positive impact on army morale, but more often than not, this was not the case.[11]

Jefferson Davis initially opposed the creation of a Southern military chaplaincy because he thought the South needed soldiers, not ministers, and because like most Southerners he believed such religious concerns were best left to the individual states and churches. Although the Richmond government later reluctantly organized a chaplaincy to placate the spiritual concerns of Southern churches, Southern chaplains received inadequate pay, few instructions concerning their duties, and little support from their government. As a result there was always a severe shortage of chaplains serving in the army, and less than half of the Confederate units would ever receive one. Lacking detailed orders concerning their military status, the few who did serve often became "fighting chaplains" and were thus far more likely to be wounded or killed in combat than their Northern counterparts.[12]

Although ambitious in its scope, even Lincoln's government-mandated chaplain program proved far less effective than other private religious outreaches to the soldiers, such as the U.S. Christian Commission. Given the Northern chaplains' failure to meet the spiritual and physical needs of the soldiers, the services of this private, para-church organization were clearly needed. When religious soldiers discussed the work of their regimental chaplains in their letters, their opinions seemed mixed. Some expressed the greatest respect for their wartime spiritual shepherds and strongly approved of their work, but the majority seemed profoundly disappointed with their chaplains' ministries. In their letters, however, almost to a man Union soldiers enthusiastically praised the work and delegates of the U.S. Christian Commission.[13] As New England soldier Wilbur Fisk explained, the soldiers preferred the Christian Commission delegates to their chaplains because the delegates seemed more committed to their ministries:

> They give their time and their services, and generally work
> hard, and work willingly. Their term is short, and they en-
> deavor to make the most of it. . . . We who receive their mini-
> strations are not asked or expected to give them anything for
> their work, but on the contrary, they distribute their gifts
> to us most liberally. Testaments . . . are given freely to any
> and all who wish to receive them, and so are religious books,
> newspapers, tracts in enormous quantities, and these gifts are
> received, read and appreciated. . . . We shall remember with

gratitude what has been done for us here, and some will have
all of eternity to be grateful.[14]

Although the vision for this benevolent, religious outreach originated with the evangelical leaders of the New York YMCA in November 1861, a host of other Northern evangelical organizations also endorsed this interdenominational missionary enterprise. The original purpose of the commission was strictly evangelistic. Aware of the "temptations" facing young soldiers in Union camps, the commission decided to send missionary volunteers, or "delegates," to what many considered was the largest and most important mission field in the world at that time: the Union armies. Although delegates initially spent most of their time and resources assisting local chaplains with their ministries, they soon discovered they could achieve much better results by directly addressing both the soldiers' physical and spiritual needs themselves. Christian Commission delegates began to deliver prodigious supplies of books, newspapers, food, and clothing directly to the troops. This evangelical strategy proved highly effective, as soldiers were far more interested in hearing the gospel from a missionary who demonstrated his genuine concern for their souls by also ministering to the physical needs of their bodies.

The U.S. government and even relatively nonreligious generals such as Ulysses S. Grant and William Tecumseh Sherman seemed to recognize the Christian Commission's positive influence on Union army morale. As Gardiner H. Shattuck related in *A Shield and Hiding Place,* in the fall of 1863, after Grant assumed command of the Union forces in the western theater, "he ordered that Commission delegates should have free and unhindered access to his troops. Since this order coincided with an intense revival among Northern soldiers at the time of the Chattanooga campaign, Grant was probably aware of the effect of the revivals in strengthening the confidence of his units, and . . . the morale of this army." As a result of this highly successful religious experiment, when Grant "became general-in-chief of all the Union forces, commission agents in every theater of the war found an almost universal reception by Federal officers and men."[15] As Northern casualties continued to mount in 1864 and Grant's bloody war of attrition in Virginia showed no signs of abating, Northern chaplains and especially private interdenominational religious organizations such as the Christian Commission helped sustain the Army of the Potomac's morale during some of the most difficult fighting of the war.[16]

Soldiers Are Christians If Anyone Is

Given the important spiritual dimensions of the sectional conflict, both sides eagerly touted their generals' and soldiers' Christian credentials. In terms of leadership, the South clearly had the advantage with many of its best commanders—Robert E. Lee, "Stonewall" Jackson, J. E. B. Stuart, D. H. Hill, and John B. Gordon, among others—all well known and respected for both their brilliant military acumen and deeply felt religious convictions. Although their Union counterparts seemed much less skilled in the arts of war, the Northern public was just as proud of its Christian generals: George B. McClellan, William Rosecrans, and Oliver O. Howard. Also men of deep faith, these generals' religious beliefs often influenced their subsequent military conduct during the war.

Shortly after taking command of the Army of the Potomac, General McClellan converted to Christianity. As an enthusiastic new convert, he immediately ordered the Army of Potomac to henceforth observe, whenever possible, a Sabbath day rest and Sunday morning religious services. Exhibiting a streak of self-righteousness often seen in zealous new converts, McClellan vowed to fight the war "upon the highest principles known to Christian civilization," and then, as a fastidious observer of the rules of war, he proceeded to castigate everyone—from his subordinates and peers to Lincoln himself—who disagreed with his narrow interpretation of the moral guidelines.

Another strict sabbatarian, Gen. William S. Rosecrans, refused to pursue Braxton Bragg's Army of Tennessee as it slipped away from the Stones River battlefield on Sunday, January 3, 1863. A devout Roman Catholic, Rosecrans could not do so in good conscience, as it would have involved issuing marching orders to his army on a Sunday.

Gen. Oliver O. Howard, as a West Point–educated veteran of the Third Seminole War and an outspoken evangelical staunchly opposed to slavery, seemed to have one foot planted in the army and the other in the church. Having seriously contemplated entering the ministry on the eve of the Civil War, Howard instead rallied around the flag and traded an arm for the Congressional Medal of Honor at the Battle of Seven Pines. His distinguished military record was subsequently tarnished by the route of his "Dutch" corps at Chancellorsville, and again at Gettysburg, but transferred to the West, Howard redeemed his military reputation while gallantly serving with Sherman's armies in the Atlanta, March to the Sea, and Carolina campaigns. A devout Congregationalist, and teetotaler who sometimes preached to his command when the services of a chaplain or minister could not be secured, Howard was popularly known as the North's "Christian Soldier."[17]

Despite their religious fastidiousness, thousands of soldiers trusted these generals implicitly, fully convinced that officers who shared their Christian faith and cause could not fail on the battlefield. This uncritical, emotional allegiance to leaders who shared their faith, however, was not always helpful. For example, when their favorite commanders were defeated in battle, soldiers often speculated that these "great strategists" had not been defeated by the enemy but had only lost because they were not adequately supported by the government and people back home. This blind allegiance to generals who shared their Christian faith, and some religious generals' refusal to take responsibility for their defeats, helps explain why some mediocre generals, such as McClellan and Rosecrans, were retained far longer than they should have been.

In any event, the war was prolonged, and as it dragged on and grew increasingly bloodier, the Northern commander in chief also increasingly turned to religion for spiritual comfort and meaning. Lincoln, who had previously rejected orthodox Christianity in favor of a more fatalistic "doctrine of necessity," claimed his religious beliefs underwent "a process of crystallization" after the death of his beloved son Willie in early 1862. Devastated by his favorite son's premature death, Lincoln sought out the spiritual counsel of his family's Presbyterian pastor, Phineas D. Gurley, who assured the president his son was not dead, but had merely passed on to heaven. Lincoln seemed vastly comforted by the thought that he might someday see his son again. Wartime events over the next few months, however, cruelly seemed to contradict Gurley's spiritual teachings about the just and merciful intentions of a sovereign God. Lincoln watched helplessly as the government's armies were first driven back from Richmond that spring and then decisively defeated again in August on the old Bull Run battlefield. In less than seven months the providential unfolding of God's will had robbed Lincoln of a son, immediate victory, and the lives of thousands of his countrymen. As news concerning the full extent of the Union catastrophe at Second Bull Run slowly filtered in, Lincoln became distraught. Completely exasperated with his administration's wartime failures and the seemingly arbitrary judgments of his Creator, the president fell into a deep depression after the battle.[18]

Over the next couple of days Lincoln must have experienced a profound spiritual and intellectual crisis as he sought to reconcile the unprecedented suffering of "an almost chosen nation" with what the church had taught him about God's beneficent attributes. Unwilling to address this grave matter with mere sentiment or emotional beliefs, as usual Lincoln systematically applied his more objective and logical legal reasoning to the problem. According to one of Lincoln's secretaries, John Hay, Lincoln secluded himself in an office and set aside an entire day to both intellectually formulate the boundaries between his presidential responsibilities to human duty and divine power, and reevaluate what God's purposes in the war might be. In a private September 2, 1862, memo titled "Meditation on the Divine Will," which was "not written to be seen of men," Lincoln shared the logical reasoning and answers that brought his troubled soul some much-needed peace. Having carefully reassessed some of his presuppositions, Lincoln reconfirmed his beliefs in the justice of the Union's cause and an immanent and transcendent God who ruled over the affairs of men. Given the superior justice of the Northern cause and God's sovereign control of wartime events, Lincoln could only conclude that for some reason God had ordained the war and wanted it to continue.[19]

Humbly acknowledging that God's purpose in the war might be something completely "different from the purpose of either party," Lincoln spent the rest of the war trying to ascertain what it might be. The progress of his quest for spiritual meaning was elegantly recorded in subsequent public declarations, such as his Gettysburg Address and 1863 Thanksgiving Proclamation, which were increasingly filled with overt religious themes and spiritual imagery. Lincoln's spiritual journey culminated in his second inaugural address. In a public address Frederick Douglass later called "a sacred effort," Lincoln eloquently articulated his own religious justification for the prolonged wartime suffering. Lincoln's profuse use of biblical names and language in the speech also suggested that some dramatic shifts had occurred in his earlier spiritual thinking.[20]

For every Christian officer in the Union army, there were a dozen or more enlisted men who shared his Christian faith. Indeed, most modern scholars acknowledge there was a pronounced intensification of Northern religiosity during the war. As in America's past wars, the entire country rallied around the flag and the cross, and given the clear and present dangers of the next battlefield, many soldiers sought religion's comforting assurance of an afterlife. In *For Cause and Comrades,* James M. McPherson observed there were few atheists in the Union trenches because the baptism of fire usually led to Christian baptisms. There were numerous examples of hardened sinners embracing Christianity as they lay mortally wounded on the battlefield or seriously ill in Northern hospitals but few of soldiers openly renouncing their faith in God. In most cases, those who were already religious became more so during the war, and thousands more embraced faith as a means of coping with the terrible carnage they witnessed on the war's battlefields. As the war continued and the fighting grew more savage, public religious rituals and confessions of faith proved vital in sustaining the will of the Christian soldier and were thus pragmatically embraced by fence sitters and grudgingly tolerated by skeptics and atheists.[21]

Even nonreligious generals sometimes admired the common soldiers' faith or publicly acknowledged that the war was fueling a spiritual awakening in the Union armies. Gen. William Tecumseh Sherman, who rarely spoke of God except when using his name in vain, publicly defended the personal integrity of his bummers: "Christian army I've got— noble fellows—God will take care of them—war improves character." While a minority of Northern clergymen feared the war was undermining soldiers' moral character, based on his own wartime experiences, Sherman was convinced that "soldiers are Christians if anyone is" and that if anything, the war was making his troops more religious. Henry Ward Beecher and many other Northern clergymen would have heartily endorsed Sherman's claim that the war was having a positive influence on Northern soldiers' religious attitudes. Many believed that the soldier's battlefield experiences would constantly remind him of his own mortality and encourage him to come to terms with his Creator. They also thought military life would help teach soldiers to be more disciplined and respectful of authority and encourage them to embrace causes that were larger than themselves. In short, instead of spiritually corrupting the soldier, army life and war would improve his Christian character.[22]

Others, however, believed this cut both ways, or that the Christian faith itself often made men better soldiers. For example, Northern evangelicals were among the most enthusiastic volunteers in the opening months of the war, and given their natural deference to authority, they were far more likely to submit to army discipline and obey their officers' orders. In *For Cause and Comrades,* James McPherson also noted that religion frequently helped soldiers perform their battlefield duties more courageously than their nonreligious counterparts. This was because the religious soldier, having already set his heart on heaven, was less likely to fear physical death on the battlefield. Finally, religious soldiers who sincerely believed that an immanent and omnipotent God was fighting on their side were more likely to make unprecedented sacrifices for that cause and retain their faith in final victory, regardless of what transpired on the battlefield.[23]

When wartime events often confirmed these presuppositions about Christian soldiers, both side's generals and politicians began supporting private religious efforts to promote wartime revivals in their armies.[24] The first major wartime revivals in the Southern camp occurred shortly after the Confederate defeats at Antietam and Perryville in 1862, but these were soon dwarfed by the larger revivals of 1863 and 1864. Although small revivals broke out periodically in the Northern armies throughout the war, the largest revivals began after the victorious 1863 summer campaigns at Gettysburg and Vicksburg and continued through the end of the war. Just like their peacetime equivalents, most of these wartime revivals took place in or around the winter season, when poor campaigning weather usually forced armies to enter their winter camps. As the war continued, these wartime revivals grew in size and intensity.[25]

Historians debate the timing and meaning of these revivals. Were the revivals that occurred in the camps of both sides in the last two and a half years of the war a response to the prolonged wartime suffering or had each side's ministry to its soldiers simply become better organized by this stage of the war? Regardless of their timing and meaning, Timothy L. Smith and Gardiner Shattuck have suggested that the original vision and evangelical nature of these army revivals originated in the "Businessman's Revival" or noonday prayer meeting revival of 1857–58. Many of the YMCA evangelical leaders who played such an instrumental role in the 1857–58 noonday prayer meeting revival also spearheaded the wartime revivals in the Northern camps. The businessman and wartime revivals shared many characteristics. They were both organized around popular inter-denominational prayer meetings, emphasized lay leadership or democratic participation in the meetings, avoided religious ritual and doctrinal controversies, and were completely focused on winning souls for Christ.[26]

In *While God Is Marching On,* Steven E. Woodworth provocatively argued that while historians have traditionally viewed the various wartime revivals that occurred in both camps as isolated, independent events, they were really a "single large revival, approximately two and a half years long, occasionally interrupted by military operations."[27] Woodworth's observation merits further reflection. Given both sides' intense desire to "prove" *they were* the genuine Christians advancing God's cause, and both armies' frequent informal communications with each other during the intervals between campaigns and battles, might not news of "spiritual revival" in the enemy's camp in the fall of 1862 and 1863 have prompted the opposing armies' spiritual leaders to initiate their own counterrevivals? After all, we are learning more and more about the intricate relationship between revivals in the camps and the soldiers' local communities. Hometown revivals often set the stage for spiritual awakenings in the camps or were themselves sparked by religious enthusiasm in the army. Was there a similar symbiotic relationship between the various wartime revivals in the opposing armies?[28]

According to Reid Mitchell, the fruits of the wartime revivals belie the popular stereotype that Southern enlisted men were somehow more spiritual than their Northern adversaries. This traditional understanding is largely based on the work of postwar Southern apologists, such as J. William Jones's bestseller *Christ in the Camp* and William W. Bennett's *Narrative of the Great Revival.* Although Southern officers *were* generally more religious than their Yankee counterparts, over the course of the revivals up to 10 percent of *both armies* may have converted to Christianity.[29]

The wartime revivals had a significant impact on the military history of the war. For example, most historians believe that the Southern revivals played a decisive role in sustaining Southern morale and prolonging Confederate resistance.[30] Long after their cause was lost, many Confederate soldiers continued to pray for a miraculous divine intervention, hoping their mass repentance, conversion, and revival might still somehow secure an eleventh-hour victory. The Northern revivals, meanwhile, apparently helped bolster the Northern armies' spiritual will to see an increasingly brutal war through to the bitter end. Beginning in the fall of 1863, a series of major revivals preceded the North's more successful 1864 and 1865 campaigns. These religious awakenings apparently both reflected and contributed to the growing élan of the Union armies.[31]

This first major Northern revival took place during the late 1863 fighting around Chattanooga. After the disastrous Union defeat at Chickamauga, the demoralized Army of the Cumberland withdrew to Chattanooga, where it soon found itself besieged by Bragg's victorious Army of Tennessee. Shortly after taking command of the Federal relief operation, Ulysses S. Grant gave the Christian Commission unprecedented authority to pursue its evangelical work in the Union camps. Within a few weeks a major revival had begun in the Army of the Cumberland. Convinced this army was still too demoralized to fight, General Grant only gave the Army of Cumberland a secondary mission in the subsequent Union campaign to lift the siege. Ordered to make a feint against the strongly held Confederate center on Missionary Ridge, Grant and Gen. George H. Thomas watched incredulously as the inspired soldiers from the Army of the Cumberland first overran the Confederate trenches at the base of the ridge and then, without any orders, proceeded to advance straight up the steep ridge, not stopping until they had captured the Confederate trenches at the crest and routed Bragg's entire army. Some of the Union army officers and officials who witnessed the attack later described this remarkable Union victory as "the miracle of Missionary Ridge," one of "the greatest miracles in military history," and a "visible interposition of God." While there were a number of factors contributing to the Army of the Cumberland's success on that day, as Gardiner Shattuck has suggested, the ongoing revival undoubtedly played a crucial role in the Union victory.[32]

Later, major revivals also swept through Sherman's army while it was encamped at Ringgold, Georgia, in the winter of 1863–64 and during its subsequent marches to the sea and through the Carolinas. As the tide of war turned increasingly against the Confederacy, the "Spirit of the Lord" began to move mightily throughout Sherman's army: "Whenever soldiers stopped for the night . . . they gathered in churches they found along the way and gave thanks for the successes they had won each day." As the revival intensified, membership in the army's formal and informal religious groups swelled: "The Christian association of one brigade in the XX Corps . . . grew from an original 50 men to more than 300, and it welcomed several hundred others as onlookers at its nightly meetings."[33]

During the brutal bloodletting in Virginia in the last year and a half of the war, Grant's army was also awash in religious revivalism. During the winter of 1863–64, the Army of the Potomac built sixty-nine chapels to meet its soldiers' growing demand for spiritual comfort and assurance. Soldiers hurriedly made their peace with God as then pinned their names and addresses to their uniforms so their families could be informed when they fell in the next attack. Each side seemed locked in a terrible spiritual contest to save their soldiers' souls in the winter camps before their bodies were destroyed on the summer battlefields. The winter of 1864–65 marked both the climax and end of the Northern revivals, as "Union forces everywhere celebrated their approaching victory with not only worldly but spiritual enthusiasm."[34]

From the beginning to the end, religion played a decisive role in the Northern war effort. When the nation was finally torn asunder, each section had aggressively competed to prove it was the true Christian country that merited God's favor. Recognizing the powerful role religion could play in mobilizing armies and sustaining their soldiers' commitment to victory, the Northern government and churches had introduced a chaplaincy and the U.S. Christian Commission to meet the physical and spiritual needs of their soldiers. When the war dragged on far longer than anyone expected, and from a human perspective all appeared lost, the wartime revivals helped renew and sustain Billy Yank's faith in final victory until the North ultimately prevailed at Appomattox. The next chapter will examine why religion was so critically important to the generation that fought the Civil War.

Chapter 2

Covenant and Revival

> Thus stands the cause between God and us, we are entered into Covenant with him for this work, we have taken out a Commission. . . . We must be knit together in this work as one man . . . always having before our eyes our Commission and Community in the work . . . . For we must consider that we shall be as a city upon a Hill, the eyes of all people are upon us.
>
> John Winthrop, "A Model of Christian Charity," 1630

> But ye *are* a chosen generation, a royal priesthood, a holy nation, a peculiar people, that ye should show forth the praises of him who hath called you out of darkness into his marvelous light.
>
> 1 Peter 2:9

TO GAIN A proper understanding of the various arguments Christian soldiers used to rationalize their wartime participation, one must first examine the antebellum religious beliefs that inspired them. The generation that fought the American Civil War was one of the most religious in American history. According to Reid Mitchell, the "mid-century North was imbued with evangelical values" and "the army it produced shared them." Phillip Shaw Paludan observed that in the Civil War such faith was "ubiquitous wherever the armies fought and camped." In both armies "there were constant religious meetings and camp revivals," and while "the extent of religiosity is hard to determine, . . . it was by no means small." Steven Woodworth, Drew Faust, and Gardiner Shattuck have also written extensively about the Northern armies' Protestant evangelical faith. But if many religious Northern soldiers were evangelical Reformed Protestants, where did they obtain this religious perspective and how did it influence the development of their community's institutions and beliefs? The answers to these questions lie in the unique origins and beliefs of the evangelical Reformed Protestant churches that socialized the North's future soldiers.[1]

Legacy of the Puritans' Covenant Theology

Although John Winthrop's original vision of a Puritan "City upon a Hill" was largely forgotten by the nineteenth century, the popular evangelical sects that arose in its wake had embraced many of the key presuppositions under girding the Puritans' "holy experiment." Antebellum evangelicals believed that they too were a chosen people, destined by God to conquer an apostate continent and redeem the world. As C. C. Goen noted, this was due to "the particular form of religion that spread most widely throughout the United States—Puritanism transformed into evangelicalism and adapted to the methods of revivalism and reformism." According to Goen, "Both sections shared a common evangelical heritage, and that was one of the strongest bonds between them until it succumbed to the controversy over slavery."[2] Over time, other religious historians have also noted the significant influence of seventeenth-century Puritanism on the evolution of evangelical Protestantism in the United States. In the early nineteenth century Philip Schaff reported "Puritan Protestantism forms properly the main basis of our North American Church." More than a century later, the intellectual historian Perry Miller agreed and persuasively argued that many of America's early political and religious ideas and institutions were deeply rooted in what he described as "modern" Calvinist, or Puritan, theology.

Samuel S. Hill Jr., however, qualified this overwhelming Puritan influence, noting that while Northern and Southern religious doctrines were both "dominantly Calvinist," the theology that ultimately shaped Northern society "was clearly an English Puritan version of Calvinism." So while the Reformed tradition influenced the religious development of both sections, there was an important distinction. Churches in the North were modeled after a New England "City upon a Hill" vision of English Puritanism, which fostered a more progressive, public, and communal society, whereas the churches in the South were initially grounded in the more traditional, private, and individualistic doctrines of the Church of England, and only later influenced by the evangelical Baptist and Methodist branches of Reformed Protestantism. These ecclesiastical differences in origin, temperament, and timing had a dramatic impact on each section's future development.[3]

John Winthrop's original vision of a godly commonweal that would first save the families of Puritan settlers and then eventually reform all of England had its origins in English Puritan covenant theology. According to Perry Miller, the Puritans introduced covenant theology to replace the mysterious, unknowable, and seemingly arbitrary God of Calvin with a more understandable and predictable God whose ways could be understood and favorably influenced by appropriate human behavior. It was based on the Old Testament idea that a person or people could voluntarily enter into a binding contract with God in which man could obtain heaven's favor and blessings as long as he faithfully submitted to God's laws and fulfilled his covenantal mission, or kept his end of the bargain. Of course, the fine print of the contract specified that a jealous God reserved the right to chastise wayward customers and, if absolutely necessary, destroy habitual offenders with long track records of delinquency and theft. By reducing God to a divine businessman, or set of understandable natural laws, the Puritans in effect gave their community an incentive for performing good works and something Calvin's religious scheme had never offered—the assurance of eternal salvation, or winning the divine lotto.[4]

The church and government covenants were two of the most important covenants under girding New England's Puritan community. The church covenant was organized by local religious leaders to save their community from eternal damnation. Its terms specified that if the elect, or God's chosen spiritual leaders, created a local church where the gospel was routinely and effectively preached, and they diligently upheld the moral integrity of their communities, then a just and merciful God would save both the elect and perhaps some of their immediate family members. The covenant of government was based on the frequently repeated Old Testament theme that God blessed nations that honored him and punished recalcitrant nations that stubbornly defied his will. The government covenant's terms stipulated that if a people faithfully submitted to the authority of their God and government, and their rulers diligently pursued justice, the nation would be blessed. But if a nation or its leaders ever became morally compromised with sin and did not swiftly confront and eradicate these evils, then the entire community would be subjected to God's terrible judgment.

Over the course of their lives, every Puritan believer was also responsible for upholding three personal covenants: their faith commitments to honor and obey God, their church, and the government. According to Perry Miller, this set of mutually reinforcing personal covenants was the cornerstone of the Puritan state. They strengthened community ties by constantly reminding believers that they lived under the authority of both God and their religious and political leaders. This meant they needed to learn how to govern both their private and public lives so they could properly fulfill their respective roles in Puritan society. This triad of covenants also reminded believers of the awful consequences of failing to submit to God's established order. Left unaddressed, one individual's rebellion against God, the church, or government could spread like a cancer, corrupting other believers and institutions until the entire community was compromised. If the people stubbornly clung to such sin, God himself would inevitably intervene with terrible judgments to purge the community of its sins and redeem his chosen people. Always mindful of the terrible consequences of such disobedience, every Puritan believer thus had a strong incentive to monitor their own behavior, as well as the conduct of their families, friends, and leaders, to ensure everyone was fulfilling their proper, God-ordained roles.[5]

Blurring of the Lines Between Church and State

The Puritans' covenant theology also had a tremendous influence on the relationship between church and state in Northern society. Given the overt religious nature of their holy experiment, in addition to fulfilling its primary roles of defending the colonists and their property, the Puritan government was expected to support the church's work by punishing evildoers and enforcing religious orthodoxy in Massachusetts Bay. Convinced that they had been chosen by God to save an apostate church back in England, the Puritans feared that any serious moral corruption in the community would breach their covenant with God, invite his wrath, and sabotage their English rescue mission. So to ward off God's judgment and ultimately accomplish their colony's central mission, the church and state had to work closely together to preserve the spiritual integrity of the city upon a hill.

Puritan politicians' understanding of the duties of their office was thus completely different from that of modern U.S. politicians. Although early government figures such as John Winthrop were expected to rule justly, they were far more concerned with upholding God's laws than winning popular approval for their administration's policies. Since any sin in the Puritan camp might provoke a communal judgment, the state took an active interest in promoting true religion by enacting compulsory church attendance laws and vigorously suppressing any perceived public immorality or spiritual challenges to the established order.

As Roger Williams and other dissenters repeatedly warned, however, this Puritan political intervention in ecclesiastical affairs often led to a blurring of the lines between church and state. For example, in addition to its compulsory church attendance laws, the Winthrop administration also required colonists to swear a religious oath to uphold the Puritan faith, allowed only church members to become "freemen" or voters, collected religious taxes to support the colony's churches, and imposed a strict code governing personal conduct, with stiff fines and humiliating public punishments meted out for dress-code violations, blasphemy, fornication, and adultery.

While historians have disagreed over time as to whether the Puritan government was a commonwealth, quasi-theocracy, or outright theocracy, one point seems clear—the proper jurisdictions of church and state were clearly not respected in Massachusetts Bay. The Puritans consciously sought to avoid the historic evils associated with Europe's church-state combinations by preventing colonial ministers from running for public office, but regardless of such safeguards, the clergy were always intervening in local political affairs. Congregational Church elders helped John Winthrop establish the first authoritarian government in the colony, and Winthrop later considered other clergymen, such as Samuel Gorton, John Cotton, and John Wheelwright, his chief political opponents. Several Puritan preachers also used their pulpits and religious writings to address current public policy concerns, promote their own political agendas, or attack their political enemies. This blatant politicization of religion foreshadowed the inappropriate commingling of church and state that would occur in the sectional conflict leading up to the Civil War.[6]

The clergy also played a prominent and inappropriately political role in the Salem witchcraft trials. When the Massachusetts Bay governor appointed a special court to try the alleged witches, local reverends enthusiastically supported a "vigorous prosecution" of the suspected witches. Cotton Mather, the most influential Puritan clergymen in New England and a widely recognized expert on witchcraft at the time, urged the court to exercise "exquisite caution" when using spectral evidence to convict the accused, but it was Mather's own scientific tracts documenting the reality of New England witchcraft that encouraged the court to believe the girls' testimony, employ spectral evidence, and later condemn the accused witches.

Having inadvertently contributed to the unfolding tragedy, to their credit the New England clergy also belatedly used their political influence to end the Salem trials. After returning from a trip abroad and learning of the trials, Cotton Mather's prestigious father, Increase Mather, urged the court to reject the use of spectral evidence. Convinced that it could easily be manipulated by a politicized court to convict the innocent, Increase Mather argued that spectral evidence ought to be discarded—even if it hurt the prosecution's case—because it would be "better that ten witches should escape, than one innocent person should be condemned." Horrified by the subsequent execution of many innocent victims, Increase Mather and a group of other prominent Congregational ministers formally asked the governor and special court to halt the executions and show leniency and restraint to the rest of the accused. The governor immediately convened a new court that ultimately acquitted the remaining 150 defendants.[7]

The Puritan clergy's strategic error of initially supporting the witchcraft trials seriously undermined their future political influence in colonial New England. But their quasi-political role in the City upon a Hill had nonetheless set an important Northern precedent for churches and clergymen to interject themselves in political affairs and influence the formulation of public policy. When the antebellum revivals once again restored America's clergy to a prominent place in society, they would reassert their political influence with a vengeance.

The Religious Goals of the Northern Churches

As Perry Miller has suggested, the Puritan's original "errand into the Wilderness" to save both themselves and, hopefully, their English kin was, at heart, a communal experiment in human salvation. Although every individual was responsible for securing his own salvation, Puritans recognized that individuals did not exist in a social vacuum but a larger human community that both influenced their behavior and was in turn shaped, either positively or negatively, by the individual's own moral choices. There was thus no such thing as "personal privacy" or "private sins" in the priesthood of Puritan believers since what modern Americans sometimes call "private sins" could conceivably set off a chain reaction of other evils that might subject the entire community to God's judgment. Because sin, in any form, posed such a serious threat to the community's present and future welfare, the Puritans believed their government should govern society "as much as possible," regulating both individual and public morality. This meant the government was constantly intervening in the religious and economic affairs of the colony. But when combined with human beings' natural tendency to focus on other people's moral shortcomings, New England's communal obsession with sin ultimately set the stage for a future conflict between the North and the South.[8]

At the turn of the nineteenth century most Northern Protestants still shared their Puritan forefathers' vision that the United States was a chosen nation and it was the church's duty to reform society. They had adapted the original mission, however, to suit their unique circumstances and purposes. Between the colonial and revolutionary periods, the mission had lost much of its original meaning. The Puritans' original purpose of creating an ideal spiritual community in the American wilderness to inspire repentance in England had been sabotaged a hundred years earlier by both the increasing prosperity and unfaithfulness of their descendants and the dramatic religious reforms introduced by Oliver Cromwell after the English Civil War. A few bits and pieces from the original covenantal framework were later resurrected to promote and sustain the patriots' revolt against England. But the rapid decline of evangelicalism in the decades leading up to the Revolution suggested that the American religious motif needed a new emphasis. Indeed, by now the Puritans' rigid covenantal frameworks and zealous self-righteousness seemed increasingly passé in America's more progressive, post-Enlightenment society.

Well aware of their churches' declining numbers and social influence in the new Republic, where new American generations seemed to share the Puritans' descendants' predilection for reaping the rewards of this world rather than those of the next, the Northern clergy shifted their focus from perfecting individual spiritual lives to promoting larger societal reforms and consolidating their Protestant religious monopoly in the United States. As Samuel Hill observed, just as Southern religion was becoming more private and individualistic, Northern religious life was "increasingly directed away from individualistic religious experience toward public responsibility and social reform." Having established Reformed Protestantism as America's dominant religion, the Northern clergy now seemed more interested in expanding their ministries to the West and fiercely defending their religious monopoly from would-be usurpers. Given America's growing numbers of Roman Catholics, Deists, and Unitarians in the 1790s, some Protestant leaders feared their forefathers' "Christian society" was in a state of serious decline. Churchmen who shared Jonathan Edwards's belief that a chosen American nation was destined to lead the rest of the world to Christ feared this growing apostasy might ruin the United States' millennial mission.[9] In this national spiritual crisis, however, few clergymen expected to receive any help from their new, more secular Republican government.

Like their Puritan predecessors, most antebellum Protestant leaders in the North believed that the church and state shared an equal responsibility to defend their society's Christian institutions, but the postwar disestablishment of state churches by the federal government and emergence of a new voluntary religious arrangement seemed to mark the end of this once intimate church-state cooperation. Deprived of their predecessors' political influence and establishment tax revenue, Northern religious leaders turned to revivalism to reenergize their flagging churches and employed new quasi-political religious organizations and movements to advance their religious and social agendas.

The Rise of Evangelical Protestantism

At the turn of the nineteenth century, many American religious leaders were deeply troubled by the state of religion in the Republic. A new generation, enamored with the rationalist writings of Thomas Paine, Voltaire, and Jean-Jacques Rousseau, seemed to be abandoning the faith of its fathers. Presbyterians and Baptists lamented this "general dereliction of religious principle and practice among our fellow-citizens" and the "melancholy and truly alarming" state of Christianity in the United States.

Looking back on his religious education at Yale during this period, Lyman Beecher recalled that his "college was in a most ungodly state. The college church was almost extinct. Most of the students were skeptical, and . . . intemperance, profanity, gambling, and licentiousness were common." Many of the powerful Congregational churches that had once ruled New England were now poorly attended and unable to provide competent ministers for new frontier parishes. The spiritual condition of the Southern Episcopal Church after the Revolutionary War was even worse, with more than half of its Virginia and Maryland parishes either bankrupt or vacant. Given the country's dismal state of religious affairs, no one—and least of all America's traditional religious elite—suspected that "the dominant theme in America from 1800 to 1860" would be a "continuing, even though intermittent, revival."[10]

Religious historians have sometimes disagreed about what exactly caused America's turn-of-the-century spiritual vacuum, but nearly all of them have concluded that evangelical revivalism filled it. A series of evangelical revivals swept through the United States in the 1800s, 1830s, and late 1850s, converting or restoring thousands of European immigrants, unchurched settlers on the western frontier, and East Coast backsliders to Christianity. Observing the initial fruits of this aggressive new expansion of the Protestant faith, in the late 1830s Alexis De Tocqueville observed that "there is no country in the world in which the Christian religion retains a greater influence over the souls of men than in America." Two decades later Philip Schaff echoed this sentiment, noting that with the possible exception of Scotland, "there are in America probably more awakened souls . . . than in any other country in the world." By the middle of the nineteenth century, European visitors—who had once been ready to write off American Protestantism—considered the United States to be the world's greatest Christian nation.[11]

An impressive array of statistics confirms this increasing nineteenth-century American preoccupation with evangelical Protestantism. At the turn of the century, there were roughly 5.3 million people living in the United States and less than 10 percent of them belonged to *any* church. By 1855, the population of the United States had expanded to 27 million, and despite the encroachments of Catholicism, Deism, Unitarianism, and Transcendentalism, more than 15 percent of them held membership in Protestant churches. While there had been more than a fivefold increase in population between 1800 and 1855, America's *Protestant sects alone* enjoyed nearly an eightfold increase in membership, increasing from roughly half a million members in 1800 to nearly four million communicants by 1855. Although the country's Protestant churches were by no means exclusively evangelical, the vast majority of this growth occurred in the evangelical wings of the Baptist, Congregational, Methodist, and Presbyterian denominations. By 1855, the predominantly evangelical Methodist and Baptist churches alone accounted for nearly 70 percent of the nation's Protestant membership.[12]

Indeed, one could easily argue that more than any other denomination, it was the Methodists who spearheaded this nineteenth-century evangelical explosion. Given their pivotal role, perhaps it would be helpful to review the spectacular evolution of the American Methodist Church and consider the factors behind its success. Although they were the last, smallest, and initially least influential of the four major evangelical denominations to arrive in America, the Methodists ultimately achieved the greatest success in the antebellum period and helped usher in the golden age of Protestantism. Originally a tiny, early-eighteenth-century English Bible study group, by 1855 the American Methodist Church contained almost a million and a half members.

The first Methodists were Oxford University students renowned for their "methodical" study of the Scriptures and powerful outreach to Oxford's prisons. Their leader, an Anglican clergyman named John Wesley, and his brother Charles later felt called to leave England and serve as Anglican missionaries in James Oglethorpe's new American colony. Their idealistic missionary visions were dashed, however, when an early ministry to the Georgia colonists and Indians proved a dismal failure. Utterly despondent and even entertaining doubts about their faith, both men returned to England, where they later experienced highly emotional spiritual conversions that completely transformed their lives. Although the Wesley brothers always maintained that their "true" conversion to Christ had occurred outside the Anglican Church, and John preached an unorthodox Anglican gospel emphasizing Arminianism and the possibility of Christian perfectionism, throughout his lifetime John Wesley urged Methodists to pursue their revival ministry within the Church of England.

Refusing to abandon his earlier missionary vision for America, in the mid-eighteenth century Wesley dispatched several missionaries to the colonies. As late as 1771, however, there were only four Methodist preachers ministering to roughly three hundred converts. These early converts quickly multiplied in the years leading up to the Revolution, and gradually several churches were planted in New York and Philadelphia. These new congregations, however, were all plagued by a critical shortage of ordained preachers. To help address the growing American spiritual demand for their more passionate, democratic, and individualistic Gospel, the Methodists introduced a system of itinerant preachers, or "circuit riders," who spent their days traveling between isolated backcountry communities in the middle colonies and upper South, ministering to potential converts scattered along the western frontier.[13]

Although Wesley had planted its seeds, the future American church would probably have withered on the vine had it not been for the extraordinary life and ministry of a young itinerant Methodist missionary named Francis Asbury. Asbury was a Methodist circuit rider who traveled more than three hundred thousand miles on horseback or cart over the course of his forty-year career, up and down the early United States and back and forth across the Appalachian Mountains spreading the "good news" of a more inclusive Methodist gospel, where theoretically all could be saved. While other Methodists returned to England during the Revolution, and Wesley himself condemned the American rebels, Asbury remained behind and sided with the colonies. This astute wartime diplomacy later paid off handsomely, as Asbury's decision to side with the colonists ensured the survival of the post–Revolutionary War American church and made him its undisputed leader. Although Wesley later ordained Thomas Coke to serve as the superintendent of the American church, both Coke and Asbury were widely recognized by the colonists as the bishops of the postwar American Methodist Episcopal Church.

Asbury used his tremendous postwar popularity to organize a highly advanced circuit system that helped spread the Methodist revival beyond the Appalachians. This extraordinarily efficient system for delivering the Methodist gospel to the frontier—modeled off the apostolic ministry of the Scriptures—involved having each Methodist circuit minister preach at twenty or more "appointments" per trip, thus exponentially expanding the potential outreach and postconversion ministry of what then was an extremely limited pool of Methodist preachers. After conducting their first open air meetings and extending an invitation to the lost, the Methodist missionaries would organize the frontier converts into "classes," or embryonic churches, and appoint talented lay persons as interim ministers. One of Asbury's typical circuit rides (1791–92) began in New York and took him south to Charlestown, South Carolina, then west across the mountains to the wilderness frontier town of Lexington, Kentucky, and then finally back north again to New York, while traveling along the western side of the Alleghenies.

The combination of Asbury's ambitious circuit program and Methodism's highly democratic theology, which rejected the Reformed Protestant doctrine of predestination and instead emphasized God's willingness to save every unbeliever who placed his or her faith in Christ, helped spread Methodism across the frontier like wildfire. In their fervent desire to spread the gospel, Methodist innovators also introduced new religious practices to reach a wider audience of potential converts, including popular religious hymns, children's Sunday school classes, and huge outdoor camp meetings to gather in the faithful. The results speak for themselves. Over the course of Asbury's lifetime a regional American church that once numbered slightly more than three hundred members and four preachers in 1771 had expanded into a national church of more than two hundred thousand black and white members by 1813. In addition to the regular church membership, nearly one million people—or one out of every eight Americans—were attending annual Methodist camp meetings. By enthusiastically introducing a simpler, more readily understood and democratic gospel to America's frontier masses, and inspiring their rivals do the same thing, the Methodists did more than any other denomination to jump-start and direct the revivalist currents of the Second Great Awakening.[14]

In their enthusiasm to spread the faith, however, the Methodists also inadvertently created one of the national's largest grass-roots political networks. Given the church's strong evangelical roots, more democratic gospel, and traditionally marginalized frontier constituency, the church seemed perfectly situated to exploit the prevailing political currents of the early nineteenth century. It would have been difficult enough to resist such political temptations in normal times, but these were extraordinarily good times for the church. It was the height of the Second Awakening, the new evangelical churches were expanding faster than anyone could have imagined, and disestablishment had created a mutually beneficial alliance between the federal government and the evangelical churches. It was thus probably inevitable that the nation's largest Protestant denomination would ultimately be subjected to the pressures of politicization, but when it succumbed to them, the consequences for a country divided by slavery proved disastrous.

For example, even a more democratic and progressive faith such as Methodism could not escape the increasingly divisive sectional controversy surrounding slavery. Wesley and Asbury had earlier strongly condemned the peculiar institution, but Southern Methodists and the Methodist General Convention quickly equivocated on the issue. By the time the convention finally took a firm stand against slavery in 1844, by refusing to allow a Southern slaveholding bishop to preside over Northern conferences, it was too late. Unwilling to accept this obvious moral condemnation of their institution, the Southern churches seceded and a bitter legal war ensued over the ownership of the church's border state properties, religious presses, and other assets. The Methodist Episcopal Church that emerged in the North from the bitter schism retained more than eight hundred thousand members, or about fifty thousand more members than the combined black and white membership of the Methodist Episcopal Church in the South.[15] Both factions, of course, would continue to maintain that they were the true Christian church conscientiously upholding what the Bible really said about slavery, thus further fanning the flames of sectional discord.

As Timothy L. Smith and others have argued, by the mid-nineteenth century evangelical Protestantism had achieved its greatest social and political influence in the United States. Although only 15 percent of the population belonged to a Protestant church in 1855, more than one in three Americans were regular churchgoers, and as C. C. Goen and T. Scott Miyakawa have demonstrated, an even greater percentage of Americans were part-time attenders. Goen writes, "Even though the total enrollment . . . was still a small percentage of the entire population . . . this should not mask the fact that nearly every minister preached regularly to congregations three or four times the size of the church membership."[16] Based on his extensive research concerning nineteenth-century weekly church attendance, Miyakawa observed that while the figures for nonmember attendance provided by ministers and laity initially seemed exaggerated, they were often confirmed by external sources:

> A British Congregational delegate to America, Dr. Andrew Reed, reported in 1835 that the two Presbyterian churches in Lexington, Kentucky, had twelve hundred at the services and three hundred members, the two Baptist meetings about one thousand attendants and two hundred communicants, and the two Methodist societies about eleven hundred regular visitors and four hundred members. . . . The denominational influence was far wider than the stated membership [might indicate].[17]

Protestant churches in the North struggled to keep up with the demand. While the U.S. population increased 88 percent between 1832 and 1854, during the same period the number of Protestant clergymen serving that population grew 175 percent. Although Robert Baird optimistically estimated there was roughly one evangelical preacher to every eleven hundred Americans in 1844, according to Allen Nevins, by 1860 "the country had one church for every 580 people, [and] the churches had facilities for seating three-fifths of the population at one time." Not content to merely preach the gospel in pulpits and at camp meetings, evangelical clergymen soon discovered numerous other means to promote their revivalist agenda.[18]

In the early nineteenth century many evangelical leaders feared America's Christian religion and republican form of government would be undermined by mass American migrations to the uncivilized West and a rising flood of Catholics, immigrants, and heretical sects in the East. Convinced that America's future millennial role and status as a Christian republic were jeopardized by a religious "conflict for the education of her sons," Lyman Beecher called upon his coreligionists to "educate the whole nation while we may." Evangelical leaders from other denominations shared Beecher's vision, and as a result, a massive, new Protestant religious empire gradually emerged in the antebellum United States.

Comprised of dozens of new national religious societies, such as home missionary, Bible, tract, Sunday school, charitable, and other religious organizations, the goals of this "Benevolent Protestant Empire" were to promote evangelical missionary activity on the frontier and evangelical revivalism in the East while harnessing the tremendous power of evangelical enthusiasm to new temperance and sabbatarian reform movements. This evangelical battle plan would help ensure the triumph of Protestantism in the West, preserve religious orthodoxy back East, and simultaneously confront some of America's most flagrant antebellum sins. The development of this new national network of religious societies enormously expanded the evangelicals' power and influence in American society.[19]

Since evangelicals recognized that revivalism on this scale would require more efficient communication between the popular Northern churches and their growing national constituencies, evangelicals developed their own publishing industry. To meet Americans' voracious appetite for news, each religious denomination began publishing its own newspapers, and as a result the number of newspapers circulating in the United States increased from fourteen in 1790 to more than six hundred by 1830. To spearhead this national revival, evangelicals also obtained their own modern printing presses. In their enthusiasm to share the "good news," they pioneered several innovative printing technologies and distribution methods. New steam-powered presses and stereotype plates halved printing costs and dramatically decreased the time it took to get the message from the pulpit to the press. By the 1830s these religious presses were turning out one million Bibles and six million religious pamphlets a year. In 1855, the American Tract Society alone sold or distributed more than twelve million tracts to eager American readers. Even secular presses were influenced by this Protestant ideology. Staunch Methodist evangelicals controlled the editorial content of most of America's leading antebellum magazines, including *Harper's Monthly, Harper's Weekly,* and the *Ladies Repository.* The widespread popularity of "Christian" fiction written by female evangelicals incensed Nathaniel Hawthorne, who later complained that "a d—d mob of scribbling women" had debased American literature with their sentimental "domestic" novels filled with overt religious themes.[20]

Nineteenth-century evangelicals also shared their Puritan forefathers' strong commitment to public education. Convinced that religious education was the best way to advance the faith and preserve religious orthodoxy, and that many of America's older religious colleges created during the Great Awakening—such as Princeton and Brown—were becoming increasingly secularized, the popular Methodist and Baptist denominations decided to organize their own set of religious colleges. Although many of these small religious schools would later fail, it was an impressive effort. Dozens of new evangelical schools were opened, and some—such as Oberlin College—would later become world-renowned institutions. In 1844, Robert Baird estimated that 62 of the nation's 103 colleges had been opened since 1819, and that nearly all of them were religious. By 1860, the Northern

Methodist Church had an education empire of 26 colleges and more than 100 private institutes and academies. Baptists had organized a college in nearly every state and were operating 33 colleges and 161 secondary schools.[21]

Besides more than doubling the number of colleges in the United States, evangelicals also took an active interest in their children's education. To ensure children attending America's new public schools were properly introduced to the Protestant God, evangelical representatives from most of the major Protestant denominations joined forces to create an interdenominational Sunday School Union. The Union organized Sunday Schools in nearly all of America's largest cities and conducted a series of aggressive public relations campaigns to persuade Protestant parents to enroll their children in the evangelical staffed schools. The Union never achieved its ambitious goal of enrolling all of America's children; nonetheless, it achieved impressive results. An independent European observer later observed that in some cities, including Boston and Philadelphia, almost 80 percent of the public school children attended Sunday schools on the Sabbath.[22]

Evangelical Protestantism thus clearly assumed a dominant place in mid-nineteenth-century U.S. society.[23] The Protestant clergy had become the vanguard of the nation's social reform movements, the national guardians of public virtue, and the moral conscience of the nation. Albert Barnes reported that "no class of men" exerted "more influence than the ministers of the Gospel," and European visitors noted that the ideals of evangelical Protestantism seemed to dominate the national culture.[24] As C. C. Goen concluded, all the evidence and statistics suggest the United States' "popular evangelical denominations" exercised "more than a generally pervading 'influence'; they document a massive social reality. These churches of the people constituted a powerful visible structure shaping the common experiences and folkways of large numbers of American citizens nationwide. No other organization in the country was in closer direct touch with more people."[25]

Samuel S. Hill Jr. has suggested that the Northern churches' increasing concern with secular, political issues was the logical consequence of a communal Puritan vision that sought to create not just a perfect church but also a perfect Christian society in America. In the long run, the Puritans were so successful at effecting a union of the ecclesiastical and political in New England "that they helped elevate interest in the corporate, the public, the societal—in a word, the political—to the point where secularly political concerns displaced their explicitly Christian-based goals for the common weal." Organizing dozens of new, interdenominational religious societies and social reform movements, the clergy, in effect, inadvertently created their own "national constituencies" and special interest groups. The sheer size of this rapidly expanding evangelical electorate helped persuade the federal government to once again recognize the Protestant churches' role in influencing the nation's public policy. Clergy in the North eagerly reinserted themselves into political affairs and began using their newfound "political power" to advance their evangelical agenda. In fact, according to James E. Wood Jr., "at no time was organized religion in the United States more active politically than in the twenty years prior to the war."[26] But the Northern churches' political resurgence came at a high price. The incredible expansion of these churches' evangelical wings in the early nineteenth century ultimately translated into greater political power, but as the church increasingly used its growing political influence to advance its public moral agenda, it gradually lost sight of its more important spiritual mission. Churches in the North were, in effect, victims of their own success. The Puritans' original goal of creating a perfect spiritual community to save individual souls had evolved into a more secular political crusade to redeem all of American society.[27] This increased politicization of antebellum religion would have dramatic consequences when the churches embraced their sections' stands on slavery and secession.

The Evangelical Reformed Protestant Worldview

The four largest and most influential denominations in the antebellum North were the Congregational, Presbyterian, Baptist, and Methodist churches. All but the latter were Reformed Protestant churches or branches of various Western European Calvinist religious sects.[28] Although there was no monolithic "Protestant worldview" dominating the antebellum United States, the most popular evangelical factions within these churches did share many of the same Reformed Protestant beliefs. In *Revivalism and Social Reform,* Timothy L. Smith cautioned his readers that "there was neither a typical Protestant point of view on religious and social matters nor even, in most cases, one which was common to the great body of believers within any major denomination." Each denomination reflected a wide variety of different religious opinions and experiences, and most had significant nonevangelical factions. The latter was particularly true of the older, more established Congregational and Presbyterian churches, which dominated the eastern section of the country. With that said, these denominations' common theological heritage in Reformed Protestantism and increasing evangelical emphasis in the nineteenth century meant that the most rapidly expanding evangelical factions within these churches often subscribed to some of the same core religious tenets. For want of a better term, these popular, mutually shared evangelical beliefs within America's antebellum churches will be identified as an evangelical Reformed Protestant worldview.[29]

A number of scholars have emphasized this popular Reformed Protestant allegiance to a small body of core beliefs. In the early 1840s, religious commentator Robert Baird was one of the first scholars to note the existence of certain fundamental similarities between the large evangelical populations of America's antebellum churches. Although Baird noted that "much has been said in Europe about the multiplicity of sects in the United States," he thought this superficial observation missed a larger and more important point, "if we take all the evangelical communions that have fallen under review, and contemplate the confessedly fundamental doctrines maintained by each, it is surprising to observe how nearly they are agreed. . . . Indeed the evangelical Christians of the United States exhibit a most remarkable coincidence of views on all important points."[30]

More recently, religious historian Donald G. Mathews's research confirmed and carefully qualified this emerging evangelical consensus among "conversionist Presbyterians, Baptists, and Methodists." As Mathews explained, "Historians have understood the phenomena that united them as Evangelical." Although "evangelical truth and experience retained variations associated with the faith communities within which they were preached," ultimately "there was essential agreement on what was valued even if there were disagreements on ritual and the precise meaning of shared terms."[31]

In *Broken Churches, Broken Nation*, C. C. Goen agreed that the similarities between the religious groups that "'bore the stamp of Geneva' in one way or another . . . far outweighed the differences." Congregationalists and Presbyterians were united "and most other Protestant groups shared with them a sense of common identity, purpose, and mission," and the bonds between them would be further strengthened "as these groups revived and proliferated through common experiences shared in the evangelical awakenings." Smith himself concluded the "line dividing Evangelical Arminians [Methodists, Cumberland Presbyterians, and Freewill Baptists] from Evangelical Calvinists [most Congregationalists, New School Presbyterians, and Regular Baptists] seems, in retrospect, to have been more a matter of custom than creed" and discovered a number of cross-denominational values and movements flowing across American Protestantism. Some orthodox Calvinist factions naturally continued to oppose the evangelical agenda as they stubbornly clung to their predestinarian theology and high church methodology, but by the mid-nineteenth century, the orthodox Calvinism that Old School Presbyterians, Antimission Baptists, and Conservative Congregationalists generally subscribed to "was a dying dogma."[32]

In many respects at the popular level, antebellum Northerners' religious beliefs were not that different from those held by their Puritan forefathers. Evangelical Reformed Protestants generally shared four core beliefs. First, they believed in a sovereign creator God who was both transcendent and immanent, or who existed outside the universe but was still there actively sustaining it. Second, they were convinced that Americans were a chosen people destined by God to perform some special divine mission. Third, like their Calvinist predecessors, they were committed to the principle of *Sciptura sola*, or the idea that people should ultimately turn to the Scriptures—not some ecclesiastical figure or body—for the final word regarding problems of faith. Believers could and should interpret the Bible for themselves in a literal, commonsense fashion. And fourth, evangelicals were deeply committed to interdenominational revivalism and perfectionism. They were convinced that their God had unleashed a new manifestation of the Holy Spirit to help antebellum Christians perfect their moral lives, reform American society, and usher in God's millennial kingdom on earth.

Reformed Protestant evangelicals' traditional understanding of God's attributes was thoroughly grounded in a literal, commonsense reading of the Scriptures, especially the books of the Old Testament. According to Sydney E. Ahlstrom, one of the principal foundations of modern Calvinism was the concept of "God's awful and absolute sovereignty." As a sovereign Creator who was both omniscient and omnipotent, he exercised absolute authority over the universe. God's sovereignty gave him the legal authority and jurisdiction to rule over his creation, and his omnipotence and omniscience gave him the power and wisdom to govern it. Although he often voluntarily limited his exercise of power to preserve humans' free will, as a sovereign and omnipotent Creator he had both the authority and power to do whatever he wished. Because God was also transcendent, standing outside the natural laws, time, and matter of his universe, he was completely independent of his creation and could thus impartially judge and govern it.[33]

America's Reformed Protestant masses also believed in an immanent God, not some distant or absent watchmaker. Although the Enlightenment faith of Deism had flourished briefly in the late-eighteenth-century colonies, by the mid-nineteenth century, America's antebellum Protestants had largely returned to their Puritan forefathers' understanding of God's immanence, or the idea that God had not abandoned his universe but was still there actively sustaining it from moment to moment. Reformed Protestants thus worshipped a God who was still actively intervening in human history, listening to his people's prayers, and ultimately answering them as he deemed best.[34]

The second popular belief of the Reformed Protestant worldview was that the United States was a chosen nation, or new Israel, that had been created for the divine purpose of converting the world to Christianity and establishing God's kingdom on earth. The Puritans were the first Americans to appropriate the mantle of Hebrew covenant theology and use it to establish a new Jerusalem in the North American wilderness. But as religious historians Perry Miller, Harry Stout, Mark Noll, and others have demonstrated, the Puritans' covenant concept survived in the American consciousness, became one of the cornerstones of the Revolution, and later convinced many antebellum Americans that the United States was indeed God's new Israel. Northerners increasingly saw themselves as a peculiar people charged with the awesome responsibility of spreading the nation's superior republican institutions and evangelical faith to the rest of the world. By 1861, most would have heartily endorsed the evangelicals' assertions that "Americans were a chosen people, and the Constitution was a national covenant." Over the next four years they were given a terrible opportunity to demonstrate their commitment to those divine propositions.[35]

Evangelical Protestants also shared the Puritans' belief that God's word, as revealed in the Scriptures, trumped all other ecclesiastical authorities, and that believers could literally interpret its moral meanings for themselves. As the nineteenth-century religious historian Philip Schaff asserted, America's modern Calvinists were fierce "contenders for the absolute supremacy of the Holy Scriptures." Based on his empirical observations of antebellum Christendom, Robert Baird also concluded that the principle "the Scriptures are the only authority in matters of faith" was being "more and more practically acted upon" in antebellum America, and theological science and religious opinion were both moving more and more "towards the simplest and most Scriptural views of the Gospel as God's gracious message." According to Mark Noll, evangelical Protestants also subscribed to a literal biblical hermeneutics, or a "distinctly Reformed Protestant approach to Biblical authority ('every direction contained in its pages as applicable at all times to all men') and a distinctly American intuition" that promoted a "commonsense reading of scriptural texts [or] ('a literal interpretation of the Bible')." Although many American elites had embraced Deism or a more liberal Christianity before and especially after the Revolution, and the country had witnessed a massive influx of Roman Catholic immigrants, at the popular level most antebellum Americans still believed they should literally interpret their Bibles and that they did not need a special education or priest to discern its meaning.[36]

The final component of the Reformed Protestant worldview, introduced earlier by the Second Great Awakening, was the widespread belief that a new dispensation of the Holy Spirit was fueling interdenominational revivalism and perfectionism throughout the United States. During a prewar tour across the country, Robert Baird witnessed many examples of this interdenominational cooperation between evangelicals promoting revival:

"There is a frequent exchanging of pulpits. . . . They scruple not, when there is no service in their own places of worship, to attend others, though of another communion; and . . . Christians regularly attend lectures of pastors not of their own communion" with "the members of one evangelical communion often join[ing] with those of another in receiving the Lord's Supper in the same church." Indeed, according to Baird, there was unprecedented cooperation among the evangelical branches of the country's churches: "A very catholic spirit happily prevails. . . . Numerous occasions . . . bring all evangelical Christians together. The Bible, Temperance, Colonization, Sunday School, and Tract Societies, not to mention such as are formed from time to time for . . . local projects."[37]

By the late 1830s, major Protestant factions that had earlier embraced revivalism were beginning to turn to the doctrine of Christian perfectionism. Ministers such as Charles Grandison Finney had long argued that the best way to reform American society was to convert individual sinners and, once saved, to perfect these new Christian saints. Now other Reformed Protestant churches also embraced one of the principal lessons of the Second Great Awakening: The same Holy Spirit that convicted sinners could also help perfect or sanctify Christian saints and their surrounding society. By thoroughly grounding new believers in the faith with extensive Bible study, spiritual mentoring, and regular Christian fellowship, the churches hoped that individual perfectionism would open the door to societal reformation as well. Based on the churches' earlier experiences in the Second Great Awakening, this would occur when the newly refined converts, like Christ, were so moved by compassion for other lost souls that they would sacrificially devote themselves to the redemption of their society so that others could be saved as well.

The popular waves of revivalism and perfectionism which arose in the wake of the Second Great Awakening, and continued to shape the United States' social landscape until the eve of the Civil War, seemed to confirm the wisdom of this ecclesiastical strategy. In the eyes of the church, these visible manifestations of the Holy Spirit's power in the United States fueled hopes that perhaps God was preparing the nation for the special role of consummating his millennial kingdom on earth. To earn the right to serve as God's regents, however, church leaders reminded their congregations that they first needed to convert more of their countrymen to Christ and address the most recalcitrant sins of their society. Between the 1830s and 1850s, extensive revivals, the popularity of Christian perfectionism and moral reform, and growing interdenominational cooperation all seemed to point to the imminent arrival of the millennium. But increasing moral division over the country's original sin of slavery and the sudden outbreak of war in 1861 would dash these religious aspirations to pieces.[38]

Chapter 3

FORWARD INTO THE RED SEA OF WAR

We are Coming, Father Abraham, Three hundred Thousand More,
From Mississippi's winding stream and from New England's shore.
We leave our plows and workshops, our wives and children dear,
With hearts too full for utterance, with but a silent tear.
We dare not look behind us but steadfastly before.
We are Coming, Father Abraham, Three hundred Thousand More!

> James Sloan Gibbons, "War poem," *New York Evening Post,*
> July 16, 1862

The noise of a multitude in the mountains, like as of a great people;
a tumultuous noise of the kingdoms of nations gathered together:
the LORD of hosts mustereth the host of the battle.

> Isaiah 13:4

ON SUNDAY, April 21, 1861, as Southerners happily reflected on a week filled with military parades, speeches, and nighttime illuminations commemorating the fall of Fort Sumter, hundreds of ministers throughout the North were preaching fiery sermons condemning the South's treacherous attack on the U.S. flag. Until the actual outbreak of hostilities, most of the Northern clergy had actually opposed a war to save the Union. Most shared *New York Tribune* editor Horace Greeley's opinion that the evils of civil war clearly outweighed any perceived advantages of retaining the Southern states in the Union. It would be in the country's best interests if the Northern states just let their "erring sisters go in peace." In the wake of the fervent national response to the Southern attack on Fort Sumter, however, most of the Northern clergy joined the patriotic groundswell and dutifully rallied their churches around the flag. With the lower South already out of the Union, the upper South teetering on the verge of secession, and the loyalty of certain border states in question, the Lincoln administration could use all the help it could get. Over the next few months, as Northern governors competed against each other to see who could supply the national government with the most soldiers and weapons, most Northern clergymen enthusiastically enlisted their churches in the Union war effort. While the vast majority of Union soldiers did not believe they were enlisting in a religious crusade against the South in the spring of 1861, evangelical leaders, beliefs, and practices played a vital role in the initial Union recruitment drives.

The Northern Churches Mobilize for War

Many Northern churches that previously had urged patience in the sectional crisis, further political compromise, or even letting go the erring sister—in short, any principled strategy that might preserve the peace—enthusiastically embraced the administration's battle cry after the fall of Fort Sumter. Northern churches that had dabbled intermittently in politics became almost completely politicized once the war was officially underway. Abandoning their previous policy of cautious self-restraint, most Northern clergymen strongly encouraged their young men to enlist and vigorously defended the administration's wartime policies throughout the conflict. As George M. Fredrickson related:

> Ministers in several denominations lost their remaining inhibitions about the propriety of political preaching, and sermons with "loyalty" for their theme were widely reprinted so that those beyond the preacher's voice might become aware of their God-given duty. As propagandists for the Union, ministers succeeded in giving the war a religious sanction and thus played a vital role in maintaining northern morale and determination during the long struggle. It seems likely, in fact, that the Protestant pulpit was the single most important source of northern patriotic exhortation.[1]

In his study of the Northern clergy's attitude toward the South, religious historian Chester Forrester Dunham also agreed that after Fort Sumter "by and large, the Northern clergy, in most cases officially, and in almost all other instances unofficially, loyally supported the Federal Government."[2]

The major Northern Protestant churches' support for the Lincoln administration's war policies was not universal, but as the war continued, it nearly became so. This was because, as David B. Chesebrough and others have pointed out, dissenting Northern clergy were branded "disloyal" by the administration and severely persecuted by their respective churches. This charge of disloyalty was frequently leveled against Northern "copperheads" or democrats who sympathized with the South and opposed the Lincoln administration's war policies. But it was also used to discredit a wide variety of other ecclesiastical responses to the war ranging from pacifism and neutrality to refusing to preach political sermons or support the work of Union Leagues.[3] While such dissent certainly existed, Harry Stout recently quantified it. In *Upon the Altar of the Nation,* after completing an exhaustive study of both sides' religious publications and wartime sermons, Stout concluded that only "a small minority" of clergymen called "the Republican Party into question, and with it the conduct of the war and the bald "political preaching" of Northern evangelical Protestant denominations."[4] This ecclesiastical failure to maintain a proper distance between the church and state during the war would have ominous implications for the Northern churches' future prophetic role in Northern society.

Byron C. Andreasen's study of dissenting Illinois preachers and their democratic allies in the Midwest illustrates how even this small but vocal minority in the major churches was gradually suppressed by the Reformed Protestant establishment as the war continued. Since the governing bodies of their churches generally remained firmly committed to the Lincoln administration's wartime policies, dissenting preachers who openly questioned or opposed the Republican politicization of their churches were first censored and then either withdrawn from active duty or expelled from their congregations. Subjected to widespread persecution and death threats from their pro-Union congregations and official censure from their superiors, many dissenting preachers abandoned their ecclesiastical establishments and joined a newly created, dissenting church called the Christian Union. Although they condemned the pro-Republican politicization of their own churches, the dissenters' rough treatment at the hands of the Northern ecclesiastical-political establishment often inspired them to embrace an equally politicized copperhead gospel damning the Union cause.[5] The North's largest Reformed Protestant churches thus gradually lost or hopelessly politicized most of the prophets that might have kept both Lincoln's government and future Republican administrations spiritually accountable for their moral failures.

With the advent of war, the largest Northern churches deftly employed some of the same tools they had used to promote evangelical revivalism and the antebellum reform movements to encourage enlistment in the Union armies. More importantly, the clergy assisted the Northern war effort immensely that spring by using their pulpits to sanctify and help mobilize the Northern war effort. One of the North's most prominent clergymen, Henry Ward Beecher, now seemed more interested in promoting the war effort than preaching the gospel of Christ. The morning after Fort Sumter surrendered, Beecher urged the members of his congregation to stand fast during the North's hour of tribulation and dismiss any thought of further compromise or reconciliation with the South. Though he had previously expressed concerns over the horrors that might be unleashed by a sectional civil war, Beecher now asserted that "it is ten thousand times better to have war than to have slavery."[6] Like other Northerners, for Beecher, the attack on Fort Sumter was the turning point:

> I love our country. . . . I hold to corrupted silently by giving
> up manhood, by degenerating, by becoming craven . . . is
> infinitely worse than war. . . . We want no craven cowards; we
> want men. . . . They have fired upon the American flag. . . .
> Let every man that lives and owns himself an American, take
> the side of true American principles.

According to Beecher, the historical legacy of Moses, Luther, and the Puritans proved that

> safety and honor come by holding fast to one's principles; by
> pressing them with courage; by going into darkness and defeat
> cheerfully for them. And now our turn has come. Right before
> us lies the Red Sea of war. It is red indeed. There is blood in it.
> We have come to the very edge of it and the Word of God to us
> to-day is, "Speak unto this people that they go forward!"[7]

Beecher was not the only Reformed Protestant minister exhorting young Northern Christians to march forward into "the Red Sea of war." Most of the Northern clergy embraced a similar battle cry: The Lincoln administration was fighting a just war to save a Christian government from rebellion. Hundreds of Northern clergy urged their congregations to join this "fight for the Lord" and support a "Christian war" against the South. Other Northern ministers chose to lead their flocks by personal example. As Bell Irvin Wiley discovered, "in Bath, Maine, the Episcopal rector was the first to enlist, and in Madison, Wisconsin, on the Sunday after Lincoln's call for troops the Reverend William Brisbane of the Baptist church . . . preached his farewell sermon in his shiny uniform."[8]

Suddenly confronted with the evils associated with a national civil war, the Northern churches instinctively turned to their traditional and most successful weapon for overcoming community crises—the local revival meeting. To unite their communities behind the Northern war movement and spur enlistment, many clergymen attended or helped organize mass recruitment meetings in Northern towns and cities. Similar in many respects to their religious counterparts, these public meetings typically featured inspirational music, passionate oratory praising the cause and condemning the enemy, and at the culmination of the meeting, a dramatic, public call to action. Pastors, community leaders, and citizens who had attended summer camp meetings or protracted meetings were extremely familiar with these evangelical rituals and methods.

Bell Wiley described what typically occurred at such recruitment meetings:

> Leading citizens joined prospective officers in regaling audi-
> ences with oratorical outbursts full of allusions to country and
> flag and breathing defiance at slaveholders and traitors. Between
> speeches, brass bands played patriotic airs. If veterans of for-
> mer wars were available they were featured as speakers or as
> adornments for the platform. The total effect of these influences
> was sometimes tremendous, especially in the early days of the
> war, so that when the cry, "Who will come up and sign the roll?"
> was given, men rushed to the front like seekers at a backwoods
> revival, each vying with the other to be first on the list.[9]

Ironically, the same popular revival tactics that had earlier helped fuel the greatest expansion of evangelical Protestantism in American history were thus also used to mobilize the armies of the Civil War. The evangelicals' revival techniques had been deliberately designed to exert the maximum possible social pressure on reluctant converts so as to encourage the proper response at the invitation. Although originally intended for "religious" purposes, these evangelical methods proved just as potent when the state used them to spur enlistment at local recruitment meetings. With their passions aroused to a fever pitch by popular patriotic tunes and their civic and religious leaders' poignant speeches, it was extraordinarily difficult for most young men to resist their community's call to action, especially when the organizers invited the entire community to the event and placed the potential recruits on a platform surrounded by their peers. In the highly charged emotional climate of the recruitment meeting, with their friends and loved ones looking on, how could they ignore their leaders' patriotic exhortations to defend their communities—especially when their comrades began responding to the call?

Caught up in the emotion of the moment, many just followed the crowd's lead and impulsively enlisted without giving the matter much serious thought. Even those who were more deliberative about their decision to join the Union army, such as William C. Robinson of Sterling, Illinois, seemed strongly influenced by their local churches. Two weeks after the Fort Sumter attack Robinson attended a service at a Congregational Church where he heard a sermon "running over with patriotism and love to the old Union." Not surprisingly, in the same letter, Robinson revealed he too had decided to enlist since: "Every man is now expected to do his duty. . . . After careful consideration mine appeared to me, to be, a prompt response to [the] Governor['s] call for volunteers."[10] Later, Robinson, a newly commissioned private in the Thirty-fourth Illinois, traveled to the neighboring city of Dixon, Illinois. There his unit was

> presented with a beautiful Banner or flag by the ladies of
> Dixon. They had fine singing of patriotic songs, prayers and
> *war speeches* by the preachers, altogether a *good time,* such
> a time as will infuse every man with feelings of love to his
> country, and a determination to defend our noble flag to the
> last. Every man was presented with a copy of the "testament."
> . . . It is somewhat singular that the women enter into the
> movement with the heroism of soldiers, and if the prayers of
> women and the blessings of old men avail anything, we are
> *well* armed for a coming fight.[11]

Tapping into the incredible motivational powers of Reformed Protestant revivalism, the Northern clergy thus sought to transform the Northern war effort into one of America's greatest religious crusades.

The Most Spirited of Patriots

In *The Life of Billy Yank,* Wiley asserted that "women were the most spirited of patriots" and provided several examples of women's contributions to the Northern mobilization for war, but he never explained why Northern women supported the Union cause so enthusiastically in the early stages of the war. Perhaps the answer lies in women's traditional roles in American society and their socialization within the nineteenth-century middle-class cult of domesticity. Traditionally excluded from the public arenas of business and politics, from the colonial period on women frequently outnumbered men in America's churches. This was particularly true during the Second Great Awakening, when emotional revivals converted nearly twice as many women to Evangelical Protestantism as men. By legitimizing the use of emotion in American religion and sanctioning a limited public role for women, the two Great Awakenings helped set the stage for a greater public role for women in the decades leading up to the Civil War.[12]

Although initially designated the moral guardians of their families by the middle-class cult of domesticity, during the Second Great Awakening Northern evangelicals encouraged antebellum women to become the new social mothers of their communities as well. Northern women heeded this call, and embracing their new public role, they declared war on the social evils besetting their towns and cities. After addressing traditional religious concerns such as the plight of orphans and widows, Northern women aggressively confronted their patriarchal society's worst sins—public drunkenness, prostitution and slavery—and ultimately created and led some of the country's most successful antebellum reform movements.

Women who had been previously encouraged to confront the greatest evils of their age by the Second Great Awakening naturally became embroiled in the escalating religious and political conflict over slavery. The serial publication of Harriet Beecher Stowe's *Uncle Tom's Cabin* was the turning point for many Northern women. This sentimental novel awakened hundreds of thousands of Northern women to the evils of slavery, and especially the odious new Fugitive Slave Act, which required even those morally opposed to slavery to help Southerners recover their runaway slaves. A second major turning point was the Kansas-Nebraska Act. As the largest constituency group in America's predominantly evangelical churches, most Northern women knew about their clergy's active involvement in the country's antislavery parties and were probably familiar with at least the basic outlines of the "Southern slave power conspiracy."

In any event, when the South fired on Fort Sumter, many Northern women had the same emotional political reaction to the attack as their men. Socialized to be the moral guardians of their family and social mothers of Northern society, antebellum women responded decisively to what they perceived to be a serious threat to their families, community, and nation. Women joined men at the mass Union meetings that were organized across the North and "mingled their voices with the shouting." Ulysses S. Grant recalled that when the young men of Galena, Illinois, were mustered into service, the women were "quite as patriotic as the men." Indeed, as one Wisconsin resident observed at a local Union meeting, when the clergymen and politicians passionately denounced the moral crimes of the South and urged men to stand up and defend their families, the "young ladies were generally more enthusiastic than the boys."[13]

In the first weeks of war, Northern women employed a variety of means to express their intense patriotism and commitment to the Union cause. The ladies attended mass Union meetings and cheered when their young men stepped forward to enlist. Gifted writers wrote moving letters to local and national newspapers expressing their staunch allegiance to the Union cause. Other Northern women physically expressed their support by sewing thousands of American flags, which they subsequently draped on their windows and balconies, presented to newly organized regiments, or attached to their hair, bonnets, and bosoms. While society's legal and social codes prohibited females from openly enlisting as soldiers, at least four hundred left home to actively campaign in the Northern armies as nurses or cooks. A few, such as Sarah Edmonds and Rosetta Lyons Wakeman, even took the extraordinary step of disguising themselves as men so they too could join the patriotic struggle against the South. Other Northern women who remained home, such as Louisa May Alcott, expressed frustration that she and her friends were not men who could openly enlist in the armies and fight to uphold the Union.[14]

While Northern women later discovered numerous other ways they could support the Union cause, many recognized their first task was to encourage the men of their communities to enlist. In many cases Northern wives and daughters successfully used their feminine powers of persuasion to encourage their husbands, sweethearts, and male friends to respond to their country's call. Wives urged husbands to perform their patriarchal duty and protect their families and community during the wartime crisis. Cousins, sweethearts, and fiancées also showered Northern men with emotion-laden letters urging them to enlist and protect their country from a traitorous enemy. Younger women bluntly informed would-be suitors that they would not associate with men who refused to wear the uniform. An Indiana soldier smugly noted that "if a fellow wants to go with a girl now he had better enlist. The girls sing 'I am bound to be a Soldier's Wife or Die an Old Maid.'" There were entire Northern communities, such as Philadelphia, where the young women pledged to have nothing to do with the men who stayed home and where the soldiers who had enlisted were being singled out for special attention.[15]

To ensure the men accepted their new wartime roles, patriotic Northern women sometimes reminded their male counterparts of the military duties they were expected to perform in Northern society by modeling the appropriate martial behaviors. According to Wiley, women engaged in a number of warlike rituals, including sewing and "displaying flags, singing martial songs . . . making [military] clothing for the volunteers." In one New England town, the women even rolled out their community's "village artillery piece and treated their neighbors to 'a salute of thirty-four guns.'" As the young men of their city prepared to enlist, some of the finest ladies of New York City publicly admired their soldiers' swords, pistols, and muskets. Other women felt compelled to demonstrate their own martial skills. After learning the country was at war, Clara Barton marched out to the Monument grounds, set up a target, and successively put nine balls "within the space of six inches at a distance of fifty feet." When a few men initially seemed reluctant to fulfill their wartime duties, patriotic women sometimes publicly shamed them by offering to serve in their place. Few had to be asked twice.[16]

Religious soldiers were extremely interested in women's attitudes about the war and seemed anxious to adopt a course of action that would please them. After arriving at Camp Defiance, in Cairo, Illinois, Pvt. Dietrich Smith immediately informed his wife Carrie that "contious [conscious] of the right and justice of the cause," he was proud to perform his duty to the country, "but not those motives alone give me pleasure in volenteering to defend our glorious Country; but the assurance of your Love and your justification of my action make me one of the happiest persons." Soldiers like Smith often felt a deep sense of satisfaction enlisting in a just war to defend the Union but only if their loved ones back home supported their wartime mission. In the first months of the war, this was rarely a problem. Most women strongly encouraged a beau's decision to enlist, mainly because, just like everyone else, they assumed it would be a short conflict and they had little or no experience with the horrors of war.

In the end, this potent combination of popular revivalist tactics and feminine persuasion proved extremely effective at mobilizing the men of the North. In the first few months of the war, hundreds of thousands of young men volunteered. In fact, so many stepped forward that the government had a difficult time supplying them all with weapons and uniforms. Some patriotic Northern communities did such a good job recruiting soldiers for the Union armies that by the second year of the war they had virtually exhausted their pool of eligible volunteers. In the summer of 1862, young Lutie Bennett wrote a letter to her Uncle Ned explaining how the war was transforming their hometown:

> The most important news is that *everybody* is enlisting. . . . It is nothing but war, war, all the time, holding war meetings, talking about the war and who is gone and who is going. . . . It is generally believed they will go to draft in this state in about a week. That has sent a great many that otherwise would not have gone. Mr. Wilson, our school teacher is raising a company here and everybody in the neighborhood that can go is going with him. . . . Harry wanted very much to go with him as all the rest of his companions were going but our doctor says he must not do it. . . . He could not stand that sort of life. . . . There are only three single gentlemen over eighteen left in the neighborhood (and they would go if they were healthy enough).[17]

Northern Christians were also caught up in this popular flood of national patriotism in the spring and summer of 1861, and just like their less religious counterparts, they often emotionally enlisted in the passion of the moment, without seriously considering the potential consequences of their decisions. Once in uniform however, some later had second thoughts about their hasty and emotionally driven decision to volunteer. Pvt. John Jones warned his mother and father, "I would not advise anyone to enlist unless he has given it a great deal of thought beforehand, some have regretted enlisting because they had not given the matter sufficient thought." In similar fashion, a young Illinois soldier confessed to his grandfather that he was "already satisfied that a camp life is a hard one and would not advise any of my friends to join the army unless it becomes necessary."[18]

This was not always the case, however. Some young men managed to somehow detach themselves from the patriotic frenzy swirling around them and carefully consider the ramifications of enlisting. One thoughtful Wisconsin boy named Abraham Boynton addressed a letter to his friends and family, carefully outlining his reasons for joining the Union army:

> I have volunteered. . . . You may desire to know my reasons for this. I will endeavor to explain them. Our country is in need of men to sustain it at the present time and it is desirable to have

those persons volunteer for. . . . If there are not enough that
volunteer men must be drafted and in drafting they may take
men from their families when they should stay at home. . . . I
have thought you could get along without my aid for a time. . . .
Before I took this step I carefully considered. But if I have acted
rashly I pray that it may turn out right and do good to all.[19]

But in carefully deliberating the consequences of enlisting to fight in a civil war, men like
Boynton were usually the exception.

Caught up in the frenzy of the moment, most Christians just unthinkingly volunteered
to serve in what they considered to be a righteous cause, without any thought as to how
their service might impact their future or the lives of their loved ones. In their defense, it
should be remembered that at the time, the vast majority of Americans believed the war
would be very brief—perhaps settled by just one big battle. They had no idea they would
spent months anxiously awaiting battle in dreary military camps, that so many of them
would die, and that most of those who perished would die from communicable diseases
contracted from their friends in camp. Volunteers rarely understood the full meaning of
their wartime commitment until their first baptism of fire, or what soldiers referred to
as "seeing the elephant." After this experience, which many later vividly described as "a
living nightmare," most volunteers lost their former enthusiasm for soldiering.

When soldiers learned about the harsh realities of combat and their families' increasing
struggles back home as the war dragged on, they frequently reexamined their original
motives for enlisting and the morality of warfare. In the end few Christian soldiers expressed any regrets about enlisting or serious doubts about the righteousness of their
cause. To cope with the war's terrible violence, however, some later had to modify certain
conflicting religious beliefs or learn how to live with their guilty consciences. But most had
little trouble justifying their wartime participation and those who did come to question
the morality of the killing had little choice but to persevere and pray that God would
someday forgive them. Pvt. John MacLachlan of the Thirty-sixth Wisconsin Volunteers
probably spoke for the latter group when he told his wife, "If I only knew as much before
I enlisted I never would have been a soldier but I am in it now and I cant help it."[20]

The Christian Justification of War

Northern Christendom had to overcome two potentially serious theological problems
during the war. First, how could evangelical preachers who had previously emphasized
Christ's message of love, forgiveness, and personal redemption during the antebellum
revivals now abruptly reverse course and encourage their converts to serve as "killer
angels" and instruments of God's judgment without appearing morally inconsistent?
Second, how could Christians who were taught to live in "peace with all men" and to
"love thy neighbor as thyself," maim and slaughter their Southern brothers in Christ
without compromising their faith?[21] As James McPherson observed, "One of God's most
prominent commandments is 'Thou shall not kill.' Jesus advised his followers to turn the

other cheek. The message of his ministry was peace, not war. How could a true Christian take up arms to kill his fellow man?"[22]

Some prominent Northern clergymen, such as Henry Ward Beecher, resolved the first challenge by replacing Christ's New Testament gospel of mercy and forgiveness in their early wartime sermons with the more militant Old Testament stories of conquest and judgment. To foster appropriate martial attitudes within their congregations this new wartime gospel substituted the Puritan's traditional image of God as a fearful and inscrutable judge of the universe for the more compassionate Savior of the New Testament. God's Old Testament attributes were also emphasized in the wartime sermons—his mysterious ways, perfect righteousness, uncompromising demands for justice, and terrible judgments against the wicked. These new theological emphases strongly influenced how many Northern Christians ultimately interpreted and justified their wartime experiences.[23]

Northern ministers also helped Northern Christians justify their role as soldiers by arguing that war was sometimes a necessary evil. Beecher himself saw no moral contradiction between Christianity and war, and his widely published sermons helped many Northern Christians justify all the subsequent killing. As he explained in his early wartime sermon "The Battle Set in Array," war was an unmitigated evil, but it was sometimes necessary because in a world hopelessly corrupted by sin, there were even worse iniquities that could only be combated with physical force.[24] This argument rested on two presuppositions: When God created the universe he also created a hierarchy of vices, and Christians living in a fallen world might sometimes have to choose between the lesser of two evils.

While the idea of ranking various moral offences might strike some as being pragmatic or theologically suspect, it was a common Judeo-Christian practice. The Scriptures contained examples of the patriarchs apparently violating various religious laws or principles as they completed their divine missions.[25] The Hebrew legal code laid out in Deuteronomy also seemed to make distinctions between various religious "crimes" by meting out different degrees of punishment depending on the severity of the sin. The more orthodox position, however, was not so much that God distinguished between different types of human sin but that, as the ultimate and omniscient moral authority of the universe, he was the final arbiter of right and wrong, and thus his conception of justice sometimes differed from man's.

Moral confusion concerning the proper prioritization of these spiritual principles often arose, even in self-proclaimed Christian societies, because peoples and governments did not always anchor their legal and moral codes in God's laws, believers sometimes interpreted the same biblical passages differently, and the Scriptures did not address every life situation. When confronted with these ethical dilemmas, however, the church urged believers to consult the Scriptures and use their reason and knowledge of God's natural laws to discern the greater good. More ominously, it also reminded them that they would ultimately be held accountable for their proper ordering of these principles.

In defending the morality of just war, Beecher did not gloss over the baneful consequences of such human conflicts but asserted that if Northern Christians did not finally stand up and manfully resist a recalcitrant South, even worse evils would follow. On the eve of the war, Henry Ward Beecher told his anxious congregation:

> I go with those that go furthest in describing the wretchedness
> and wickedness and monstrosity of war. The only point on
> which I should probably differ from any is this: that while
> war is an evil so presented to our senses that we measure and
> estimate it, there are other evils just as great, and much more
> terrible, whose deadly mischiefs have no power upon the
> senses. I hold that it is ten thousand times better to have war
> than to have slavery. I hold that to be corrupted silently by
> giving up manhood, by degenerating, by becoming cravens, by
> yielding one right after another, is infinitely worse than war.[26]

War and death were terrible evils, but if Christianity was true and there was life after death, then moral compromise and eternal damnation were infinitely worse.

Numerous Christian soldiers seemed to share Beecher's opinion that as terrible as the war might be, it would save the country from an even worse fate. Sgt. Charles Mumford of the Third Wisconsin Cavalry, who favored a "prosecution of the war to the *Bitter End*," believed that the war was a choice between two evils:

> Of two Evils let the People chuse the least the war is certainly
> a great evil yet if the Rebels Suceed in dismembering the
> government of the United States the evil I think will be far
> greater if the Rebels should suceed I do not believe we should
> have peace but a short time for by the same rule of State Rights
> the whole North would be cut up into petty governments or
> dynasties in a few years such undoubtedly will be the end of
> our once glorious Republick if the Rebellion is not put down.[27]

Since the horrors of a national civil war could conceivably be dwarfed by the evils of further governmental breakdowns and perpetual future conflict, Mumford urged his fellow Douglas Democrats and Wisconsin friends to "rally to the *Battle cry* and help to put down this damnable rebellion."[28] As his unit prepared to enter the battle at Stones River, Capt. Alexander Ayers agreed that "*war is a most terrible thing* but since it must be let it be done up soon as possible and [then] let us go home to enjoy our families." In their letters to loved ones, countless other religious soldiers echoed Ayers's opinion that the war was indeed a terrible, unavoidable evil but was something that simply "must be."[29]

Most Northern Christians ultimately reconciled their military duties with their faith by embracing their churches' biblical teaching that Christians might sometimes have to embrace war as a necessary evil to preserve their Christian institutions. Although Christ's teaching seemed to contradict this proposition, antebellum Northerners who interpreted the Bible in a literal, commonsense fashion could find scriptural evidence that supported the idea of "Christian warfare." Like so many other moral controversies in Christendom, it often depended on which passages or interpretations were emphasized.

The New Testament gospels enjoined Christians to be peacemakers and suggested that most wars were fought for immoral purposes such as greed, hatred, ambition, or revenge. Many Christians also questioned the moral legitimacy of waging war in light of Christ's teachings and the early church's practice of Christian pacifism. The church abandoned its pacifist stance after it was integrated into first the Roman and then medieval political orders and sanctioned the limited use of violence to defend Christian states. But it had never officially disavowed its pacifist origins or strong opposition to warfare. Indeed, when combined with a commonsense exegesis of the New Testament gospels, the historical practices and teachings of the early Catholic Church seemed to present an authoritative and unambiguous Christian condemnation of most nineteenth-century warfare.

Over the centuries, however, the Reformed Protestant churches had gradually developed their own Scriptural case justifying the limited use of force to combat physical threats to the state. Indeed, a commonsense reading of the New Testament convinced many antebellum Protestants that there was nothing inherently immoral about the government's lawful use of force against a dangerous enemy or serving one's country as a soldier. After all, when soldiers visited John the Baptist, the prophet did not morally condemn them or their occupation. He only said they should exercise their authority responsibly and be content with their pay. Jesus could also have chastised the Roman centurion who asked him to heal his servant with his usual admonition to go and "sin no more." But Jesus instead healed the man's bondservant and then commended the centurion for his extraordinary faith. Protestants thus rejected the notion that Christ's New Testament Gospel categorically condemned the art of soldiering and use of force. Perhaps most damning of all to this notion was an obscure reference in Revelation which suggested the Christ who had once come preaching peace, mercy, and forgiveness would someday return bearing "a sharp sword, that with it he should smite the nations," and tread the winepress of the "fierceness and wrath of Almighty God."[30]

To strengthen their contention that the Bible supported the just use of force, the Northern clergy and religious soldiers often turned to the Old Testament. The books of Joshua, Judges, and 1 Samuel contained numerous examples of God's people yielding the sword as a last resort to defend their communities or more aggressively to establish and preserve a Christian enclave in a wicked world. Since American Protestants practicing a literal hermeneutics of the Scriptures believed the God of the New Testament was the same God as the old, they ultimately embraced both a God of peace and war. Given their preferred form of Scriptural exegesis, this was perfectly consistent. After all, they believed that the same God who had blessed the peacemakers had also ordered the complete extermination of the seven nations inhabiting the Promised Land—to the last man, woman, child, and animal. And that the New Testament God of "mercy, and peace" had also called the fierce Hebrew warrior David a man patterned "after mine own heart."[31]

Although Christ had come bearing a new covenant, antebellum Protestants did not believe God himself had changed. Jehovah's character and attributes were immutable, and the Scriptures explicitly declared that he was a God who both trained his people's hands for war "and fingers to fight" and ordained a time for peace and "a time of war."[32] So while Northern Christians believed they ought to practice mercy and forgiveness and generally pursue a life of peace, they also thought there were times when a Christian people might, as a last resort, have to forcefully combat the physical manifestations of evil in this world to preserve God's kingdom on earth.

In the end, soldiers intimately familiar with these biblical passages and Reformed Protestant teachings came to the same conclusion. They may have had their initial doubts about the morality of killing their coreligionists, but the temporal moral authorities they most implicitly trusted—their churches and women folk—assured them their cause was just. Now it was their duty to come to their country's aid.

Chapter 4

FOR FAMILY AND COUNTRY

So nigh is grandeur to our dust,
So near is God to man,
When duty whispers low, *Thou must,*
The youth replies, *I can.*

> Ralph Waldo Emerson, "Voluntaries,"
> *Atlantic Monthly,* October 1863

And Moses said unto the children of Gad and to the children of Reuben,
Shall your brethren go to war, and shall ye sit here? And Moses said unto
them, If ye will do this thing, if ye will go armed before the LORD to war
. . . until he hath driven out his enemies from before him, And the land
be subdued before the LORD: then afterward ye shall return, and be
guiltless before the LORD.

> Numbers 32:6, 20–22

IN SEPTEMBER 1863, a plucky New England war correspondent named Wilbur Fisk
found himself stationed just outside New York City. His unit had recently been transferred from the Gettysburg battlefield to New York City to help suppress the Irish draft
riots. In a letter to his readers back home in Vermont, Fisk described the chief character
traits that distinguished him and his comrades from the Irish rogues they were battling
in New York:

> Unless a man has patriotism of the most exalted kind, a high
> sense of duty, and an undoubting faith in the righteousness
> of our cause to lean back upon in his hour of trial, he has
> poor support. It is only the man who truly loves his country,
> and believes that we are fighting for God and humanity, that
> can cheerfully submit to his fate when drafted. It is utterly
> impossible for others to do so. Standing target for the rebel
> minnies, is one of the most uncomfortable positions a man was
> ever placed in, as I can tell you from experience, and we do not
> wonder that some men pray to be excused when the country
> calls for such work.[1]

While Fisk and other Christian soldiers sometimes shared the Irish protestors' fears about what might await them on the war's battlefields, a stronger sense of duty to their country and families, and firm belief they were engaged in a just war for Union and liberty, compelled them to rally around the flag. As Benjamin Webb Baker related in a poignant letter to his grandfather:

> I ask forgiveness for going contrary your wishes in joining
> the army—I feel that I have only discharged a duty which
> as a good citizen I owe to my country, to my friends, and to
> liberty. And now I ask your blessings as with my face to the
> enemy's land I go forward—as long as this arm has strength to
> wield a sword or handle a rifle; as long as these feet can carry
> me forward and these eyes can see to direct my steps I expect
> to march forward.[2]

The Meaning of Duty

One of the most popular arguments Christian soldiers advanced to justify their participation in the Northern war effort was that they were merely performing their Christian duty. When most Northern soldiers spoke of duty, they were usually referring to their responsibility to defend their families and country. This was no accident. They had first learned about the importance of duty in their homes, schools, and churches. Indeed, from the cradle to the grave their patriarchal Christian society constantly reminded them of men's duty to respect their elders and social superiors, protect and provide for their families, and submit to their God and government. Northern soldiers also knew their church and society would ultimately hold them and their families morally accountable if they failed to observe these social obligations. Few men needed to be told it was their duty to protect their families and communities, but the new evangelical churches also encouraged Northerners to defend the republican government that upheld their political and religious freedoms. With the advent of war, many Northern clergymen began preaching inspirational sermons couched in patriotic themes to remind men of their civic responsibility to defend the national government.

In their wartime letters Union soldiers constantly spoke of their "duty" to defend their Christian government and families, but few if any ever defined precisely what they meant by the word "duty." When most soldiers invoked the idea, however, the connotation seemed to be some vague, unspoken obligation an individual owed to another party. This outside party might be another person, his family, church, government, or even God himself. While not legally binding, these commitments were considered socially and morally binding, and those who broke them would soon find both themselves and their families ostracized from society. According to Gerald F. Linderman, this was because there was an intimate relationship between courage, duty, and honor in the nineteenth-century United States. An honorable soldier was always expected to act courageously on the battlefield and fulfill his assigned duties, even if it cost him his life. In a society that always expected men to act honorably, the worst possible fate a soldier could suffer was to lose his nerve under fire and fail to perform his duty. Most considered this a fate worse than death because, regardless of his past conduct or intentions, the soldier would be permanently discredited in the eyes of his peers. There was an almost universal antebellum understanding that such men were dishonorable cowards who had betrayed their God, families, and communities, and were thus unfit for life in a civil society.[3]

Since the typical nineteenth-century reaction to such a moral failure was often permanent social stigmatization for the unfortunate soldier and his family, Christian soldiers were understandably more concerned with their military conduct than their physical safety on the war's battlefields. Indeed, in the letters they penned to loved ones on the eve of battle, Christian warriors often expressed deep concern they might somehow fail to live up to their society's expectations. As one young private confided to his mother, "I almost feel anxious to be in a battle and yet I am almost afraid. I feel very brave sometimes and think if I should be in an engagement, I never would leave the field alive unless the stars and stripes floated triumphant. I do not know how it may be. . . . Pray that I may be a true soldier." In the spring of 1862, an ambitious officer in the Forty-fifth Illinois Regiment, Capt. Luther H. Cowan, conveyed similar fears to his wife. As his unit approached enemy territory in eastern Tennessee, Cowan assured her that "if we see a battle you will never be ashamed of the way I behave in it." Three days later, as Cowan and his men prepared for their baptism of fire, he again nervously relayed his concerns about properly performing his duties as an officer by reminding his wife that God ultimately determined military outcomes, not man: "Battles are not always to the strong. We may come out best. If we do not it is not our fault nor shall it be. I would rather die than come out of a fight dishonorable." Cowan wrote these words in deadly earnest. Subsequently promoted commander of the Forty-fifth Illinois, the following summer he was killed while leading a charge on the Confederate breastworks outside Vicksburg.[4]

Other soldiers shared Cowan's anxieties about inadvertently failing to measure up once the shooting began but nonetheless expressed a firm determination that come what may, they would properly discharge their duty. As he marched South to meet the enemy for the first time, 1st Lt. Dwight Fraser told his sister, "I *hope* and *pray* to God that if I am thrown into battle, that I may stand up like a *true soldier,* and do my duty, not fearlessly, but *cooly* and *bravely.*"[5] A few days before the bloody struggle at Shiloh, Lt. James F. Drish of the Thirty-second Illinois also seemed anxious about meeting his first enemy on the battlefield.

Drish seemed torn between his natural instinct to avoid danger and his patriotic duty to defend his country. He confessed to his wife that while the prospects appeared excellent that his regiment was about to see its first battle, he had orders to visit a rear-area supply base. "I should hate to be absent when the Regiment was likely to git into a fight not that I am anxious to get into one myself but I feel it to be my duty to do my part toward puting down the rebellion that is what I volunteered for and I expect to do it," he wrote.[6]

While Drish hardly relished the thought of facing his enemies on the battlefield, like other soldiers he was determined to perform his duty. Soldiers' concerns about fulfilling the demands of duty were not always confined to the battlefield. Even as he lay seriously ill in a New Orleans military hospital, Pvt. Francis Harvey Bruce was terrified he might not live up to all that was expected of him. Bruce asked his mother and all his Christian friends to pray for him "that I may stand firm at my post to the end."[7] Regardless of their rank or physical condition, most soldiers were determined to overcome their personal shortcomings and fear of the unknown and fulfill their military obligations.

Such commitment made perfect sense given churches' grandiose claims regarding the rewards awaiting those who fulfilled their obligations to God and society. One of the North's leading preachers, Henry Ward Beecher, offered virtual immortality to those who enlisted and faithfully completed "the race":

> We will not forget you. . . . You shall return from the con-
> quests of liberty with a reputation and a character established
> forever to your children and your children's children. It shall
> be an honor, it shall be a legend, it shall be a historic truth;
> and your posterity will say: "Our fathers stood up in the day
> of peril, and laid again the foundations of liberty that were
> shaken; and in their hands the banner of the country streamed
> forth like the morning star upon the night." God bless you![8]

A grateful nation would never forget the sacrifices of the brave Christian soldiers who fought to uphold their government and glorious flag.

Other Northern clergymen supported Beecher's proposition that military service would both spiritually strengthen the soldiers and redeem the rest of Northern society. After decades of luxury and peace, the fiery judgment of war would purge the country of its chief national sins: an exorbitant self-indulgence and disrespect for authority and the country's shameful exploitation of the Indian and African. Congregational churchman S. P. Leeds rejoiced that wartime hardships would cast a harsh light on the nation's indolent pleasure seekers "while men of deeds come to the front." S. D. Phelps of the First Baptist Church of New Haven also thought that military training would make Northern men "hardier and stronger, both in physical endurance and in moral vigor." By instilling soldiers with a sense of discipline, faithfulness, and sacrifice, the war would produce both "a purer and more stable Republicanism" and a new set of American "moral and Christian heroes" whose heroic qualities and "stalwart influences" would be emulated by the next generation. Wartime suffering and sacrifices would discipline the country and once again remind Americans of their more noble republican virtues, or what was truly worth living, fighting, and dying for.[9]

The war might kill and maim thousands of men, but it would also surely improve the moral character of those who survived. At least this was Pvt. Robert Crandall's understanding. After enduring an arduous year of Union reverses in 1862, Crandall told his family, "When this wicked war is over and I return to you, I shall not only return as steadfast in morality as hitherto, but one of the luckiest men in that I have fully discharged my duty to my country and my God." Although he quickly discovered war was "awful," Pvt. T. S. Seacord also believed military service could have a salutary moral influence on a man's character. Seacord "ashured" his dear wife Anne that "if ever God spares me to return I shall Return as pure as I left you and I trust a wiser and better man." Christian soldiers such as Crandall and Seacord could thus reconcile their participation in a "wicked war," convinced that by faithfully performing their duties as soldiers of the cross, God could use even an evil war to bless them.[10]

Duty to Family and Government

While the New Testament instructed Christians to avoid conflict and "live peaceful and quiet lives," most nineteenth-century Protestants believed they also had a Christian duty to shield their families and country from danger. The Scriptures, after all, enjoined men to marry and charged them with the responsibility of caring for the physical and spiritual needs of their families. Men were to love their wives and children unconditionally, just as Christ loved the church. When taken in context with passages such as John 15:13, which said a man could express no greater love than to "lay down his life for his friends," few male believers could miss the implication. Just as Christ had obediently offered himself up on the cross to redeem the church, Christian soldiers were expected to sacrifice their lives in defense of their families.[11]

There was thus little doubt as to what the Christian's duty should be when the lives of his family and friends were at risk. Union private John Lindley Harris could not fathom how any young, able-bodied man could "conscientiously sit down at home and see his brothers engaged in this bloody struggle for the protection of himself his Father Mother sister and all that is dear to him and not rally to his support." William Robinson felt sorry for the men who stayed at home: "I think that a fellow who has to stay at home . . . deserves as much *sympathy* as the one who goes. It seems to me almost a disgrace not to be in the ranks, when there is so much at stake."[12] Other soldiers insisted they were not fighting for land or property but simply to protect their homes and families. As Pvt. Isaac Tucker assured his Wisconsin girlfriend, he and his comrades were not marching into Dixie to conquer the South but to save "our friends which we have left behind dearest by far than our own hearts Blood yes those are what we will fight for and bleed for and die for, this you may depend upon."[13]

One practical consequence of the war, however, was that it forced thousands of religious men throughout the North to choose between their traditional familial duties as fathers and husbands in their families and their civic responsibilities as citizens of a sovereign state. Although their close geographic proximity to the Confederacy rendered some Northern states vulnerable to potential Southern invasions and depredations, the vast majority of Northerners did not feel any immediate threat to their lives and property. To ensure Christian soldiers understood they owed a higher allegiance to the Union than their families, Northern clergymen strongly encouraged Christians to rally to their government's defense, arguing that this was the best way to safeguard both their liberties and their families. According to David B. Chesebrough, the predominant theme expressed over and over by Northern preachers at the onset of the war was that the Union must be preserved at all costs. Pastor A. L. Stone of Boston's Park Street Church urged the men of his congregation to "strike for Law and Union, for country and God's great ordinance of Government." Beecher admonished his congregation that it was the duty of all citizens to "maintain inviolate the territory of the United States . . . to stand up for their government; to protect its just authority . . . and to see to it that its jurisdiction is not restricted." In these and other Northern sermons, believers were constantly reminded that the Union was the principal source of their liberties and best guardian of their homes and families. To ensure Northern soldiers never lost sight of their preeminent duty to the state, their chaplains echoed these patriotic themes throughout the war.[14]

While Northern Christians often regretted leaving their families behind to fend for themselves, they believed their duty to defend the Union outweighed any familial responsibilities they had back home. For Christian soldiers such as 1st Lt. Philip Welshimer, God and country clearly took precedence over home and family. In the spring of 1861, Welshimer informed his wife that he and the rest of his company had decided to enlist for three years of government service when their "country called." Conscious of his dereliction of familial responsibility, Welshimer confessed, "My only trouble dear Julia is in leaving you and the Children and in this I can only make amends by keeping my character unsullied and by Sending you every cent of my wages." Perhaps this compromise relieved Welshimer's guilty conscience, but how did Mrs. Welshimer feel about her husband's unilateral decision, or when she later learned he had been captured at Chickamauga and sent to Richmond's notorious Libby Prison?[15]

Other Union soldiers shared Welshimer's higher commitment to national service. Maj. Joseph J. Dimock, the commanding officer of the Second New York Militia, told his sister Sallie he would prefer to be back home with his family in Hartford, "but Duty just at present keeps me here and although it would be much more pleasant to remain at home with Dora and the children [illegible word] I think I ought to be here, for I can be of some service to my country and now is the time when the country needs defenders."[16]

The soldier's temporary abandonment of certain familial responsibilities during the war also often included the postponement of marriage plans. In February 1862, a Wisconsin soldier named Daniel Webster shared his hopes of swiftly returning to his beloved fiancée, Gertrude. But between the lines of this and other letters, Webster clearly conveyed the impression that his duty to the Union outweighed any previous commitment to his betrothed:

> I hope the war *will* end before we can be got ready, I would
> rejoice to hear tomorrow morning that the rebel leaders had
> sued for peace and surrendered up all—nothing would please
> me better unless tis an immediate and honorable discharge

from the service. Yet if there *must* be fighting I feel that tis my
duty to *help do it,* and if I ever get a chance I shall do my best
at it and every blow I strike shall be for my country and *you.*[17]

Although Webster and Gertrude were safely reunited after the war, thousands of other
Northern women who lost a beau in the war probably regretted a husband's or fiancé's
decision to place the country's interests above those of his family.

The Northern soldier sometimes rationalized this subordination of the family to the
state by convincing himself and his loved ones that by fighting for his country he was
also defending his home and upholding his family's honor. This line of reasoning was
often buttressed by churches' wartime sermons, which exhorted men to forsake their
craven impulses for the comforts of home and manfully resist Southern assaults on their
government, communities, and personal honor. Soldiers also reminded their wives of the
derisive treatment that was being meted out to the men who remained behind and asked
for their support in avoiding a similar fate. Such appeals to familial pride and honor often
achieved their intended result, as thousands of Northern fathers and sons enlisted, and
often later reenlisted, for long terms of military service to ensure the ultimate triumph of
the Union cause.

With the passage of time, however, and a growing realization of what a prolonged
civil war might cost their families, some women came to regret their husbands' or boy-
friends' decision to enlist. Northern women grew tired of anxiously awaiting news of their
menfolk's fate after each battle and struggling to manage their farms and households by
themselves. When the war dragged on and casualties mounted, thousands of hard-pressed
women became concerned their spouses and sons might never return and began besieging
the Northern armies with a steady stream of correspondence begging them to come home.
Their letters often bore bad tidings—a veritable litany of home front crises that would
surely destroy the family and farm if their prodigal husbands and sons did not immediately
return. Conscientious soldiers often suffered acute mental anguish in the wake of such
letters, as they contemplated the desperate plight of their families and discovered how
difficult it could be to comfort loved ones from afar.

Most Northern soldiers, however, steeled themselves against such emotional appeals
and refused to abandon their military duties just because their families were experiencing
hardships. After receiving bad news from home, one troubled Indiana private did little to
alleviate the suffering of his grieving wife. In a sternly worded reply, Andrew J. McGarrah
briefly affirmed the harsh realities of his wife's life but then abruptly concluded, "I trust
in Heaven for your welfare during my absence be not discouraged nor grieve over things
which I can not change, we must defend our Country let our fate be whatever it may."
Even if McGarrah wanted to come home, his sense of duty compelled him to remain at
his post. Another young soldier, just back from a recent furlough, coolly informed his
family members that "leaving home this time was harder work than it was the first time,
but it could not be helped for we are needed here, and this is no time for those who can
do their country a service, to be lying at home idle."[18]

Capt. Harley Wayne of Illinois tenderly scolded his "dear Ellen" for suggesting he did not
love his family, reminding her that he was only serving to preserve the honor of his family:

> Your reproaches of want of affection for you and my dear
> boy (which I need not refute) cannot move me— My own
> honor—Your honor—Charley' honor and the good name of us
> all are dependent upon my fulfilling my vows and duty to my
> own native land—and I here promise you in the presence of
> God our master that though I die in conflict or by disease or
> languish in the prisons dangerous though it cost me all I have
> and am and *are* I will try to do my duty well that you shall not
> be disgraced of me living or dying—I shall try to do what ever
> duty calls me to do and if I live return.[19]

Harley kept this emotional promise to never dishonor his family's name. He was still courageously performing his duty when he was killed four months later at the Battle of Shiloh.

Other soldiers, such as Pvt. David Rose Simpson, tried a more diplomatic approach with their wives and sweethearts, hoping to win them over with reason. Simpson tried to deflect his wife's entreaties by gently reminding her that faithful Christian women also had a duty to perform in the war:

> I can not come home until they see fit to let me unless I desert
> and I know that you would not have me disgrace myself to that
> Extent. . . . So my dear try and be content and I will if God
> spares come home as soon as possible respectable and honored
> as a . . . Soldier of the Cross and a true Christian as becomes
> a parent and husband with tears of Gratitude I pray God to
> bless you my Dear wife give her strength to fulfill her duty as a
> mother and wife. . . . Comfort her in her Lonely Condition.[20]

A handful of soldiers invoked the legacy of republican motherhood when responding to their wives' entreaties, reminding them that just like America's founding mothers it was now incumbent upon them to make sacrifices in support of their government and sustain a new generation of patriots fighting for their freedoms. Patiently responding to his wife's withering criticism of his enlistment and the Northern war effort, an Irish color sergeant with the Twenty-eighth Massachusetts Volunteers asked his Margaret to "look at our situation in a different light." Noting the unprecedented freedoms they enjoyed in the United States, Welsh patiently explained that they both had a duty "to sustain for the present and to perpetuate for the benefit of future generations a government and a national asylum which is superior to any the world has yet known." In a similar vein, responding to his wife's repeated exhortations to return home, Capt. Alexander Ayers pointedly asked, "If all should go out where then would our country be—gone without a hope."[21]

Betrothed soldiers occasionally turned the tables on their fiancées by arguing that military service would strengthen, not jeopardize, their future families. According to these soldiers, a man who failed to fulfill his duty to his country was unlikely to honor his future commitments to his family and thus could not possibly be a good husband or father. As Lt. David Beem told his young fiancée:

> If I were now to abandon the cause I am engaged in, and
> refuse to bear arms for my country in its present distracted
> condition, I would consider myself unworthy of you, or any
> other lady. None but the brave deserve the fair. I hope, by
> dilegently doing my duty as a defender of our constitution and
> laws, to make myself a fit companion for you. And in carrying
> out this determination, I am certain that Providence will smile
> upon us both, and bring us to a speedy and happy union.[22]

Of course, one weakness with this line of reasoning was that it overlooked the fact the soldier in question might not survive this refining process. But at least such appeals clearly communicated the soldier's belief that by properly performing his duty to his country, he would advance both his personal interests and those of his country. In any event, these examples illustrate that in the ongoing competition between familial and state loyalties, during the Civil War the Northern clergy and religious soldiers clearly put the country first.

Evolution of the Christian Republic

When most Northern churches and Christians enthusiastically enlisted in the Northern war effort, they did so because they believed their duty to their country superseded their familial responsibilities. But where had this overriding sense of personal obligation to a "national" government come from and when had their secular Republic allegedly become a "Christian" nation? The religious foundations of this nascent American nationalism and emerging civil religion were firmly rooted in the Puritans' semitheocratic scheme of providential exceptionalism, the Great Awakenings, and the new Republic's disestablishment of state churches.

American exceptionalism was historically rooted in the Puritan leader John Winthrop's original vision of a "City upon a Hill." Winthrop and other Puritan apologists believed God had called their people out of an increasingly corrupted Anglican religious community in England to create a New Zion in the North American wilderness, whose Godly example might someday help spiritually redeem backslidden England. In accepting this divine invitation, the Puritans had entered into a holy covenant with God in which he promised to bless their colony as long as they remained faithful to him and their original spiritual mission. Some of America's earliest and most influential colonists thus believed that, just like the ancient Jews, they were a chosen people singled out by God to advance his kingdom on earth.

By the middle of the seventeenth century, however, various jurisdictional breakdowns of the Puritan church and state had produced a major spiritual crisis in Massachusetts Bay that would ultimately undermine the colony's original spiritual mission and identity. An increasingly politicized church's failure to focus on its spiritual role of saving the lost and sanctifying the elect had left Puritan families vulnerable to the distractions and temptations of this world. Abundantly blessed by God, succeeding generations had become intoxicated with their wealth, and their focus had gradually shifted to more worldly affairs. Self-satisfied and reliant, and above all tired of their parents' excessive wrangling over religion, many had later abandoned their fathers' faith, or as Cotton Mather neatly summarized matters, "Religion brought forth Prosperity, and the daughter destroyed the mother." Although the City upon a Hill's spiritual redemption mission had been irretrievably compromised, nearly a century later the preachers of the First Great Awakening planted the seeds for a much broader and expansive notion of American exceptionalism by drawing from the Puritans' religious experiment and adapting its form and meaning to better suit their own eighteenth-century circumstances.

Largely a reaction to what many devout colonists considered to be a general spiritual decline in the thirteen colonies at the turn of the eighteenth century, or more accurately, a growing distaste for the authoritarianism, predeterminism, and strict doctrinal standards of the established Puritan and Anglican churches, the Great Awakening had its origins in the evangelical zeal and spiritual enthusiasm of seventeenth-century German Pietism. The Pietists were religious reformers who believed Luther's new Protestant church was gradually being undermined by corrupt, state-run churches, savage interchurch religious conflicts and confessionalism, or the practice of placing more emphasis on church dogma, ritual, and the performance of good works than the study of the Scriptures.

To combat this growing spiritual nominalism, the Pietists reintroduced Luther's original teachings about God's grace, humans' free will, and believers being justified by faith alone. Rejecting the Puritans' mysterious, distant Sovereign who predestined people to heaven or hell, the Pietists spoke of a loving, personal God who graciously offered salvation to all who were willing to examine their consciences, confess their sins, and embrace Christ's atoning sacrifice on the cross. Shifting believers' focus away from empty ritualism and endless doctrinal disputes and back to the central message of the Scriptures, a spiritually corrupted people's desperate need of a Savior, proved a winning formula for both the Pietists and American evangelicals who embraced their theology. After it was imported to the New World by Irish and English evangelists such as William Tennant Sr. and George Whitefield, and embraced by new American enthusiasts, this "back to the basics" revivalist gospel unleashed a tidal wave of religious enthusiasm in the thirteen colonies. This unprecedented American spiritual awakening soon crossed geographic and generational lines and flooded the colonies with a host of new evangelical converts. The sheer magnitude of the ensuing revivals impressed even confirmed skeptics like Benjamin Franklin, who noted, "it seem'd as if all the World were growing Religious." Convinced they could no longer submit to the authority of their spiritually corrupted, state churches, many new evangelical converts, or "New Lights," decided to leave them and create their own churches.

The First Great Awakening only strengthened Northerners' traditional tendency to mix religion and politics by encouraging them to focus not just on their own personal sins but also the public virtues of their church and larger society. Believers were thus encouraged to hold their churches and public institutions accountable for promoting Americans' spiritual and social welfare and fostering a society that was receptive to evangelical outreaches. As relations between the mother country and colonies soured in the mid-eighteenth century, evangelical preachers shifted the focus of their critique from local establishment churches and colonial assemblies to the policies of the English Crown.

Fully persuaded that the English were conspiring to deprive them of their religious and political liberties, the Northern clergy helped promote and spiritually justify the colonists' resistance using some of the same revivalist tactics and moral appeals they had employed earlier in the awakening. This strategy proved so successful that by the time the country finally went to war in 1775, most patriots were fully persuaded of the "Christian" nature of their cause. Having incorporated key presuppositions from the City upon a Hill's covenant theology in their new revolutionary gospel, evangelicals naturally embraced their predecessors' belief that the future success of their own "republican" experiment depended on their churches' ability to preserve the country's public virtue and their government's active support of religious freedom. Given their own denominations' declining influence in the new Republic, this conclusion initially produced significant dismay in the evangelical camp. But rapidly unfolding, turn-of-the-century events were about to prove them spectacularly wrong.[23]

Having effectively co-opted the Puritan community's spiritual identity and redemptive purpose, during the interlude between the two awakenings, evangelicals broadened their ministerial outreach. Ultimately rejecting the rigidity and exclusivity of the Puritans' institutionally based vision of providential exceptionalism, evangelicals removed the intermediating ecclesiastical institutions and opened the game of salvation up to everyone. Repudiating their Puritan forefathers' doctrine of Predestination, antebellum evangelicals preached that a loving, personal God would extend Christ's gift of atonement to all who sincerely read his Word, repented of their sins, and allowed the Holy Spirit to transform their lives.

With the American masses enthusiastically responding to their message at Creedance Clearwater Church, Cain Ridge, and other camp meetings, evangelicals invited Americans to join a new religious crusade to redeem not just their own communities, or England, but the entire world. Redemption no longer rested with a particular group, religious form, ceremony, or creed; in the evangelicals' scheme everyone could be a winner. Indeed, the very success of the evangelicals' grass-roots revivals seemed to indicate that God was preparing the United States to become his chosen instrument for saving all of humanity. Given the tremendous success of their far more ambitious agenda, evangelicals now questioned whether the Puritans' understanding of providential exceptionalism had only partially grasped God's greater design. Perhaps they had simply cast too narrow of a net and God's redemptive plans were even bigger than they imagined. Or maybe the real purpose of their journey into the wilderness had simply been to foreshadow America's larger spiritual mission, and like a kernel of wheat, the original vision of a City upon a Hill had to die before a truly American sense of national exceptionalism could be born. In any event, like their Puritan predecessors, evangelicals expected their church and state to play key roles in the redemption of their society. Determined to avoid the jurisdictional breakdowns that had proven fatal to the Puritans' experiment, evangelicals were determined to have their churches and public institutions strike a better balance between working closely together to advance religious freedom and respecting one another's proper areas of jurisdiction. After the Revolution many statesmen shared evangelicals' belief that the best way to achieve this institutional balance was by disestablishing the country's churches.

Ironically, however, instead of weakening religion and the close relationship between church and state in the United States, the early Republic's disestablishment policy revitalized American Protestantism and vastly expanded the churches' political influence. Membership in the antiquated state churches had been steadily declining in the decades after the Revolution and was in freefall by the turn of the century. Steeped in the secular republican ideology of the Enlightenment and Revolution, a new generation of Americans largely rejected organized religion. And those who did not generally seemed more comfortable with the progressive doctrines of Unitarianism than with the legalistic authoritarianism of Congregationalism and Anglicanism. The established churches' historic use of mandatory attendance laws, compulsory religious taxes, and religious tests to prop up their ministries also seemed incompatible with republicanism. Indeed, by the turn of the nineteenth century, most Americans viewed the country's historic state churches as relics of the past, hopelessly outdated and completely out of touch with the spirit of a new age. Thus most Americans were happy to learn that the new federal Constitution prohibited religious tests for holding public office and included a First Amendment barring Congress from making "any law respecting an establishment of religion." These national enactments sent a strong signal to the states that republican government would be best served by the disestablishment of official state churches.

State governments quickly followed suit, and the disestablishment of their churches finally gave Americans the freedom to choose their own religious institutions, if any. The introduction of this new "voluntary" system reinvigorated American Protestantism by liberating it from a rapidly deteriorating religious establishment and promoting greater diversity and competition. This created an ideal environment for the growth of the country's popular new evangelical sects. Finally freed from the official economic and political persecution they had endured under the establishment regime, the more popular and democratic Baptist and Methodist faiths thrived. Their success in turn provided the country's rapidly expanding population with new churches better suited to match antebellum Americans' more democratic political sentiments. Disestablishment thus removed the chief barriers blocking the natural evolution of the country's religious institutions. In doing so, it also set the stage for a second, even larger awakening that culminated in the greatest expansion of Protestant Christianity in American history.

Thanks to this Second Great Awakening, churches and Protestant religion became the most important "mystic chords" uniting the nation. As historian C. C. Goen observed:

> For the great mass of ordinary Americans, it was evangelical
> Christianity that helped to define their experiment in freedom
> and that shaped their visions of national destiny. The revivals
> and multifaceted activities they generated laid the foundation
> for a religiously based nationalism that transcended sectional
> differences, tamed the "barbarism" of the frontier, and
> heightened Americans' sense of fulfilling a special vocation in
> the purposes of the Almighty.[24]

Evangelists promoting this second religious revolution preached an even more aggressive social gospel than their eighteenth-century predecessors, firmly convinced that the gospel that rescued individuals could also "renew the face of communities and nations." The result, according to Perry Miller, was that "in the minds of evangelicals" there was increasingly a "complete identification of the cause of the Revival with that of the Federal Union."[25] Protestant Christianity had become the cornerstone of the Republic.

In *Democracy in America* Alexis de Tocqueville observed that while religion played "no direct part in the government of society," in America it was nevertheless "the foremost of the political institutions of that country" and Americans considered it "indispensable to the maintenance of [their] republican institutions."[26] Tocqueville and other European visitors were fascinated by the intimate relationship between America's popular Christian churches and republican government. Both the new evangelical churches and the Republic seemed to celebrate and uphold the same principles of individual freedom and democratic equality. Indeed, as Tocqueville asserted, "Americans combine the notions of Christianity and of liberty so intimately in their minds, that it is impossible to make them conceive the one without the other."

There certainly were plenty of examples of this intermingling of church and state in the decades leading up to the Civil War. Prominent antebellum preachers did not have any qualms about freely inserting political messages or election advice in their sermons, and prewar politicians, like Lincoln, increasingly added overt religious language and symbolism to their public speeches. The nation's popular and rapidly expanding Baptist, Methodist, and New School Presbyterian churches experienced unprecedented growth in the West thanks to the government's voluntary religious system, and in return, these churches urged their members to cherish and defend the republican governments that secured their freedoms.

Indeed, the act of disestablishment itself seemed to affirm the democratic and spiritual nature of the new government. For by removing public funding from a few old-line churches the national and state governments had both given Americans the democratic freedom to choose their own Protestant sects and inadvertently united the country around a common evangelical Protestant culture. The practical consequences of government disestablishment thus transformed the antebellum United States into the world's leading "Christian Republic."[27]

So if most Northern Christians were willing to sacrifice their lives for their national government in 1861, it was partly because, like Lincoln, they had developed an almost religious regard for the Union. Indeed, many had come to venerate the federal government and all the patriotic symbols associated with it, as if the Union itself was the spiritual foundation of the North. There were manifest reasons for this. For years evangelical ministers had informed them that their national government was the chief guardian of their religious and political rights and was founded on Reformed Protestant religious principles—such as covenant theology, religious freedom, the innate depravity of man and the separation of church and state. Those looking for proof of this government support of religion need only consider the new Republic's disestablishment policy, under which the nation's largest evangelical churches were thriving. Given this state of affairs, it is easy to understand why prominent antebellum preachers such as Henry Ward Beecher sincerely believed their country was a "true Christian democracy."[28] Having only recently obtained their political enfranchisement and religious freedom from the new Republic, antebellum evangelicals naturally came to view the national government as the principal source of their new-found liberties. In the minds of many Northerners, the cause of the country and Christ had become one.

Till Victory or Death

Given Northern Christians' newfound loyalty to the central government, it was relatively easy for ministers and politicians to transform a political war to save the Union into a war to save the world's only Christian republic. After their leaders had persuaded them that the Union was the world's last, best hope for advancing God's kingdom on earth, most Northern Christians enthusiastically enlisted in their government's armies and later reenlisted for the war's duration, convinced it was their Christian duty to keep fighting until the North emerged victorious.[29]

Pvt. John Harris of Illinois refused to place any time limits on his service to a Christian nation. In a letter to a female admirer back in Illinois, Harris declared he was prepared to fight "until the bitter end": "I am soldiering as a private and expect to continue to untill this rebellion is put down if it takes 20 years. I think it is my duty to be in the army and there I shall stay as long as I am able." Sylvester Bishop, a young Hoosier away from home for the first time in his life, sadly wrote his mother on Christmas morning 1861, "Little did I think last year this time that I would spend my next Christmas as a soldier in a sister state and I hope this may be my last in such a capacity, Though if need be I am willing to serve my country till every foe is subdued." Chagrined by his present circumstances and surely tempted by warm thoughts of home and family, Bishop was nonetheless resolved to keep fighting until the bitter end, no matter how many family Christmases he missed.[30]

After surviving his first battle at Fort Donelson, Pvt. William Dillon told his father, "I of course know not what awaits me in the future but one thing I do know and that is I will stand by the Stars and Stripes (should I be spared) until the funeral knell of Secessionism shall be heard and the union flag shall wave in triumph over the palmeto flag."[31] Another Union soldier wounded in the Fort Donelson battle told his sister that while he missed home and was enduring many "hardships and deprivations," he did not regret his decision to enlist and was not ready to come home yet. As he earnestly explained to her, "I enlisted to defend the rights of my country. I came here for the purpose of fighting. I expect to fight till the last armed foe expires." Although many soldiers had initially only volunteered to serve for ninety days, and then reenrolled for a three-year term, most vowed to keep fighting until the Confederacy was destroyed and backed up their boasts by reenlisting again in 1864.[32]

Like Sullivan Ballou, the Rhode Island volunteer forever immortalized in producer Ken Burns's documentary series on the Civil War, many Christian soldiers expressed the conviction that if necessary, they were "willing—perfectly willing to lay down" their lives to preserve the government and freedoms secured by their forefathers. In September 1862, an Indiana boy named Hiriam Reid informed his friends he had enlisted and was prepared to make the ultimate sacrifice in defense of his Christian government. Convinced a Christian could serve God just as well in the army as in the church, Reid wrote, "My faith is that in Serving my country that I can serve my god also and I am resolved to live up to that faith if I die in the attempt."[33]

Some Christian soldiers sounded almost stoic as they discussed their likely death in a desperate war to save the Union. On the eve of a battle with Joseph Wheeler's Confederate cavalry raiders, Sgt. Amos C. Weaver confidently assured a certain "Miss Mirriam" that "before tomorrow eve death may have settled on my brow and my cheeks that glow with the vigor of life and youth may be palid and cold. . . . But this thought does not alarm in *the least* I am ready and willing to sacrifice my life for my country if required." Pvt. James McIlrath of the Thirty-first Illinois also questioned whether he would survive the war, but as he told his wife, "We never intend to act the cowert and if we die we will die in an onerable causs." After all, every man eventually died, but how many could claim the honor of having died for a truly just and holy cause? As Wisconsin private Daniel Webster related to his fiancé in the fall of 1861, what Northern patriot would refuse to "wade through bloody seas, [and] suffer every thing but *death* its self," and suffer, "*all*—aye *more* than all this, even,—for right and justice[?]" Fighting near Corinth, Mississippi, Pvt. George Russell of Illinois idealistically concluded his letter with the grim observation that "as the poet sang we will live and die and Die for the union What is the cost of any one ore any number of men if we can uphold what our forefathers upheld?" Victory in a just war would be sufficient compensation for the lives of a few good soldiers.[34]

From the perspective of the Christian soldier who believed the Union was destined to become the redeemer nation that brought salvation to the world and ushered in the millennium, such reasoning made perfect sense. Christian soldiers, whose souls were already assured a place in heaven, could help save the Union—and hence the rest of the world—by sacrificing their lives for their country. So, would it not be better if, like Christ, a few Christian soldiers died so the rest of the world could live?

Origins of the Just War Code

After the fateful summer of 1863, when the tide of war finally appeared to be shifting in favor of the North, a veteran of the Sixty-third Indiana urged his youngest brother not to enlist. Pvt. Andrew McGarrah told his teen-aged brother "to *stay at home*. I do not give you this advise because I think this is an unjust *war* but that I think you are needed more at home." While McGarrah's letter failed to achieve its intended purpose—his brother enlisted a few weeks later—it illustrates the critical importance many nineteenth-century Christian soldiers attached to the idea of waging a just war. Most religious soldiers would not have enlisted in Lincoln's armies if they had entertained serious doubts about the just nature of their cause or the means used to advance it.[35]

Many of the United States' antebellum political, religious, and military leaders were at least vaguely familiar with the basic principles, if not the formal language, of just warfare, a set of internationally recognized legal principles for governing the use of violence in warfare. These guidelines helped them distinguish between just wars civilized nations could legitimately wage and unlawful wars they should avoid. In a just war a nation only resorted to violence after first exhausting every peaceful means for resolving the conflict. The war could only be initiated by a legitimate government authority and had to be fought with the right intentions, or to uphold international justice and not just to loot or vindictively punish a traditional enemy. The war should be defensive in nature, with the enemy attacking first and ideally striking the first blows. Enemy civilians should be spared, and retaliation should be proportionate to the original offense, with nations never inflicting greater violence and destruction on their enemy than had been directed against them, thus avoiding an escalating spiral of reprisals. The just war also had to be at least theoretically "winnable," and could only be waged using certain lawful and limited means, or a reasonable amount of legal violence.

Christians were theoretically barred from participating in wars that did not meet these criteria because the church believed such conflicts were immoral and could not be fought without irreparably damaging the moral fabric of the societies that waged them. Since God's word sanctioned the government's limited use of force to combat societal evil, Christians could participate in just wars, but they could not embrace violence for immoral purposes or employ inappropriate means to subdue their enemy.[36]

The idea that nations should wage just wars predated the European colonization of North America. It was probably the Roman lawyer and statesman Cicero who first articulated the principles girding the theory of just warfare. Later, Saint Augustine gave Cicero's just war framework a Christian context and reintroduced it to encourage the early and predominantly pacifistic church to defend the Roman Empire after it embraced the faith. In *Summa Theologica,* Saint Thomas Aquinas systematized Augustine's principles into a more comprehensive just war doctrine that was eventually recognized by the Roman Catholic Church.

Originally this doctrine concerned itself primarily with *jus ad bellum,* the legitimate or just causes for going to war. During the sixteenth and seventeenth centuries, however, Counter-Reformation theologians such as Francis de Vitoria and Francisco Suarez developed additional *jus in bello* guidelines governing wartime conduct that had to be observed if a war was to be waged justly. Unfortunately, the church proved incapable of honoring its own doctrine. During the Thirty Years' War the Catholic Church often sanctioned the use of unlimited violence in its crusade to purge Europe of Protestant heretics. The horrors of this religious warfare prompted Hugo Grotius to draft his seminal legal treatise, *On the Law of War and Peace,* which successfully merged both *jus ad bellum* and *jus in bello* criteria into a secular version of the earlier Catholic doctrine and created the international rules of war later recognized by Western Europe and the fledgling United States.

The professional Spanish, Dutch, French, and English officers who helped colonize North America in the early sixteenth and seventeenth centuries transplanted these just war practices and principles to the New World. Although Europe's early nation-states had consistently disregarded them in their religious wars against each other, we know colonial governors and military officers were familiar with the international guidelines governing warfare because they constantly accused their New World enemies of violating them. Anecdotal evidence suggests that America's early English colonists retained this tenuous Western European commitment to a code of just warfare. For example, during the New

England Indian wars, Puritan soldiers, clerics, and historians such as John Mason, religious leaders such as John Winthrop, and contemporary historians such as William Hubbard periodically invoked these "laws of nature" and "laws of nations" to justify some of the Protestants' harsher military measures against the Indians.[37]

When the colonies were later drawn into the French and Indian War and two subsequent conflicts with England, leaders such as George Washington also struggled—often unsuccessfully—to observe this professional military code. Most of the founding fathers were well acquainted with the "law of nations." George Washington, Alexander Hamilton, and Thomas Jefferson frequently cited it in defense of their foreign policies and competing political philosophies. But even when the colonial aristocracy conscientiously endeavored to fight by the book, there was little guarantee their subordinates or troops would. Given their lack of formal military schooling or training, noncommissioned officers, short-term volunteers, and men mustered from local militias were invariably the worst offenders when it came to observing the rules of war.[38]

To improve U.S. military compliance with such protocols, after the War of 1812, the army decided to add the formal study of just warfare principles to the curriculum of the United States Military Academy at West Point. In 1818 Sylvanus Thayer introduced a new course at West Point called "Geography, History and Ethics." Besides providing students with a basic understanding of American history and geography, the purpose of this required course was to provide cadets with an ethical framework for waging war.[39] By 1821, course instructors were using two required textbooks to develop this professional code of conduct for the country's future warriors: William Paley's *Principles of Moral and Political Philosophy* and the Swiss jurist and diplomat Emmerich de Vattel's voluminous work, *The Law of Nations*. Published a generation earlier in 1758, Vattel's work was enthusiastically embraced by both the country's founding fathers and America's antebellum politicians, lawyers, and diplomats, who widely considered it the most comprehensive and authoritative treatment of international law. James Kent's *Commentaries on American Law* had officially replaced *The Law of Nations* as the course legal text by 1839, but since many still considered Vattel the authority on international law, the academy continued to use his book to supplement Kent's commentaries throughout the antebellum era.[40] Thanks to Thayer's innovation, the officer candidates graduating from West Point in the antebellum era were generally well schooled in the principles of just warfare. For many of them, the Civil War would present the ultimate test of such principles.

Although the armies that fought the war were primarily made up of civilian volunteers who had little if any formal military instruction, the generals who ultimately assumed command of the North's largest armies either had been schooled at West Point or were drawn from the more educated class of antebellum society and thus likely had some prior exposure to the law of nations. Commanders issued general orders to their armies conveying their interpretation of such rules to subordinates, trusting that in a hierarchical organization like the army, this would ensure that all the soldiers in their command fought under the same ethical guidelines. As the army had discovered earlier, however, during the American Revolution, such was not always the case.

In *Upon the Altar of the Nation: A Moral History of the Civil War*, Harry S. Stout observed that the North's practical application of this moral framework underwent a significant evolution over the course of the conflict. Lincoln gradually turned from a limited fight to save the Union, which sought to minimize bloodshed, property damage, and civilian suffering, to a total war against slavery, which employed far "harder measures" to break Southerners' spiritual and physical capacity to continue resisting. Stout set aside "the question of *why* the war was fought (*jus ad bellum*) because . . . secession is a moral issue with no moral criterion for a sure answer" and instead castigated Lincoln, Sherman, and Grant for "condoning the logic of total war in the name of abolition—and victory."[41]

In Stout's opinion the Civil War was not "a just war dictated by prudent considerations of proportionality and protection of noncombatants" because "in too many instances both sides descended into moral misconduct." Most of his just warfare critique, however, is directed against the Union war effort and focused on the writings of the Northern elite—not the common soldier. Having initially embraced a just war based on the "West Point code," which emphasized a war of maneuver rather than costly battles, the protection of innocents, and minimal destruction of enemy property, Stout believes Lincoln pragmatically introduced an "Emancipation lever" to inaugurate surreptitiously a "total war" that would "obliterate prior rules." After effectively declaring war on the Southern population in July 1862 with executive orders allowing the Army of the Potomac to subsist upon the country, seize enemy property, exile unrepentant Rebels, and execute Rebel guerrillas, Lincoln next allegedly replaced the West Point code with a more liberal code of military conduct called the "Lieber code." Officially drawn up in 1863 to give the army an official handbook on just warfare guidelines, according to Stout, Francis Lieber's more pragmatic approach to warfare gave Northern soldiers the ethical freedom to do "just about anything" they wanted to Southern civilians, all in the name of "military necessity." Stout recounts how, after receiving this green light from the administration, Lincoln's generals indiscriminately waged a relentless war against the Southern population with official orders or policies sanctioning the forcible relocation of disloyal enemy civilians and the confiscation and destruction of enemy property, businesses, and unrepentant Rebels' homes. Stout also claims the North violated the *jus in bello* prohibitions against the use of excessive and disproportionate force when it later conducted an extremely costly war of attrition, introduced a brutal scorched-earth policy, and deliberately targeted noncombatants when bombarding enemy cities to finally conquer an unyielding South.

Stout's moral history of the war is a pioneering and brilliant work on many levels, but in at least one respect his just war critique of the conflict seems a bit overdrawn. While accurately tracing what happened, Stout's analysis fails to provide adequate historical context concerning either West Point's instruction in just warfare or the U.S. military's application of the doctrine in past wars. For example, although Stout discusses the West Point code of conduct that emphasized the use of limited violence to protect the lives of innocent civilians, he says virtually nothing about the principal West Point textbook that influenced future Civil War generals' understanding of just warfare: Vattel's *Law of Nations.*[42] Given Vattel's enormous influence on antebellum politicians' and generals' conception of just warfare, any moral judgments rendered on either side's ethical conduct in the war should take his guidelines into account. A systematic review of Vattel's work reveals that most of the major *jus in bello* violations Stout identified—from the confiscation and deliberate destruction of enemy property and bombardment of fortified enemy cities (Atlanta) to the sacking and ravaging of enemy communities—are both theoretically described and, when properly applied, considered legitimate just war options. Nor did any of these so-called total war measures, or for that matter even Lieber's infamous code, mark a radical departure from what had transpired earlier when the U.S. Army had fought "savage" enemies under Vattel's guidelines. In fact, the Union armies' overall ethical conduct in the war was at least consistent with, if not superior to, its performance in earlier, protracted nineteenth-century conflicts against enemies employing guerrilla warfare tactics, such as the Second Seminole War.[43]

Although the "regular" rules of war prohibited the excesses decried by Stout, according to Vattel and Lieber, there were certain occasions when the use of these "harsher measures" was justified to punish "savage" enemy nations that blatantly violated the laws of nations. In the case of the Civil War, the enemy behavior that prompted the Northern high command to introduce these more severe measures to punish the South and "bring the war to a conclusion" was Confederate guerrilla warfare. Here an important distinction must be drawn between Confederate irregular troops who, while detached from the main Confederate armies, were fighting in uniform as paid soldiers for the Confederacy and guerrilla detachments who ambushed Union supply columns and then melted back into the civilian population before Union forces could mount an effective response. In the spirit of Vattel's *Law of Nations,* Lieber's code sought to provide a clearer distinction between these two categories, treating irregulars, whom both sides were employing with increasing frequency, according to the standard rules of war, while continuing to criminalize the operation of enemy guerrillas.

Both Vattel and Lieber clearly specified the additional and more severe measures a nation could lawfully employ against enemy noncombatants who employed such means of resistance. Vattel asserted that as long as enemy noncombatants were careful to "submit to him who is master of the country, and pay the contributions demanded, and refrain from acts of hostility," they would "live in safety as if they were on friendly terms with the enemy; their property rights are even held sacred." If enemy noncombatants resisted the occupying authorities, however, they were liable to "suffer the calamities of war." According to Vattel, these wartime calamities or judgments could include the confiscation or destruction of civilian property, the taking of civilian hostages, reprisals, and the looting and destruction of civilian homes, businesses, and farms. The Lieber code also extended special protections to "the unarmed citizen," who was to be spared his "person, property, and honor as much as the exigencies of war will admit," and asserted, "No belligerent had the right to declare that he will treat every captured man . . . as a brigand or bandit." Like Vattel, however, Lieber included an important exception: "If however, the people of a country, or any portion of the same, already occupied by an army, rise against it, they are violators of the laws of war and are not entitled to their protection." In other words, to secure the safety of their commands and prevent the enemy from impeding their future operations in the South in rear areas still plagued by widespread insurrection, Union commanders were free to invoke, in the name of military necessity, the more serious wartime punishments spelled out by Vattel.[44]

Nearly all the principal Northern commanders who advocated a "harder" policy toward enemy noncombatants—Grant, Sherman, Sheridan, and Henry Halleck—had served in the West, where their commands and military operations had been repeatedly disrupted by the activities of Confederate irregular forces and guerrillas.[45] In their minds this deliberate and officially sanctioned Confederate guerrilla activity constituted a clear violation of the just war provisions prohibiting noncombatants from engaging in hostilities. They also believed the South's failure to abide by the conventional rules governing warfare fully justified the introduction of a much harsher Northern occupation policy and stern countermeasures to combat the activities of suspected enemy spies and guerrillas and discourage similar acts of resistance in the future.

According to Vattel, even Sherman and Phil Sheridan's terrible scorched-earth policies in Georgia, the Carolinas, and the Shenandoah Valley had just war precedents. While generally regarding such measures "savage and monstrous excesses, when committed without necessity," Vattel considered them lawful in two cases: (1) when "a country is totally ravaged, towns and villages are sacked, and delivered up . . . to fire and sword," for the purposes of "chastising an unjust and barbarous nation," or "checking her brutality," and (2) when a country is ravaged and rendered "uninhabitable, in order to make it serve as a barrier to cover our frontier against an enemy whose incursions we are unable to check by any other means." Although easy to condemn in hindsight, Sherman's destructive March to the Sea and judgment on South Carolina certainly seemed motivated by a quest to punish the Southern people's stubborn intransigence and martial spirit. Given the Confederacy's repeated use of the Shenandoah Valley to invade the North and threaten the Yankee capital, even as late as 1864, Halleck and Grant could arguably have used the second case to justify what the residents of the valley later bitterly called "the burning."[46]

Although Vattel's ideal conception of a just war mirrored McClellan's vision of waging a carefully limited and largely bloodless war of maneuver, Vattel was also realistic enough to understand that in some protracted wars against unjust nations, generals needed the operational freedom to employ harsher means to "procure victory and bring the war to a conclusion." In these cases, the "right of punishing him [the enemy] produces new rights over the things that belong to him, as it also does over his person." For example, although generally disapproving of the bombardment of towns, such as Vicksburg and Atlanta, Vattel thought it was "nevertheless warranted by the laws of war, when we are unable by any other means to reduce an important post, on which the success of the war may depend."[47]

In his writings Vattel even seemed to invoke a nascent doctrine of military necessity, something Stout and other scholars seem to consider an innovation of Lieber's code. Claiming that a country had the right to weaken an enemy by every justifiable method, Vattel explained, "Since the object of a just war is to repress injustice and violence . . . we have a right to put in practice, against the enemy, every measure that is necessary in order to weaken him, and disable him from resisting us and supporting his injustice; and we may choose such methods as are the most efficacious and best calculated to attain the end in view, provided they be not of an odious kind, nor unjustifiable in themselves, and prohibited by the law of nature." For, "the pillage and destruction of towns, the devastation of the open country, ravaging, setting fire to houses, are measures no less odious and detestable on every occasion when they are evidentially put in practice without absolute necessity."[48]

Given this far grimmer nineteenth-century understanding of *jus in bello,* perhaps this explains why, with the exception of McClellan—always a pronounced critic of the administration—so few Northern generals or politicians expressed any serious moral reservations with the ethical conduct of the Northern armies or paid much attention to the new Lieber code. As Stout himself emphasized, the "Union generals showed scant interest in the code and soldiers none." Concerning the war's conduct, the Northern clergy were "virtually cheerleaders all," and "on all sides—clerical, political, journalistic, military, artistic, and intellectual—the historian searches in vain for moral criticism directed at one's own cause."[49] Given their understanding of the law of nations, Northern politicians and generals clearly believed they were in fact waging a "civilized" war against the South, albeit a noticeably "harder" one after 1862. Indeed, the few critical sources that Stout musters to substantiate his charges of foul play are principally Northern Peace Democrats; Confederate civilians, writers, and generals; and devout Union chaplains and surgeons, with all but the latter obviously predisposed to criticize any effective Republican military policy, and the latter generally predisposed to reject any harsh wartime measures and empathize with those who are suffering.

Although Stout included extensive excerpts from a series of letters Sherman and Hood exchanged regarding Sherman's application of the just rules of war in the Atlanta campaign, he excluded the last letter where Sherman directly cited the "rules of war" that justified his harsh actions. In this remarkable exchange of letters, Hood first chastised Sherman for his "unprecedented" cruelty in forcibly evacuating Atlanta's civilian population after his conquest of the city. Later in the exchange, he also condemned Sherman for his immoral conduct during the siege of the city. The Northern general had not provided Confederate authorities with advance warning of his intended bombardment of the city so they could safely evacuate noncombatants and had then deliberately targeted the civilian population. Having already explained his humanitarian motives for removing Atlanta's civilian noncombatants from a potential future battlefield, in his final letter Sherman addressed the morality of his bombardment of Atlanta: "I was not bound by the laws of war to give notice of the shelling of Atlanta, a 'fortified town, with magazines, arsenals, foundries, and public stores;' you were bound to take notice. See the Books," a clear reference to one or more of the just war textbooks the two had studied together at West Point.[50]

Since Maj. Gen. Henry Halleck, the author of the 1861 West Point textbook *International Law* and one of America's prewar authorities on the subject of just warfare, also weighed in on the controversy, perhaps we should consider what he had to say about Sherman's alleged *jus in bello* violations in the Atlanta campaign:

> The course which you have pursued in removing rebel families from Atlanta . . . is fully approved by the War Department. Not only are you justified by the laws and usages of war in removing these peoples, but I think it was your duty to your own army to do so. Moreover, I am fully of the opinion that the nature of the war, the conduct of the enemy (and especially of non-combatants and women of the territory which we have heretofore conquered and occupied), will justify you

in gathering up all the forage and provisions which your army
might require. . . . We have tried three years of conciliation
and kindness without any reciprocation; on the contrary,
those thus treated have acted as spies and guerrillas in our rear
and within our lines. The safety of our armies, and a proper
regard for the lives of our soldiers, require that we apply to our
inexorable foes the severe rules of war. . . . I have endeavored
to impress these views upon our commanders for the last two
years. You are almost the only one who has properly applied
them.[51]

Halleck and Sherman's belief that Southern noncombatants were getting what they
deserved would probably have resonated well with Vattel, who urged opposing civilian
populations to "submit to the regulations imposed upon them by the enemy" peaceably
if they wished "to be spared the calamities of war."[52] Given these Union generals' understanding of early-nineteenth-century international law, it would thus seem that it was
the Southern people's actions, not Lincoln's, that ultimately persuaded some Northern
authorities to begin treating certain portions of the Confederate population as enemy
combatants.

Ironically, the *jus ad bellum* criteria Stout "set aside" because they focused on "a
moral issue [secession] with no moral criterion for a sure answer" were some of the most
frequently addressed subjects in Northern religious soldiers' correspondence.[53] Just as
Stout found only a handful of loyal Northern elites who were genuinely critical of the
North's *jus in bello* practices, only a few religious soldiers expressed serious concerns with
either side's wartime conduct. In their wartime correspondence, Northern Christians
occasionally accused the South of violating some *jus in bello* principle by, for example,
waging guerrilla warfare or deliberately mistreating Union prisoners of war. But the vast
majority seemed far more concerned with *jus ad bellum* issues—the just nature of the
Northern war effort and obvious immorality of the Southern cause.[54]

Even common soldiers who had never read anything about just warfare instinctively
seemed to recognize there were at least a few bedrock principles girding and limiting
wartime violence. After all, the Scriptures and Europe's long history of religious wars
were the principal inspiration for the original Catholic just war code, and these were
two subjects Reformed Protestants were intimately familiar with. The citizen-soldiers'
Judeo-Christian heritage and rudimentary understanding of Western European history
clearly informed them that even in times of war, civilized peoples had to obey God's
laws and observe certain diplomatic and military niceties if they wished to avoid the
irrevocable censure of this world and the next. To ensure God's favor in a war, Christian
soldiers recognized that their cause had to be just, that a legitimate government authority
had to issue a formal declaration of war before commencing hostilities, and that their
side needed to fight with the right motives, means, and degree of force while shielding
noncombatants from the violence. Given most common soldiers' belief that a faithful
adherence to such principles would ensure God's favor and ultimate victory in the war,
they naturally attached great importance to upholding them and were also quick to cry
foul when their opponents did not.

Northern Christians who believed they were engaged in a just war against the Confederacy often cited three *jus ad bellum* arguments to defend their government's war against the South, all of which revolved around the justice of their cause, the political and moral illegitimacy of the Confederacy, and the truly right and noble intentions for which the war was being fought. The first argument was that the South was clearly the aggressor in the war. Without any prior provocation, Southerners had seized federal property in the South and inaugurated a civil war by firing the first shots at the U.S. flag flying over Fort Sumter. So unlawfully attacked first by the South, the Northern government had every legal and moral right to defend itself. The North was also perfectly justified in using military force against the South because secession was illegitimate, and the Southern states were thus in a state of rebellion against a duly constituted and lawfully elected national government. Finally, the Union war against the South was being fought with the right intentions, or proper motives. Northerners were not fighting a war of revenge or to conquer the South's territory and wealth. The Lincoln administration was simply fighting to suppress rebellion and to "nobly save" the world's "last best hope" of obtaining true Christian freedom.

Most Christian soldiers had little doubt the South was the aggressor in the war. Like the Northern clergy, they agreed with Henry Ward Beecher's assessment that despite the North's "honest and long-continued effort to preserve the right by peaceful methods . . . war, has been forced upon us (not sought, nor wished, but accepted reluctantly) by the overt act of the rebellious States." For decades the leaders of the Southern states had been periodically rattling their swords and threatening to secede or inaugurate a civil war whenever they felt their sectional interests were somehow threatened.

In the 1850s, the political climate was further poisoned when Southern filibusters and statesmen had engaged in duplicitous and provocative schemes to expand their section's peculiar institution in Latin America, even at the expense of a foreign war. Then, after finally seceding from the Union in the winter of 1860–61, Southern states had compounded their "original sin" of secession by illegally seizing federal property and military supplies in the South. One of the most egregious examples was Virginian politician John B. Floyd, who used his position and political influence as Buchanan's secretary of war to ensure Union military weapons and supplies fell into the hands of Southern sympathizers. Given this long history of sectional discord, when South Carolina finally fired on the U.S. flag flying over Fort Sumter without any prior provocation, it was the last straw for many outraged Northerners. Having patiently borne their Southern neighbors' indiscretions for decades, many believed that it was high time the South's moral and political crimes be punished.[55]

For most Northern Christians, the issue could not have been clearer. A traitorous section that had long been trampling upon the rights and dignity of its sister states had now brazenly assaulted the national flag itself. It was their holy duty to defend the Union and crush the recalcitrant Southerners. Upon arriving at Camp Butler, just outside Springfield, Illinois, Pvt. William Onstot immediately dispatched a letter to his sister Lizzie declaring that he was now "one of uncle Sam's boys" and "proud to be call by so high a name as that of volunteer soldier in defense of my country's flag against traitorous hands."[56] After learning of the Confederate attack on Fort Sumter, Abraham Boynton earnestly told his friends that "the time has come when it is the duty of all that can to rally around our country's shameless flag and protect it, from the impious hands of traitors. . . . I have solemnly taken an oath to protect it and I mean to do it, while I live."[57] Boynton immediately enlisted in the Fourth Wisconsin Cavalry. The volunteer soldiers of 1861 and 1862 who survived the war would later proudly recall the sincere patriotism and idealism that prompted their enlistment. In an 1865 letter to his nephew, an Eleventh Indiana veteran named Jasper Kidwell enthusiastically shared his motives for volunteering, noting that "when the call was made to rally And protect our Noble Country we did not faltar at that Call But marched Bravely forth worthy of our Patriot Sires To quell a traiterous foe who have Ever Sought our destruction."[58]

Competent Authority and Just Intention

A second popular *jus ad bellum* argument that many Union soldiers often cited was the illegitimacy of secession and the U.S. government's right to defend itself against unlawful rebellions. The just war doctrine clearly specified that only competent government authorities could legitimately wage war against other nations, and most Christian soldiers shared their commander in chief's view that since secession was illegal, the Confederacy itself was not a lawfully established political entity empowered to make war. If true, this fundamentally altered the whole character of the conflict. It was no longer a conflict between two aspiring Christian republics but an unlawful internal rebellion that needed to be suppressed.

Reformed Protestants' biblical understanding of government, and especially the believer's duty to submit to the governing authorities, made this a particularly devastating *jus ad bellum* argument for the Union. Indeed, Romans 13:1–2 asserted that all existing government authority was derived from God: "Let every soul be subject unto the higher powers. For there is no power but of God: the powers that be are ordained of God. Whosoever therefore resisteth the power, resisteth the ordinance of God: and they that resist shall receive to themselves damnation."[59] In light of this passage, even if secession was somehow constitutionally legitimate or backed by popular opinion, the Southern states still had no moral authority to rebel against the Union because it was a legitimate Christian government instituted by God. Subsequent verses warned wrongdoers that rebellions against God-ordained governments would be severely punished because governing authorities were agents of wrath who did not bear "the sword in vain." Northern clergymen, such as the Congregationalist theologian Horace Bushnell, could thus persuasively argue that in rebelling against the Union, Southerners were rebelling against God himself. Southern states rights became "the most pestilent heresy of the nation" because it sought "to shake off Providence and law together" and take "away every semblance of right in the government." Presbyterian cleric E. E. Adams also shared Bushnell's understanding that from a biblical perspective, the Southern rebellion could never be justified because the "preservation of government was the cause of God."[60]

In making this argument, of course, the Northern clergy and Lincoln had to make a careful distinction between morally justified revolutions against tyrannical governments and unlawful rebellions lest they undermine the legal basis for America's own revolution against England. In their eyes the American Revolution was morally just because the colonists had only embraced violence as a last resort. Their forefathers initially fought to *restore* the colonial governments unlawfully usurped by the British, not create a completely new government. To buttress such arguments, the backers of the Union could cite none other than Thomas Jefferson, who had carefully laid out the patriots' legal justification in his Declaration in a manner that John Locke himself might have even approved. According to Jefferson, the founding fathers had only embraced revolution after the English government had engaged in "a long train of abuses and usurpations" and ignored the colonies repeated petitions for redress, or demonstrated by its own malfeasance that it was not the legitimate government of the colonies. Even then, the colonists had initially only sought to restore the governing authority of their colonial assemblies. Complete political independence was only embraced after their mother country made it a wartime necessity.

In the case of the Southern Confederacy, however, states belonging to an existing government had sought to secede from that regime without securing the national government or their sister states' consent. The Southern states had also unilaterally declared their independence without awaiting the requisite "proof" that Lincoln's so-called Black Republican administration would in fact over time consistently violate their rights and ignore their repeated appeals for redress. The Southern states had left the Union not because the Lincoln administration had consistently abused or usurped Southern liberties but because of what Southerners feared his administration might do in the future. For most Northern Christians these were enormous differences, and they completely discredited Southern claims concerning the legitimacy of secession and how the creation of the Confederacy was in fact a "Second American Revolution." If, as many Northerners argued, the Union was a compact or covenant predating the Constitution, then there could be no legitimate national government in the South until the Northern states agreed to let the erring states go.

Since submission to established authority was one of the cardinal principles of both Puritan and antebellum America, this was a particularly devastating *jus ad bellum* argument for Northern Christians because it undermined both the political and religious foundations of the Confederacy and hence justified the North's immediate and forceful response. By convincing Northern believers that Southern secession was really lawless sedition, the Northern clergy effectively transformed the South's "conservative, preemptive counter-revolution" into a treacherous rebellion against a God-ordained government. Northern evangelicals who subscribed to a literal hermeneutics had little trouble drawing the appropriate biblical analogies. Just as Satan had defied the Creator's lawful authority by leading a rebellion against heaven, the South was also defying God's kingdom on earth by rebelling against his chosen Christian government. And just as the Almighty had summoned his angelic armies to crush Satan's revolt in heaven, Lincoln was perfectly justified in mobilizing Union volunteers to suppress a Southern insurrection against his administration. In the end, anyone who unlawfully rebelled against a Christian government would rightfully suffer the wrath of God.[61]

That numerous Union soldiers embraced this image of the Confederacy being an unholy insurgency against a God-ordained government was clearly evidenced by the number of times Northern Christians used the terms "Rebel" and "rebellion" in their letters. In the winter of 1863, Pvt. Michael Hayes Cunningham indignantly informed his wife he was not fighting for abolition, "old Abe . . . you or any one else. The Rebles are trying to break down one of the best governments that men ever had and we are trying to keep them from doing it."[62] Another soldier, trying to explain his wartime absence to his little boy, was just as blunt. Pvt. Joseph Manson of the Twenty-seventh Iowa told his son "the Detestable Rebs have tried to Destroy this good Government. That is what I am away from home for and as soon as they are whipped and hanged I will come home and I guess no Rebel will dare to destroy the United States again will they?"[63] While such language may not have deterred Manson's Southern enemies, it made quite an impression on little James. As they marched off to war, many Northern Christians appreciated the moral clarity that stemmed from the belief that their side was engaged in a just war against an illegitimate rebellion. When other soldiers contemplated laying down their lives for the Union, however, religious soldiers searched for some other, even higher purpose that would help them justify making such a sacrifice.

Liberty and Union

Although most Northern Christians viewed the conflict as a just, defensive war against Southern aggressors, or the forceful suppression of a politically illegitimate and immoral rebellion, a few thoughtful individuals looked beyond these immediate issues, and after considering both sides' ultimate intentions in the war, they realized that far more might be at stake than just the preservation of the Lincoln administration. According to them, the outcome of the war would determine the future meaning of freedom in the United States, and perhaps the rest of the world as well. Religious soldiers who subscribed to this third popular interpretation of just war argued that while Southerners publicly professed to be fighting for their independence, the real intention of their rebellion was to expand the South's "peculiar institution" throughout the United States and extinguish the North's free institutions. Should the South prove victorious, these Northerners feared that the founders' original vision of liberty, which maintained all men were created equal and "endowed by their Creator, with certain inalienable rights," would perish alongside the Union. The war thus pitted a regressive Southern aristocracy that offered liberty only to wealthy whites against a more progressive Northern society that wished to extend freedom to all Americans and was finally taking the first hesitant steps toward implementing that ideal. For these Northerners, a war to ensure the survival and future advance of human liberty represented the purest of intentions, and this was certainly a cause worth fighting for.

The words "liberty" and "Union" might be abstract terms today, but for nineteenth-century Americans who held an almost religious affection for their Christian republic, the sentiments behind them were dearer than life itself. It should be remembered that in the mid-nineteenth century, the United States was the only republic in the world, or the only government that had entrusted its citizens with the reins of power. Its dominant

Protestant majority could also celebrate the fact that by every modern measure, their country was the most Christian nation on the planet. Absolute monarchies backed by corrupt state churches were generally the rule elsewhere. So when Northern Christians thought of the word "liberty," it reminded them of the unprecedented freedoms they enjoyed living in a Christian republic dedicated to the radical proposition that because all men were created equal, they should enjoy the same political and legal rights. The word "Union," meanwhile, denoted the national compact that united the various states under the common Constitution. By the mid-eighteenth century, however, the meaning of both terms had become so inextricably linked in the fabric of American republicanism that in the minds of most Northerners, they virtually meant the same thing.[64]

Most antebellum Northerners had learned to appreciate the deeper meaning of these words in school, when they memorized Massachusetts Senator Daniel Webster's famous reply to South Carolina's Senator Robert Hayne in the 1830 Webster-Hayne debate. After explaining to Hayne why the Union ratified by the American people in 1776 was a perpetual institution, Webster forever immortalized those mystical terms when he proclaimed that the United States could not prosper without "Liberty *and* Union, now and forever; one and inseparable." The Union had not been created by the states' ratification of the Constitution, according to Webster, but by the colonists' declaration of independence from England. It was a sacred compact between the American people and their government, not a temporary alliance between competing political entities, and Webster was convinced that there could be no true liberty outside it. For if lesser political bodies could defy the federal government's authority by seceding from the Union whenever they found it convenient to do so, then the national government was a meaningless facade and the rights and liberties it defended were illusory.

In their letters, Northern soldiers, steeped in Webster's pro-Union political philosophy, repeatedly expressed their willingness to fight and die for both the freedoms their forefathers had sacrificially secured in the Revolution and the Union that preserved them. Until 1861, Northerners believed the Union was the best defender of those freedoms. They had long suspected the Southern slave power was conspiring to rob them of their economic and political freedoms, and now by making war on the Union itself, the planter aristocracy was assaulting the chief foundation and guardian of their liberties. Unable to imagine a world in which true freedom existed outside the Union, religious soldiers suddenly realized their own families' future liberties and happiness were inextricably tied to its fate.

Evangelical clergymen reinforced these themes during the initial Northern enlistment drives, arguing that the war was a contest to determine the future meaning of freedom and liberty in the Union. Henry Ward Beecher proclaimed that the war was "a conflict for the government of this continent between two giant forces,—the spirit of Christian liberty and democracy, and the spirit of aristocratic oppression." A contest that would determine whether the United States upheld or rejected the founders' views concerning the "Divine right of liberty in man." According to Beecher, either the Northern or the Southern view of freedom would ultimately prevail—liberty for all men or just the Southern slaveholder.[65] Rather than watch a free government dissolve in an orgy of slavery and despotism, Beecher beseeched his congregation, "Take the side of true American principles;—liberty for one, and liberty for all; liberty now, and liberty forever; liberty as the foundation of government, and liberty as the basis of union; liberty as against revolution, liberty, against anarchy, and liberty, against slavery."[66]

Other Northern preachers also joined this patriotic chorus by encouraging their young men to rescue the country's political institutions from the anarchy unleashed by Southern secession. Pastor A. L. Stone of Boston's Park Street Church told the men of his congregation that they were not enlisting in a "sectional war; not a war of conquest and subjugation," but "solely a war for the maintenance of the Government and Constitution." At All Souls Church in New York City, Henry W. Bellows asserted that the North was not going to war "to force fifteen states to live under a Government they hate" but to "save order and civilization."[67]

After the attack on Fort Sumter, these saber-rattling sermons and other public demonstrations of republican patriotism helped persuade thousands of Christians who had previously favored further compromise with the South to drop their moral reservations about going to war. During the secession crisis in the winter of 1860–61, Harley Wayne abandoned his earlier opposition to a violent sectional confrontation. Writing from the chambers of the Illinois Hall of Representatives in Springfield, Wayne told his startled wife, "Actual war is upon us and we have got to make preparation for it—There is no hope for escape I mean to stand by the country and if need be fight for the liberties of the nation." Other soldiers were just as fervent in their desire to uphold, and if necessary sacrifice their own lives in defense of, their country's political traditions. In the autumn of 1863, Pvt. Andrew McGarrah of the Sixty-third Indiana indicated the intensity of his own commitment when he told his younger brother James, "I believe this is true as scripture. It is my honest sentiment and by the grace of God it shall be my Dieing sentiment. Independence *now and Union Forever.*" Illinois private Benjamin Webb Baker was also prepared to sacrifice his life on the Union's altar of liberty: As he informed his anxious mother back in Illinois, "If there is a battle and I should fall, tell with pride and not grief that I fell in defense of liberty."[68]

Convinced that the Union was the principal source of their liberties and freedom, many Northern soldiers believed they now had a moral obligation to defend it. Private Cunningham of the Eighteenth Wisconsin completely disagreed with his wife's interpretation of the war:

> I do not think as you do in regard to this war you seem to think
> it is an Abolition war I think . . . the South is is [*sic*] trying to
> break up this Union and build up an Aristocratic Government
> and we are defending the Union and a Republican form of Gov-
> ernment And you must say that it is the best government the
> Sun ever show on It has protected us so far and now when we
> are called up to protect it ought not we do it [?][69]

Despite his seemingly less important military assignment, guarding Helena, Arkansas, from the depredations of Confederate guerrillas, Pvt. James Lockney believed he too was playing an important role in a just war to sustain his government. In the winter of 1862–63 he told his mother, "I know that I am determined to defend the *God-like Cause* of *Liberty* and *Union,* for which *I* enlisted now as certainly, sincerely, truly and ably as I felt determined to fight for the Right last summer when I enlisted." Convinced that he was fighting to uphold his country's republican principles and institutions, Lockney was obviously determined to see the conflict through.[70]

Pvt. John Siperly of Wisconsin was also convinced that the war was being fought over "higher" republican principles, such as liberty and justice. In a beautifully written and highly imaginative letter to his girlfriend in Delavan, Wisconsin, Siperly compared the just nature of the Union's cause to a star rising above the Murfreesboro battlefield:

> Away in the distance can plainly be seen looming up above
> the dark horizon of civil war and oppression the bright star
> of peace and Liberty—a star that will soon flash across the
> continent with blinding brightness At those miscreants that
> have usurped their power and sought to overthrow the best
> government known to civilized man—and will infuse a spirit
> of unspeakable gladness in the hearts of all lovers of Liberty,
> Justice and Equal rights.[71]

Henry Ward Beecher told Northerners that the Southern rebellion threatened not only the Union but also all government and liberty:

> The maintenance of this government in its original jurisdic-
> tion is demanded, not alone because it is good to us, but
> because it has such signal relations to the prosperity of the
> entire world. It was an experiment,—an experiment ridiculed
> at first, then feared, and now detested, by absolute monarchs.
> This government was an experiment that caused the first dawn
> of hope upon the minds of nations struggling in fetters and in
> bondage; and has inspired the hope that there was coming a
> period when the common people, the world around, should be
> redeemed from thraldom, and when human rights should be
> respected by governments.[72]

According to Beecher, the North was thus fighting for the liberty of the entire world, for every man's right to liberty as a creature made in God's image.[73] If the Union disintegrated, monarchs and tyrants around the world would point to the American experience as proof that republican experiments in self-government were doomed to failure. The triumph of a slave aristocracy over a democratic government would make a cruel mockery of the proposition that all men were entitled to the same rights of life, liberty, and the pursuit of happiness. Southern victory would completely undermine the North's free institutions and be a major setback for every oppressed people who longed for the political and economic freedoms Americans enjoyed. Thus, for Northern Christians, the potential consequences of God's redeemer nation being compromised by Southern victory were unthinkable. The United States would lose the honor of fulfilling her millennial mission, and the rest of the world would be plunged into a new Dark Age of aristocratic tyranny and paganism.

Other Christian soldiers also suspected the war might have implications for freedom elsewhere. A highly articulate Illinois soldier named Ransom Bedell told his cousin that the war was an epic contest between liberty and despotism, a struggle for the future freedom of every nation:

> In the two great sections of our land the North and South
> we see the two great principles of *liberty* and *despotism* duly
> accepted "and defended"—maintained and supported. The
> South in accepting of despotism on a grand scale has thrown
> her whole strength, politics, money, power, time, talents,
> and the life of thousands of her noblest sons,—all into the
> scale for the upbuilding of a grand system of oppression, and
> tyranny, of the darkest dye.—While the north in the pride of
> her strength, and a sense of truth and justice has arisen, and
> thrown her money, politics, time, talents, and thousands of her
> noble Sons, on the side of truth, justice, liberty, equality, free
> govt, and free institutions, And on many a field of fearful and
> deadly strife have we caused the vile minions of Rebellion to
> quail, not before our numbers, but before our prowess, skill,
> and invincible courage, arising from a just cause—having in
> view the future good of all Nations.[74]

Another Northern soldier tracking the successful advance of Sherman's army in Georgia seemed to understand exactly what was at stake when he contemplated the meaning of Northern victory in the war:

> The Rebellion will be crushed and we will have a Govern-
> ment that the world will admire and respect. . . . And here
> will be the great temple of liberty from which shall spring the
> liberation of all nations and the equality of all men and then
> we can look up to that grand old flag for which we have fought
> and blead and Know that under its folds the freedom of all
> men is recognized.[75]

Victory in the war would vindicate the North's free institutions and usher in a new birth of freedom around the world.

In the end, the just war framework offered Northern believers both an ethical rationale for enlisting in a war against their Christian neighbors and much-needed moral assurance that they were engaged in a righteous cause. When churches asked the men of the North to serve out of a sense of duty to their families and country, and to the higher cause of freedom itself, the churches were appealing to the better angels of their nature. But in their intense desire to assist the Union war effort, the evangelical churches also appealed to men's baser instincts when they sanctioned a holy war against the Confederacy that demonized the South.

Chapter 5

THE GREAT NORTHERN CRUSADE

He has sounded forth the trumpet that shall never sound retreat
He is sifting out the hearts of men before his judgment seat
Oh be swift my soul to answer him
Be jubilant my feet
Our God is marching on

> Julia Ward Howe, "Battle Hymn of the Republic"

Hear, O Israel, ye approach this day unto battle against your enemies: let not your hearts faint, fear not, and do not tremble, neither be ye terrified because of them; For the LORD your God *is* he that goeth with you, to fight for you against your enemies, to save you.

> Deuteronomy 20:3–4

Bear witness, O Thou wronged and merciful One!
That Earth's most hateful crimes have in Thy name been done!

> John Greenleaf Whittier, "The Gallows," 1842

IN THE FIRST YEAR of the war, Pvt. Henry Hole of Illinois confidently told his friends, "I have no fear for the result of the war. We will surely conquer because we are right."[1] Hole's certainty regarding Northern victory in the war stemmed largely from his Reformed Protestant belief that an immanent God would ensure that the more righteous side won. The Old Testament, after all, was filled with stories of Jehovah dramatically intervening in human history to deliver his covenanted people from evil. Convinced the United States was God's new chosen nation and that they were fighting to preserve a Christian government, Hole and other Christian soldiers had little doubt God was on their side. Throughout the war, the Northern clergy promoted such thinking by emphasizing the Christian nature of the Northern cause and the utter depravity of the South.

The Northern churches' campaign to depict the war as a holy crusade against a wicked Southern Confederacy essentially rested on four religious propositions, which the Northern clergy vigorously defended throughout the war. The first proposition was that the North enjoyed God's special favor in the war. While both sides may have been corrupted by certain prewar sins such as materialism and slavery, in the end, God would still favor the side that was upholding true Christian government and liberty. A second assumption was that while the crusade against the Confederacy might be long and hard, and the forces of evil might sometimes appear to be triumphing, the more righteous Northern side would ultimately prevail. This "historic truth" was borne out by the stories of the biblical patriarchs, men such as Moses, Joseph, and David, who had all endured relatively long periods of personal defeat and suffering before God finally delivered them from the hands of their enemies. Given Reformed Protestantism's teaching about God's immanence, Christian soldiers also believed that their God would somehow supernaturally intervene in the conflict and personally direct military and political events in such a way as to ensure final Northern victory. Finally, a small minority of religious soldiers believed that the faithful warrior who perished in the struggle for freedom would be guaranteed a place in heaven.

Fighting in the Army of the Lord

Like most other Northern clergymen, Henry Ward Beecher believed the Civil War was an epic struggle between the forces of good and evil, between Northern civilization and Southern barbarism, and that God was naturally on the side of civilization. According to Beecher, the North was the quintessential foundation of American civilization. Before hostilities even broke out, Beecher maintained the "distinctive idea of the Free States is Christian civilization." Later he expanded this idea, asserting the North was the source of the nation's most vital institutions:

> The heart is here; the trunk is here; the brain is here . . . the
> source of all that is godlike in American history. . . . It is the
> foundation of industry; it is the school of intelligence; it is
> the home of civilized institutions; it is the repository of those
> principles which are the foundation of our political fabric.[2]

Although Beecher certainly exaggerated New England's role in American history, his comments reflected many religious soldiers' belief that God favored the more progressive and public-spirited North. Other ministers defended the Christian nature of the Northern cause by contrasting it with the cause of the South. In an 1862 sermon, Congregational minister James D. Liggett argued that God could not possibly favor the Southern cause in the war:

God does not in fact look with favor upon such schemes of
conspiracy against liberty and humanity as the authors of this
rebellion are endeavoring to carry out. . . . All the attributes
of his nature are clearly against that system of human bondage
which they are avowedly fighting to establish; which they
have boastingly laid down as the corner stone of the frail
superstructure of the aristocratic and military government
which they hope to erect upon it. We cannot come to the
conclusion that our enemies are in the right and that God is
with them; and if they are in the wrong God cannot be the
friend of their cause.[3]

The North thus enjoyed God's special favor by Southern default. The South's peculiar
institution made it impossible for God to bless its cause.

Young Christian soldiers serving in the Union army had little trouble determining
which section enjoyed God's favor in the war. After returning from a tour of duty in the
lower South, a grateful Union private told his parents, "It makes me feel like a *human being*
to be once more where I can attend the religious institutions to which I am accustomed in
God's country (as 'the boys' call the North in significant distinction from the South)."[4]

Benjamin Webb Baker employed a similar parlance to differentiate the two sections in
a letter to his cousin expressing his dissatisfaction at having to be stationed "in Dixie."
According to "Webb," his lot there was all the worst because he "did not get papers or
anything else to read except now and then a letter from a friend up in God's land."[5] If the
rolling farm-fields and townships of the North represented God's country, then surely the
army recruited from that region was the Lord's. This, at least, was the popular perception
of Protestant evangelicals serving in the Union armies. Soldiers who viewed themselves
as holy warriors engaged in a crusade against a morally depraved enemy were proud when
other young men from their communities enlisted in the same sacred cause. In 1861,
Pvt. William Robinson declared it was a glorious sight to see "this mighty uprising of the
people who are determined with every means in their power to *crush out* the inglorious
and unholy rebellion."

During a subsequent recruiting drive, Pvt. John Harris of the Fourteenth Illinois
Regiment told his friend Susan it was "Soul cheering news" to learn that most of his friends
were also "inlisting in the army of the *Lord*," and he was firmly convinced that they too
would make "brave soldiers of the cross." According to Harris, such soldiers performed
a valuable service "in the regular Army of the Lord, fighting his battles, to clear the way.
so that all mankind will be brought to see the importance of claiming protection in his
government."[6] In the final year of the war, Stanley Lathrop expressed similar sentiments
when he told his father that he was "proud and thankful that our family has such a bright
record on the pages of these stirring times that there is not a blot upon our escutcheon
in this great struggle. Nearly *all* the able-bodied males of our family (both paternal and
maturnal branches) either are or have been in the army of freedom."[7]

Having persuaded their congregations that God was fighting on the side of the North,
it was relatively easy for the Northern clergy to prove their side would ultimately prevail

in the contest. Ministers simply argued that since the Northern cause was God's cause, a just and immanent God would ensure that the North won. As Beecher told his New England congregation in May 1861:

> I have not the least doubt as to where victory will issue; I have
> not the least doubt as to which side will triumph. I forsee the
> victory. I rejoice in it . . . not because we are North and they
> are South, but because we have civilization and they have bar-
> barism, because we stand on the principle of equity and liberty,
> and they stand on the principle of slavery and injustice.[8]

Christian soldiers frequently shared Beecher's belief that the North would eventually prevail because it stood on the side of God, justice, and civilization. The forces of evil might occasionally triumph over the armies of righteousness on the battlefield, but these were only temporary setbacks. With the Union armies fighting alongside God to uphold the freedoms of a Christian government, in the end there could be only one possible outcome. As a young Northern soldier named Ransom Bedell explained just before he enlisted, "Having God—eternal truth, and right, on our side, our cause must prevail." In early 1864, Sgt. Henry C. Matrau of the Iron Brigade could also easily dismiss news that the "Rebels are getting a big army in the field" because he was confident they would be "whipped in the end, for right must eventually conquer." Likewise, in the final year of the war an Illinois private told his brothers and sisters that he had no fears concerning the final outcome of the war because "with the right on our side we must succeed."[9]

Other religious soldiers also shared this religious-borne optimism. Pvt. James H. Leonard told his friend Mary that his growing appreciation of the spiritual dimensions of the war had strengthened his belief in final union victory: "Believing that God is on our side and feeling that we have such prayers as you prayed in your letter that God would prosper us and bring us off victoriously and restore peace to our country once more, we are enabled to have stronger hopes that we shall succeed."[10]

Convinced they were enlisted in God's "army of freedom" and fighting alongside "the armies of Heaven," devout Northern warriors believed they enjoyed a distinct advantage over their Southern foes. Wilbur Fisk, a Union soldier serving as a war correspondent for Vermont's *Green Mountain Freeman,* informed his readers that while the Confederate armies might fight desperately and achieve temporary successes, their efforts were all in vain for God had preordained the outcome:

> We have no fears. A Revolution against such a Government as
> ours is too foul a thing for God to permit. The Confederacy
> is doomed. Cut asunder now in two vital points, their armies
> pent up, they can only struggle and die. Their victories, if
> they have anymore, will be few and feeble, and may possibly
> lengthen out the contest a short time, but not long. Trusting
> in God we know the issue cannot be doubtful.[11]

Christian soldiers might have to march through the valley of the shadow of death, and lose some of their number, but surely God's army would triumph in the end.

While most religious soldiers were convinced that the righteousness of their cause would secure God's favor and ultimate Northern victory in the war, some apparently believed an immanent God was directly intervening in the contest and personally influencing wartime events to ensure a favorable outcome for the North. Religious soldiers had an important part to play in the Union war effort, but in the end God had reserved the most important role for himself, so there would be no doubt as to who was ultimately responsible for the final victory. An invisible, divine hand was leading the faithful Northern armies across oceans of blood to the distant shore where final victory awaited.

Several Union soldiers readily acknowledged God's decisive role in affecting the war's final outcome. Fighting with the Fourteenth Indiana at Antietam, the bloodiest one-day battle in American history, Capt. David Beem had witnessed firsthand the sacrificial death of his friends and comrades in a holy cause. After experiencing the battlefield's awful carnage, Beem told his wife his wife he was ready "to see an end to this wicked, cruel war" but that he still retained his faith in final victory, "believing as firmly as ever that God is on our side, and that the issue will be brought about by Him."[12] James Connolly seemed certain that God was orchestrating all the Union victories in the Atlanta campaign: "The 'God of Israel' is wielding his sword in our behalf and we know no such word as fail."[13] Wilbur Fisk also thought a divine power was working behind the scenes and periodically intervening on the Union's behalf at the decisive moments of the contest. According to Fisk, Union victories at Atlanta, Mobile Bay, and especially Phillip Sheridan's decisive defeat of Gen. Jubal Early's Confederate raiders, just weeks before the November 1864 election, were clear signs of this providential support:

> The material fruits of that day's work were great, but its moral effect upon the nation's welfare at that critical time, just on the eve of a Presidential election, is beyond the power of figures to estimate. Just imagine the result had our corps been sent to Petersburg, as we thought we had got started to go Oct. 13th, leaving Early to defeat the remaining portions of the army, and cross once more into Maryland and Pennsylvania, to wreak his vengeance for the property we had destroyed in the Valley. How many timid men would have been frightened to cast a vote for peace, that ever afterward they would have been ashamed of, though ashamed too late to do any good? Can there be any doubt on whose side God's Providence was there?[14]

With God himself personally intervening in the war's military and political events on behalf of the Union cause, how could the North possibly lose?

Christian Martyrs in a Holy Cause

While most religious soldiers were convinced that the North would inevitably win the contest, they were considerably less certain that they themselves would be alive to witness the victory. Ironically, this was because the same Reformed Protestant worldview that guaranteed the success of their cause could not offer them similar assurances concerning their own survival. Various Scriptures seemed to suggest that believers would almost certainly experience hardships, religious persecution, and perhaps even martyrdom in a world corrupted by sin. And while Christ had commended the faith of the centurion, over the course of his earthly ministry one of his only obscure references to those who bore arms was his advice to Peter in the Garden that "all they that take the sword shall perish with the sword." This was a rather ominous passage for the prospective soldier and seemed to challenge the whole concept of Christian soldiering being promulgated in Northern churches. So the Northern clergy often ignored it. However, at least one Northern chaplain used this passage and an equally problematic text from Revelation 13:10, "He that kills with the sword must be killed with the sword," for a Sunday sermon to some new Illinois recruits. Few could have missed the implication, especially when the chaplain concluded his sermon by warning his young charges to make proper spiritual preparations for their potential deaths in battle.[15] Another Union sermon, delivered to Sherman's troops in Tennessee during the winter of 1863–64, must have seemed in hindsight eerily prophetic to the men who would soon be marching on Atlanta. As the wife of a Union officer recalls, the text was, "'It is appointed to all men once to die and after that the Judgment.' It was an exhortation to be ready when Death comes."[16]

Apparently the evangelical God who offered spiritual salvation to everyone who placed their faith in him did not always shield his followers' physical bodies from suffering and death. While Christ assured his disciples he would always grant them the spiritual strength to endure the many troubles and tribulations they would confront in a wicked world, he never promised to supernaturally shield them from such suffering. As the apostle Paul observed to the would-be saints of the church of Corinth, he and his fellow believers were "troubled on every side, yet not distressed . . . persecuted, but not forsaken; cast down, but not destroyed. . . . Always delivered to death for Jesus' sake, that the life also of Jesus might be made manifest in our mortal flesh." So if God miraculously "saved" all those who called on his name, clearly it was not always in a physical sense. Indeed, nineteenth-century believers seemed far more concerned about avoiding an eternal "spiritual death" than escaping their own inevitable physical death.[17]

Antebellum Americans were generally more comfortable with the reality of human death because it so completely pervaded their nineteenth-century world. As the intellectual historian Lewis O. Saum observed:

> Death was an ever-present fact of life. A normally unreflective
> Maine farmer cited the conventional wisdom: "in life we are
> in the midst of death." Few cultural commentaries on that era
> fail to remark the intimacy most people had with death. Theirs
> was an immediate, not a derivative or vicarious awareness. . . .
> As Perry Miller remarks about Concord, "the supreme fact was
> death."[18]

Antebellum Americans lived in an age when thousands of people, young and old alike, were routinely struck down by smallpox, flu, and malaria epidemics. Mothers and children still frequently died during childbirth, and hundreds of families—like the Lincolns—

lost two or more of their children to fatal childhood diseases. So if nineteenth-century American literature seems permeated with a strong sense of tragedy, perhaps it is because the authors lived in a world stricken with sickness and death, where human life was tenuous and Americans were constantly reminded of the fact that one day, they too, would die. For an Indiana soldier, the implications were obvious. "Life is uncertain," he recorded in his wartime diary. Then, echoing a phrase from the Episcopal Book of Common Prayer, he noted that "in the midst of life we are in death. How careful then ought we to live so that when Death comes, we may be ready."[19]

Antebellum believers' understanding of death was heavily influenced by their Evangelical Reformed Protestant worldview, which approached the subject of death from a distinctly "spiritual" perspective. After examining thousands of letters and diaries from this period, Saum noted that for most believers, death was not something to be feared and mourned because it represented "an escape from the world's sadness, an end to the 'pilgrimage' through spiritual and bodily hostility."[20] Death marked the moment of divine deliverance, when those who had labored faithfully as aliens in an often harsh and cruel world were delivered from the evils of a physical universe cursed by sin. It was not the end of human existence, only the beginning. As one thoughtful Union soldier explained to his loved ones, "This world is but a short period of our existence."[21] Most Reformed Protestants believed that life on earth was merely a brief test, to see whether an individual would ultimately strive to gratify himself and secure his own physical salvation or learn to humbly serve others and place his trust in a higher power he could not always see. In a fallen world everyone inevitably experienced physical death, or what Protestant evangelicals referred to as the "first death"—some sooner than others—but the human spirit or soul would live on forever, with individuals either being rewarded with a more meaningful and pleasurable life with God and their loved ones or being condemned to a second "spiritual death" of everlasting torment and separation.

Antebellum Christians, intimately acquainted with the transient nature of their nineteenth-century existence, were far more concerned about escaping this second, everlasting, spiritual death than avoiding their inevitable and rapidly approaching physical death. As little children, the *New England Primer* had always reminded them that "*Xerxes the great did die; And so must you and I.*"[22] It was impossible to escape "the first death," but by willingly submitting their lives to God, believers could look forward to spending eternity in a place where there was no more pain or sorrow. True reality was the eternal spiritual world that could not be seen, not their visible and obviously flawed physical world. As one Pennsylvania soldier tenderly reminded his wife:

> These are trying times and we should all humble ourselves and
> try to live as we should and as we will wish we should have
> done when we come to die. We should live always with God
> before our eyes and endeavor to serve him continually. At best
> our days are few and evil, and we should live agreeable together
> in this world so that we may be better prepared to enjoy our
> heavenly home above; a few days, weeks, months or years at
> farthest we will be called upon to leave our earthly home if we

> live right the days allotted to us here below the change will be a
> good one. If not it will certainly be a very bad one.[23]

Few soldiers expressed any interest in prolonging their time on earth beyond the day and hour assigned to their death because they thought that their life in this world was merely a trial of their faith, and a few even seemed to look forward to the end of their earthy sojourns. One Illinois cavalryman, for example, actually looked forward to "the destruction" of his "gross, material body" so he could enjoy a far richer and less troublesome life in heaven. From his perspective a soldier's death was thus "not a fate to be avoided, but rather almost to be gloried in." A Pennsylvanian private also seemed willing to trade his life as an infantryman for paradise: "If we keep faithful dying is merely changing worlds for a better home." Indeed, for most nineteenth-century Christians, immortality would have been the worst imaginable punishment—an eternal extension of their trials and tribulations in a wicked world. Just like their Puritan ancestors, most antebellum Christians thus accepted the inevitability of their death with a spirit of divine resignation and concentrated on living and dying in a manner that might win God's favor and a better home in heaven.[24]

Ironically, a few religious soldiers actually believed that the war offered them an unprecedented opportunity for guaranteeing their salvation. In the opening months of the conflict some Northern clergymen began preaching that soldiers who perished in the struggle against the South would be holy martyrs and receive a heavenly reward for sacrificing their lives to save a Christian nation. This echoed a persistent if rather unorthodox religious tradition in Christendom, dating back to the Crusades, that Christian soldiers who perished in just wars would be guaranteed a place in paradise. Of course, there was a caveat to this rule: The faithful soldier had to sacrifice his life in a just war. Most Northern Christians, however, were confident that this was the case, because in the spring of 1861 virtually all their spiritual, military, and political leaders were constantly reassuring them of the justice of their cause. As one Illinois recruit later told his friend, "I went to the Congregational Church and listened to a sermon that was sound to the core. . . . It was quite war-like, and proved that every man who fell sustaining the government, fell in a just cause."[25] Over the course of his research into the religious life of the Civil War armies, Civil War historian Gardiner Shattuck also discovered that one of the most popular wartime sermons delivered by chaplains in the Northern armies was that faithful Christian soldiers who sacrificed their lives for the Union's holy cause would surely go to heaven. According to Shattuck, the sermons revolved around a common theme:

> The pious soldier who died in service of his country had
> nothing to fear in death, for if his soul was prepared, he
> would immediately receive his reward in God's kingdom.
> As a chaplain advised his men in a sermon, those who gave
> themselves sacrificially in the "baptism of blood" of the war
> would be truly blessed by God.[26]

These sermons generally specified that only soldiers whose souls were prepared, or those who had embraced Christ's atoning work on the cross and not subsequently jeopardized their salvation by their backslidden behavior, would be saved. However, given the blurring of republican and evangelical lines in America's nineteenth-century civil religion, a few ministers and soldiers apparently embraced the heretical proposition that in the eternal scheme of salvation, a soldier's faithful allegiance to the flag was just as important as his relationship with Christ. In their eyes, service to country was synonymous with faith in Christ, and those who died in their country's service would thus be guaranteed a place in heaven, regardless of their personal spiritual state. If some theologically naïve common soldiers embraced this heresy, however, at least part of the blame lies with their clergy and their political and military leaders, who occasionally promulgated or tacitly approved this unorthodox vision of religious martyrdom. At the 1863 flag presentation ceremony for the newly formed Fifty-fourth Massachusetts Regiment, after "a very impressive prayer" by Reverend Grimes of Boston, Governor John Andrew assured the new enlistees that if, "in the battle's rage, you cast your eyes on this Christian banner. . . . Though you fall in your country's defense, with a just and sincere appreciation of the teaching inculcated by that banner, your spirit will soar to that home in store for those who faithfully do their duty to Humanity, their Country and their God!"[27]

This patriotic vision of holy warrior martyrdom was hardly confined to New England. Midwestern Union soldiers, such as William Wiley of the Seventy-seventh Illinois, heard virtually identical messages at their units' flag presentation ceremonies: "We were treated to a rousing speech by E. C. Ingersole [Ingersoll] which was perhaps more patriotical than orthodox. He told the boys they need not fear to go into battle that any one who was killed in such a holy cause was sure to go strait to Heaven."[28] Maj. John H. Halderman of Kansas also made sure that the men of his regiment understood that if they died fighting for the Union flag, they would undoubtedly be rewarded with a new heavenly home.[29]

Rightly fearing they might perish on the next battlefield, a few religious soldiers apparently embraced this heretical teaching, fully persuaded that if they and their comrades faithfully discharged their religious and military obligations, God would surely usher them into paradise. From roughly the fall of 1862 on, some soldiers began to parrot their chaplains and officers' claims about slain Northern troops being martyrs for the Union cause. For example, when expressing his grief for a fallen comrade a Pennsylvania soldier, William McCarter comforted himself with the thought that his friend had died "a martyr to the cause of liberty and humanity."[30] Other Union soldiers joined this growing chorus. After Sherman's decisive repulse at Chickasaw Bayou, R. W. Floyd thought the fallen Union soldiers had proven their commitment to the Union cause "as did the Martyrs of old prove themselves true to their God."[31] After the Battle of Antietam, Seymour Dexter of the Twenty-third New York described the Union dead as holy "martyrs to the cause of freedom, justice and our union."[32]

For a generation steeped in the evangelical Protestant worldview and caught up in a seemingly merciless and never-ending civil war, this language of religious martyrdom sometimes conveyed a deeper spiritual message about the eternal fate of the deceased. Northern Protestants who in normal circumstances would have categorically rejected the idea that dying for a cause, even a good one, could assure one's place in heaven seemed more inclined to entertain the idea when they were struggling to ascertain the meaning and ultimate purpose of their closest friends' deaths. For example, after mourning the death of another comrade who had sacrificed his young life "upon the altar of his country" the previous spring, George H. Allen was more explicit when discussing the eternal fate of a Rhode Island friend at Antietam: "We trust that his noble and heroic sacrifice in giving his young life to his country has gained for him a crown of glory in that better land beyond the skies."[33] Indeed, by 1864 even Northern ministers were sometimes comparing their fallen heroes to the great martyrs of the early Christian church.[34] For most religious soldiers, the implication was obvious and heretical, but in the terrible stresses accompanying a savage and unremitting civil war, a small minority of them apparently embraced it.

If a few Northern Christians and clerics readily embraced this teaching, however, perhaps it was due in part to the increasingly politicized nature of their churches. Already hopelessly intermingled by the Republic's evolving civic religion, in early 1861 the Northern churches further blurred the distinctions between church and state by pledging their unconditional support to the Union war effort. This made it increasingly difficult for spiritually immature believers to distinguish their Christian republic's cause from the cause of Christ. Given their leaders theologically confusing if not completely heretical public pronouncements, it was thus only natural that some soldiers misinterpreted their leaders' patriotic exhortations to mean that those who sacrificed everything for the Union would earn themselves a place in heaven.

In some respects the motifs of holy war and martyrdom were mutually reinforcing and self-fulfilling. By nobly volunteering to sacrifice their lives in a conflict they sincerely believed was being fought to save the world's only Christian republic, in one sense Northern Christians did ultimately help sanctify the Union's war effort. Their subsequent deaths in battle for the Union also seemed to confirm their status as religious martyrs, and lend further weight to the idea that the Northern war effort itself had to be a holy war. After all, if God was not on the Northern side, then why were so many young Christians eagerly enlisting, fighting, and dying under the Union flag?

In any event the concepts of holy war and martyrdom often proved very empowering to Christian soldiers. Believers were less likely to question the purposes and methods of a holy war and could thus focus their energies more on the proper performance of their military duties. Faithful soldiers could also rest assured that should they fall in battle, they would be spiritually redeemed by their death in a holy war and someday reunited with their loved ones in heaven. Those who sincerely believed they could obtain their salvation by sacrificing their lives in a holy cause thus often lost their fear of death, convinced that even if the enemy destroyed their physical bodies on the battlefield, their eternal fate was secure. Holy wars were a win-win proposition for the would-be Yankee saint. A few days after his first brush with the enemy, Pvt. William H. Onstot tried to relate the practical consequences of this Christian understanding of holy war to his sister Lizzie. Just before the battle, Onstot confessed he felt extremely anxious for his safety:

> I naturaly thought of the coming scenes of that bloody day.
> I knew many that was radient with life would before night
> be laid lifeless on the Field of Battle. Possible nay propable
> I might be among that number. . . . This was the dark side

of the picture. My thoughts returned to the other side. I
was engaged in a holy cause. I was to fight for the cause of
Constitutional liberty and everything that was dear to men
against a treasonable horde. . . . With these Reflections I
resolved to do my duty though it might cost the last drop
of blood in my veins.[35]

When a holy warrior focused on the righteousness of his cause, death lost its sting, and
there no longer seemed to be any reason to be afraid. The enemy might kill his temporal
body, but they could not harm his eternal soul.

These twin themes of holy war and Christian martyrdom surfaced in many religious
soldiers' letters. On the eve of Grant's first unsuccessful Vicksburg campaign, Pvt. Robert
Steele repeatedly assured his parents that he would perform his duty and thus they need
not worry:

I have no particular desire to be in an engagement but don't
feel like shrinkin from any duty I may be called upon to perform. I go feeling that our cause is just and I can claim the
protection of the All Mighty and I feel that if I should fall on
the field of Batel all is well. Don't feel to anxious about me.
Our staying in this world is short at the longest. Let us live so
we can welcome death and be prepared to meet where wars
and sin and parting are no more.[36]

After losing his father and cousin's husband in the desperate fighting at Stones River,
Pvt. Andrew J. McGarrah could also comfort himself and his cousin with the thought
that their loved ones were now in a far better place:

Tis true that you and I have both met with Sad losses, me the
loss of my father you with the loss of your dear Companion but
let us try and be consoled as much as possible for although our
loss is very great yet your dear Companion fell on the dread
Battlefield of Stone River fighting to rescue our country from
the hands of Traitors. My father who was my only hope also
fell in this great Struggle for liberty but as great as my loss is I
will try and do the best I can Hoping that he now rests in the
bright regions above.[37]

Death might temporarily separate the Christian soldier from his loved ones, but he and
his relatives could take comfort in the hope that their loved one's death in a holy cause
would ensure that they someday met again.

As the war progressed, these patriotic wartime sermons promoting martyrdom for the
Union cause became so prevalent that other, more orthodox, clergy back home finally felt
compelled to address them. After learning that his own Catholic priests had condemned
this heretical wartime gospel from the pulpit, a soldier in the Irish Brigade, Peter Welsh,
tried to reassure his wife that few religious soldiers took such sermons to heart:

> My dear wife you tell me of the admonitions of the fathers of
> fifty ninth St that dying on the battlefield will not save a mans
> soul unless he is in a state of grace shurely no Catholic is so silly
> or ignorant of the teachings of the Catholic church as to believe
> that dying on the battlefield would gain their salvation.[38]

Most religious soldiers shared Welsh's skepticism and seemed to hold both a more orthodox and pragmatic view of religious martyrdom. As orthodox believers they knew their salvation depended on faith in Christ's atoning work on the cross, but from a more pragmatic perspective, they also believed that their wartime service would ultimately help ensure their salvation, namely, because their close proximity to death on the battlefield would always encourage them to be spiritually prepared for death. After contemplating his own potential fate, a soldier in the Ninety-third New York wrote, "All must die. Let us be prepaired."[39] Confronting the same predicament, William Gould reassured his sister, "I have endeavored to live in such a way that come life or death all will be well."[40] In hindsight, this was probably one of the greatest advantages Christians enjoyed as soldiers. After all, how many men received advanced warning of the likely hour of their death so they could make proper spiritual preparations before facing judgment?

Many religious soldiers thus followed the lead of their Reformed churches in defining the American Civil War as a religious war, or crusade, to defend their Christian republic from a new generation of barbarians. Those who embraced these wartime interpretations found them helpful in that they confirmed the religious soldiers' belief that God was indeed fighting on the North's side, relieved them of any doubts about the final outcome of the war, and offered them eternal hope in the event they did not survive the struggle. But the Reformed Protestant religion that convinced religious soldiers that God was manipulating wartime events to ensure Northern victory offered them no guarantee they would live to see that glorious day. So like the ancient holy warriors of the Christian crusades, a few Northern soldiers embraced the doctrine of religious martyrdom to cope with the painful reality they might not return from the next battlefield. Although the symbols and ideas associated with holy war helped many religious soldiers cope with their wartime doubts and fears, other Union soldiers inappropriately used this motif to demonize their Southern adversaries.

The Prewar Demonization of the South

In October 1861, Henry Hibben was serving as the chaplain of the Eleventh Indiana when it occupied the pro-Southern city of Paducah, Kentucky. Hibben wrote his sister that he was somewhat puzzled by the local citizens' irrational fear of the Northern occupiers:

> Many of the people have fled and left their houses, fearing
> that we would murder them—They seemed to think that we
> are savages and would devour them. I cannot conceive how
> intelligent people can be so ignorant and deceived about their
> Northern brethren.[41]

Although Hibben apparently had a difficult time understanding this emotional reaction by the citizens of Paducah, his experience with the Southern people was hardly unique. Like most warring peoples, Southerners initially feared and hated their conquering enemy. As Union armies marched south in 1862 and began to occupy various strategic locations throughout the Confederacy, other Union soldiers were also surprised to discover how vehemently Southerners hated and feared them. A Hoosier private, Sylvester Bishop, found Southerners' preconceived stereotypes about Yankees so extreme they were actually humorous: "They expected to see men with blue bellies and horns on their heads and one eye on their foreheads but after seeing the Yankees they exclaimed 'Why they look just like our men!'"[42]

Hibben and Bishop may have poked fun at their opponents' naïveté, but Northerners were often just as guilty of embracing and propagating similarly negative stereotypes about Southerners. By 1861 Northerners and Southerners had increasingly come to view their sectional opponents as devils, and much of this irrational hatred was rooted in the prewar sectional conflict over slavery.

By the time of the Missouri Compromise in 1820, slavery had become one of the nation's most controversial issues and was beginning to divide the country along Northern and Southern lines. From the Colonial period on, the North and South had been rapidly evolving into two distinct regions with their own political and economic goals and competing visions concerning the future of American slavery. Although Southern control of the White House over the next few decades insulated the South from a rapidly growing antislavery movement in the North, the militancy of abolitionism in the 1830s gradually forced the South to mount an aggressive defense of its "peculiar institution." Hundreds of Northern preachers, such as Congregationalist Nathaniel Hall, joined the antislavery camp and began to speak of a "higher law" than the U.S. Constitution that "we are bound to obey" when human laws "conflict with the law of God, as made known in our souls and in His Word."[43]

Southern preachers now sprung to their peculiar institution's defense, and instead of just quietly defending slavery as a necessary evil, some began to proclaim that slavery was a positive good for both the slave and the slaveholder. In the increasingly bitter sectional conflict over slavery, radicals on both sides adopted insulting stereotypes and epithets to disparage their sectional opponents. Southerners accused Yankees of being godless materialists who favored free love, religious anarchy, abolitionism, and racial amalgamation. Yankees, meanwhile, fired back, reproaching their Southern neighbors for being brutal, backward aristocrats who had been spiritually and sexually perverted by their "peculiar institution."

As war drew closer, leading politicians and preachers on both sides increasingly began to depict the sectional conflict in harsh black-and-white terms, often deliberately choosing the most offensive rhetorical language and symbols to castigate their political rivals. For example, in Massachusetts senator Charles Sumner's 1856 "Crime against Kansas" speech, Southern senator Andrew P. Butler was no longer Sumner's esteemed colleague from the state of South Carolina but "the maddest of zealots" and one of the chief "propagandists of slavery" because he had "a mistress to whom he has made his vows, and who, though ugly to others, is always lovely to him; though polluted in the sight of the world, is chaste in his sight I mean the harlot, Slavery."[44] Shortly after delivering his bitter invective, Sumner himself bore the brunt of the South's fury, as he was viciously caned on the Senate floor by Butler's nephew for several minutes while other Southern senators prevented anyone from intervening. Condemning the caning as a "cowardly assault on a gentleman unarmed and pinioned to a desk," a clergyman from Maine accused the South of inaugurating a "Reign of Terror" as it continued to engage in a "conspiracy to crush the freedom of congressional debate" on the subject of slavery.[45] The use of such inflammatory rhetoric was bound to breed further violence between the sections.

In the process of waging this divisive political and cultural war over slavery, some clergymen and politicians even began to question their sectional opponents' faith, convinced that anyone who held such radically different views of slavery, social reform, and freedom could not possibly be an orthodox believer. As a result of this joint political and religious onslaught, both sides gradually transformed their sectional enemies into larger-than-life monsters intent on destroying all their society's traditional institutions. The outbreak of war in 1861 only further intensified this process of spiritual vilification. As both sides mobilized for war, the North's evangelical churches used their considerable moral authority to sanctify the Union war effort while damning that of the enemy's.

As a result of this bitter prelude, by the time they joined the great Northern crusade in 1861, many Northern Christians were generally convinced that the Southern cause was evil and had cursed the South and its white inhabitants. While most Northern soldiers believed the South's chief sin was its rebellion against a God-ordained government and thought the South should be punished for its violent attack on the U.S. flag, a significant minority of Christian soldiers maintained that the South's principal moral crime was its stubborn refusal to give up its "peculiar institution." According to them, chattel slavery was an abomination before God that had physically blighted Dixie's landscape and spiritually corrupted Southerners. And unless the South immediately repented of the evil, God would subject the cotton belt to even more grievous judgments in the future.

Although many Northern preachers and believers considered slavery a national sin that both sections had illegitimately profited from, others found it easier to ignore their own section's sins and cast stones at the South. In an 1863 essay, Andrew McGarrah blamed South Carolina for introducing the evils that had cursed the Southern Eden and divided the Union: "Slavery and Rebellion, reared in the same congenial clime, in the Sunny South, illegitimate twin children of the Same Monstrous Mother South Carolina having one father the *Devil:* may they both go down to the grave, never, never more to arise."[46]

If one purges the supernatural elements from McGarrah's essay and tempers his remarks about South Carolina bearing all the responsibility for the national sins of slavery and rebellion, one sees that his arguments are based on a couple of historical truths. South Carolina did play a very important role in the evolution of both America's chattel slave system and the theory of secession. The first Africans in America came ashore at Jamestown in 1619, but Virginia law initially treated most of these Africans more like indentured servants than chattel slaves. Although the gradual evolution of the institution can readily be traced in Virginia's legal statute books over the next several decades, Virginia planters continued to use black and white indentured servants on their tobacco plantations until the latter half of the seventeenth century. But there was no such "temporary window of equality" when Charles Town, South Carolina, was settled nearly half a century later, in 1670. Chattel slavery was there almost from the beginning. Predominantly colonized by the descendants of English planters from the Caribbean Island of Barbados, the land-hungry settlers of Charles Town hoped to duplicate the success of their parents' sugar cane plantations in America. When early experiments growing sugar, trading furs, and employing Native American slaves failed, the ambitious Barbadian transplants decided to transplant their parents' brutal chattel slavery system to Carolina where the slaves later provided the principal labor force for the colony's new rice and cotton plantations. These chattel slave–based cotton plantations proved so lucrative that they later multiplied across South Carolina like an ugly rash, eventually spilling across colonial lines and dotting the entire Lower South.[47]

McGarrah also correctly identified South Carolina's prominent role in the evolution of the political theory of secession in the United States. While the theory of states' rights and secession gradually evolved from a series of historic American political and legal precedents, such as James Madison and Thomas Jefferson's Kentucky and Virginia resolutions, it had never really been fully developed or articulated until John C. Calhoun made it South Carolina's pièce de résistance. In his brilliant political tract, *The South Carolina Exposition and Protest,* Calhoun explained exactly how a state could legally go about "nullifying" an unconstitutional federal law and "interposing" itself between the federal government and its citizens. South Carolina's attempted nullification of the Jackson administration's "Tariff of Abominations" in 1832 had mixed results—intimidated by Jackson's ominous military threats, South Carolina had backed down and moderated its political demands—but Calhoun and his allies learned an important lesson from their defeat. The next time South Carolina defended its state sovereignty from a tyrannical federal government it would act in unison with other Southern states. Over the next three decades, Calhoun and his allies worked tirelessly to build that Southern coalition. Thus it was no accident that South Carolina was the first Southern state to take the fateful step of seceding from the Union in December 1860 or that so many other lower Southern states promptly followed its example.[48]

While McGarrah's letter may have been predicated on certain historical realities, his accusation that South Carolina alone was responsible for these national "sins" was not one of them. Like other deeply religious Northerners, McGarrah had been quick to judge his Southern neighbor's sins while conveniently overlooking Northerners' moral shortcomings. For example, although McGarrah vigorously rejected the legitimacy of secession, he expediently ignored the fact that Southerners were basing their doctrine of secession and the "Second American Revolution" on some of the same English legal precedents and natural law arguments that McGarrah's forefathers had cited to justify their rebellion against England. McGarrah had also conveniently forgotten that long before Calhoun introduced his doctrine of nullification, the North too had once flirted with the principle of secession. In the waning months of the War of 1812, New England's Federalist leaders had contemplated seceding from what they considered to be a tyrannical national government at the Hartford Convention.[49] Finally, McGarrah's vehement condemnation of South Carolina's sins completely overlooked New England traders' and bankers' eager participation in the economic development of the Southern colonies and especially its peculiar institution. The entire country had morally prostituted itself to reap some of the economic benefits of slavery.[50] As Lincoln himself later acknowledged in his second inaugural speech, the sins associated with secession and slavery were never historically confined to a single state or section.

McGarrah, however, was not the only Union soldier who found the locus of the nation's evils in the South. In a letter written from a camp outside Brandy Station, Virginia, in 1864, a Vermont soldier named Wilbur Fisk expressed his conviction that slavery had always been the spiritual cornerstone of the South. Neatly cataloging the South's various sins, Fisk personified "Slavery's" role in provoking the war:

> Slavery was jealous of the comlier strength that Freedom pos-
> sessed; and maliciously envied her irresistable march onward to
> a higher destiny. Slavery drew sword, and would have stabbed
> Freedom to the heart, had not God denied her the strength.
> She could not bear that her more righteous neighbor should
> be prospered, while she herself was accursed, and in her foolish
> madness she has tried to rend the Union in twain.[51]

Benighted by the curse of slavery, the South had only heaped further judgment upon itself by coveting the rapidly growing political and industrial power of the North and seeking to destroy a national government it could no longer dominate.

A Cursed Land

Religious soldiers who believed the South alone bore all the responsibility for America's sins of slavery, rebellion, and anarchy were also convinced that a righteous and immanent God was already judging the South for its sins. Before the war, religious abolitionists sometimes noted that the South had the highest murder rate in the antebellum United States and cited this as "evidence" of both the South's endemic immorality and God's judgment on a wayward section. When Northern soldiers later began marching into the land of Dixie during the war, they discovered other evidence that suggested the South had already long been reaping what it had sown in terms of the curses associated with slavery.

Many religious soldiers believed the best example of this divine judgment on the South was its primitive economic condition. Most Northern soldiers had never traveled more than twenty miles from their childhood home, so they were shocked by the enormous economic differences they witnessed during their travels through the South. In their letters and diaries, Union soldiers constantly compared the farms and towns of the South with those of the North. Juxtaposed against "God's Country," with the exception of the Gulf Coast and the hills of Tennessee, the South virtually always fared worse. Compared to the rich and well-developed farms of the mid-Atlantic states and Midwest, the Southern landscape seemed largely undeveloped and barren. Thanks to the South's heavy investment in agriculturally intensive cash crops, even lands that had once been inhabited and developed were now abandoned, depleted, and covered with undergrowth.

Confronted with such scenes, perhaps some religious soldiers recalled Moses' warning to the Israelites. If God's people did not observe his laws in the Promised Land and defiled it with their sins, their crops would fail "and the land itself" would "vomiteth out her inhabitants." In any event, numerous religious soldiers shared their conviction that the Southern landscape had been cursed by the sins of slavery and secession.[52]

While campaigning in Tennessee during the spring of 1862, Pvt. William Moore shared his opinion regarding the practical consequences of slavery and secession on the South:

> The country around Bowling Green looks as though it de-
> served a better fate. But the garden of *Eden* was polluted
> with sin, and was visited by the *great Father of Secession.*
> . . . From the mouth of the Tenn, to Hamburgh eight miles
> above Pittsburgh Landing, the Country presents a wild and
> uncultivated appearance. Every thing shows a want of energy
> and enterprise. And I could not help thinking, how different
> it would be if that beautiful Stream had been laid in one of
> our Northern States, where the accursed blight of human
> bondage does not blind the intellect of man with a chain of
> iron, forged by Aristocratic hands as it does in States where
> Slavery is worshipped as the "God of Day."[53]

Since one of the central themes of the Old Testament was that a jealous God punished apostate lands with natural disasters, famine, and pestilence, Moore believed the South was reaping the physical consequences of having honored slavery more than God's laws.[54]

Other soldiers also noted the deleterious effects of slavery on the economic development of the South. Pvt. Charles Webb, a former seminary student from Maine, believed slavery was the South's chief sin and source of the "squalid poverty" he witnessed in Virginia. Thanks to slavery, the South was "fifty years behind the time in all improvements and fashions and all that tends to make men good and great." Webb, however, optimistically predicted that if border states such as Maryland abolished slavery and purged their "great sin," God would again bless them and they would become lands "flowing with milk and honey."[55]

A Cursed People

Christian soldiers who believed the Southern landscape had been cursed by its inhabitants' carnal relationship with slavery were even more pessimistic when they contemplated the long-term moral influence of the "peculiar institution" on Southerners. The demonization of Confederates by Northern soldiers and clergy manifested itself in various ways, but it was usually grounded in a complete or partial denial of Southerners' civilization and Christian faith. Although hardly unique to the United States, by now it had also become a familiar American pattern. To justify the destruction of rival New World civilizations, Americans needed only depict their Native American, Spanish, or Mexican adversaries as uncivilized heathen. These savage peoples and their untamed land needed to be conquered so they could be assimilated into the kingdom of Christ. In similar fashion, some Northern clergymen and Christians now denigrated a Southern culture and faith they found wanting. In casting such aspersions on their enemies, the Northern church was subtly undermining the humanity of Southerners themselves, but just as in the ante-bellum debate over slavery, no one seemed concerned with the long-term consequences of their rhetorical assaults.[56]

Although Northern Christians often condemned the civilization and faith of their Southern opponents, they did so to varying degrees and with an important qualification. For example, while Northerners found much to like about the South, they generally believed Southern civilization would always be impaired, and its future development stymied, by the presence of slavery. In matters of religion, there was widespread skepticism and doubts about the sincerity of Southerners' commitment to Christianity. When holding the "secesh" accountable for their spiritual and political betrayal of a Christian republic, however, religious soldiers thought it was important to distinguish between the poor Southern farmers who were mistakenly supporting the slave aristocracy out of a sense of duty or ignorance and the planter elite who had deliberately provoked the war. Unfortunately, this moral distinction was lost on a few vindictive Christian soldiers battling enemy irregulars and guerrillas behind Union lines, who seemed eager to consign the entire "traitorous" people to hell.

As usual, the Northern clergy led the charge in disparaging the culture of the South's traditional agrarian society. In their minds, slavery had set Southern civilization back a century or more. Henry Ward Beecher considered chattel slavery "an academy of corruption" that tended to "narrow men, to make them selfish; to unfit them for public service." According to Beecher and other Northern evangelicals, the spirit of slavery had corrupted Southern education, compromised the Southern church, and fostered an un-American and demonic spirit of aristocratic tyranny in the South. Horace Bushnell agreed, noting that the "scholarship, the philosophic and esthetic culture, [and] the originative art [of the South] . . . are barbarized of necessity by the element of slavery."[57]

After touring Union occupied regions of Kentucky and Tennessee, the Reverend Nathaniel Hall was equally impressed with the South's primitive society. He told his congregation that for the would-be Northern visitor examining the local culture, it seems as though "he has fallen back generations from the civilization he has left. . . . You seem . . . to have come among a different nation, upon a different age; among those who have been slumbering, while the rest of the world moved on." After Lincoln's assassination, Northern ministers dropped any previous self-restraint they had exercised and openly shared the intense prejudices that had colored their wartime sermons. Congregational reverend Daniel C. Eddy seemed ready to inaugurate a second war against the defeated South when he claimed that the

> Southern people are a different race. Slavery has given them
> a different idea of religion. . . . Slavery has barbarized them,
> and made them a people with whom we have little in common.
> We had an idea of Southern civilization . . . when Sumner was
> bleeding in the Federal Senate, . . . when ornaments were made

for Southern ladies of the bones of the brave soldiers killed
at Bull Run, . . . in the atrocities perpetuated on our poor
soldiers. . . . And now we have another exhibition of it in the
base, wanton, assassination of the President.[58]

In their letters home, Northern soldiers also frequently mentioned the significant dearth of cultural refinements and civilization in the South. According to Bell Irvin Wiley, one of Billy Yank's most frequent complaints during his sojourn in the land of Dixie was how the schools, newspapers, and even the farming methods were at least "a hundred years behind the times."[59] Having long heard Northern stereotypes about the primitive nature of Southern society in their newspapers and churches, religious soldiers now believed they were witnessing the evidence firsthand. The relatively few schools, and squalid nature of the ones that did exist, convinced William Gould that Southerners were a backward people:

> Just look at the difference between the north and the south.
> This is the first slave state that I have been in yet where they
> have free schools. And here they do not have school onley
> three months a year and there are but few school Houses
> at that. This gives but poor chance for the poor class to get
> aney education at all. . . . There is more papers printed in old
> Delaware county than there is in this whole state. The South
> has a great reformation to make before they get on an equal-
> ity with the North.[60]

After another successful raid of the North Carolina coast in 1863, a New England soldier named A. L. Butler delivered a Thanksgiving address to his company in which he emphasized the fundamental differences between Northern and Southern society:

> Much of the success and prosperity of New England of to-day
> can be traced to the principles, habits, and institutions that our
> forefathers practiced and established. . . . What man among us,
> during our late march through a portion of this State, could
> help contrasting the want of industry, prosperity, and intelli-
> gence, with the neatness, thrift, and happiness of a New Eng-
> land village?[61]

While serving with the 121st New York Volunteers, Surgeon Daniel M. Holt's interactions with the Southern population apparently confirmed his worst fears. Holt thought there had never been a people more in need of "the influence of religion, conjoined with free schools."[62] Disgusted with the bitter fruits of their society's chattel slavery system, Holt sarcastically condemned his Southern hosts' arrogance and extreme provinciality:

> We pass through the village of Purcellville—*small in dimen-*
> *sions,* but taking the word of the people for it, next to Rich-
> mond, which they look upon as being the greatest city in
> the world, and in the very center of creation, a sentiment I

find universally adopted of the Babel of treason, by all half
civilized, half educated bigoted rebels who have never traveled
beyond the precincts of their own country or associated with
a higher order of talent than the *"human chattels"* around
them.[63]

Holt seemed equally disappointed with what he saw of Southern architecture. When
he visited the infamous Charlestown courthouse and jail where John Brown had been
housed and put on trial, Holt thought the jail was "the most conspicuous object of the
town, it is the most disgusting spectacle which can be conceived of. It is a fair specimen
of Southern Institutions—full of holes, frowning grates and bars, chains, bolts, and
tumble-down pillars and colonnades."[64]

While marching down to Atlanta with Sherman's army, Charles Wills also lost whatever
respect he once felt for Southern civilization. Inspecting one of Johnston's defensive works
south of Dalton after the Confederates withdrew, Wills observed that the enemy had run
their works "through a graveyard . . . and torn down all the palings inclosing graves, to
make beds for themselves, and unnecessarily destroyed everything of beauty around."
Condemning the vandals' sacrilegious desecration, Wills asserted that his side would "not
have done so in our own country, and *I* would not anywhere. I don't give these Rebels
half the credit for humanity or any of the qualities civilized beings should possess, that
I used to." Convinced the war would only end when one side or the other was utterly
defeated and destroyed, Wills had earlier concluded that "the world and civilization will
lose the least by losing the South and slavery."[65] Generally concurring that the South was
plagued with various cultural deficiencies, many religious soldiers shared Henry Ward
Beecher's belief that the progress of Southern civilization had been severely retarded by
the Southern church's compromise with slavery.

If the Southern church had foundered on the rock of slavery, the Northern church had
only recently begun to negotiate a passage around the obstacle. The Northern church's
own tardy moral response to slavery did not really begin until the mid-1830s, when the
Second Great Awakening inspired a handful of New England ministers to vigorously
address one of the country's oldest and most significant compromises with sin—the
importation of African slaves and legalization of chattel slavery. In 1835 Presbyterian
minister E. P. Barrows Jr. declared that slavery was "a violation of love, was unjust and evil,
and did great moral and mental harm to both slaves and masters." With each succeeding
year a few more Northern clerics enlisted their congregations in the antislavery struggle,
so that by the time the war finally arrived, there was generally a growing consensus in
the Northern evangelical churches that chattel slavery was a sin.[66]

Although most Northern clerics were careful to emphasize that both sections had been
complicit in the genesis and growth of the national outrage, the moral stridency accompanying their new antislavery gospel carried with it the subtle, if unspoken, corollary
that those who refused to recognize the error, or who stubbornly defended its practice,
must in fact be sinners. An 1834 antislavery sermon delivered by James Taylor Dickinson
illustrates this well. After conscientiously reminding his flock that the country's guilt over
slavery "must be shared by the entire nation which had permitted . . . [its] perpetuation,"

Dickinson asserted that it was every Northern Christian's "duty to warn slaveholders of God's certain judgment and punishment if slavery persisted." Although the vast majority of these new antislavery converts in the North remained, for the time being, staunchly opposed to abolition, they now increasingly viewed their spiritual counterparts in the South as Godless heathen who had never really known Christ, or worse, spiritual traitors who, having once known God, had now effectively abandoned their faith.[67]

A common theme of such sermons was that a slave system which treated men made in the image of God as animals was an abomination before God and that Southerners' compromise with this sin had subjected the South to a host of other evils. In 1854 Eden B. Foster, a Congregationalist minister from Massachusetts cataloged some of these sins in a sermon more reminiscent of the Puritan era. Declaring that the evils of "cruelty, ignorance, immorality, and sin" were all "inherent in the slavery system," Foster argued that the Union would never become a "high, Christian civilization" until it purged itself of this evil.[68] Of course, Foster was hardly the first Northern cleric to issue such a warning about the baneful spiritual influences of slavery. Since the late 1830s, the Northern revivalist Charles G. Finney had been preaching that slavery was an "abomination" and "iniquity" which had severely compromised the nation's churches.

Nor were such warnings the exclusive province of the clergy. Given her intimate familial connections to some of New England's most prominent abolitionist preachers, Harriet Beecher Stowe incorporated many of these antislavery themes in her novels. Two of the chief themes of *Uncle Tom's Cabin* were that the "peculiar institution" had transformed even "good Masters" into aristocratic tyrants and made the antebellum South an inherently violent place. Slavery had completely corrupted the good people of the South, both slaveholders and nonslaveholders alike, according to Stowe, by making it possible for a people to earn more than their daily bread by robbing other workers of their wages and exercising absolute power over the lives of other human beings. Nor were the Southern sins associated with chattel slavery confined strictly to slave owners. In Stowe's novels, planters needed the support of their communities' poor whites to maintain their cotton fiefdoms and suppress "any spirits of rebellion" on their plantations. Even lower-class, nonslaveholding whites could thus be corrupted when planters used their immoral profits from slavery to purchase their white neighbors' goods and services or hire the sons of nonslaveholders to work as overseers on their plantations.

Harriet's famous brother, Henry Ward Beecher, apparently shared his sister's belief about slavery's pervasive corruption of Southern society. After the successful repulse of Lee's first invasion of the North, Beecher informed his national audience that the North would ultimately prevail in the contest because the spirit of slavery had cursed the Southern cause. By allying themselves with the slave power, Southern churches had spiritually compromised themselves and opened up a Pandora's box of other evils: pride, sloth, ignorance, racial hatred, murder, and sectional envy and discord.[69] So while the Confederacy might briefly prevail on some of the war's battlefields, its prewar compromises with slavery had already sown the seeds for its destruction. A highly profitable chattel slavery system may have blessed Southerners with great material wealth, but it had also spiritually poisoned their hearts and souls, and in the end this would ruin them. Given Beecher, Stowe, and other religious abolitionists' vigorous prewar denunciation of the South's peculiar institution, many Northern religious soldiers marched off to war convinced that the sin of slavery had already virtually extinguished the light of Christ in the South.

Although few religious soldiers devoted precious letter space to a detailed theological discussion of Confederate religion, the adjectives and descriptive labels they applied to their Southern enemies are revealing. For example, numerous soldiers used the pejorative adjective "heathen," or some other form of the word, when describing the Southern landscape and its inhabitants. William Fifer, a private serving in the Eighty-third Indiana Infantry, believed that the Southern Confederacy was a "heathen" land inhabited by a "heathen" people. During his wartime service in Dixie, the religious soldier William Webb Baker also equated the land of rebeldom with "heathendom," and Wilbur Fisk thought that any kingdom founded on slavery must be "accursed." Other religious soldiers were probably conveying a similar message when they spoke of a "wicked" or "unholy" rebellion. James Magrill told his loved ones he would continue fighting until "this wicked rebellion" was suppressed. A soldier in the Tenth Massachusetts, Berea M. Willsey, also expressed his disdain for an "unholy rebellion," while a corporal from the same state commended the sacrifices of his brave comrades "who have so cheerfully and nobly gone forth to put down this wicked rebellion."[70]

Given the antebellum South's extensive spiritual degeneration, some religious soldiers apparently believed that part of their wartime mission was to restore a wayward section to the kingdom of God. Several soldiers used the term "christianize" or "christianizers" when referring to their military goals in the South, and the tools they were using to subdue the Confederacy. After his corps thrashed Hood's army in the Atlanta campaign, Illinois private Charles Wills speculated that with Hood's army now neutralized, perhaps "Sherman intends to use us to Christianize this country." Another private in the Thirty-third Illinois told his niece that given Southerners' determined resistance, he thought his "cannons and mortars are the best christianizers we can use just now."[71]

While some religious soldiers used adjectives such as "heathen" and "wicked" to describe their Southern adversaries, it is difficult to establish the precise meaning they attached to such stereotypes. In the case of the word "heathen," for example, did most soldiers really intend to convey the idea that their Southern enemies were, as Webster defined the word, a people who did not "acknowledge the God of the Bible" or imply that they were truly "uncivilized and irreligious" savages? Or were they asserting that their Southern counterparts' behavior had somehow become "strange" and "uncivilized"? Ascertaining the connotation of another human author's language is often challenging, especially when an intervening time span separates the reviewer from the historical context, culture, and values of his subject. But it is difficult to imagine that most Union soldiers sincerely believed Southerners—a people who shared their same language, political history, Reformed evangelical heritage, and in some cases family tree—were now the cultural equivalent of heathen savages.

The roots between the two peoples simply ran too deep. It thus seems much more likely that in the majority of these cases, soldiers had the latter definition of "strange" and "uncivilized" in mind when they repeated the slur. Southerners were considered heathen not because they were fundamentally irreligious but because from the perspective of

Reformed Protestantism, their sinful compromise with slavery had been causing them to behave in a "strange and uncivilized" manner for decades, or more like badly backslidden believers than genuine Christians. This was an important distinction, because in past holy wars, the fate of most uncivilized heathen had usually been extermination or exile. In this uniquely American religious war, however, the backslidden enemies who survived would be spared in the hope that they too could someday be reformed and sanctified.

In any event, having conveniently disassociated their Southern adversaries from the priesthood of believers, religious soldiers could enthusiastically pitch into their enemies and then look on remorselessly as Confederate widows mourned the loss of their men and homes. Elisha Hunt Rhodes was anxious to "see Richmond soon and humble the pride of the men who brought on this war," but he also believed the Southern people needed to be held accountable for their complicity in waging war against the Union. While attending an Episcopal Church service in a Union-occupied Virginian town, Rhodes immediately noticed that "most of the ladies were dressed in black, and it seemed almost like a funeral. Several families lost friends in the late battle. . . . It made me sad to see the people so sorrowful and weeping, but when I remembered that they brought their troubles on themselves and that the women encouraged the men to make war on the Government, I could not help but feel their punishment was just."[72]

After his own experience fighting Confederate irregulars and guerrillas in Tennessee, William Gould could only conclude Southerners were a "barbarous race of people." Gould was particularly incensed with the Rebels' treatment of East Tennessee's Unionists: "They not only take all their cattle hogs and sheep and c. but take all the provision that they can find in the house and leave the inmates in maney instances to Die. . . . If the people offer aney resistance they are shot down like Dumb Brutes. Is this the acts of Southern arristocrats that is so much admired by England, France and the Northern Peace Democrats?"[73] When his unit was later transferred to Virginia, these impressions left Gould with little sympathy for the plight of Virginia's civilian population:

> Half of the houses where we have been in Va . . . have been
> destroyed. Va is now suffering for her rashness and in the part
> of cession. It will throw this state more than one hundred years
> behind, by plunging its self in this unnecessary warfare. As I
> frequently tell those people when they come and complain of
> grivences, the way of the transgressor is hard.[74]

Although many Northern Christians believed that Southerners' conduct belied their Reformed Protestant beliefs, when meting out punishment for their moral and political crimes others thought it was important to distinguish between the wealthy planter cabal which had long conspired to dismember the Union and the poor, Southern whites who were dutifully fighting on the slave owners' behalf. Convinced they were less educated and cultured than themselves, most Northern soldiers believed their Southern counterparts were the poor, ignorant dupes of the Southern planter class. Southern whites were simply too ignorant and politically naïve to understand that just like the slaves, they too were being exploited and oppressed in a slaveholder society and that they would ultimately bear the brunt of the South's wartime sacrifices. After invading a North Carolina coastal community, Massachusetts corporal Zenas T. Haines noted the civilian population's general ignorance, reporting that "the poor white people left behind here, and even those of respectable appearance, are unable to read or write. They considered it unlawful to send their children to school." In the last year of the war Union surgeon Daniel Holt also increasingly sympathized with the poor Virginian refugees he encountered on the march. Observing one hapless refugee family that had latched onto his unit, Holt noted they were a "fair specimen of *'poor white trash'*—a set of men and women far less attractive than the poorest Negro. Snuff-dipping, tobacco-chewing and smoking creatures filled with domestic whiskey when they can get it—trading with and consorting with slaves who look upon them as inferiors as they *really* are.—No people or set of people I ever met so deserve our pity." Like Holt, many Northern Christians gradually developed a special empathy for the Southern enlisted men and their families.[75]

Although his wartime experiences in the South sometimes caused Illinois private Charles Wills to question the vitality of Southerners' faith and civilization, he also found ample evidence to support the popular charge that the conflict was a rich man's war and a poor man's fight: "You can't go into hardly a house here and they'll ask you if you know anything of 'my son,' 'my brother,' or 'my husband,' that was taken prisoner at this place or that place, and then the poor creatures will cry as though their hearts were broken and . . . I can't stand at all. It hurts me . . . to see these poor women suffering, for maybe not the fault of those they mourn, but of rich men and politicians who have by threats and lies induced these poor devils to leave their families to die of starvation, to fight for, they can't tell what."[76]

These religious soldiers did not believe the Southern masses should bear the brunt of the wartime punishment because, though not entirely innocent, they had for the most part been tricked into the war and were now being just as victimized by it as the Northern population. Throughout history, armies have frequently unleashed their frustrations on enemy civilians during civil wars. The Northern armies, however, exercised remarkable restraint during the war—especially given the protracted nature of the conflict and the Confederate population's widespread participation in guerrilla warfare. Most Northern soldiers reserved their harshest wartime judgments and punishments for the enemy leaders whom they thought had provoked the war.

Northern Protestants often singled out Jefferson Davis for their most vituperative personal attacks. Few entertained any doubts about the spiritual condition of the Confederacy's anointed leader. Unlike Lincoln, the Confederate commander in chief publicly professed his commitment to Christianity by converting to Episcopalianism in 1862. Although Confederate propagandists were quick to trumpet the alleged spiritual superiority of their leader and generals, Northern religious soldiers continued to question the sincerity of Davis's religious commitment. After attending a religious service in occupied Virginia, where a Southern minister asked the congregation to pray for all Christian leaders, Elisha Hunt Rhodes sarcastically observed, "I hope this included Jeff Davis, for he certainly is in need of prayer." When Lewis Chase learned that Grant had broken through Lee's Petersburg defenses, he told his mother that he thought it was funny that "Grant should give poor Jeff such uneasiness when he was worshipping that he had to leave before he had finished worshipping toward the holy Jerusalem Ain't he a sainted

Cuss I don't think it was wrong to say that about the old sinner do you Mother." In the spring of 1864, J. N. Deforest probably thought Davis's spiritual condition more closely resembled that of the Egyptian pharaoh in Exodus than Moses or Jesus. For just as the pharaoh's stubborn refusal to submit to God's commands had destroyed his kingdom, Deforest thought the only reason that Davis and the Confederate Congress were not suing for peace was because "God Almighty won't let them until slavery has been fully abolished and these men have wrought their own destruction."[77]

If Union soldiers expressed skepticism concerning the sincerity of Davis's religious beliefs, they were utterly cynical about the alleged "Christian nature" of the Confederate cause and leadership. Thanks to James Henley Thornwell's prewar "Spirituality of the Church" doctrine, religion in the antebellum South had largely been relegated to the private sphere of Southern society. For the Southern elite in particular, it usually remained a private matter between a man and his God. With the possible exception of defending chattel slavery from Northern religious attack, the church was to eschew politics and war and devote itself to the pursuit of individual salvation. The prewar South was thus preserving its historic commitment to maintaining a strict separation between the church and state.

Ironically, however, with the advent of war, this policy was completely reversed as leading Southern politicians and generals, such as Jefferson Davis, Braxton Bragg, and John Bell Hood, openly converted to Christianity in prominent, well-advertised public ceremonies. Confederate leaders constantly boasted, both privately and publicly, of the superior Christian nature of their government and emphasized this distinction by adding an official invocation of God's blessings to the preamble of their new constitution.

Perhaps noting the inconsistency in this sudden emergence of a civil faith in the South, a number of Northern Christians rejected the so-called Christian nature of the Rebel cause and the Confederate leadership—some more forcefully than others. The latter could always follow the lead of their officers. During the fighting in front of Richmond in 1865, one religious soldier observed that when his commanding officer offered a prayer "to the God of battles" for the troops fighting at the front, he "didn't choose soft words at all. He took it for granted that the Almighty regarded the cause of Jeff Davis and that of Satan in the same light, and he prayed for the complete overthrow of the rebel army, and their utter annihilation." On the eve of the Battle of Murfreesboro, Capt. Alexander Ayers also seemed fairly certain as to the eternal fate of the Confederacy's leaders. In a letter written to his wife Ayers noted, "There is certainly no use of any Hell if those who have brought on this war do not get a place in its lowest depths." Wilbur Fisk thought the blood of every martyred Northern soldier and the tears of their widows and orphans would someday require a moral reckoning from the "band of traitors who caused this calamity." Contemplating the "fearful load of guilt" such men would bear "when the Father of the fatherless and the Judge of the widow calls them to their final account," he could only speculate: "If there is a pit in hell deep enough to receive them it must be a very deep one indeed."[78]

Davis and other Confederate luminaries could try to prove their side's alleged moral superiority with public wartime conversions, regular appearances at Richmond's St. Paul's Episcopal Church, and by including a reference to "Almighty God" in their constitution, but in the minds of most Northern Christians they would always be spiritual counterfeits. Some religious soldiers thus pinned the blame for the war on a generation of morally corrupt Southern leaders, who like Lucifer, had boasted of their spiritual superiority, even as they rebelled against a God-ordained government. Other religious soldiers maintained, however, that if the Confederacy's leaders were spiritually corrupt, it was because they were the chosen representatives of a morally depraved people.

A few Northern Christians apparently believed that Southerners genuinely were a reprobate people, who after tasting the goodness of the Lord had, like Judas, abandoned their Savior for a silver idol of slavery and then compounded their original sin by politically betraying their Christian republic. Refusing to countenance any moral distinction between the leaders who created the Confederacy and the masses who followed them, these zealous Northern Christians compromised Christ's command to "judge not, that ye be not judged" and damned their traitorous enemies to hell.[79]

If anything, from a Reformed Protestant perspective, the Southerners' Judeo-Christian heritage made their moral predicament even worse. For as religious soldiers familiar with the Scriptures knew, while Christ had proven extraordinarily merciful to repentant sinners, he reserved his harshest judgment for hypocritical, false teachers and religious apostates who despite their knowledge of God's saving grace and outward confession of faith had turned back to their old sins. As in Dante's *Inferno,* the Scriptures suggested such religious apostates or spiritual traitors would suffer an even worse fate than the unconverted heathen. As Saint Peter ominously warned in his second epistle, "If after they have escaped the pollutions of the world through the knowledge of the Lord and Saviour Jesus Christ, they are again entangled therein, and overcome, the latter end is worse with them than the beginning." For Northern Christian who viewed their Southern enemies in this light, when so-called Southern Christians vigorously defended the moral legitimacy of slavery and secession, they were merely confirming their own guilt and utter depravity.[80]

In early 1861 a young Northern Christian still wrestling with his decision to enlist felt certain that chattel slavery had completely corrupted the Southern populace. As he discussed recent events with his cousin, Ransom Bedell thoughtfully recalled:

> One of God's holiest men "Wesley" when measuring slavery
> by the Divine law—denounced it as the Sum of all *"Villianies"*
> embracing in the vile system of oppression all human crimes
> offensive in the sight of God. . . . And what must be the moral
> condition of that people who can sacrifice so much to uphold
> a thing, so vile and ruinous in its results, who hug it to their
> Bosom, nourish it with their life's blood, and sacrifice their
> sons in its maintenance.[81]

Bedell was probably alluding to Ezekiel 23:36–39, where the fierce Old Testament prophet had condemned God's chosen people for abandoning his commandments and their faith by sacrificing their sons and daughters to the false Canaanite gods of Molech and Baal. In similar fashion, Bedell believed that Southerners had also traded their Savior for the golden idol of slavery and were now sacrificing their sons in a misguided war to preserve their false god. In the end, the master of the slave had been mastered by the sin of slavery.

The actions of the South spoke louder than its words, and in the eyes of these religious soldiers, the cotton kingdom stood self-condemned. Having enthusiastically enlisted in their leaders' rebellion and made war against the Union, Southerners were too blinded by their previous sins to recognize the extent of their treachery. Perhaps this explains why later, when Northern armies began to invade and militarily occupy the South, some religious soldiers had no faith in their Southern hosts' assurances they had always been for the Union or were genuinely "reformed" former Confederates. As Pvt. John Harris of the Fourteenth Illinois Infantry Regiment explained to a female friend, "They profess to be well pleased with the change of power here, but that may be so or may not. They are awfully deceptious. A traitor is a traitor in every thing. no matter where he lives or what his occupation may be."[82]

Other Christian soldiers took this process of demonization even further and began to associate their treacherous Southern enemies with the traditional spiritual enemies of Christendom. When he scolded his "dear little wife" for constantly expressing her negative feelings about the war, Capt. Philip Welshimer warned his wife to reform her behavior, lest she too one day she become a devilish "She Rebel." Welshimer clearly detested the female arm of the Confederacy: "I do not know that I ever saw an imp of hell unless it was one of these She Rebels and I have sometimes thought they were realy the imps of hell let loose among men." Joseph Whiney thought "the best sermon I ever heard in my life" was the one in which his unit chaplain "compared the sesess to the Devil."[83]

The Union soldiers who were desperately battling Confederate irregulars and guerrillas behind Union lines in Missouri, Kentucky, and Tennessee probably came the closest to embracing a complete demonization of their enemy—and perhaps an un-Christian spirit of vengeance as well. With Southern civilians directly assisting the Confederate rear-area raids on vulnerable Union supply units, occupation garrisons, railroad lines, and bridges, or in some cases targeting them themselves, these vindictive soldiers did not seem particularly interested in ensuring that only the guilty Southern parties were punished.

Initiating their own, more traditional holy war against those they genuinely perceived to be uncivilized heathen, a few religious soldiers seemed intent on relegating every white Southerner to Hades. As he fought Confederate partisans in Missouri, Charles Wills told his loved one that he would "hate mightily to get killed by such a pack of murderers." Convinced the Confederate bushwhackers "would murder Jesus Christ if they thought he was a Union man," Wills regretted his unit's failure "in doing what we wanted to the last trip, but I believe we'll get even with them yet." Maj. Oliver L. Spaulding of the Twenty-third Michigan Volunteers was seeking similar vengeance after his regiment's failure to corner John Hunt Morgan's rampaging Confederate cavalry in June 1863. Nor was Spaulding feeling very charitable toward Morgan's numerous civilian allies in Kentucky and Tennessee: "Everything looks as if it is going to the devil and I know the citizens ought to, and I have faith they will." Pvt. John Harris had expressed similar sentiments to his father the previous year. Convinced the civilians of Tennessee were still waging their own private guerrilla war behind Union lines against vulnerable railroads and rear-area supply units and garrison, Harris declared that the whole Southern people—men, women, and children—were guilty of rebellion: "God send the time that all of them will have to pay the debt they owe the devil for to him they have all pledged their souls long ago and their day of redemption has passed, and I say give the devil his due." In the minds of a few religious soldiers, the bitter partisan war in the West had thus apparently transformed Christ's admonition to love one's enemies into a gospel of unmitigated hatred and vengeance. In their overwhelming desire to see their holy war enemies punished—preferably by Satan himself—a few vindictive religious soldiers may have embraced and been battling their own personal demons.[84]

In the end, there probably could not have been a true holy war against the Confederacy without a corresponding demonization process that partially stripped away Southerners' special status as human beings made in the image of God. Converting their Confederate adversaries into uncivilized heathen, hopeless spiritual reprobates, or inhuman devils made it easier for religious soldiers to wage a total war against the South and justify their enemies' destruction or suffering. A soldier of the cross might find it morally troublesome to rob, wound, and kill fellow Protestants, but not heathen savages already damned to hellfire— especially when he believed that by doing so he was accomplishing God's will.

From the perspective of the Northern religious soldier, in the end the South stood guilty as charged. Seduced by the idol of slavery and corrupted by other evils accompanying their "peculiar institution," Southerners had abandoned the God of their fathers and subjected both themselves and their communities to the wrath of God. A proud and utterly wicked people had then compounded this original sin by seceding from their Christian republic and unjustly attacking it. For most Northern Protestants, grounded in a literal reading of the Scriptures, there was no moral ambiguity concerning the South's crimes or the Northern soldier's duty to punish them. The South was a modern-day Canaan awaiting divine judgment, and now, like Joshua's army of old, the Christian soldiers of the North would serve as the instrument of God's judgment and forcibly restore a wayward section to the kingdom of God.

Chapter 6

God's Will

The purposes of the Almighty are perfect, and must prevail, though we
erring mortals may fail to accurately perceive them in advance. We hoped
for a happy termination of this terrible war long before this; but God
knows best, and has ruled otherwise. . . . We must work earnest in the
best light He gives us, trusting that so working still conduces to the great
ends He ordains. Surely He intends some great good to follow this mighty
convulsion, which no mortal could make, and no mortal could stay.

> Abraham Lincoln, Letter to Mrs. Eliza P. Gurney,
> September 1864

Father, if thou be willing, remove this cup from me: nevertheless not my
will, but thine, be done.

> Luke 22:42

IN AUGUST 1862, Charles Wickesberg, the oldest son of a German immigrant family
living near Sheboygan, Wisconsin, enlisted in the Twenty-sixth Wisconsin Volunteers. A
devout German evangelical, Wickesberg sincerely believed it was God's will that he enlist
and that as long as he and his loved ones faithfully submitted to God's will for their lives,
everything would turn out for the best. Before Wickesberg left Milwaukee for service in
Virginia, perhaps feeling a little nostalgic and homesick, he penned a short note to his
family that included the following verses from an old German hymn:

1. God will see to it that things go as
they should
Let the waves rage and roar
(they will not harm you) as long as you
are with Jesus.

3. He who worries because he thinks Jesus
has gone from him
Will torment himself until he learns
to believe better.

5. Be strong in your faith that the best
has been decided for you. If only your
own will is quiet, you will be free from
all sorrow.[1]

Promoted to corporal after serving only a few months in Virginia, Wickesberg was subsequently wounded in the heavy fighting at Gettysburg. In the spring of 1864, he was promoted to sergeant and his regiment was reassigned to the Army of the Tennessee for service in Sherman's Atlanta campaign. Perhaps sensing he was approaching a major crossroads in his life, in January 1864 Wickesberg again spoke of his deep faith in God's providence: "Dear Mother, I hope, God willing, the war will be over soon. Please pray for me as long as it lasts, and trust in God, He will bring everything to a good end." Four months later, Wickesberg was mortally wounded while leading an attack against a heavily fortified Confederate position at Resaca, Georgia. In the end Jesus had *not* saved him from the "waves" that raged and roared. What had gone wrong? Had Wickesberg misinterpreted "God's will" for his life? Had his faith failed to withstand a terrible wartime test? Or was this somehow God's "best" or God's idea of a "good end" for Charles Wickesberg and his family?[2]

Defining God's Will

Before addressing these questions, one must first gain a proper understanding of what nineteenth-century soldiers such as Wickesberg meant when they used terms such as "providence" and "God's will" to interpret their wartime experiences. Most mid-nineteenth-century Americans' understanding of "God's will" was shaped by their socialization in an evangelical Protestant society. From their earliest years, these men had been carefully socialized with an image of God based on a literal, commonsense reading of the Scriptures. According to these sacred texts, God was a mysterious higher being whose nature could best be understood by describing his divine attributes.[3]

When they described the character of their Judeo-Christian God, most antebellum theologians usually referred to his sovereignty, omnipotence, omniscience, and providential nature. As the Creator of the universe, God held complete sovereignty over his creation. His spoken word had created the realities of human existence, and he could still alter or erase them at will. God had complete authority over everything that happened in his universe—nothing could occur without his explicit consent. His supreme authority over the spiritual and physical realms, his chosen children, and even unrepentant sinners were strongly emphasized in the Scriptures.[4]

Modern theologians often define God as being transcendent and immanent, but such language would have been completely foreign to many antebellum believers. Most simply took God's existence for granted and assumed he was still inhabiting their universe and actively sustaining it from moment to moment. The Creator existed outside of nature, but he was still there answering believers' prayers and intervening in human history to accomplish his higher purposes. The Hebrew name for God, "Yahweh," or its English language equivalent, "Jehovah," perhaps captured this concept best, as it employed the *hiphil* tense of the Hebrew verb "to be" to identify God as the great "I am" or "He who causes everything else [past, present, and future] to be."[5]

The Judeo-Christian God of the universe was also an omnipotent and omniscient higher being. As the Creator of worlds, the Almighty had unimaginable, unlimited, and inexhaustible powers for accomplishing his purposes on earth, and nothing could successfully resist his will. Jehovah not only had the power to do whatever he wished, but as the chief Sovereign of the universe, he also possessed the proper authority to do it. So while others might abuse their power to exploit those beneath them, believers could trust that whatever their God did would ultimately be just. Reformed Protestant theology thus completely rejected the idea of a dualistic universe, where two equally powerful forces of good and evil competed for the hearts of their people. According to the Scriptures, God had already defeated Satan, restricted his activity on earth, and condemned him to a fiery everlasting punishment. As an omniscient deity, God also had a "universal knowledge of all things" and was "all-seeing." The Creator of the universe was intimately familiar with both the natural laws that governed the physical universe as well as the "higher" supernatural laws that governed eternity. Since God stood outside time, he had already witnessed the beginning and end of human history and therefore knew exactly how the lives of individuals and nations would unfold. Given God's perfect righteousness and inconceivable knowledge, believers could always trust that his judgments were fair and infallible.[6]

This Christian understanding of a mysterious higher God who both transcended a wicked universe yet immanently sustained it provided great solace to soldiers locked in the life-and-death struggles of the Civil War. Because a sovereign and immanent God was controlling the events of history, Christian soldiers could rest assured they were not morally responsible for wartime horrors they had not foreseen or intended. Christian soldiers also need not feel too anxious about going into battle because a sovereign God was superintending the events of their life and already knew the time and place of their death. Nothing could happen apart from his perfect will. Since they had placed their faith in this God, and knew he would work everything out for their best, they had nothing to fear on the battlefield. Finally, the concept of a sovereign God relieved religious soldiers of the burden of believing final victory or defeat rested on their shoulders. Since God was sovereign over human history, nothing they did or failed to do in the war could possibly sabotage the perfect unfolding of his will.

Most antebellum Americans also held a providential view of God that shaped their understanding of his nature and will. According to Lewis O. Saum, in the "popular thought of the pre–Civil War period, no theme was more pervasive or philosophically more fundamental than the providential view," which "simply put . . . held that, directly or indirectly, God controlled all things."[7] While helpful, Saum's definition provides only half the picture because it fails to convey the motivation for this divine superintendence and its ultimate purpose. The definitions of the words "providential" and "providence" in Webster's 1828 dictionary provide additional context.

Webster defined "providential" as "proceeding from divine direction or superintendence; as the providential contrivance of things; a providential escape from danger" and illustrated the word with a quotation: "How much are we indebted to God's unceasing providential care." "Providence," meanwhile, was "the care and superintendence which God exercises over his creatures" and was illustrated by a quotation: "A belief in divine providence, is a source of great consolation to good men." This additional context suggests that in the providential view of the world, the principal motivation of the sovereign Creator who "controlled all things" was his sincere affection for his creation and strong desire to care for it, especially the creatures that bore his image. Implicit in this definition of providence was also the idea that the main goal of God's supervision and care of human beings was to prepare them for their eternal future. In short, God intended to have a loving, long-term relationship with his creation, and good men had nothing to fear in the unfolding of his perfect will.[8]

This image of a sovereign, all-powerful, all-knowing, and providential God had a dramatic influence on Protestant soldiers' understanding of God's will. Since God was the sovereign, omnipotent Creator as well as the providential Sustainer of the universe, it logically followed that nothing could occur apart from his will. This, at least, was one of the meanings conveyed by the 1828 Webster Dictionary's definition of the word, which defined "will" as "to decide in the mind that something shall be done or forborne; implying power to carry the purpose into effect. In this manner, God wills whatever comes to pass."

Antebellum Protestants thus avoided some modern Christians' tendency to blame Satan for all the evil they witnessed in their world. Although a good God was not the *source* of such evil and did not approve of it, as Sovereign of the universe, nothing could exist without his consent. So for some reason, known perhaps only to himself, he both tolerated these terrible evils and used them to advance his higher purposes. After all, if a providential God truly controlled everything in the universe, then everything that happened there—both good and bad—must ultimately be his will.[9]

Since the events of the late 1850s, and especially the spring of 1861, had made a violent conflict between the sections virtually inevitable, most Northern Protestants concluded the Civil War must be God's will. After analyzing dozens of antebellum and Civil War era sermons, the late historian David B. Chesebrough concluded that throughout the conflict, clergymen on both sides proclaimed that God had ordained the Civil War.[10] The North's most popular wartime preacher, Henry Ward Beecher, used his congregation's Reformed Protestant understanding of providence to present the war as a foregone conclusion: "If we could have prevented it, this should not have taken place. But it is a fact! It hath happened! The question is no longer a question of choice. The war is brought to us. . . . Hearing the voice of God in his providence saying, 'Go forward!' shall we go?"[11]

If some Northern Christians failed to draw the appropriate conclusion from Beecher's line of reasoning, Northern preachers such as Boston's Zachery Eddy stated the obvious: "IT IS THE WILL OF GOD! IT IS THE WILL OF GOD!" Northern soldiers raised with a providential view of history could thus rest assured that for some reason the divine architect had preordained the slave states' rebellion against the Union and that he now wanted Northern Christians to save that government by crushing the Confederacy. While soldiers sometimes later had second thoughts about whether God had really intended for them or especially some incompetent Northern officers to serve in the Union armies, they rarely doubted the providential nature of the war itself or their belief that the North would ultimately prove victorious.[12]

Understanding God's purposes in the past or present was not easy, but the real challenge was attempting to discern what the future unfolding of God's will might hold for the religious soldier and his family. Would a merciful God help him survive the war and return safely to his family or would he die a lonely death on one of the war's distant battlefields? When religious soldiers realized they would soon be going into battle, many turned to their faith as they contemplated their potential wartime fate.

When writing what possibly could be their last letters to their loved ones, Christian soldiers often shared their own understanding of God's will, especially concerning their potential wartime fate. They generally expressed one of the following three beliefs concerning God's will. Some thought God's will could be accurately discerned from the Scriptures and his providential ordering of events. These soldiers generally believed God would spare their lives either because he had almost always delivered his chosen servants in the Scriptures or because they were faithfully performing their duty in a holy cause. Other soldiers were equally convinced that God's will could not be discerned from a commonsense reading of the Scriptures or the unfolding of earthly events. Those who held this perspective often emphasized God's inscrutable nature as a "Higher Being." In their minds, the final outcome of the war and their personal fate in the contest were an enigma. Finally, there were those who expressed their belief that the war was a divine test or prolonged period of trials designed to test the Northern church and strengthen the faith of true believers. These latter soldiers seemed more concerned with their proper spiritual response to the wartime judgment than their physical fate on the battlefield. For they believed that those who ultimately proved faithful in the face of such suffering would, like Christ, ultimately overcome the evils of this world.

Safe in God's Hands

There was plenty of biblical evidence to support the first theological position, or the propositions that God's future will for the believer could be discerned from the Scriptures and that his word revealed the faithful warrior would be delivered from his enemies. Like the ancient Hebrews, most antebellum Christians believed there was a prophetic dimension to the Holy Scriptures. The Old Testament was filled with biblical prophecies concerning the coming of the messiah, which Reformed Protestants believed had already been fulfilled in the Christian gospels. In an age when American Protestants spent long hours poring over apocalyptic passages to discover the proper meaning and correct chronology of millennial "end time" events, some religious soldiers understandably assumed that God's will for their future lives could also be partially discerned through intense Bible study and prayer.[13]

A plain reading of God's word seemed to indicate that while the religious warrior would not be shielded from danger, hardships, military defeats, or life-threatening wounds and diseases, God would ultimately deliver the faithful soldier from a premature death. Both Testaments, and especially the book of Psalms, were filled with divine assurances that the God of Abraham would not forsake his chosen servants during times of trouble or danger. Many religious soldiers took comfort in passages such as Psalm 91:

> He that dwelleth in the secret place of the most High shall
> abide under the shadow of the Almighty. I will say of the LORD,
> *He is* my refuge and my fortress: my God; in him will I trust.
> Surely he shall deliver thee from the snare of the fowler, *and*
> from the noisome pestilence. He shall cover thee with his
> feathers, and under his wings shalt thou trust: his truth *shall*
> *be thy* shield and buckler. Thou shalt not be afraid for the ter-
> ror by night; *nor* for the arrow *that* flieth by day; *Nor* for the
> pestilence *that* walketh in darkness; *nor* for the destruction *that*
> wasteth at noonday. A thousand shall fall at thy side, and ten
> thousand at thy right hand; *but* it shall not come nigh thee.[14]

Numerous other passages echoed the hopeful words of Jeremiah: "But I will deliver thee in that day, saith the Lord; and thou shall not be given into the hand of the men of whom thou art afraid. For I will surely deliver thee, and thou shalt not fall by the sword . . . because thou hast put thy trust in me." Religious soldiers who believed such passages were God's living word, or his promises to all believers, simply applied them to their own circumstances and struggled to become the sort of believers a faithful God would shield on the battlefield.[15]

Some Protestant soldiers, however, believed that while faith in God's promises was vital, in the end such faith would not save them on the battlefield unless it was also accompanied by human action. They were convinced that if God saved some soldiers on the battlefield, it was only because they were faithfully performing their duty in a just and righteous cause. After all, the Old Testament heroes of faith had not only believed God's promises, they had physically acted upon them. According to Lewis O. Saum, the popular evangelical belief that God would help those who struggled to work out their salvation reflected an inherent tension within Reformed Protestantism between the doctrines of dependence (faithful submission to God's saving grace) and human activity (the need to secure one's own redemption).[16]

Like the biblical controversies over predestination versus free will and faith versus good works, this apparent contradiction between divine submission and human action was based on a literal interpretation of the Scriptures. According to Philippians 2:12–13, believers were to work out their "own salvation with fear and trembling" while recognizing that it was the "God which worketh in you both to will and to do of *his* good pleasure" who was conforming their lives, desires, and external events to accomplish his higher purposes. In other words, believers were to act as though everything in life depended on their own efforts while simultaneously believing that only God, working through them and others, could ultimately save them and use their lives to advance his kingdom on earth.

In a universe ruled by a sovereign God but inhabited by people with a free will, physical and spiritual salvation required both human faith and action as well as divine intervention. It was impossible for depraved human beings to please a perfect and holy God without placing their faith in his son's atoning sacrifice on the cross. But believers also had to demonstrate the reality of their faith by obeying Christ's commandments and modeling his example. As Jesus' alleged brother James asserted in his epistle, believers were supposed to place their faith in Christ and work out their own salvation, illustrating their faith in Christ by what they did. For faith alone, "if it hath not works, is dead." In a similar vein, some Christian soldiers believed their physical salvation on the battlefield depended on both their belief in Christ and how well they performed their military duties as faithful soldiers of the cross. After the war, this complex theological construct lost much of its deeper spiritual meaning when it was more simply articulated in the popular Southern expression: "God helps those who help themselves."[17]

During the war this gospel of "Self-Help" or "faith and action" proved extremely popular among soldiers and chaplains with Arminian leanings, and they eagerly shared its hopeful message with their comrades and loved ones. While attending a religious meeting at the neighboring Thirty-third Massachusetts, John McMahon was so impressed with their chaplain's message he summarized its theme in his diary: "It was not [so] much of a sermon but an exhortation for us to work as well for a blessing as we would pray for one."[18]

At the height of Lincoln's 1864 reelection campaign, an Ohio soldier named Henry Kaufman also seemed to recognize man's crucial role in advancing God's purposes on earth. After reminding his siblings of their responsibility to ensure Lincoln won in November, Kaufman added, "It is no use for us to talk about it, for if we trust in God he will make it all right, yet although we must do our part and do it right."[19] Perhaps this was also David Beem's theological understanding. After serving in McClellan's successful 1861 West Virginia campaign, Beem told his fiancée why he had no fears about his physical safety on the battlefield:

> We had only 13 men killed in all, 4 from this regiment, and 11 wounded. We killed several hundred of the enemy and took 13 prisoners—Providence is certainly on our side, or we would not have come off so well. . . . It is true that I have been in some danger, but I never felt like being afraid in the least. I am in a good cause and intend to do my duty. It seems to me the good Lord will keep me safe, so I do not fear evil.[20]

As he walked through the valley of the shadow of death, Beem was convinced that as long as he faithfully performed his duty for a holy cause, God would deliver him from evil.

Other soldiers shared Beem's understanding that those who faithfully fulfilled their duty to a higher cause would be spared. If man did his part, a faithful God would surely reciprocate. Maj. Joseph Dimock of the Second New York Militia assured his father, "I shall do my duty and trust in Providence for the result. I have no fear for myself and no fear but that in the end the *right* will prevail."[21] In Dimock's mind, the best way a soldier could ensure that both he and the Union survived the war was by faithfully performing his military duties. Pvt. Caleb Clark would have agreed with that sentiment. Declaring that he had abandoned everything he held "dear on Earth" for God and country, Clark was certain he and his parents could now "look forward to the Future with Brightest Hopes Trusting in the God of Battles who is able to carry us through the Storm of Life."[22]

Few soldiers expressed the direct relationship between the performance of duty and acquisition of divine protection more explicitly than Pvt. Abraham Boynton of the Fourth Wisconsin Cavalry. After participating in a Union offensive in Louisiana, Boynton confessed to his friends that he was badly frightened when his regiment suddenly came under heavy enemy fire during an attack on some Confederate fortifications, "but as soon as I discharged my gun all feeling of fear left. I thought I was shielded by a higher power and this thought nerved me to be calm and cool." Through the simple physical act of pulling a trigger, Boynton had fulfilled his sacrament of duty and thereby obtained his physical salvation.[23]

The Christian soldier who believed God was only protecting him because he was serving in a holy cause or performing his duty often shared some of the same theological presuppositions as the nonreligious soldier who suddenly turned to religion or some other source of comfort on the eve of battle. Both believed that by doing something—such as performing their duty better than their peers, discarding a deck of cards, or just vowing to live a holier life in the future—they could somehow strike a bargain with God and persuade him to spare their lives. The irony was that this was precisely the sort of works-based salvation formula that their Puritan forefathers had so vehemently condemned in the Anglican and Roman Catholic churches.

Other Reformed Protestant soldiers rejected this gospel of good works. Although they still believed God would miraculously shield their bodies on the battlefield, they sincerely doubted whether they had done, or ever could do, anything that merited such special dispensation. After all, did the omnipotent Creator of the universe really require their assistance to accomplish his purposes? Did man have anything of value that God had not given him or could not create? The members of this second group maintained that if God delivered religious soldiers from a premature death on the battlefield, it was only because he was a loving and merciful heavenly Father who wished to spare the lives of his chosen servants.

Many Scriptures testified to God's extraordinary love for his creation and especially for the creatures who bore his image. In the beginning, God had declared that all of creation "was very good." Although Adam and Eve's fall in the Garden had cursed a previously perfect world and people, instead of completely destroying them, a righteous and merciful God had both punished the sin and set a plan into motion to redeem the sinner. In the full course of time, God had sent his only son, the second Adam, to atone for the sins of his fallen people and offer salvation to all who called upon his name.

So far from being presumptuous or egocentric, religious soldiers' claims that God would save them because he loved his chosen servants were perfectly consistent with a literal interpretation of the Scriptures. In the Judeo-Christian interpretation of history, human beings occupied the center stage. "History" was the deterministic, linear story of man's creation, fall, and redemption as well as his future judgment and millennial reign with Christ. It revolved around two simple themes, God's unconditional love for his creation and eternal quest to find a few good, faithful men and women who would reciprocate his love.

In the Scriptures, the God who noted the fall of every sparrow and knew the exact number of hairs on every human head had repeatedly warned those who bore his image not to be concerned about their physical needs or safety because they were "of more value than many sparrows." Psalm 23 depicted God as the Good Shepherd who cared for his sheep and was willing to lay down his life in their defense. Indeed, Jesus' parables about the lost sheep, the lost coin, and the prodigal son seemed to demonstrate God's extraordinary concern for every human life. Numerous other Psalms and Old Testament passages also promised that if believers put their faith in God, he would always deliver them from evil.[24]

Northern soldiers' letters clearly revealed they were familiar with such Scriptures. An Irish veteran of the bloody Peninsula campaign earnestly reassured his anxious sister that "all our lives are in the hands of God" and that he could "save from danger those who put their trust in him, tho' encompassed by hosts of enemies." Other soldiers were more frank. After a sharp clash with Stonewall Jackson's army in the Shenandoah Valley, which Pvt. Ransom Bedell of Illinois described as "the most fierce and Bloody Battle I have ever been in," Bedell suddenly realized how fragile and insignificant his life was in the larger scheme of things. As he wrote to his cousin on a hill overlooking the battlefield, Bedell expressed how lonely and vulnerable he felt "in this vast scene of Desolation," wondering perhaps how much longer it would be before he too joined the countless dead littering the field below him. But then Bedell seemed to draw renewed strength from his faith, as he observed, "I am in the Hands of him who noteth even the sparrows fall and He will surely have some object in the fate of one even poor as I am."[25]

Writing from the Union trenches surrounding besieged Vicksburg, a lieutenant in the Twelfth Indiana also took comfort in God's promises to care for his children's physical and emotional needs:

> I am safe in God's hands my dear wife. You have put me there
> and I have I hope committed myself to the same safe keeping.
> Let us rest there. One of the surest promises for today in my
> book is from John 14:18. "I will not leave you comfortless; I
> will come to you."[26]

Likewise, although William Gould of the 144th New York Volunteers expressed concern about his weakened physical constitution, he told his sister that he felt certain God would providentially provide him with the strength he needed:

> Although I have not that strength I used to have, but this I
> trust will come in God's own good time—aint it, Hannah,

a great consolation to have Christ and God our Friend in
affliction and to read his word and there to find this holy
promise that all things shall work together for good to them
that love and serve our God and also this all sustaining
assurance that my *Grace* is sufficient for now.[27]

Other Protestant soldiers placed their faith in certain Old Testament passages that
spoke of God sending invisible armies of angels to protect his chosen servants and Christ's
testimony concerning the existence of guardian angels.[28] Convinced these Scriptures
reflected timeless, universal spiritual realities, a few religious soldiers apparently believed
that just like the Old Testament prophet Elisha, they too were shielded by a protective
canopy of heavenly warriors. Pvt. William G. Baugh, for instance, was convinced a desperate supernatural battle was being waged in the skies above his earthly battlefields that
would ultimately determine both the outcome of the war and the physical fate of the men
struggling below.

After losing some of his comrades in a desperate clash at Resaca, Georgia, Baugh wrote
his mother to tell her how thankful he was that God's angels were protecting him: "O
how thankful I ought to be for the protection they keep over me. I do not see how I can
ever repay them for what they have done. . . . Oh, it must of caused them sorrow to see
me in such danger, but thank God, I escaped all right." Later, at Kennesaw Mountain,
Baugh told his mother to stop fearing the worst: "I put my trust in God, and I think all
will be well in the long run. I think I am better off than [the other] boys for I have help
from above that the other boys have not got." In this case, a young Christian's childlike faith in his heavenly Father's protection was vindicated. Baugh survived Sherman's
Atlanta campaign and march through the Carolinas and returned safely to his mother
at the end of the war.[29] Sgt. Charles N. Mumford, a battle-hardened veteran of the
Third Wisconsin Cavalry, may not have shared Baugh's belief in guardian angels, but he
remained convinced that "the same Power that has protected us all our lives can protect
ours on the terrible field of Blood and Carnage."[30] Though strict, uncompromising, and
dreadful in his judgments, Mumford and Baugh knew their God was also a doting and
protective Father who would always try to shield his children from harm.

If It Be Thy Will

Although the previous group of religious soldiers optimistically expressed their belief
that God's plans could be discerned in the Scriptures, other thoughtful believers seriously doubted whether God's will could be ascertained so easily. Many seriously doubted
whether the Scriptures had anything meaningful to say about the particular life circumstances of any modern believer. While the Bible was prophetic, its prophecies were primarily
concerned with the historic nation of Israel, the coming of the messiah, and the final day
of judgment, not the wartime fate of Union soldiers.

This second and far more popular understanding of God's will maintained that the
future could not be divined with any certainty from the Bible and that there was thus no

guarantee that believers would survive the war. Religious soldiers in this camp emphasized the inscrutable nature of their sovereign Creator and man's frequent inability to discover or accurately interpret what God was doing today, let alone what he planned to do at some distant point in the future. Since no one presumed to know the mind of God, all a Christian soldier could do was echo Christ's Gethsemane prayer that "if it was God's will," they wished to be delivered from the perils of the battlefield.[31]

If the first group tended to view God as a faithful and loving heavenly Father or a God who rewarded those who served him, this second group embraced their Puritan ancestors' view of God as a terrible, righteous judge whose thoughts and ways were so much higher than man's they were often inscrutable. The Puritans' depiction of God as a distant and mysterious Sovereign bears little resemblance to the more intimate and understandable God of the nineteenth-century revivalists, but according to Lewis O. Saum, Sydney E. Ahlstrom, and others, this harsher Puritan view of God was still widely held by America's antebellum masses. While the revivalists' God had been responsive to human beings' good intentions and behavior, this second group of soldiers served a silent and inscrutable God who randomly predestined some soldiers for survival and others for destruction. A mysterious Sovereign who blessed believers with life one moment might just as easily take it away again the next, with no apparent explanation. But as the omniscient Creator, whose thoughts and ways transcended the time, experience, and wisdom of his creation, God owed no explanation for his seemingly arbitrary judgments.[32]

This vision of a fearful and inscrutable Higher Being was also well grounded in a literal hermeneutics of the Old Testament. The Hebrew God was a mysterious deity whose thunderous voice echoed from fiery mountaintops, thunderstorms, and whirlwinds. Multiple passages declared that the fear of the Lord was "the beginning of wisdom." Believers were also told to serve the Lord their God with "fear and trembling" lest they unintentionally provoke the terrible "wrath of the Lord," which would one day purge the wicked "off the face of the earth." God's judgments were said to be "unsearchable" and his ways "past finding out." As Job and King Solomon had so bitterly discovered, no one could ever presume to know the "mind of the Lord," and who could possibly give him advice? Indeed, the Scriptures confidently asserted that the world's greatest wisdom was "foolishness" in God's sight and would ultimately come to nothing. God's thoughts and purposes were so vastly superior that human beings could scarcely imagine the sort of heaven God had prepared for those who loved him.[33]

So instead of searching the Scriptures to ascertain a mysterious God's future intentions, or naïvely assuming their bodies would always be shielded from a deadly foe, this second group of soldiers did not speculate much about their future lives, or even God's ultimate purposes in the war. They could hope and pray for a particular outcome, but in the end, such matters rested with a God whose goals frequently did not coincide with theirs. After all, by prolonging and intensifying the wartime suffering, God had already demonstrated his purposes in the war differed vastly from those of Northern and Southern believers. Antebellum Christians had been taught that it was better not to have many personal expectations, because a Higher Power was orchestrating the events of their life. In fact, a common theme of these soldiers' letters was man's utter powerlessness to shape his destiny in a universe superintended by an omnipotent and inscrutable God.

So even as they expressed great faith in the morality of their cause and ultimate Northern victory, these religious soldiers could not reassure their families they would live to see the Union's final victory. A corporal serving with the Twenty-ninth Maine Regiment seemed more confident about the Union's prospects in the war than his own. A. H. Edwards informed his friend Anna that he felt comfortable asking God for "good health and courage enough to take me through all our hardships and privations," but

> as for the future I can say nothing. If I can return home again
> when our Country is once more at Pease I think I can settle
> down and I *think I can* enjoy the *Peace* that cost us so much to
> gain. For I can certainly believe that we shall yet be victorious
> Dear Anna I hope that not many more months will elapse
> before we can talk over the *war that was.* Till then I must be
> content with what fortune gives me.[34]

Likewise, in a letter to his brother in law, Wesley Gould encouraged his family to be in "good spirits until I do get home. When that will be I cannot tell. Perhaps never. I am not sorry that I enlisted in the United States army."[35] Gould had no doubts about the morality of his wartime service or the righteousness of the Union's cause, but he simply could not be sure that God's will for him in the war was the same as his family's.

In the fall of 1862, after suffering another humiliating Union defeat at Second Bull Run, a despondent president also wrestled with the problem of conflicting human and divine purposes. Fortunately for posterity, Lincoln recorded his personal musings about the enigmatic nature of God's will in a private memo one of his secretaries later titled *Meditation on the Divine Will.* Convinced that God wanted the "human instrumentalities" of the North to "effect His purposes" by upholding the biblical principles of lawful government and human equality, Lincoln had earnestly struggled to accomplish these goals as expeditiously as possible. After two years of frightful defeats, however, he openly expressed his frustration with a God who seemed to be deliberately prolonging the dreadful wartime suffering: "He could have either *saved* or *destroyed* the Union without a human contest. Yet the contest began. And having begun He could give the victory to either side any day. Yet the contest proceeds." Lincoln could only conclude that despite all his earlier efforts to avoid a civil war and more recent attempts to bring a swift end to the terrible violence, "God wills this contest, and wills that it shall not end yet."[36]

For Lincoln, the spiritual lesson gradually crystallized over the succeeding months. Although he had been convinced that his wartime policies were successfully advancing God's will, the Union cause had been stymied and a chastened president was ready to acknowledge that perhaps God's purposes in the war differed from his. As Lincoln later related in a letter to Thurlow Weed after his second inaugural speech, "Men are not flattered by being shown that there has been a difference of purpose between the Almighty and them. To deny it, however, in this case, is to deny that there is a God governing the world."[37]

Like their commander in chief, some soldiers were understandably frustrated as they wrestled to reconcile their own goals and plans with the predestined, but as of yet undetermined, will of their Creator. Their religion sometimes seemed to confront believers with a logical contradiction. The Scriptures admonished believers to work out their own salvation and help advance God's kingdom on earth, but how could believers confidently make any future plans when an inscrutable God was charting their destinies?

Pvt. Andrew J. McGarrah's correspondence in the spring of 1864 depicted one religious soldier's heart-wrenching struggle to balance his biblical commitments to family and parents with a God whose ways sometimes seemed capricious. After the North's decisive victories at Gettysburg and Vicksburg, McGarrah believed that the tide of war had finally turned against the Confederacy. Conscious of his parents' failing health and inability to manage the family farm on their own, when McGarrah learned his younger brother had left home over the winter to join the Union army, McGarrah wanted to return home and assist them. Torn between his duty to the Union and his Christian responsibility to care for his ailing parents, McGarrah hoped and prayed for a swift Union victory so he could go home. But despite his deep faith in God and the Union cause, he could not be sure this was God's will. So in subsequent letters to his parents, McGarrah could not offer them any concrete hope regarding either an imminent Northern victory or his swift return home. "I hope this wicked rebellion will soon end so that we may return home to our aged parents and see and tend to you, you shall never lack anything while it is in my power for you to get it," he wrote. "But let us trust in Providence if its his will to save us as a nation of people he will do so."[38] In hindsight, perhaps McGarrah was right to withhold such comforting reassurances. He was killed three months later at the Battle of Resaca.[39]

Religious soldiers such as McGarrah, who refused to make firm predictions about the war's outcome or extensive postwar plans with loved ones, believed it was pointless if not downright sinful to engage in such idle speculation. The Scriptures clearly warned believers against trying to discover or chart out their own destinies apart from God. Biblical passages such as James 4:13–16 sharply rebuked those who arrogantly presumed to know God's will, or believed they could control their own destinies:

> Go to now, ye that say, To-day or to-morrow we will go into
> such a city, and continue there a year, and buy and sell, and get
> gain: Whereas ye know not what *shall be* on the morrow. For
> what is your life? It is even a vapor, that appeareth for a little
> time, and then vanisheth away. For that ye *ought* to say, If the
> Lord will, we shall live, and do this, or that. But now ye rejoice
> in your boastings: all such rejoicing is evil.[40]

There was nothing wrong with religious soldiers making tentative, short-term plans for the future, and optimistically hoping and praying that God's will might sometimes mirror their own. But assuming that God should always make allowances for their plans or stubbornly insisting that God's purposes should parallel theirs was a sin of pride that failed to respect God's sovereignty. This was Satan's original sin: believing that he could map out his own destiny and live a life independent of Heaven, or essentially become his own god. Since it was man's duty to obey his Creator, whose ways were always superior to man's, all a Christian soldier could do was trust God and hope for the best.

Reformed Protestants who shared McGarrah's theological perspective thus either conscientiously avoided making unwarranted assumptions about the future or carefully qualified such speculation by prefacing it with proper Christian catchphrases such as "God willing" or "If God wills." For example, in a December 1862 Christmas letter, an Irishman in the Twenty-eighth Massachusetts named Peter Welsh admonished his wife to have a merry Christmas without him and stop worrying so much: "Do not let your care for me fret and worry you God is good he brought me safe out of this last battle and he can just as easily bring me safe home to you if it is his holly will."[41] Unfortunately, it was not God's will. Welsh was killed two years later in the fighting around Spotsylvania Courthouse.

But if these men's families were more prone to "fret and worry," perhaps it was because soldiers with a more ambiguous understanding of God's will either could not or would not assure their loved ones that they would survive the war. After all, if God was an inscrutable grand puppeteer, whose mysterious ways sometimes required the wide-scale death and destruction of his people, then loved ones might sometimes have to perish to advance his higher purposes. So maybe the families' fears were not misplaced.

In letters written to their loved ones on the eve of major battles, these soldiers were far more likely to discuss the subject of death or even entertain premonitions about death. As the Union army approached Corinth, Mississippi, in May 1862 and a major battle appeared imminent, Sgt. Amos C. Weaver inconsiderately informed his mother that a number of men from his outfit would "have to die" the next day: "We expect to make a general atack tomorrow we expect a desperate struggle but we are anxious for the fight to commence although we know that numbers of us will have to die. . . . If I get killed in this battle I want to be taken home and buried in our old burying ground."[42] William H. Walling of the 142nd New York expressed similar misgivings about his survival. After watching several men from his regiment get picked off by enemy snipers near Gaine's Mill, Walling stoically informed his loved ones to be prepared for the worst: "Everytime out we lose some. God only knows who will be 'next.' . . . Surely we know not the day nor the hour when He will call for us." Such thoughts often encouraged soldiers to live each day as though it might be their last. As the men of his unit prepared for another battle outside Atlanta, LaForest Dunham likened the war to a giant game of chance and told his Illinois sister, "If thare is any place that a person ought to lade a criston life heare is the place, for a person don't know what time he will be cald up. . . . If it should be my lot to fall, I hope and trust that we will all meat in a better world."[43]

Those who lived in the constant shadow of death sometimes questioned how much freedom human beings really enjoyed in a world ruled by the arbitrary judgments of Providence. While trying to reconcile his marriage plans with the unknown will of his Maker, Pvt. Daniel Webster confessed he could almost be a fatalist:

> Death may step between us and such enjoyment upon earth;
> but we are not to calculate for his interference as he *will* come
> sooner or later any way; and the chances are he will over
> look us for years yet to come, while they are equally as great
> that one or both of us may be called home before the close
> of another month. I have frequently thought that if I could
> become a firm believer in *fatalism* I should become perfectly

> happy and contented but I cannot really subscribe to its
> doctrines in to to [*sic*].[44]

Embracing fatalism might have helped religious soldiers cope with the uncertainty of their wartime predicament, but in the end it could not alter their divine destiny. God was superintending every event in their universe, and if for some reason he had preordained their death on a particular battlefield or decided that this time both the just and the wicked would perish together, there were no grounds for appeal.

God's Divine Testing

Many soldiers may actually have found the idea of an inscrutable Sovereign who arbitrarily predestined believers to life or death helpful in that it relieved them and their families of any spiritual responsibility for securing the soldier's spiritual and physical salvation. A generation increasingly familiar with the new and more hopeful doctrines of Protestant Arminianism, however, also seemed interested in discovering what their role might be in the wartime drama. A third popular option for religious soldiers interested in theologically defining God's will in the conflict was to embrace the belief that the war was a spiritual trial of their faith. Emphasizing God's perfect righteousness, this last group of soldiers believed a righteous God was using a bloody Civil War to test the authenticity of his followers' faith and strengthen the faith of the elect. Thus the war that was so severely punishing their country for its prewar sins would also help refine and strengthen the Northern church.

For many religious soldiers, the Civil War was the most trying period of their lives, and they looked to God's Word to interpret the meaning of their suffering. The early disciples had warned believers they would invariably experience all kinds of trials and tribulations in the world because of their faith. Just as he had tempted Jesus in the wilderness, Satan would also try to undermine the Christian's faith by buffeting him with a host of troubles and doubts. But God permitted such suffering because it was the only way to verify the authenticity of believers' faith and draw them into a closer relationship with him. As the Apostle Peter explained, Christians were to resist the adversary, "stedfast in the faith, knowing that the same afflictions are accomplished in your brethren that are in the world," for after "ye have suffered a while," Christ Jesus would "make you perfect, establish, strengthen, [and] settle you." Christians were thus told to "count it all joy when ye fall into divers temptations; Knowing this, that the trying of your faith worketh patience." The spirit of steadfastness and perseverance, which could only be produced from weathering such trials would help perfect the believer's faith by making it more mature and complete. The Hebrew prophet Malachi had also proclaimed a coming day of judgment, when only those who faithfully served God would be spared, so that everyone could see the distinction "between the righteous and the wicked, between him that serveth God and him that serveth him not."[45]

In light of such Scriptures, many Christian soldiers eventually concluded the purpose of their wartime suffering was to test and strengthen the faith of the Northern church.

The Northern church was being deliberately purified in the furnace of war. The "chaff," or various religious counterfeits in the church, would be consumed in the resulting flames, and only those who remained faithful through their fiery ordeal would be delivered from an untimely death or rewarded with eternal life. In the end, life was just a divine test to determine whether individuals would come into a submissive accommodation with Providence or chart their own destiny like Satan. In classic Arminian tradition, the ultimate spiritual fate of the religious soldier thus largely rested in his own hands.

A private in the Fourteenth Illinois, B. P. Bruce, tried to describe this arduous trial of faith to his mother: "My hope in god is as strong as ever yet I have many triles to encounter but I no that if [I] trust in him I no that it will be well at the end and I will be permited to ware the crown if I holed out faithful."[46] Pvt. Joseph Manson also believed the war was a spiritual test of his family's faith. Reflecting on his wartime service in 1865, Manson told his wife:

> Notwithstanding all the trials we have passed through in our
> past lives and especially for the last two years, We have great
> reason to praise our heavenly Father for his tender mercies to
> us. While life lasts we must contend with the world, the Flesh
> and the Devil. [But] fight the good fight and our great High
> Captain is shure to bring us out Conquerors.[47]

Believers might not be able to escape the physical consequences that accompanied life in an evil world, but God promised that those who remained faithful in suffering would ultimately triumph over evil.

The war that winnowed out the wicked and matured the faith of the elect frequently offered religious soldiers some basic lessons in applied Christianity. A private serving with the Thirty-ninth Indiana Infantry believed God was using the war to teach him some lessons about man's inherently evil nature and the importance of loving his neighbor. Chastened by his wartime experiences, Jacob Bartmess told his wife:

> I firmly believe the Lord is laying out a work for me to do, and
> that it was necessary to give me a lesson of three years from my
> family, in the army, first probably to learn me to love my family,
> and second to learn me human nature, for no better chance is
> afforded one, than in the army to learn human nature.[48]

For some religious soldiers, struggling to remain faithful in the midst of terrible suffering was literally a matter of life or death. Pvt. Amaziah Hadden was certain God would keep him safe—as long as he and his wife remained faithful:

> Oh my dear wife let us strive to be faithfull in serving god
> that we may be counted worthy of a seat in his kingdom where
> parting is no more. I feel to trust in god and fear no evil
> though I am with the friends of Satan I know that god is able
> to bring us safely through the jaws of death. He has promised
> to be with us in all times of trouble and I believe that he will,

if we are faithful which I trust we will try to be god being our
helper.[49]

Proud soldiers were thus reduced to a state of complete dependency on God. Their
physical salvation required a strong, unquestioning faith in God, but they soon realized
they could not possibly obtain such faith without divine assistance. So all they could do
was hope and pray that their merciful heavenly Father would provide what was missing.
As Pvt. John Jones of the Twenty-third Wisconsin Volunteers discovered, the religious
soldier's future existence completely depended on God's continued mercies:

> I am alive and within the bounds of hope, praise be to the
> Lord for his loving care towards us who are so base and
> unworthy. We should give thanks without ceasing that we are
> still amongst the living for to the living there is still hope. . . .
> We hope that we shall remain under the hand of Him who is
> able to protect us.[50]

A hardy German volunteer from Wisconsin was even more explicit in drawing a connection between wartime faithfulness and personal survival. After surviving another
disastrous Northern defeat at Fredericksburg, Adam Muezenberger told his lonely and
miserable wife:

> This hard lot is merely a test for us. If God wills I can return
> and we will have wonderful—in fact the most wonderful days
> of our life together. Now don't give up. God still lives and I
> trust that he will let me return in the best of health and will
> reunite us.[51]

Captured at Gettysburg, in subsequent letters to his wife Barbara, Muezenberger desperately clung to his belief God would restore him to his family—if only he and his
wife Barbara proved faithful. Traumatized by the news of her husband's imprisonment,
however, Barbara ultimately turned to the unbiblical practice of divination to discover her
husband's fate and was devastated by what she learned. This dark prophecy was seemingly
confirmed a year later when her husband finally succumbed to disease in Richmond's
notorious Libby Prison. Had Barbara's sin of divination somehow compromised her
husband's physical salvation? Or like so many other religious soldiers had Muezenberger
simply assumed too much concerning his Father's will?

Thy Will Be Done

The death of faithful Christian soldiers like Muezenberger, who trusted so implicitly in
God's deliverance, could be spiritually devastating to those who shared their faith in a
just and righteous God. Muezenberger had apparently been faithful to the very end, but
had God? Although a relatively rare occurrence given the nature of their assignments,
the death of a faithful chaplain presented an even greater spiritual challenge to believers.

In their letters, Christian soldiers often carefully documented any misfortune or tragedy that befell their unit chaplains because they viewed them as divine barometers of God's will. Effective chaplains were viewed as God's chosen spiritual leaders whose mere presence symbolized God's special favor and blessing. So the premature death of a faithful chaplain could sometimes prompt even the most religious of soldiers to question God's will. How could a good and just God let one of his most dedicated servants, a faithful shepherd who had dedicated his entire life to the ministry, suffer such a terrible death so far away from his home and family?

A Wisconsin private named Robert Steele apparently experienced such a crisis when his unit's extremely popular chaplain became ill during a campaign then suddenly died during a raging nighttime thunderstorm. Steele's faith seemed badly shaken by the incident. After all, if God had not seen fit to spare the life of this beloved man of God, what hope was there for him? As he struggled to retain his faith in a righteous and loving God, Steele sought comfort in the reassuring words of William Cowper's hymn, "God Moves in a Mysterious Way":

> Heaven only knows the horrors of war. Still I hope to live to
> get home again and to greet once more the ones I love for this
> I trust to the guidance and protection of our Heavenly Father.
> Judge not the Lord by feeble sence, But trust him for his grace.
> Behind a frowning providence Thee hides a smiling face.[52]

Steele might question God's ways, which on this occasion appeared cold and arbitrary. But did an omniscient God perhaps have some other, higher purpose for taking his servant home that night which simply surpassed Steele's limited human understanding? With his own life in constant mortal danger, Steele chose to retain his faith in a good God and trust that an inscrutable but merciful heavenly Father would still somehow deliver him from evil.

The assassination of the Northern commander in chief in the closing days of the war also severely tested many religious soldiers' faith in God. As the divinely appointed leader of the Union, Lincoln had led the nation through the darkest days of the war and never swerved in his commitment to defend the "last best hope of earth." In April 1865, however, the religious soldiers' heroic captain lay dead under the capitol rotunda, struck down by the cowardly hand of an assassin. Capt. Wilbur Fisk initially questioned how a righteous God could have permitted such a tragedy:

> As we think of this mournful calamity we can hardly keep
> from asking, Oh why did a just and merciful Providence permit
> this thing to happen? Why was not the assassin's hand stayed
> before it had stricken down the man we all so much loved to
> honor. . . . But we must quote, in view of this event, the same
> words that Mr. Lincoln quoted in his second inaugural The
> judgements of the Lord are true and righteous altogether.[53]

Confronted with meaningless tragedies over which they had no control, like the senseless assassination of their commander in chief after the war had already been decided, many religious soldiers ultimately took comfort in the idea that a mysterious but just and loving God was directing the events of the war. If he had permitted these terrible calamities to take place, they must surely be intended to accomplish some greater good that the faithful simply did not yet understand.

When God's purposes no longer made sense, all a good Christian soldier could do was trust and obey. After becoming badly disillusioned with the war and learning about his family's terrible hardships back home in Indiana, John Blackwell reminded his wife that, like him, she too had no choice but to remain faithfully submitted to God's will. As the troubled Hoosier noted, "It is *good* when such conclusions are forced upon our minds, to remember that, God is light and in him is no darkness at all and that we may walk in his light. It is *good* to trust him *always*. What else can we do[?]"[54] Since the will of the enigmatic Being who ruled over the peoples of the earth could not always be discerned, all a religious soldier could do was imitate the biblical example of Job or submit to God's judgments and trust that he was working everything out for some greater, future good.

For religious soldiers, learning to submit to God's will in all circumstances was the ultimate lesson of their wartime testing. Regardless of their physical fate in the war, the Scriptures informed religious soldiers that their eternal destiny might well be determined by their response to life's troubles, injustices, and meaningless tragedies. When confronted with such inexplicable human loss and suffering, would believers retain their faith in a just God, even when his ways seemed arbitrary and unjust, and continue submitting to his judgments? Or would they reject a seemingly indifferent or impotent Deity and chart their own moral destiny? In the end, most religious soldiers clung to their faith and to Scriptures such as Romans 8:28, which assured them that a just and infinitely wiser God was somehow providentially working everything out "for the good of those who love him, who have been called according to his purpose."

Perhaps one reason so many soldiers ultimately deferred to their God's "inscrutable" judgments was because the United States' antebellum masses still widely subscribed to the old Puritan doctrine of submission. According to Webster's 1828 dictionary, submission implied "resignation; a yielding of one's will to the will or appointment of a superior without murmuring." Webster underscored the importance of this Christian virtue by inserting an illustrative sentence: "Entire and cheerful submission to the will of God is a christian duty of prime excellence."[55] The religious meaning of submission thus stressed God's complete sovereignty as the Creator over the lives of his created beings. As the apostle Paul argued:

> Therefore hath he mercy on whom he will *have mercy,* and
> whom he will he hardeneth. Thou wilt say then unto me, Why
> doth he yet find fault? For who hath resisted his will? Nay but,
> O man, who art thou that repliest against God? Shall the thing
> formed say to him that formed *it,* Why hast thou made me thus?
> Hath not the potter power over the clay, of the same lump to
> make one vessel unto honour, and another unto dishonour?[56]

As the sovereign Creator, God had the right to fashion some human beings for honorable purposes and to make others vessels examples of his "wrath," predestined for destruction,

to remind his people of the limited and transient nature of human life and ultimate consequences of human sin. Only time would tell which category the religious soldier fell into.

This religious definition of submission has often been misunderstood by subsequent
American generations. It did not, for example, release believers from personal responsibility for their actions or necessarily imply a fatalistic approach to life. Indeed, Saum notes
that while "logic suggests that providentialists and others with determinist ideas should
appear in the garb of contemplative quietism. . . . Calvinists and others have been notorious activists." God expected believers to be good stewards of their talents, and would one
day demand an accounting for how they had spent the limited time he had given them
on earth.[57]

After humbly acknowledging God's sovereignty and seeking out his will, submitted
believers were expected to fulfill his purpose for their lives "without murmuring" or
complaining about their assigned roles. This was often easier said than done, but the
biblical account of the Jews' exodus from Egypt demonstrated the terrible consequences
that awaited those who complained about their divinely appointed missions. When the
Jews constantly questioned God's purposes in leading them out of Egypt, and grumbled
that it would have been better for them to die in Egypt or the wilderness than perish at
the hands of the Canaanites, God granted their wish by blocking the path to the Promised
Land until all the original transgressors had perished in the wilderness.[58]

Reformed Protestant soldiers thus concluded that regardless of their wartime fate, it
was their religious duty to submit to God's will without murmuring. They were simply to
trust and obey, leaving the final results up to God. Perhaps one of the secrets to achieving this quiet resignation to God's will was learning how to live with fewer expectations
about the future. In the fall of 1862, Pvt. T. S. Seacord told his wife, "I hope God in
his providence will soon permit us to meet again but we must submit to his will and be
prepared for the worst and hope for the best."[59] Soldiers who were always psychologically
prepared for "the worst" were less likely to be disappointed by subsequent events.

Other Northern Christians were also prepared to accept their assigned lot in life—for
better or for worse. Amaziah Hadden, the young Illinois private who believed the war
represented a divine test of his family's faith, wrote his "dear and affectionate wife," telling her, "I hope that we shall meet before long but how long it will be god only knows I
don't. The will of god be done, not mine. I trust that he will preserve us that we may meet
on earth again but if we should not may god grant that we may meet in heaven."[60]

Other soldiers shared Hadden's resignation to God's will—whatever that might be.
Marching south in the spring of 1864, Dwight Fraser, a lieutenant serving in the 128th
Indiana, wrote his sister Lizzie, "I am willing to trust to God for the consequences,
believing that whatever may come to pass concerning us will be for the best."[61] After being
wounded in battle, a pious Indianan named Hiriam Reid seemed prepared for the worst
when he cited a line from the funeral rites of the Book of Common Prayer in a letter to
his wife and wife and children:

> According to the decrees of god a man born of woman is of
> few days and full of trouble not withstanding it is wright to
> quietly Submit to the will of the Lord. So let us be Resind to

thes things and try to walk worthy of the vocation Set before
us So that when we are called up before the Judgement Seat of
christ we may not be a Shamed of our conduct hear below.[62]

The troubles of life and the inevitability of death were all part of the natural order of
things and did not excuse the faithful from their duty of humbly submitting to God's will.
God's purposes might not always coincide with man's, but his judgments were "true *and
righteous* altogether." The principal evil to be avoided was the temptation to complain
or oppose the will of the Lord.[63]

This was sometimes extremely difficult in the army, where idle soldiers were fond of
complaining about everything from their food to their officers. Suffering the same wartime evils, and living side by side with murmuring comrades, religious soldiers frequently
struggled to restrain their negative spirits. After complaining about his hard lot in the
army, Private Seacord suddenly checked himself in mid-sentence:

> We may stay here all Winter and we may have to leave in less
> than six ours we are like the waves of the sea driven by the
> wind not knowing when or where we are to go or how long we
> are to stay it is a dog's life without much prospects of it ending
> very soon. . . . Many of our soldiers are almost discouraged
> the armys moove so slow but may we all feel to say thy will Oh
> God be done.[64]

Pvt. Abraham Boynton, a Union prisoner of war who had been badly mistreated during
his time in captivity, likewise tried not to question his providential fate. After his release
Boynton told his friends he was "so grateful to the Director of events for getting out
of the confederacy that whatever ill luck befalls me through life I shall endeavor to not
murmur."[65]

Resisting temptations to murmur was sometimes difficult for men who constantly
risked their lives on the battlefield. Traveling aboard the Union transport ship *John
Dickey* on his way to Sherman's ill-fated December 1862 diversionary attack on Vicksburg,
Robert Steele tried to encourage his disconsolate wife: "Try and content yourself as well
as you can my dear for the time will soon come when I shall be home if spared if not
the will of the Lord be done."[66] Far too often "the will of the Lord" turned out to be
a seemingly senseless death on an indecisive battlefield. But despite such risks, religious
soldiers repeatedly placed their lives in peril, convinced that whatever fate befell them,
their heavenly Father would somehow work everything out for the best.

As he marched South with Grant's victorious army in the spring of 1862 to meet his
own divinely appointed fate near a quaint log church called Shiloh, Sgt. William Edmund
Brush urged his father to stop worrying about him because regardless of what happened
in the future, his son was now safe in God's hands:

> I for one am ready for the fray and having put my faith and
> confidence in Him who knows and directs all things for the
> best, in Him who has said I will never leave or forsake those
> that come unto me in faith and sincerity, what ever may be

> my fortune in war be assured that in Him I have put my trust
> and commended myself to the mercy of his all seeing power
> knowing that all will be well. have no fear for my welfare.[67]

In the end, submission required a religious soldier to surrender his own individual rights to life, liberty, and happiness and trust in an all-seeing and -knowing Creator. Although frequently disappointed or frustrated with his judgments, most religious soldiers ultimately retained their faith in his love and justice, partly because they believed God's purposes must somehow be superior to theirs. And more important, because they still shared their Puritan ancestors' belief that those who submitted to God's will in life had nothing to fear in death.

Chapter 7

A DIVINE JUDGMENT

> I John Brown am now quite *certain* that the crimes of this *guilty, land:*
> *will* never be purged *away;* but with Blood. I had *as I now think: vainly*
> flattered myself that without *very much* bloodshed; it might be done.
>
> John Brown's Last Words, Charlestown, Virginia,
> December 2, 1859

> For the time *is come* that judgment must begin at the house of God:
> and if *it* first *begin* at us, what shall the end *be* of them that obey not the
> gospel of God? And if the righteous scarcely be saved, where shall the
> ungodly and the sinner appear?
>
> 1 Peter 4:17–18

AS HE SURVEYED "the absolute emptiness" of the heavily foraged countryside around Raleigh, North Carolina, William Walling wrote his sister, "If ever a people have been brought low it is here." Recalling the terrible devastation his New York regiment had inflicted on the Confederacy during its march with Sherman through Georgia and the Carolinas, Walling expressed no regrets, as he believed Southerners had brought this judgment on themselves with their "crimes against God, humanity, and good government." Walling's belief that soldiers like himself had appropriately administered God's judgment on the South reflected one popular wartime view concerning God's judgment. Another, completely different perspective was shared by the father of an Ohio religious soldier. In a letter to his soldier-son Henry, Joseph Ankeny explained that while he was confident God would "speed the right" and "eventually preserve this union," he also believed God would probably have to "scourge us first severely. We as a nation have all greatly sinned and abused our high privileges. It may be for our benefit to be thus scourged, to teach all how to use our great and glorious privileges bequeathed to us by our fathers." Although Walling and Ankeny obviously had different parties in mind, when they contemplated the object of God's wrath in the war, they both ultimately shared a belief that the war would last as long as it took for the guilty to be thoroughly chastised and purified of their sins. Throughout the war, these two contrasting visions of God's judgment—one that only contemplated hellfire for the South and another that also contemplated sackcloth and ashes for the North—would dominate the correspondence of Northern religious soldiers. Ironically, both views were rooted in the tradition of the New England jeremiad.[1]

The jeremiad has its origins in the Old Testament ministry of the fierce Hebrew prophet Jeremiah and was essentially a prophetic speech or sermon warning God's people to repent and turn back to God before they were punished for their unfaithfulness. In the Old Testament book bearing his name, Jeremiah had repeatedly warned the inhabitants of Judah and Israel to turn back from their sins and honor the covenant their forefathers had made with Yahweh before they aroused the wrath of a jealous God. But the people had stubbornly persisted in their sins and so judgment and destruction had come anyway. In the archetypal jeremiad, the prophet virtually always employed the same three-point formula: first identifying the sins that had provoked God's wrath, then discussing in great detail the likely judgments awaiting those who failed to heed his warnings, and finally concluding his message by beseeching his listeners to humble themselves and repent before it was too late.

The American Jeremiad

In the Puritan commonweal, the clergy frequently turned to the jeremiad to keep a chosen people focused on their larger messianic mission. It reminded Puritans of their exceptional status and higher purposes, but its principal purpose was to warn spiritual backsliders of the dangers of compromising their faith and covenant. By the last half of the seventeenth century, the Puritan preachers of New England could empathize with Jeremiah. Lamenting the spiritual declension of their own chosen community, the Puritan clergy had begun preaching jeremiads warning their congregations of the terrible judgments that awaited those who did not immediately repent and restore their covenant with God. During the 1660s and 1670s, for example, various jeremiads condemned a younger generation for replacing their parents' god with a golden idol of prosperity and predicted that a long-suffering but righteous God would someday hold them accountable for their unfaithfulness.

In the 1674 jeremiad, "Day of Trouble Is Near," the Puritan minister Increase Mather warned that such punishment was imminent, and the following summer it providentially arrived. A local Wampanoag tribe led by Metacom (King Philip), with whom the Puritans had earlier negotiated a treaty, suddenly launched a series of devastating raids on New England's outlying villages and towns. Although probably motivated by the Puritans' increasing encroachments on traditional Indian lands, the raids soon sparked a much wider, intercolonial Indian war that eventually killed one out of every sixteen male colonists of military age in New England. At the time, Mather and other Puritan clergymen claimed that this horrific war—America's deadliest conflict in terms of the proportion of casualties to total population—was a manifest example of God's judgment on a wayward people. To ram this message home, Mather in 1677 crafted an official history of the conflict, *A Brief History of the Warr with the Indians in New-England,* documenting his version of the events and, more important, the ultimate spiritual meaning of the war: God had providentially used Metacom as a tool to chastise a spiritually compromised colony.[2]

The Puritan tradition of the jeremiad survived the demise of the original City upon a Hill and was later embraced by the Puritans' colonial and republican successors. During some of the darkest days of the American Revolution, the Protestant clergy once again invoked the jeremiad to inspire would-be patriot volunteers and resurrect a seemingly lost colonial cause. Convinced the God of battles would look kindly on a cause that humbly acknowledged him and repented of its sins, clergymen preached patriotic jeremiads and organized public days of fasting and thanksgiving to secure the Almighty's favor and ensure ultimate American victory. After playing this crucial role in shaping and sustaining colonial resistance to England, the jeremiad was retained in the new Republic and institutionalized in both American memory as the government periodically invoked its spirit on official days of fasting and Thanksgiving.

Antebellum Americans who embraced the Puritans' visions of American exceptionalism and adapted it to their times were well aware of the responsibilities incumbent upon a chosen people and the potential consequences of betraying this sacred compact. The Judeo-Christian god the founding fathers had covenanted with was an eternal, unchanging, and transcendent being. This meant that just like the ancient Jewish patriarchs, the colonists had ratified an eternal contract that permanently bound them and their descendants to a subordinate, contractual relationship with God. And now, just as Yahweh had held succeeding Hebrew generations accountable for upholding their forefathers' covenants, a Judeo-Christian God would providentially ensure that the Puritans' descendants were faithful to theirs. The heavenly Father who richly blessed the faithful would also severely chastise them if they went astray. For the classic Puritan jeremiad ominously warned that if the religious community was compromised by sin and refused to repent of such evil, judgment would begin with the house of God. This severe judgment, or "scourging," could consist of manmade calamities such as rampant crime, rebellion, unexpected enemy attacks, and prolonged, costly wars; or it could manifest itself in the form of natural disasters such as unprecedented floods, fires, earthquakes, plagues, insect infestations, famines, and droughts. As Sacvan Bercovitch has observed, the ultimate purpose of such punishment, however, was not to destroy the elect but to redeem them: "God's punishments were *corrective,* not destructive. . . . His vengeance was a sign of love, a father's rod used to improve the errant child. In short, their punishments confirmed their promise." The principal purpose of judgment was thus to convict a wayward people of their sins so they could be restored to a proper, submissive relationship under God.[3]

The New England jeremiad thus continued to serve two valuable purposes in antebellum society. First, it gave communities a model for interpreting the cause and meaning of wide-scale human suffering in their midst and helped emphasize the community's responsibility for securing its spiritual and physical salvation. And second, it provided a means for restoring spiritually compromised communities. If a people stumbled into sin, and the Scriptures suggested this was inevitable, then the community could deliver itself from the coming judgment by sincerely repenting of its collective sins.[4]

While the themes and purposes of the Puritan jeremiad remained relatively the same, the central mission of the covenanted American community had fundamentally changed over time as succeeding generations modified it to advance their own, and increasingly more secular, purposes. For example, the purpose of the Puritans' original errand into the wilderness had been to erect a perfect Christian community that would save their families and England from a godless Anglican church. But a less religious Revolutionary War generation had employed the jeremiad to defend their religious and political freedoms and reclaim their natural rights as Englishmen. After erecting what they believed was a morally superior system of popular republican government and disestablished religion, a new uniquely *American* generation now believed it was their duty to preserve the liberties associated with their free institutions and share them with the rest of the world. As Harry Stout observed, the revolutionary generation's "democratic stepchildren retrieved the rhetoric of most-favored-nation, but in place of theology attired it in democratic garb celebrating religious liberty and republican ideology."[5]

Convinced that slavery posed the greatest threat to the United States' new republican and evangelical institutions, in the 1830s religious abolitionists introduced their own antislavery jeremiad. Although most of their moral appeals were ignored or never seen by the general population, Southerners were enraged when Harriet Beecher Stowe covertly marketed a powerful antislavery jeremiad to the American people in the pages of her best-selling novel *Uncle Tom's Cabin*. After gently introducing Americans to some of the sins associated with the South's "peculiar institution" in *Uncle Tom's Cabin,* Stowe prophetically warned her readers that the United States' long moral compromise with slavery had aroused the wrath of a righteous God. According to Stowe and her radical abolitionist allies, unless the church immediately repented of its sinful compromises with slavery, and especially for ignoring the awful plight of slaves in the South, God would surely punish the entire nation. Throughout most of the 1850s, however, this radical antislavery jeremiad remained a "voice in the wilderness" that was largely ignored or rejected by the rest of the Northern church. It was only after John Brown's infamous 1859 Harpers Ferry Raid that other Northern preachers began to echo Brown's prophetic warning at the gallows, that the crimes of a guilty land might have to be purged with blood.[6]

As the country prepared to go to war in 1861, Northern preachers once again returned to the timeless themes of the Puritan jeremiad, convinced that America was about to undergo a terrible but well-deserved day of judgment to set it back on the path of righteousness. But there was a considerable diversity of ecclesiastical opinion concerning the causes and purpose of this divine retribution. Initially, most clergymen thought the South would bear the brunt of the wartime judgment for its sinful rebellion against a God ordained government. Echoing the government's official position, Northern ministers carefully emphasized that the war was being fought to save the national government, not destroy Southern slavery. Methodist minister Ichabod Simmons told his Simsbury,

Connecticut, congregation that "the war is not being fought for the purpose of liberating the Southern slaves; it is the government saving itself." Likewise, in April 1861 Reverend A. L. Stone informed his Park Street Church in Boston, "It is not an anti-slavery war we wage . . . it is simply and solely a war for the maintenance of the Government and the Constitution." While he thought the war would deal "death blows" to the institution of slavery, the brilliant Congregationalist theologian Horace Bushnell also believed the war was primarily being fought to vindicate the supremacy of the national government and the rule of law.[7]

Other ministers, however, believed that God might also be using the war to punish the United States for its past moral, economic, and political crimes. In an 1861 address to the Yale College alumni, the Congregationalist reverend J. M. Sturtevant declared that the adversities of war would reform a country corrupted by a "morbid philanthropy; an ostentatious and costly self-indulgence; a lack of . . . reverence for a strong and energetic government; and a disposition . . . to substitute the wills of majorities . . . [for] the will of God."[8] Henry Ward Beecher also thought the nation was being disciplined for a host of private and public sins. In his 1861 Fast Day sermon, "Our Blameworthiness," he argued the North was being spiritually disciplined for its selfish pursuit of materialism and pleasure, criminal mistreatment of the Indian and Mexican, and shameful compromises with slavery. Having sacrificed their moral convictions for economic and political gain, Northerners would now reap what they had sown.[9]

Instruments of God's Judgment

Once the fighting was underway, most Northern sermons coalesced around a common theme: the South's guilt in rebelling against a Christian government and the Christian soldier's duty to crush this slaveholders' uprising. Henry Ward Beecher and other Northern ministers immediately encouraged their congregations' young men to enlist in a national crusade to defend their Christian government and freedoms. In the process of rallying the troops, the clergy reassured Christians that violence against evil reprobates, or hopeless sinners, was justified because "God used both the persuasive power of the Gospel and the deadly power of the sword" to advance his kingdom on earth. In word and song, religious soldiers were encouraged to imitate John Brown's example and enlist in a holy war against an evil Southern slave empire so they too could become instruments of God's judgment.[10]

Based on their letters, it seems clear that many religious soldiers fully embraced this mission. Most sincerely believed that the South bore all the responsibility for the breakup of the Union and resulting war, in part, perhaps, because like many modern Christians they found it easier to focus on the crimes of their neighbors than scrutinize their own consciences for sins that might offend God. In any case, firmly convinced that the war was a divine retribution against the South, some Northern Christians eagerly accepted their new wartime role as instruments of God's judgment. If the war truly had been ordained by Heaven to set a wayward people back on the path of righteousness, it was not only morally permissible for soldiers to mete out God's judgment, it was their Christian duty.[11]

In embracing such a mission, however, Northern preachers such as Henry Ward Beecher warned their charges not to fight in a spirit of vengeance but righteous indignation: "Let not our feelings be vengeful nor savage. We can go into this conflict with a spirit just as truly Christian as any that ever inspired us in the performance of Christian duty. Indignation is very different from anger. Conscience is very different from revenge." Union soldiers were not to embrace a blind spirit of revenge because such vengeance ultimately belonged to the Lord and would be more perfectly meted out by him on the final judgment day. Religious soldiers were thus told to punish evildoers in a carefully measured way that met the requirements of God's justice but did so without promoting an endless cycle of violence.

Indeed, a careful reading of the Exodus passages associated with the Old Testament principle of *lex talionis,* or an "eye for an eye," suggests that the principal goal of *lex talionis* was restitution or a just recompense for some wrongdoing, not vengeance, or spitefully seeking to avenge some enemy crime with even greater violence. The governing principle of the Hebraic legal system was compensatory justice, or the proper restitution of the victim, the offender, and their larger society. So if anything, the principle of *lex talionis* was probably introduced to *restrain* Semitic blood feuds, not justify retaliatory killing. This principle of compensatory justice was later incorporated into English common law and thus became an important component of the United States' nineteenth-century legal system. Perhaps these biblical and legal distinctions explain why most religious soldiers preferred to use the words "retribution" and "punishment" when discussing the fate of their Southern enemies instead of the King James Bible's more commonly used words of "revenge" and "vengeance."[12]

These subtle but important moral distinctions, however, were sometimes lost in the intense hostility many religious soldiers felt for their traitorous Southern enemies. Indeed, thanks to their clergy's demonization of the South, most seemed eager to serve as the agents of God's wrath. As he completed his training at Camp Defiance in Cairo, Illinois, in May 1861, Pvt. Dietrich C. Smith told his friends, "I do not expect to feel much southern steel I intend to make them feel mine at least I will try pretty hard those miserable traitors. Excuse me for this hard language; but every time I think of their actions it makes me feel all over." A year later, while stationed near the Fair Oaks battlefield along the Chickahominy River, James H. Leonard told a Wisconsin acquaintance, "The graves of every soldier here seemed to cry out for punishment on those who instigated this war. The leaders of this rebellion must receive that punishment which is justly theirs, Mercy to *them* would be *Cruelty* to *Civilization.*" After helping to repulse Braxton Bragg's invasion of Kentucky a month earlier, Capt. Alexander Ayers of the 125th Illinois explained his wartime role to his wife: "*Cursed* Kentucky, she must pay the penalty she has incured in her bloody traffick—May her citizens beg for bread and her soil be purified by fire—we are doing it."[13]

Wartime events sometimes intensified this Christian passion to punish a wicked section. After leading the remnants of his brigade in a costly but successful last-ditch stand against the Army of Northern Virginia at Gettysburg, aide-de-camp Frank Haskell prayed that God would help him utterly destroy his Southern enemies:

> By God's help they shall pay for their sin. May I be one of the
> instruments of their desolation and punishment, and to bring
> it about, that the places that know them shall know them no
> more forever, and to teach such as they how sacred a thing is
> the Constitution, and how terrible is the wrath of the offended
> Republic.[14]

Other Union soldiers shared Haskell's righteous anger. Pvt. Peter Weyhrich of the Forty-fourth Illinois Infantry Regiment confessed:

> I never destested a set of men more in my life than when after
> the battle of Stone River I went over the field of Carnage and
> there saw our dead stripped of their clothing. . . . A cause
> which will tolerate such acts of barbarism can not in my
> opinion find favor in sight of Heaven. But retribution is going
> to overtake them yet so let us leave them in their guilt.[15]

Weyhrich obviously had difficulty restraining his strong desire for revenge, but as a Christian, he apparently took comfort in the thought that any earthly punishment he could imagine for his enemies would pale in comparison to the terrors that awaited them in hell.

Soldiers serving in Gen. William Tecumseh Sherman's victorious Army of the Tennessee also viewed themselves as the enforcers of God's justice. After conquering Atlanta in 1864, Sherman was convinced that the South would never abandon its stubborn predilection for waging war until the North made "war so terrible" for the Southern people that they lost their taste for it. Perhaps heeding their commanding general's advice, that "those who brought war into our country deserve all the curses and maledictions a people can pour out," Sherman's soldiers made Georgia howl as they swept irresistibly to the sea in the fall of 1864. Singing religious songs such as the "Old One Hundred" as they marched, many religious soldiers considered themselves avenging angels of the Lord as they cut a swath of destruction twenty miles wide through the heart of rebeldom. Having abandoned their railroad lifeline to the North, Sherman's troops foraged liberally from the rich Georgian farms they passed. Although some religious soldiers were clearly troubled with the extensive theft and destruction of Southern civilians' property, seeing little moral difference between foraging and outright theft, others justified it as part of the "hard hand of war." Charles W. Wills apparently thought the Southern planters were simply getting their just desserts:

> [I] Begin to see where the "rich planters" come in. This is
> probably the most gigantic pleasure excursion ever planned. It
> already beats everything I ever saw soldiering, and promises to
> prove much richer yet. . . . Our men are clear discouraged with
> foraging, they can't carry half the hogs and potatoes they find
> right along the road.[16]

Destroying railroads, cotton gins, and anything else of military value they encountered during their march through Georgia, Sherman's troops made off with all the farm animals and foodstuffs they could carry away and then often destroyed the rest. Even the planting seed was taken or ruined.

Another Christian in Sherman's army, William Henry Walling, was morally troubled by the "hard foraging" of his New York comrades. In his opinion, they were seizing much more than they needed. "All is taken and the people are left in many instances with broken furniture or none at all," he wrote.[17] Despite his moral reservations as a believer, as a soldier Walling had to admit that Sherman's new strategy was devastatingly effective:

> If the saying be true that all things are right in times of war
> which distress ones enemies then the warfare of Gen. Sherman
> is the one after for me (though I cannot admit it in clear
> conscience). Where he has been there will be no seed time,
> consequently there can be no harvest. He seems to be the
> avenger of the slave as well as his liberator.[18]

After pragmatically justifying Sherman's policies, however, Walling added a line that suggested he was troubled by the whole business. He offered a brief benediction for Sherman and his troops: "May God bless him, him and us."[19]

Sherman's troops reserved their greatest wrath for the state they considered to be the spiritual heart of the Confederacy—South Carolina. Upon entering this hotbed of secession, in addition to the "hard foraging" and destruction of potentially useful "military property," soldiers began to burn some of the Southern homes and farms in their path. A few officers later described how they could trace the progress of Sherman's columns by watching the gradually advancing plumes of smoke in the sky.[20] Although Sherman's troops generally exercised greater restraint in North Carolina, according to Pvt. William G. Baugh, some soldiers were still seeking retribution when the army occupied Fayetteville: "As fast as we would try and save the public buildings, the crowd would cut the hose, and set fire in a different place. The soldiers were bound to burn the secession place, and they done it."[21]

Sherman's troops were not the only Union soldiers who had an insatiable desire to punish an unrepentant slave aristocracy. As early as 1862, the radical religious abolitionist Capt. Francis Russell thought the North should embrace extreme measures in its war against the Southern slave power: "I am for giving rebeldom *hell* giving them the *horrors of war*. . . . I would burn rebel houses. . . . I would *pursue* and destroy their army and the towns that contained them taking feed and [?] from the rich and even giving it to the poor and *starving families*."[22] Like other religious soldiers, Russell believed the war was God's long-awaited punishment of the wayward South, and that by ruthlessly punishing the section for its sins he and his friends were helping to purge the infernal region of its sins. When the war's fiery judgments had consumed everything predestined for destruction, Dixie and her inhabitants would finally be redeemed. There were also other, far more temperate soldiers who shared Russell's vision, if not his extreme rhetoric. Cpl. Zenas T. Haines of Massachusetts thought that "the more we learn of the despicable social condition of the South, the stronger appears the need of the purification which, in the Providence of God, comes of the fire and the sword." As a native of Massachusetts, Haines naturally interpreted the war along familiar jeremiad lines: Having stubbornly persisted in its sins, a compromised community would now be providentially subjected to the terrible scourge of war in the hopes that those who survived would finally be spiritually purified of their more stubborn sins. In this fashion, the instruments of God's judgment would also serve as his arm of redemption.[23]

Other religious soldiers—just as dedicated to punishing the South as Russell and Haines—took a more charitable view of their Southern enemies' plight when they realized how truly dreadful it was to fall into the hands of the living God. Although Union surgeon Daniel M. Holt had not "in the smallest degree become less enthusiastic in a desire to see traitors punished," as the wartime judgment continued to grow increasingly severe, he exhibited a greater magnanimity toward his sworn Southern enemies. As he observed Sheridan's devastation of the Shenandoah Valley—"The whole Valley [is] in a blaze. Heavy clouds of smoke hang over it like a funeral pall"—Holt could not help but feel "compassion [for] the case of the poor deluded people."[24]

Equally awed by the terrible magnitude of the wartime judgment, when Pvt. Michael Cunningham contemplated the awful fate of Southerners, he could not help but pity them:

> It is hard to look at the country through which we have passed this spring and summer five years ago it was the pride of America and was the home of her most wealthy Sons and daughters and now these homes are heaps of mouldering ruins and the owners of them fill an unknown grave I hope and pray that the day be not far distant when our glorious old flag shall wave free to the breeze in every city town and Hamlet in the United States and the din and tumult of war be heard no more in our broad land.[25]

A National Judgment

While some Northern Christians had once prayed that their God would intervene in the sectional conflict over slavery and punish the South for its sins, none had dreamt how terrible that punishment might be or realized how much the North would also suffer as a result of that judgment. When the war was not resolved with one big, glorious battle, and the Union armies began to suffer one defeat after the other, the Northern clergy and religious soldiers began to suspect what some radical abolitionists had realized from the beginning. The war was not just a divine judgment of the South. God was punishing the entire country for its prewar sins: from the evils associated with chattel slavery to the excesses of Northern capitalism. Materially blessed by the fruits of slavery and a rapidly emerging industrial economy, both sections had arrogantly assumed they could chart their own economic and political destinies independent of God. As the North's Episcopal bishops noted in a joint ecclesiastical letter published in 1862, God was providentially "chastening" the North for its sins: "God has loaded us with benefits and with our benefits have grown our ingratitude, our self-dependence, and self-sufficiency, [and] our pride."[26]

Weighed on the scales of divine justice, a chosen nation had been found wanting and would now reap the consequences of violating its covenant with God.

Over time, a larger number of religious soldiers ultimately embraced this belief about the war being a national judgment, probably because it was more consistent with their traditional understanding of the Puritan jeremiad. After all, the principal goals of the original Puritan jeremiads had not been to destroy evildoers but to draw attention to the existence of certain evils within the church and warn believers that if they failed to address this sin in a timely manner, God would hold their entire community accountable for it. Although it had been relatively easy for some Northern Christians to feel indignant about the moral crimes of the South, it took the harsh realities of an endless civil war to convince others that God might also be punishing the North for its sins.

Most soldiers did not offer a precise explanation for this national judgment, but they believed that the God who had providentially unleashed the calamitous wartime scourging would remove it just as soon as it had accomplished its intended purposes. Indeed, it almost seemed as though an immanent and omnipresent God had, throughout the war, been trying to convey this spiritually comforting message to an almost-chosen people. On the same day Abraham Lincoln was publicly sharing his own nuanced understanding of the war's purposes at the second inaugural in Washington, D.C., Richard R. Crowe articulated a similar, albeit much abbreviated, version of the same message to loved ones from Sherman's army in the Carolinas: "An all wise Providence will end the strife and misery, as soon as the purposes for which it was ordained is accomplished." Another godly soldier gently reminded his anxious wife and children, "This war is sent by our Lord" and once "the People are punished enough for their national sin then it will soon be settled." With even the lowest ranks now conveying their understanding of the jeremiad to loved ones, the Northern clergy had clearly done their job.[27]

Pvt. Wilbur Fisk believed that like Christ, the North was now paying the price for the South's sins. The South was rightfully reaping its just punishment for the sins of secession and slavery, but since the Southern and Northern states were all members of the same American family, the entire country would have to endure the wartime judgment. And this meant that innocent Northern soldiers would now have to suffer alongside their Southern brethren to redeem their country from the curse of slavery:

> Virginia is a guilty state, and the day of her retribution seems to
> be at hand. . . . Omnipotent wisdom alone can tell when the end
> will come, or the extent of ruin that will be accomplished when
> the end does come. If Virginia and her sister conspirators against
> our good Government were obliged to bear the whole burden
> of their guilt, it would be well, but this cannot be. The whole
> nation is involved, and deep grief and poignant sorrow must be
> borne by the North, to expiate the crimes of the South.[28]

By nobly offering themselves up as sacrificial lambs in atonement for their nation's sins, religious soldiers could thus fulfill a righteous God's demand for retribution and save their country from further destruction.

This popular wartime vision of young Christian soldiers sacrificing their lives to save others was perhaps best articulated after the war by the New England Congregationalist pastor and theologian Horace Bushnell. In *The Vicarious Sacrifice*, Bushnell offered a new interpretation of the meaning of Christ's sacrifice on the cross. The orthodox view held by most antebellum Americans was that the problem of human sin had been resolved by Christ's sacrifice on the cross. At Calvary, Christ had satiated the righteous demands of a perfect God by taking full responsibility for all human sin and atoning for it by sacrificially dying on the cross in man's place. This traditional meaning of Christ's death—the sacrificial death of a perfect God to redeem mankind from the wages of sin and death—meant that good works were therefore no longer necessary to enter the kingdom of heaven. As long as people sincerely embraced the broken Savior's sacrifice on the cross, what they did in the future or had done in the past no longer made any difference—they would be saved.[29]

In *The Vicarious Sacrifice*, however, Bushnell resurrected the more traditional Catholic understanding that while faith in Christ's redeeming act at Cavalry might be sufficient to save the individual, Christians were also called upon to imitate Christ's example, or illustrate the reality of their newfound faith by what they subsequently did. This meant that, like Christ, believers needed to develop such a compassion for the lost that they too would be willing to take up their crosses and sacrificially lay down their lives itself to redeem their fallen society. According to Bushnell, this was precisely what had happened during the Civil War. Morally outraged by the terrible consequences stemming from the national sins of slavery and rebellion, the young men of the North had marched off to combat them and, in many cases, had sacrificed their lives to atone for the sins of their country. As Sydney Ahlstrom observed, by seeking to understand the meaning of the war's suffering by meditating on Christ's crucifixion, Bushnell discovered that in both cases "the expiation of corporate sin and guilt had opened the way for atonement." By restoring a spiritually compromised people, the war had thus resanctified the nation so it could complete its glorious millennial mission. Given this understanding of the conflict's purposes, a horrific Civil War could thus become something good in the same way the purpose behind Christ's tragic death on a cross had ultimately rendered the evil Friday of his crucifixion "good."[30]

Other prominent Northern Protestants also shared this unorthodox idea that Christ's sacrifice on the cross was somehow insufficient to atone for the country's sin of slavery. In her *Battle Hymn of the Republic* lyrics, abolitionist poet Julia Ward Howe suggested that just "as He [Christ] died to make men holy," Northern Christians would now have to march into battle with God at their side and "die to make men free." In the fall of 1862, Harriet Beecher Stowe joined this swelling heretical chorus. After learning that several thousand women in the British Empire had delivered a petition urging their sisters across the Atlantic to bring an end to the fratricidal conflict, Stowe penned the official American rebuttal, *Reply to An Affectionate and Christian Address of Many Thousands of Women of Great Britain and Ireland to Their Sisters the Women of the United States of America:*

> Yes, our sons must die, their sons must die. We give ours freely;
> they die to redeem the very brothers that slay them; they give

> their blood in expiation of this great sin, begun by you in Eng-
> land, perpetuated by us in America, and for which God in this
> great day of judgment is making inquisition in blood.[31]

Why anyone still had to die to expiate such sin, given Christ's universal act of atonement on the cross, was the unasked question. While Stowe claimed Yankees were dying to spiritually redeem their Southern enemies, other Northern politicians and clergymen were either more orthodox or honest when they asserted that Northern soldiers were dying for their country. The Christian soldiers of the North were being sacrificed to create and preserve a new American civil religion, based on secular patriotism to the state, not traditional spiritual commitments to God's Church.

As they witnessed the terrible consequences of the war unfolding before them, some religious soldiers were dismayed when they suddenly realized their own side was being subjected to the same divine scrutiny that had earlier condemned the South. Would the sins of the Northern armies and people back home somehow deprive their cause of God's blessings, or worse, expand and intensify the current wartime judgment? As 1st Lt. John Blackwell watched the stunned women of Jackson, Mississippi, meandering aimlessly through the burning streets of their city in 1863, he wondered if the Northern armies and people might not be the next objects of God's wrath:

> When I left the streets were becoming crowded with drunken
> soldiers and I dare not think of the scenes of brutal violence
> that may disgrace our army still more. The scenes already
> baffle description. I was not made for a soldier I find. I can
> face bullets if need be for my country but such things I can
> not countenance and will not. It may be it is just retribution
> on the destroyers of our good government and on those who
> for so long dealt in the bodies and souls of men, but I cannot
> but think that those who thus riot in these scenes will one day
> reap God's wrath for their sins.[32]

The terrible God who had found the hearts of Southerners wanting would also surely judge the secret sins of the North. Two months later, Blackwell was so demoralized by his comrades' sins that he was no longer certain whether the union armies merited heaven's favor. "For my own part war becomes daily more distasteful to me," he wrote. "There is nothing but the justice of our cause that supports me. . . . Even with this consideration I cannot see sometimes how God can bless us when there is so much envie vandalism and lust and impurity in our army."[33]

Other devout soldiers also wondered how a righteous God could possibly ignore the sins of the North while punishing those of the South. After describing the shell-pocked landscape, bombed out homes, and innumerable graves of the Murfreesboro battlefield to his wife, Jacob Bartmess contrasted man's terrible wickedness with the peaceful harmony he found in nature and marveled that God did not wipe man off the face of the earth:

> Alas while nature is peacable and acting in harmony with
> her laws, man is rebellious disobeying law and order and is

> engaged in deadly strife. Why is man the only portion of
> God's creation that does not live in harmony and peace. Ah
> the reason is plain. it is because his imaginations are evil, his
> heart is wicked. he is constantly seeking the advantage of, and
> superiority over his fellow. Is it not a wonderful mercy that the
> Blessed God does not blot man out of his remembrance. But
> why should I consider thus. God bless the right.[34]

An aberration of nature, man was rebellious and violent and always seeking to destroy that which he could not control. In his human wisdom, Bartmess believed God would be perfectly just to destroy such creatures, but he hoped that a more merciful Providence could somehow overlook such sin and still side with the North.

Mercy Triumphs Over Judgment

Although many religious soldiers acknowledged their nation was desperately wicked and no doubt deserved to be mercilessly punished for its sins—the South for its sins of sectional pride, secession, and slavery, and the North for its growing materialism, secularism, and past compromises with slavery—they could take comfort in the Scriptures' assurance that they served an extremely merciful God who might still intercede on their behalf. The gospels assured believers that they would be judged by the same measure they used to judge others, and that those who acted mercifully would in return receive mercy from God. Perhaps most comforting of all was the apostle James's promise to early Christians that God's mercy triumphed over his judgment. The same God who mercilessly destroyed the unrepentant sinner also generously offered forgiveness and eternal life to those who would receive it. Swift and unrelenting in his judgments, he also often delayed them, not wanting anyone to perish in their sins.[35]

Indeed, the principal lesson of the wartime judgment seemed to be that the Northern church needed to repent of its corporate and private sins and ask a merciful God to spare their country from further judgment. This at least was one young Wisconsin soldier's understanding. Having just lost his best friend in battle, Harlan found it difficult to be optimistic as he discussed the dreadful consequences of America's sins with his girlfriend:

> I hope your cousin will be spared to you. This war makes many
> hearts sad. An' almost every breeze is born to no the news of
> the loss or suffering of some dear friend. How earnestly should
> Christians pray for peace. When our nation repents of our great
> sins—then and not till then shall we have peace. Sometimes
> when I feel our great wickedness as a nation—I feel that God
> would be but just to destroy us. He is merciful—to that we do
> trust.[36]

The tragedy of war had clarified a truth that was often obscured in peacetime. The fate of men and nations had always been in the hand of God, and everything depended on his future mercies.

The need for national humility and repentance seemed underscored by the intensity and duration of the nation's wartime suffering. After all, if a truly righteous Northern government was waging a holy crusade against an evil rebellion, why had the Lord not crowned the Union armies with greater success in battle? In the first two years of the war, despite the North's morally superior cause, the Confederate armies had repeatedly and decisively defeated its armies in the East. Based on their study of Israel's Old Testament conflicts, some Northern believers could only conclude that the disastrous Union defeats and excessive casualties were evidence of some secret, unconfessed sin in the Northern camp that was preventing Jehovah from blessing the North with victory. This, after all, had usually been the spiritual lesson when God's "other chosen people" had suffered defeat in battle.[37]

Sanctification of the Northern Cause

Based on their literal, commonsense understanding of the Old Testament cycle of sin and redemption, other Northern Christians concluded that if God planned to use the Northern armies as a tool to punish Southern reprobates, he might first have to sanctify his chosen instrument of judgment. Indeed, according to some Northern clergymen, such as Henry Ward Beecher and Horace Bushnell, sanctification was the primary purpose behind the North's wartime suffering. In his 1864 sermon "Popular Government by Divine Right," Bushnell seemed to endorse John Brown's prophecy that the sins of a guilty land could only be washed away with the shedding of blood: "Blood, blood, rivers of blood, have bathed our hundred battle-fields and sprinkled the horns of our altars! Without this shedding of blood, how could the violated order be sanctified?" This spiritual purification of the Northern people, however, was a necessary prerequisite, not only for defeating a wicked slave power in a civil war but also for realizing the United States' more important, millennial destiny. When the conflict ended in Union victory, Baptist pastor James T. Robinson vividly described how a spiritually refined country would finally achieve its glorious God-ordained mission: "The great Republic, tried by fire . . . but terrible and glorious, ascends through smoke and flame to unending sway and splendor."[38]

Mid-nineteenth-century Reformed Protestants were extremely familiar with the doctrines of sanctification and perfectionism, which essentially held that salvation was not the climax of the believer's life in Christ, but only the beginning. It was not enough for a believer to be saved. According to these doctrines, true Christians "proved" their faith by asking Christ to come into their heart and transform them into his likeness. In effect, the believer's subsequent life as a Christian would demonstrate the authenticity of their conversion. This meant that the believers' everyday life should increasingly reflect Christ-like qualities as the indwelling of the Holy Spirit transformed them into new creatures, gradually purging them of hidden sins and helping them live a more godly life. The ultimate goal of this process of sanctification was to create an army of saints that would spiritually redeem their society and usher in the millennial reign of Jesus Christ.

Instead of concentrating their efforts on facilitating this process of sanctification, however, both sections' antebellum churches had effectively ignored or abandoned it when they shifted the focus of their ministries to expanding the size and political influence of their ministries and supporting their section's stand on slavery. This compromise of one of the church's central spiritual missions had potentially blocked or reversed the process of sanctification in the country's churches and thus spiritually blinded them to the nation's increasing wickedness. A merciful God, however, had chosen to intervene decisively at this point and use a terrible war to save his Church from the eternal consequences of its prewar digressions. And now, thanks to their churches' prewar compromises, many Northern families would have to endure the fiery trials of war until hearts long hardened by the sins of sectionalism, selfish ambition, and moral apathy were finally melted and believers once again humbly renewed their commitment to inner sanctification.

Christian soldiers, overwhelmed by cruel wartime events that defied traditional religious explanations, frequently invoked sanctification to rationalize a seemingly endless war, an unexpected defeat, or the loss of a close comrade. In the end, many were comforted by the thought that God was using the terrible wartime suffering to perfect their faith. When a young Illinois private's moral universe was turned upside down by the war, instead of abandoning his belief in a good God, he attributed the wartime chaos to America's spiritual blindness and trusted Providence would someday restore his countrymen's vision:

> The America of a few years ago is not the America of to day.
> The brow of an American is clouded and sad and he looks
> upon the deeds of his country with grief. Once harmony now
> distraction once love now hatred once peace now War. God
> choose the day may come soon when the eyes of man will be-
> come opened. When they will see the enormity of their crimes
> and peace and quiet will spread their rays of light over our
> distracted country.[39]

Pvt. John S. Copley also thought that personal and corporate acknowledgment and repentance for certain prewar sins were the keys to ending the war. He told his loved ones the war would continue until there was "an acknowledgment of God's dealings with us because of our great national and individual sins. . . . Until we as a nation and as individuals acknowledge this and repent of ours sins and turn to God and respect his laws I cannot expect this strife to cease."[40] Despite his country's sins, Indiana major James M. Shanklin believed God would ultimately bless the Union with victory, but only after its sinful people had undergone the fiery wartime judgment and had a fundamental change of heart: "I believe God is on our side, but I believe also it is His design to humble us first before allowing us the victory. If that is so, our humility should be speedy and deep."[41] Copley and Shanklin may well have been alluding to a popular jeremiad passage found in 2 Chronicles, chapter 7, which explained what a chosen people should do when they found themselves suffering under God's judgment: "If my people, which are called by my name, will humble themselves and pray and seek my face and turn from their wicked ways; then will I hear from heaven and will forgive their sin, and will heal their land."[42] According to Northern clergy, if the church faithfully adhered to this biblical formula, God would not only remove the supernatural impediments blocking final Northern victory and heal their broken land but also use what man had intended for evil to accomplish a greater good. The prolonged sectional conflict would spiritually sanctify the Northern church by purging it of its prewar sins. Individual believers' faith would be strengthened by a terrible war that drew them closer to God, and taught them to be more selfless and to embrace causes higher than themselves. In the end, if Northerners sincerely repented of their prewar sins and recommitted themselves to Christian sanctification, the Union would prevail. Genuine repentance and sanctification were thus the keys to Northern victory, and Northern preachers and religious soldiers trusted that, when the Union finally did prevail, just like the biblical patriarch Job, God would bless their spiritually refined nation even more in the future than he had in the past.

Northern clergymen and chaplains promoted national repentance and sanctification throughout the war. As many soldiers soon discovered, they could almost always expect such a sermon on official government-sponsored days of fasting and prayer, which sought to secure God's blessings at the beginning of Northern military campaigns or plead for his forgiveness and clemency after serious Union defeats. Lt. John Blackwell received a letter from his brother summarizing the major points of one such sermon: "At Eleven O'clock the people assembled in the old school Church and listened to a good Union discourse on the subject of our national Sins and the duty and necessity of repenting of them in order to secure the favor of God."[43] A jealous God's wrath would not be satiated until the religious soldiers of the North had sincerely repented of their prewar sins and submitted themselves to his higher purposes.

Lincoln's Wartime Jeremiad

Oddly enough, the individual who best defined and articulated the North's wartime jeremiad was not even a publicly professed Christian or formal member of a church. Since Abraham Lincoln never formally joined any Christian church, as Mary Todd Lincoln later observed, by the standards of his time he was "not a technical Christian." Like his Separate Baptist parents, Lincoln believed a higher power was directing all the events of his life, but as a young man he had subscribed to a more deistic and fatalistic view of God called "the doctrine of necessity." During the war, however, Lincoln's religious beliefs apparently underwent "a process of crystallization." He read his Bible more frequently, occasionally attended a local Old School Presbyterian church, and gradually adopted a more Calvinistic perspective concerning the doctrines of providence and immanence. In a Protestant age where the lines separating church and state were less sharply drawn, Lincoln also followed the now-well-established American tradition of proclaiming national days of prayer, fasting, and thanksgiving to secure God's favor in times of crisis.[44]

Lincoln frequently expressed his own interpretation of wartime events in popular jeremiad-style language, but over the course of his presidency he developed a greater appreciation for the jeremiad's rich theological foundations and power to pierce the hardened hearts of an almost-chosen people. For example, Lincoln's 1861 proclamation of a national day of fasting and prayer is an uninspired rote recitation of the classic Puritan jeremiad. Lincoln acknowledged that God was using the fierce judgment of war to punish the sins of a wayward people and that only sincere national repentance for these sins, and intense prayer and fasting, might persuade him to relent and restore America to its former greatness:

> And whereas, when our own beloved Country, once by the blessing of God, united, prosperous and happy, is now afflicted with faction and civil war, it is peculiarly fit for us to recognize the hand of God in this terrible visitation, and in sorrowful remembrance of our own faults and crimes as a nation and as individuals, to humble ourselves before Him, and to pray for his mercy,—to pray that we may be spared further punishment, though most justly deserved; that our arms may be blessed and made effectual for the re-establishment of law, order and peace, throughout the wide extent of our country; and that the inestimable boon of civil and religious liberty, earned under His guidance and blessing, by the labors and sufferings of our fathers, may be restored in all its original excellence.[45]

Two years later, however, something had clearly changed. After his own faith had been severely tested the previous spring by the death of his beloved son Willie, Lincoln no longer seemed to be dutifully reciting the empty words of a meaningless religious formula. In his March 1863 fast day proclamation, Lincoln's words seemed touched with emotional reverence and personal meaning, almost as if he himself had been personally chastened and was imploring the Almighty to absolve him and his family of some private sin:

> And insomuch as we know that, by His divine law, nations like individuals are subjected to punishments and chastise ments in this world, may we not justly fear that the awful calamity of civil war, which now desolates the land, may be but a punishment, inflicted upon us, for our presumptuous sins, to the needful end of our national reformation as a whole People? We have been the recipients of the choicest bounties of Heaven. We have been preserved, these many years, in peace and prosperity. We have grown in numbers, wealth and power, as no other nation has ever grown. But we have forgotten God. We have forgotten the gracious hand which preserved us in peace, and multiplied and enriched and strengthened us; and we have vainly imagined, in the deceitfulness of our hearts, that all these blessings were produced by some superior wisdom and virtue of our own. Intoxicated with unbroken success, we have become too self-sufficient to feel the necessity of redeeming and preserving grace, too proud to pray to the God that made us! It behooves us then, to humble ourselves before the offended Power, to confess our national sins, and to pray for clemency and forgiveness.[46]

Troubled with frequent bouts of depression and melancholy throughout his life, perhaps because a mysterious and inscrutable Sovereign had prematurely struck down virtually all the people he loved best in this life—his beloved mother, sister, first love, and second-born son—Lincoln had now once again experienced the heartache of personal loss: the death of his favorite child. As Allen Guelzo noted, virtually none of the Northern clergymen and devout believers who wanted to Christianize Lincoln so badly after the war "ever penetrated to the real heart of Lincoln's personal religious anguish, the deep sense of helplessness before a distant and implacable Judge who revealed himself only through crisis and death."[47]

Already increasingly burdened by the thought that he, as the Union commander in chief, was personally responsible for all the lives being lost in the war, Lincoln had apparently come to a critical crossroads in his faith.[48] He could either reject a heartless God whose judgments seemed arbitrary and cruel or continue humbly submitting to a Providence whose contrary purposes often proved inscrutable. After repeatedly seeking spiritual counsel from his Presbyterian preacher on the matter, Lincoln placed his faith in an immanent and ultimately just Providence and took another important step in his religious journey.[49]

Lincoln's own intense wartime suffering heightened his awareness of human sin and its tragic consequences, but it also awakened him to the deeper spiritual meaning of the war. If a good and just God had allowed an innocent boy like Willie to die, perhaps to providentially chastise Lincoln's family for its sins or deepen their faith, perhaps God was using the deaths of thousands of other boys to expiate the country's sins and redeem an almost-chosen people. In any case, by late 1864 Lincoln believed he had finally discovered the principal cause and purpose of his country's suffering, and he used the occasion of his second inaugural address to share his own wartime jeremiad with the American people.

Speaking in the third person to humbly remove himself from what followed, Lincoln declared that both sections' sinful compromises with slavery had provoked a just God's wrath. He then shared his recent revelation that the wartime judgment would likely continue until enough men had sacrificed themselves in atonement for the nation's sins and the country had sincerely demonstrated its commitment to ushering in a new birth of freedom for all Americans. Having done all he could to set his country on a path he believed would deliver it from evil, Lincoln urged Americans to submit patiently to their God's "righteous" judgments and rededicate themselves to advancing his kingdom on earth "with malice toward none; [and] with charity for all."

The speech generally received lukewarm praise in the Northern press and few accolades from other international observers. Lincoln himself acknowledged that it would not be "immediately popular." Frederick Douglass thought the problem lay with Lincoln's extensive use of the Scriptures. With Lincoln invoking God fourteen times, prayer three times, and quoting biblical passages four times in a four-paragraph speech, "the address sounded more like a sermon than a state paper."[50] At least one American observer, however, recognized the full import of what had just transpired in a speech modern religious historians Harry Stout and Mark Noll consider "American's Sermon on the Mount" and one of the most "profound theological interpretations of the War between the States."[51] Having witnessed Lincoln's address firsthand in Washington that day, Union officer

Charles Francis Adams Jr. shared his own personal assessment with his illustrious father, who was serving as America's minister to England at the time:

> That rail-splitting lawyer is one of the wonders of the day. Once at Gettysburg and now again on a greater occasion he has shown a capacity for rising to the demands of the hour which we should not expect from orators or men of the schools. This inaugural strikes me in its grand simplicity and directness as being for all time the historical keynote of this war.[52]

For some religious soldiers, Lincoln's revelation merely confirmed what they had instinctively sensed from the beginning: A just and righteous God was providentially using the war to chastise their country for its national sins of self-indulgence, apostasy, secession, and slavery. But a compassionate and gracious God had also provided believers with a means of ending their wartime judgment. According to the formula laid out by Moses in the Pentateuch, all Christians had to do was humbly submit to God's righteous judgments, sincerely repent of their country's national sins, and renew their commitment to personal and corporate sanctification. These three keys would unlock the doors to final Northern victory and a glorious American future. This, at least, was Pvt. Wilbur Fisk's understanding. After emerging unscathed from the fighting around Cold Harbor and Petersburg in 1864, Fisk told his Vermont readers, "A war like this, once begun, will not close without achieving important results. What the result will be, unless our national sins are past forgiveness, no one that believes in a God of justice, can for a moment doubt."[53] Fisk and some of his Christian comrades ultimately concluded that the best way they could demonstrate their commitment to such repentance and hasten final Northern victory was to join the fight against slavery and help eradicate America's original sin.

Chapter 8

EMBRACING EMANCIPATION

> Radicalism is what we want,—a radicalism which shall strike at the root
> of the evil, and so end the rebellion.
>
> Henry Ward Beecher, "Our Good Progress and Prospects,"
> November 27, 1862

> For ye are all the children of God by faith in Christ Jesus. . . . There is
> neither Jew nor Greek, there is neither bond nor free, there is neither
> male nor female: for ye are all one in Christ Jesus.
>
> Galatians 3:26, 28

AS THE UNION armies prepared to embark on their first major campaigns of the war in the summer of 1861, a handful of religious soldiers shocked their families and friends when they announced it was time for their nation to embrace the radical measure of emancipation. Although a few abolitionists continued to adhere to the prewar pacifist policies of William Lloyd Garrison's New England Non-Resistant Society, almost overnight many religious abolitionists who had once savagely condemned the Union for its compromises with slavery now eagerly volunteered to defend that government to the death. This dramatic reversal in abolitionist sentiment toward the Union foreshadowed an even larger shift in religious soldiers' thinking about slavery that would occur after Lincoln issued his Emancipation Proclamation.[1]

Even as they donned the Union blue, however, religious abolitionists were careful to remind their friends and relatives they were only fighting for the Union because they believed its war against the Confederacy would inevitably destroy the South's peculiar institution. As Capt. Francis Russell of the Sixteenth Illinois told his older brother, he had not enlisted in a conflict to save the union, but in a war to eradicate slavery:

> I was born an Abolitionist. The only thing my heart has ever
> retained hatred *against* is the damnable curse of slavery. . . . I
> am never prouder than when men revile and speak all manner
> of evil against me for freedoms sake which my religion teaches
> me is the cause of God. And I tell *you,* that if I thought the
> *result* of this war would be less than the final extermination of
> slavery, I would desert the army before the setting of tonights
> sun.—I would never have enlisted.— I will not lend my arm
> feeble though it be to sustain a government that recognizes
> it, unless I believe, as in the present case, that in sustaining it,
> that most damnable curse will thereby be exterminated. No.
> Did I not think thus, I would dance by the light while an
> American Nero fiddled over the burning ruins.[2]

Like his secular allies in the American Anti-Slavery Society, as a thirty-year veteran of the crusade against slavery, Russell was not afraid to express his opinion that the North's principal military goal should be the abolition of slavery. For them, this would constitute victory in America's most important war.

The Radical Abolitionist Minority

Although they only constituted a tiny, if outspoken, minority group in the Union army, religious abolitionists such as Russell were being completely sincere when they declared they were willing to suffer or sacrifice anything, even the old Union itself, if it helped advance their goal of ending slavery. In the fall of 1862, a worsening Northern military situation seemed to be increasing the prospects that England might intervene on the side of the Confederacy. It was high time the nation struck a blow for freedom. As the Connecticut Yankee Robert H. Kellogg stridently lectured his parents, "We *must* free the blacks or perish as a nation. I have long held this view and have been sneered at and called an abolitionist, but I am content to wait. I think I'm *right*." If the North was losing the war, Kellogg explained, it was because the nation had "disregarded God's voice" and "not let the enslaved blacks go free when we had the power."[3]

While other Union soldiers worried about how England's diplomatic recognition of the Confederacy could adversely impact the Union war effort, Francis Russell considered the possible benefits English recognition held for the cause of abolitionism:

> It seems to me that present prospects indicate an early
> recognition of the Southern Confederacy by the powers of

Europe. . . . Is it possible that Monarchial England is to be the
chosen instrument of God to proclaim liberty to the oppressed
in our own *boasted land of the free?* . . . Is God in his infinite
wisdom about to tear down our present government and build
another upon its ruins. If so, I pray that it may be one having
its basis established upon the eternal principles of liberty to all
mankind.[4]

In 1862 Captain Russell may have been willing to trade a hopelessly compromised Union
for a new government purged of slavery, but by the following spring, rapidly unfolding wartime events had completely restored his faith in the Lincoln administration.

As Russell later explained to his brother, over the course of the winter there had been
a sea change in Northern opinion concerning emancipation:

Slavery has gone up. This is the inevitable result of the war, all
can see this now that are not wilfully blind. It is dieing much
faster than we had reason to hope faster than we even prayed
for expecting our prayers to be granted in God's own good
time by any means short of miracles.—Miracles have been
wrought—the great masses north and south have been caused
to think, and thinking are fast coinciding with the sentiments
of truth and liberty. The people say amen to what one year ago
they would have risen up in rebellion against.[5]

For Russell and his abolitionist allies, the divine meaning of this timely shift in Northern
opinion was unmistakable. A just God was providentially using the war to accelerate the
destruction of the South's peculiar institution.

In the minds of the religious abolitionists, the Civil War was merely an extension of their
prewar political struggle against slavery. Except now, instead of using political broadsides
and public meetings to awaken a morally apathetic country to the evils of slavery, religious abolitionists were embracing the rifle and bayonet, like their hero John Brown, and
battling the slaveholders themselves. Southern masters who did not voluntarily abandon
their system of involuntary servitude would either be struck down on the battlefield or
forcibly converted to abolitionism by defeat. While some religious abolitionists had always
deplored the use of such violence, like many of their Quaker allies they ultimately decided
to embrace the awful consequences of war to end what they believed was the far greater
evil of chattel slavery. Sustained by their staunch convictions, Russell and other religious
abolitionists dedicated all their energies to ensuring that the war to save the Union also
became a war to end slavery.

Given their theological understanding of the war's origins and purposes, some Northern Christians were abolitionists in all but name. Although he confessed he was "no
Abolitionist as an abolitionist cannot be a Christian" just before he enlisted in the Thirty-
ninth Illinois, Ransom Bedell told his cousin that emancipation was a foregone conclusion in the war. According to this idealistic midwesterner, a righteous God was using the
war as a winepress of his wrath to purge the sin of slavery from a wicked nation:

> It seems where our Nation has failed to act in putting the
> abomination away from among them that God has allowed
> war and carnage to operate—And now President Lincoln has
> offered the Border states a proposition for gradual emancipa-
> tion . . . giving a hint to the Border State Representatives that
> unless they accept of gradual Emancipation that *Emancipation*
> will certainly come . . . as the Nation now seems to demand
> the utter Extinction of the vile thing which has caused the
> untimely death of so many of our Brave sons of the *north*.[6]

Religious soldier Orra B. Bailey thought that slavery was the national sin that had provoked the wartime judgment. "We as a nation have committed a great sin in cultivating
and propping this institution up untill it has become so powerful that it has almost over
thrown the Government," he wrote. Andrew Sproul also seemed confident that slavery
was the principal issue of the war. He told his loved ones that God would "carry on the
war" until he made "all flesh free."[7]

Other religious soldiers believed that emancipation was not only inevitable but also
absolutely essential to the successful prosecution of the Northern war effort. After narrowly escaping the South on the eve of the war, a prewar businessman named Wallace
Dinslow abandoned his former sympathies for the people of Dixie and announced he
was willing to "go to any extreme and is willing even to be called an *abolitionist*," in
the war against the Confederacy. During his time in the South, Dinslow had observed
that Southerners viewed the approaching conflict over slavery as a "*holy war* for the
protection of their homes and families," and he believed the only way the North could
defeat this proslavery extremism was to mount an equally radical war against slavery.
According to Dinslow, the North could not afford to wage a largely symbolic war to save
the Union when Southerners were engaged in a life-and-death struggle to defend their
slave-based economic and political order. Other religious abolitionists warned that until
the Lincoln administration linked the battle cry of freedom to the cause of saving the
Union, Southerners fighting in defense of their homes and way of life would enjoy the
moral high ground in the war and perhaps even possess a stronger will to win. Lincoln
heard a similar refrain from the radical religious abolitionists in the Republican Congress,
who insisted that to subdue the Confederacy the North would first have to declare war
on its economic and spiritual foundation: slavery.[8]

With several key border states still hanging in the balance, however, Lincoln initially
ignored the abolitionists' advice and shrewdly pursued a more conservative course concerning slavery. Proclaiming that his administration was only fighting to preserve the
Union as it was, Lincoln said he would neither abandon his party's principled opposition
to the expansion of slavery nor interfere with slavery where it already existed. As a politician, he shrewdly judged he could safely disregard abolitionist sentiment at the beginning
of the war because most Northerners still strongly opposed immediate emancipation.[9]
Lincoln could also take comfort in the fact that some of his top commanders, such as
George B. McClellan, heartily endorsed his strategy of trying to save the Union as it was
by diplomatically protecting slaveholders' property in Virginia and the border states. Since

the Union army was largely a microcosm of the larger Northern society, only a handful of soldiers initially shared the abolitionists' commitment to end chattel slavery. In *The Life of Billy Yank*, Bell Wiley estimated that at best, only one in ten Yankee soldiers expressed any serious interest in emancipating the slaves. James McPherson put the number somewhat higher in *For Cause and Comrades*, claiming that as many as three out of every ten Union soldiers linked the abolitionists' goal of ending slavery with the administration's goal of preserving the Union. In any case, the consensus seems to be that in the first years of the war few Northern soldiers were fighting to free the slaves.[10]

Moral Failure of the Churches

If most Northern Protestants did not initially take a strong moral stand against slavery it was largely due to their churches' vacillation on the issue. In the 1830s, some New School Presbyterians and Methodists had finally joined forces with the Quakers and Unitarians to promote the early abolitionist movement, but William Lloyd Garrison's growing radicalism subsequently drove most of them out of the American Anti-Slavery Society. Over the next two decades Northern evangelicals opposed to slavery found themselves caught between their own denominations' conservative tendency to avoid this divisive spiritual issue and an increasingly radical abolitionist movement that had morally denounced America's political and religious institutions for their past compromises with slavery.

When the Northern churches finally did seriously address the issue, their belated moral response to slavery was disastrous. For example, when the New School Presbyterians stepped up their public preaching against slavery in the late 1830s, their western synods were promptly expelled from the Presbyterian Church. A similar division soon rent the Methodist Church. Increasingly dissatisfied with their church's moral ambivalence concerning slavery, a small group of dissident "Wesleyan" Methodists split from the larger Methodist Episcopal Church in 1843. But these modest early divisions were merely harbingers of the larger denominational schisms to come. In the mid-1840s the Northern Methodists' refusal to support the candidacy of a slave-owning bishop and the Baptist Convention's opposition to slaveholding missionaries triggered even bigger ecclesiastical catastrophes. First the Methodist and then the Baptist churches divided along strict sectional lines, permanently splitting the country's largest bodies of Protestant believers into rival proslavery and antislavery camps.

The country's most prominent Protestant preacher at the time, Henry Ward Beecher, later observed that the evangelical churches' failure to act decisively against slavery from the very beginning played a major role in the resulting ecclesiastical divisions:

> In about every Presbytery and ecclesiastical convention or
> assembly in the North, the determination was that there should
> not be an utterance of the religious community against slavery.
> The first great controversy was whether they ought to call it
> an evil. They did not think they could call it anything. They
> thought they ought to leave it alone. They deemed it to be none

of their business. But when they were pressed to call it, not only an evil, but a sin to be repented of and renounced, they would call it an evil, but they would not call it a sin. When, further, they were pressed, not only to call it a sin, but to discipline those that indulged in it, they would call it a sin, but they would not make it a matter of discipline. And so, step by step, the controversy went on till it divided those churches that would not let it come in.[11]

Anxious to prevent any further religious or political divisions and to preserve their future witness to potential converts from the border states, Northern evangelicals decided to steer their churches away from the explosive slavery issue. As George M. Fredrickson explained, Northern evangelicals were not so much spiritually blinded to the evils of slavery as they were afraid of the consequences of confronting them:

> Not wanting to risk the disunion and anarchy that forceful northern action against slavery might arouse, the ministers of the 1830s and 1840s, with a few conspicuous exceptions, rejected the abolitionist demand for immediate emancipation, and counseled Christians to be patient until such time as Divine Providence willed that the evils of slavery pass away.[12]

Intent on preserving their large antebellum congregations, most Northern churches found it expedient to direct their ministries in other directions. Although evangelicals would continue to frown on the worst excesses associated with chattel slavery, throughout the 1840s they seemed more concerned with the growing radicalism of the abolitionist movement.

Ironically, most Northern evangelicals were only awakened to the evils of slavery after religious abolitionists in the Liberty and Free-Soil parties—forerunners of the future Republican Party—convinced them that a growing "Southern slave power" posed a direct threat to their future economic and political freedoms. Abandoning earlier abolitionist efforts that relied solely on tactics of moral persuasion, these religious abolitionists appealed directly to the fears of Northern whites by alleging that the South was engaged in a slave-power conspiracy, a covert plan to advance its economic and political power by stripping Northerners of theirs. The basic outline of this conspiracy was that a slave power, or large network of Southern planters and Northern sympathizers, had long been engaged in a clandestine plan to gain control of the federal government's institutions and use them to spread slavery, while simultaneously undermining the free institutions of the North.

The abolitionists' charge that slavery posed a direct threat to Northern whites' economic interests in the West proved particularly effective. Many lower-class Northern whites had good reason to feel vulnerable on these grounds because they believed the frontier offered them the best hope for improving their future economic condition. Since the intense agricultural demands of cotton production required an almost continuous expansion of Southern landholdings, they rightly feared that slavery would eventually move into the western lands they so coveted. Indeed, all the recent sectional crises seemed to demonstrate that Southerners were intent on expanding slavery into the western territories.

This posed a serious problem to Northern whites because their tiny family farms could never economically compete against the large Southern plantations worked by chattel slaves, so the admission of slavery into new territories would for all intents and purposes close them off to free labor. Having already come to view Southern planters as potential economic competitors in the West, Northern whites thus readily embraced the slave power conspiracy as further evidence that Southerners were conspiring to deprive them of their future economic opportunities out West.

If this were not bad enough, the antislavery parties also reminded Northern whites that the slave power was also actively working to subvert their political and social freedoms. This seed also fell on fertile ground. Based on their limited knowledge of the South, which ironically often was based on information they had gleaned from New England textbooks, sermons, or abolitionist tracts, many Northerners viewed the region as an economically backward, biracial, and two-tiered society. An aristocratic planter elite exercised absolute power over both their slaves and a much larger body of poor, uneducated Southern whites. Arguing that a slave-based planter aristocracy in the territories would deprive western settlers of a truly representative government and the benefits of a good education, religious abolitionists asked Northern whites if they really wanted to live under the planters' thumb out West.

Religious abolitionists told Northern whites that given the right opportunity, Southerners would use the same coercive measures they used against their slaves to suppress the civil liberties of Northern whites. After all, in 1836 Southern politicians had already deprived whites of their constitutional right to petition Congress for redress of grievances by enacting a gag rule automatically tabling antislavery petitions. In that same year a Southern-dominated Congress had also banned the mailing of abolitionist literature to Southern slave states. So Northern whites had already been deprived of their political right to oppose slavery and legal right to communicate ideas hostile to it. Given this history of political suppression and the South's numerous physical threats against Northern abolitionists, as well as its jailing of Southern dissidents like Daniel Worth, Northern evangelicals could no longer have any illusions about the fate of their country's freedoms should the slave power prevail.

In the end, these more pragmatic arguments appealing directly to Northerners' fundamental economic and political concerns proved much more effective at building an antislavery political base than earlier abolitionist efforts at moral persuasion. Although still largely indifferent to the plight of the slaves themselves, many Northern Christians nonetheless concluded that their own economic and political interests would be best served by supporting politicians opposed to the future expansion of slavery. So in the wake of the controversial 1854 Kansas-Nebraska Act, Northern evangelicals increasingly joined the rest of the country's disaffected political groups in the ranks of the new Republican Party.

Sensing political change was in the air during the political crises of the 1850s, the Northern clergy also gradually shifted their previous political stand on slavery, but again, when they did so, it was primarily to promote the political and economic interests of their white congregations—not Southern blacks. For many evangelical clergymen, Stephen Douglas's 1854 Kansas-Nebraska Act marked the fateful hour when their churches could no longer ignore the tyrannical designs of an aggressive Southern slave power. Given the popular groundswell of antislavery feeling, Northern churches finally felt empowered to take strong public stands against the further expansion of slavery into the territories. More than three thousand New England ministers signed a public remonstrance opposing Douglas's act, while others opened their churches up to the first organizational meetings of the new Republican Party. The Northern church had finally joined the political war against the slave power, but most evangelicals remained as reluctant as ever to embrace the cause of abolitionism. This well-established prewar pattern of racist Northern Christians only gradually embracing limited antislavery measures, once convinced such actions also served their best interests, foreshadowed how most religious soldiers would later react to the issue of wartime emancipation.

Reluctant Emancipationists

Just like their commander in chief, most Northern clergymen and religious soldiers were reluctant emancipationists. A dreadful litany of wartime disasters would finally convince the clergy and Lincoln to embrace the Radical Republicans' idea of emancipation, but only as a necessary wartime measure. Even after emancipation, in the minds of most religious soldiers, the principal goal of the war remained saving the Union, with most viewing the abolition of slavery as an inconvenient but necessary means of achieving that end.

Absolutely convinced of the justice of their cause, in the first months of the war the clergy generally supported the administration's position that the federal government was not fighting to destroy the South's "peculiar institution" but only to defend itself from an unlawful rebellion. Given their understanding of God's providential hand in history, however, after the humiliating Union defeat at Bull Run, some Northern clerics had to reconsider whether God truly favored their existing cause or perhaps expected something more of his chosen people.

Henry Ward Beecher was one of the first nationally prominent Northern clerics to suggest that a perfectly righteous God might not be interested in saving a Union still compromised with the original sin of slavery. After the disastrous defeat at Bull Run Beecher thought that God might be impeding the progress of the Northern war effort because the government had failed to take a decisive stand against slavery. Perhaps disillusioned by the North's early failures to defeat a cause he associated with the devil, in his 1861 Thanksgiving address, "Modes and Duties of Emancipation," Henry Ward Beecher hinted at the main reason for that failure—the North's unwillingness to attack the South's peculiar institution. According to Beecher, the North would never win its war to save the Union until it first struck a decisive blow against slavery—the spiritual root of the rebellion and economic engine that sustained the Confederacy. Until now the North had found it politically expedient to pretend that the war was not being fought over the issue of slavery. But a righteous God was not interested in such diplomatic niceties. According to Beecher, the disappointing outcome of recent wartime events seemed to suggest that God wanted Northern believers to confess that slavery was indeed the stumbling block that had divided the nation. Final victory would continue to elude the Northern armies until God's people acknowledged their own guilt for having tolerated and profited from slavery and took remedial actions to atone for it. In the end, Beecher thought the conflict was being fought over one question: Were the founding fathers right when they declared that all men were created equal, or were Southerners right when they asserted that some men were born to be slaves?

To support his claim that slavery was the principal cause for which the South was fighting, Beecher made extensive use of excerpts from a recent speech delivered by the Confederate vice president, Alexander Stephens, at a political reception in Savannah. In his speech, Stephens had recalled Thomas Jefferson's prediction that slavery would be the "rock upon which the old Union would split," and noted:

> He was right. . . . But whether he fully comprehended the great truth upon which that rock stood and stands, may be doubted. The prevailing ideas entertained by him, and most of the leading statesmen at the time of the formation of the old Constitution, were, that the enslavement of the African was in violation of the laws of nature; that it was wrong in principle, morally, and politically. . . . Those ideas, however were fundamentally wrong. They rested upon the assumption of the equality of the races. This was an error. . . . Our new government is founded upon exactly the opposite ideas. Its foundations are laid, its cornerstone rests, upon the great truth that the negro is not the equal to the white man; that slavery, subordination to the superior race, is his natural and normal condition.[13]

According to Stephens, slavery—or the principle that Africans had been and always would be physically and spiritually inferior to whites—was the cornerstone of the Southern Confederacy. If this was true, Beecher believed the best way the North could hasten the Confederacy's defeat was to strike at this foundation by finding some lawful means of immediately emancipating all the South's slaves. Beecher's advice to the country was probably best summed up nearly a century later by the renowned Civil War historian Bruce Catton: "To save the Union the North had to destroy the Confederacy, and to destroy the Confederacy it had to [first] destroy slavery." Other Northern clergymen later drew the same conclusion. If the evils of slavery had provoked God's fierce wartime judgment, and slavery was the linchpin of the Confederacy, then the administration would have to embrace the radical cause of emancipation to defeat the South. But with the Lincoln administration still cautiously attempting to placate the border states and appeal to the better angels of the elusive Southern unionists, for the time being Beecher's cry for immediate emancipation went unheeded.

As the Union armies continued to suffer disastrous defeats throughout 1862 and the casualties continued to mount, however, other Northern clergymen also subjected the administration's wartime goals to greater moral scrutiny. After all, if the Northern cause was just, and the clergy were certain it was, then why was God withholding victory from the Union armies? Indeed, the very nature of the spectacular Confederate victories—from the providential timing of the enemy's movements and reinforcements to the extraordinary incompetence of the Union commanders—convinced some evangelical leaders that God himself must be engineering the defeats. But what message was the Almighty attempting to convey through these military disasters?

Congregationalist minister James D. Liggett believed the answer could be inferred from the Old Testament story of Israel's punitive war against the Tribe of Benjamin. In a fall 1862 sermon, Liggett's used an exegesis of this intertribal biblical conflict to convey his understanding of God's purposes in the war. According to the book of Judges, the conflict began when the Tribe of Benjamin unlawfully gave safe refuge to some tribes-men who had viciously raped and murdered a young Levite's newlywed wife. When the Benjamites refused to surrender the guilty party, the other tribes of Israel turned to the sword for justice. As Liggett recounted the story, all of Israel mobilized for war. The "cause was doubtless just; the nation was united in its support; the symbols of national authority were with them"; the Benjamites were outnumbered more than fifteen to one— and yet the Israelites were unexpectedly and disgracefully beaten in the first battle:

> After their first defeat they were greatly mortified . . . but evidently had not really discovered the true cause of their failure and disaster. They encouraged themselves, instead of seeking direction from God, and set themselves in battle array the second time, and then after having done so, sought God's advice whether to fight or not. Having first decided the question of duty for themselves, the act of submitting it to God was doubtless a formal rather than a sincere submission to his will. . . . Israel had one Bull Run disaster, and had passionately resolved to avenge it. . . . [Now] they are defeated [again] and massacred in heaps on the same bloody and fatal field. This second defeat brought them to a proper sense of their own weakness and error. While in their vain glory and zeal, they undertook the correction of other transgressors, they found themselves corrected. This time their tears are not those produced solely by regrets for their losses . . . but there are also tears of penitence for their own sins forgetting and departing from the Living God; and they for the first time humbly and honestly submit the question to him.[14]

Convinced that "almost the same history is being acted over again in our country," Liggett cogently laid out the historical parallels. Just as the indecent assault on the Levite's young bride had provoked a popular war of retribution, after the dishonorable Southern attack on Fort Sumter, the rest of the country's "unanimous decision was that the rebellion must be subdued." As Liggett explained:

> And for this object it was determined that whole power of the nation should be at once employed. The campaign [McDowell's] was inaugurated, and after some successes, ended with a great defeat. The people wept sorely and were greatly disheartened, but they encouraged themselves, and again set themselves

in battle array against the enemy. The second campaign
[McClellan's] was inaugurated on a scale much larger than
the first. We felt that no power could withstand our new
armies. . . . This campaign also ended in failure; and [now]
our national existence, involving the cause of liberty and justice is in greater peril than ever.[15]

After rhetorically asking why a God of justice would permit the more righteous of the
two sections to suffer such horrendous human carnage and suffering, Liggett argued it
could not be because God favored the Southern cause and its cornerstone of human bondage. For this would have clearly been contrary to all his well-known attributes. Returning
again to the story in Judges, Liggett asserted that these disastrous defeats must be the
result of some unconfessed sin in the Northern camp that needed to be identified and
addressed if the Union was to prevail. Then he paused and asked Northern Christians and
the Lincoln administration to reconsider, for a moment, what they were fighting for:

If it is for the Union as it recently was, corrupted and perverted by the very men who have destroyed it . . . then that
is one of the things that can never be again. . . . Let us break
away from the fallacies and prejudices of the past . . . and in
manly strength grapple with the living issue of the agonizing
Present. That issue is Liberty or Slavery. The rebels have resolved to destroy the nation that they may establish Slavery.
Shall we hesitate to destroy Slavery that we may preserve the
nation? Because it has come to this, that the nation must
perish or that which strikes the nation's life must perish. Our
President has said, and all his policy has been, to preserve the
national life and slavery too, if he can. He has tried it, and
the experiment has certainly been tried long enough. The
nation faints under the terrible and protracted torture. God
thunders in his ears from the rivers and valleys of the West and
mountain fastnesses and plains of the East, which the blood
of our slain had made red in vain—"You cannot."[16]

According to Liggett, the administration had made a grievous error in its categoriza-
tion of wartime priorities. Lincoln had wanted to save the Union first and worry about
slavery later, but this was putting the cart before the horse. A perfectly righteous God
could not possibly save a government hopelessly compromised with sin. So God was
now providentially using battlefield events to reveal his purposes in the war. If Liggett's
theological reasoning was sound, then the North would ultimately prevail in the contest,
but only after Lincoln made the war to save the Union into a crusade to end slavery, and
more importantly, the Northern people confessed their section had also been corrupted
by the evils stemming from the South's peculiar institution.

Turning more directly to the Northern people's culpability in the Union's defeats,
Liggett identified an even more serious problem with the Northern cause—Americans'
pervasive racism: "I hear God saying to us—'Are you ready as a people, after all, ready to

do justice? The rebels are fighting for Slavery; are you fighting for liberty in the true sense and from principle? Is it from a sense of justice to the slave, or a feeling or revenge and hatred towards the master that you ask Slavery to be destroyed? Is this nation fit in heart to do this great work of God?'" Liggett then ominously predicted, "If not, then must he, by still greater reverses and afflictions, prepare our hearts and make us fit to receive upon our brows the wreath of victory." Since the Northern church served a jealous God who "looks on the heart," Liggett believed the decisive issue was the Northern people's attitudes toward the Negro. Had Northern Christians learned to embody Christ's love for the Negro, or to love their Negro neighbors as they loved themselves? Liggett had his doubts:

> Let us endeavor, through outward signs, to look a little fur-
> ther into this nation's heart. . . . What means the recently
> enacted black code of the great patriotic and Liberty profes-
> sing State of Illinois? . . . What means all the howl of objec-
> tion against allowing black men, who were good enough to
> fight the battles of our country under Washington and Jackson
> to bear arms and help fight the same battles under Lincoln?
> What means the most extraordinary spectacle of the President
> of our great nation, inviting to his own council chamber a
> large number of as intelligent and respectable colored men
> as he could find, to insult and degrade them by telling them
> "Your presence in this country is offensive, injurious and
> intolerable to the white race, and . . . your expenses shall be
> paid, if you will be gone from our sight and the land of your
> unfortunate birth forever?" What mean these and very many
> other things . . . but that there is yet in the heart of this nation
> a deep-seated and unjustifiable hatred of the enslaved race of
> this country?—a spirit which is at once the root and the fruit
> of Slavery. "Whosoever hateth his brother, is a murderer"
> And shall we not, from this divine rule of judgment, also say
> that whoever hateth an oppressed race of men in our midst
> is an oppressor? . . . Judged by this rule, we are a nation of
> slaveholders still. Is this nation then prepared in heart to take
> off the shackles from four millions of black men and do justice
> by them? If God will punish the slaveholder for his sin, as we
> believe He will, is it not just in him first to correct the spirit
> of the slaveholder in the hearts of those whom he intends to
> make the instruments of his judgment?[17]

Liggett then concluded his brilliant sermon using some of the same language and themes Lincoln would employ two years later in his Second Inaugural Address:

> In the vast changes wrought already in the hearts of the people
> by the defeats we have suffered and not by the victories we
> have won, we can plainly see that God and not man is working

a mighty and rapid revolution for us. It may seem to move too slowly, too slowly while the life of the nation is wasting away in torrents of blood, but the engine of God's power propels it; and it must and will move on, through all the friction and weight of man's opposition. . . This is our faith; and let it be the ground of our hope. In the meantime let us be patient and not despair, but work on, seeking to work in the line of God's direction. . . . But for this interpretation of what is otherwise dark and inscrutable, I should despair of the present and future of my country. . . . Let our constant prayer be—"Thy will be done, O God, and fit us to do it."[18]

A Great National Curse and the Chief Cause of the War

Religious soldiers could probably discern the gradual shift in Northern sentiments about slavery from the reams of religious literature they received from their chaplains, missionaries, and the U.S. Christian Commission. Their opinions about slavery were also undoubtedly influenced by their personal observations of the peculiar institution while serving in the South. But their commander in chief's decision to issue a preliminary emancipation proclamation in the fall of 1862 undoubtedly had the greatest impact on their attitudes toward slavery and emancipation.

Many religious soldiers who shared their opinions about slavery with loved ones generally agreed with their ministers back home that slavery was a great national evil and that it might well have been the chief sin that provoked the wartime judgment. In September 1862, Sgt. John F. L. Hartwell took advantage of a lull in the fighting to write his wife from the Antietam battlefield. After describing his march through Maryland and his unit's role in "the severest battle of the war," Hartwell wrote, "The more I see of the south the more I detest slavery and all those that upheld and fight to establish it." In an April 1863 letter, Pvt. James B. Lockney thanked "God, who is now angry with this nation for its sins, that we our family are all free of the crime for which our nation is suffering so severely. From what I have seen of *Slavery* I am now more opposed to the hellish thing than ever and I hope you are too."[19]

Soldiers who believed slavery was the main cause of all their suffering often expressed their hope that the war would finally put an end to this festering national sore. As Pvt. James T. Miller told his sister, "i [*sic*] do hope that old Abes emancipation proclimation will have universal success for as far as i can see there is no other cause for this war but Slavery and the sooner it is done the better for us." Amos Hostetter of the Thirty-fourth Illinois believed the war was God's judgment on Americans for having embraced or tolerated the sins of slavery and racial miscegenation in their country for so long. In January 1863, he told his brother and sister, "Any country that allows the curse of Slavery and Amalgamation as this has done, should be cursed, and I believe in my soul that God allowed this war for the very purpose of cleaning out the evil and punishing us as a nation for allowing it."[20]

George T. Chapin, a second lieutenant in the Twenty-seventh Indiana, also thought slavery was the principal reason for the United States' divine judgment and shared his hope that wartime events would soon destroy the South's peculiar institution:

> Slavery is most undoubtedly the great curse of our country
> the cause of all our trouble, misery, the cause of the war, and I
> hope the war will have the good effect to wipe it from the face
> of the country forever. . . . And if it does not we will have spent
> our lives in vain. . . . Alas my country how thou art suffering
> for *this* sin! And yet will *hardly* repent.[21]

On September 22, 1862, Lincoln finally moved decisively to ensure that slavery did not survive the war. He issued a preliminary Emancipation Proclamation, which promised to free the slaves of any state that was still under rebellion as of January 1, 1863. Lincoln's emancipation became one of the major turning points of the war. The proclamation effectively transformed a political war to save the old Union into a moral crusade to free the nation from the curse of slavery. It also added a new spiritual dimension to the Northern war effort, which finally united evangelical Protestants, abolitionists, and Radical Republicans behind the Lincoln administration's war effort. And without their support the North could not have sustained its wartime commitments during the awful bloodletting of the 1864 campaigns.

According to James McPherson, the Union army's initial reaction to Lincoln's Emancipation Proclamation was somewhat mixed, with roughly half the army supporting it and the other half evenly divided between those who fervently opposed the measure and those who ventured no opinion on the subject.[22] This author's research, however, suggests that Northern religious soldiers were some of the earliest and most enthusiastic supporters of Lincoln's emancipation scheme. There are several possible explanations for this. First, at least a few of the soldiers were religious abolitionists who had always favored immediate emancipation. Since they frequently corresponded with loves ones from their home communities, others may just have been following the lead of their churches, which had sometimes already embraced the idea of emancipation. In some cases religious soldiers were converted to the cause of emancipation by the terrible fruits of slavery they had witnessed in the South. Since Christianity strongly emphasized the importance of proper submission and obedience to authority, religious soldiers were also more likely to support their government's wartime policies, even when they did not personally agree with them. As was the case with their less religious comrades, however, most Northern Christians ultimately embraced emancipation because, in the end, they believed it was in their best interests to do so.

Ironically, some of the same soldiers who enthusiastically supported Lincoln's proclamation often retained their racial contempt for the blacks freed by it. In their letters, some religious soldiers expressed strong personal distaste or veiled contempt for the "Niggers" they encountered in the South. Others openly ridiculed their dress and speech, cruelly mocking people they considered less human or civilized than themselves. Yankees disliked the slaves in part because of their preexisting racial attitudes, but also because many of them thought slaves were somehow responsible for the war. Convinced that the war was being fought over slavery, some racist Christians thus blamed both Southern slave-holders and blacks for their wartime suffering.

Midwesterners were invariably the most racist. With the exception of abolitionists, however, New Englanders could also be extremely condescending toward the freedmen. Illinois adjutant Charles W. Wills's comments were fairly representative of the average midwestern Christian's attitude toward African Americans:

> The blacks are scrambling in this direction to a very lively
> tune. . . . I am thoroughly opposed to receiving any more
> than we have work for within our lines. You have no idea
> what a miserable, horrible-looking, degraded set of brutes
> these plantation hands are. Contempt and disgust only half
> express one's feelings toward any man that will prate about
> the civilizing and christianizing influence of slavery. The most
> savage, copper savage, cannot be below these field hands in
> any brute quality. Let them keep their Negroes though, for
> we surely don't want our Northern states degraded by them.
> . . . These nigs that come in now, say that their masters were
> going to put them in the Southern army as soldiers. I'm sure
> the Southerners are too smart for that, for a million of them
> aren't worth 100 whites.[23]

Even New Englanders, more sympathetic to the cause of abolition, could be disparaging in their description of the freedmen. A Massachusetts corporal serving as a war correspondent with his unit in North Carolina saw nothing but "niggers and soldiers" in the towns of Newbern and Washington. The correspondent, Zenas T. Haines, also offered a critique of the local Negro spiritual services, noting that the singing was "horrible. The praying and preaching better appealed to the emotions. . . . The sermon was an invocation for watchfulness. . . . It was rich in funny logic and quaint grammar."[24]

Happily, there was also always the occasional exception in which Northern religious soldiers genuinely empathized with the plight of their black brothers and sisters. New York surgeon Daniel Holt wrote his wife a letter recalling his reaction as he watched soldiers from his command raze a Virginian plantation:

> The most pitiful sight of all was when all had been swept
> away. . . . These people hailed their deliverance from the
> hands of their inhuman task masters, as did the Israelites
> upon the return of the Jubilee. Cold and apparently freezing,
> as they stood upon the hard frosty grounds in the month of
> December, with eyes streaming tears, they blessed the hand
> of their deliverer and called upon their God to bless *"de dear
> gentlemen"* who wrought their deliverance. Contrasting my
> own with the case of a poor mother who stood before me
> with two little ones—one an infant at the breast, and the
> other fellow of about two years who stood at her side crying

piteously for a blanket to keep himself warm, I thought how
blessed was I, with wife and little ones in a home where every
comfort filled the house. . . . Oh, Louisa, the sight of these
emancipated slaves at that hour, standing bareheaded and
barefooted on the worst night I ever was out . . . was one
which I can never forget and never wish to see again. . . .
God help and bless the poor mortals. I cannot think of them
even now, without (as I did then) shedding tears for them.
It may be a weakness but I can't help it.[25]

Embracing Emancipation

Racist or not, most Northern Christians eventually embraced the cause of immediate
emancipation—but each for his own reasons. Some simply supported the government's
emancipation plan because they believed it was their duty to do so. Capt. Alexander
Ayers told his wife he was prepared to perform whatever patriotic duties his government
required: "I came out in good faith to serve this the best government the world ever
saw and I want to help save it and free the niggers and mean to do what I can to do
both." Other religious soldiers who thought certain practices associated with slavery
were immoral—such as the breaking up of families and preventing blacks from reading
the Bible—ultimately embraced emancipation because it seemed like the most ethical
solution for addressing these abuses.[26]

Wartime correspondent Pvt. Wilbur Fisk severely rebuked those who made light of
such moral concerns:

> I almost lose my temper sometimes (what little I have got)
> when I hear men that really ought to know better, call this a
> mere crusade to free the negroes, "a nigger war" and nothing
> more. But even if I was fighting to free the negroes simply, I
> don't know why I should be acting from a motive that I need
> be ashamed of. I verily believe that He who when he was on
> the earth healed foul leprosy, gave sight to the blind beggars,
> and preached the gospel to the poor, would not be ashamed
> to act from such a motive, And if he would not, why should
> I? Fighting to free the "niggers!" Why yes dear fellow, we
> are doing just that and a great deal more. . . . Should such
> an event, however, rather help than hinder the success of this
> war, we trust that you will acquiesce in the result, and when
> the future of this country shall have become by this means
> more glorious than the past has ever been, we hope that you
> will find your own liberty and happiness has not been at all
> infringed upon by giving the same liberty and happiness to
> a few ignorant and despised sons of Africa.[27]

Northern Protestants were sometimes gradually converted to the cause of abolition by their wartime experiences in the South. This was evidently the case with Pvt. James T. Miller, who noted that the behavior of the South's so-called Christian Gentlemen was converting Union soldiers like himself into abolitionists. After discovering that one local master, a prominent member of the local Baptist Church, had in addition to his own white family three Negro mistresses and more than a dozen mulatto children, some of whom he had subsequently sold, Miller told his brother:

> I tell you that Uncle Tom's Cabin bad as it was fel far short of portraying the evils of slavery in as bad a light as they really exist. You will say that i am getting to be a radical Abolitionist and i don't know but i am and in fact the great share of the army as far as i am acquainted are in the same fix and i believe that these two years of war have made more Abolitionists than the lecture of Wend[ell] Phi[l]ips and Ger[r]it Smith and William L[l]oyd Gar[r]ison would have made in one hundred years.[28]

By the spring of 1863, Capt. Jefferson Newman's views on slavery had also evolved. As he shared his epiphany with his sister, Newman explained that the South's peculiar institution "is one of the greatest sins that man ever committed" and "until this is ended there can never be any peace in the United States. We are a nation that has boasted [of] our freedom and at the same time have been holding millions of human beings at the South in bondage, and now if God ever punished a nation for anything He is punishing the whole United States for doing and allowing such things. . . . Slavery and freedom cannot exist together and one or the other must go down and it is for us to say which it will be."[29]

In the end, however, most religious soldiers embraced the cause of emancipation for the same reason their churches had earlier embraced the antislavery cause—they believed immediate emancipation would also advance their interests. Like their secular counterparts, many religious soldiers who rejected abolition before the war supported wartime emancipation because they believed it was a military necessity that would hasten final Union victory. If slavery was the foundation of the Southern cotton kingdom, the best way to defeat the Confederacy was to strike decisively at its cornerstone.

Slavery strengthened the Confederacy economically, militarily, and psychologically. Slaves provided Confederate soldiers with their food and clothing and cared for their families in their absence. They helped supply the Rebel armies with guns and ammunition, constructed field fortifications, and forged the Confederacy's cannons. As economically and emotionally valuable members of the paternalistic planter's extended "Christian family," Southerners' beliefs about their institutions and slaves may have even initially given them a stronger will to win the war. The Southern masters' sincerely held beliefs that slavery was God's ordained role for the African and that blacks actually appreciated being slaves on their plantations gave Southerners the psychological advantage of believing they truly were the spiritually superior side fighting to preserve a more Christian economic and familial order. God had established and blessed their extended biracial "families" and plantations, and slaveholders would now gladly sacrifice everything to defend their ideal but illusory world.

The early Northern policy of confiscating Southern slaves, or treating them as contraband of war, deprived the South of some of its best field hands, factory workers, and conscripted military laborers. But when Lincoln issued his Emancipation Proclamation, he mortally wounded the Confederacy by directly challenging its false psychological and spiritual underpinnings. In early 1863, as word spread throughout the South that the administration had freed the slaves, Southern planters were shocked when their supposedly "happy" Negroes abandoned their plantations and fled toward the nearest Union armies. Later, they were even more perplexed when the North was not severely chastened by God for challenging the divine ordinance of slavery, but on the contrary seemed to be enjoying greater military success after issuing the proclamation. Southerners may not have lost their will to win or belief that God favored their cause, but they did lose some of their former certainty concerning God's purposes and the fundamental nature of their society.

Many religious soldiers thus embraced emancipation as a radical but necessary war measure that would help hasten the end of the war. Having already confiscated Southern field hands and military workers as contraband, religious soldiers had little difficulty grasping the strategic value of an act that stripped the Confederacy of its manual labor force. Thus most came to view Lincoln's Emancipation Proclamation as a vital war measure that would contribute decisively to final Northern victory. Pvt. Amos Hostetter confessed to his brother and sister that before the war he was one of those who "did not believe in interfering with slavery but we have changed our opinions. We like the Negro no better now than we did then but we hate his master worse and I tell you when old Abe carries out his Proclamation he kills this Rebellion and not before. I am henceforth an *Abolitionist* and I intend to practice what I preach."[30]

Richard Brown also supported the administration's new emancipation policy despite his obvious racial prejudice: "For my self I endorse the efforts of the government in putting down this rebellion niggers and all Since they [Confederates] have compelled this most mild most patient most forgiving and benign Government to Strike at the root and Cause of their folly and wickedness." Later, when hundreds of thousands of African Americans began to pour into their camps, racist Northern whites such as Brown may have cursed the efficiency of Lincoln's emancipation program, but few could question its ultimate wisdom.[31]

Black Bodies Can Stop Rebel Bullets Too

As black laborers abandoned their Southern plantations and began to filter into Union lines in increasing numbers, government officials immediately considered where they might best be employed to assist the Union war effort. Most contrabands performed a variety of manual labor projects for the Union army, and many resumed their former work as field hands on newly liberated plantations. Nearly two hundred thousand African American men, however, were eventually enlisted in the Union armies, where they performed rear-area garrison and supply duties, and in many cases—such as that of the Fifty-fourth Massachusetts at Fort Wagner—served gallantly at the front.

Most Northern soldiers, religious and nonreligious alike, were initially strongly opposed to the use of black soldiers. They believed Africans would make poor soldiers and complained they did not want to serve alongside "niggers." Some Northern whites were also insulted that the government was planning to provide people they considered racially inferior with the same military uniforms, duties, and honors white soldiers received. As with the issue of emancipation, however, most Northern Christians were eventually persuaded that the government was acting in their best interests when it added black regiments to the Union armies.[32]

Whites soon realized that the introduction of black troops would benefit them in several ways. Enlisted men who coveted officers' commissions learned they could easily obtain them by volunteering to serve as officers in the new black regiments. Black soldiers also relieved white soldiers of unpopular rear-area duties such as guarding prisoner-of-war and contraband camps, defending vital bridges and railroads, and garrisoning occupied enemy cities. Black troops were also typically assigned some of the army's most difficult manual labor projects, such as digging fortifications and building bridges and roads. But above all, the introduction of black regiments to the Union army meant that blacks would now be performing their fair share of the fighting and dying.

After watching "Burnside's negroes" charge the Confederate fortifications outside Petersburg, Wilbur Fisk thought the black soldiers had performed their duty just as well as any white soldiers and their white peers seemed to respect them for it:

> The negroes were remarkably well pleased with their prowess
> on this occasion. It was a glorious day for them. They won
> great favor in the eyes of white soldiers by their courage and
> bravery. I am sure I never looked upon negroes with more
> respect than I did upon these soldiers, and I did not hear a
> word of disrespect towards them from any of the boys.[33]

Fisk's comrades were probably surprised that soldiers whom they considered to be physically inferior to themselves had performed so well on the battlefield, and some may have even admired the black soldiers' courage. But as they watched them charge straight into the enemy breastworks "under a terrible fire" and then observed "the stream of wounded that came pouring back, some leaning on a comrade and some carried on stretchers," they could hardly ignore the fact that black soldiers were now suffering and dying in their place.

Although it was a base motive, racist Northern soldiers such as James T. Miller were more willing to support the use of black troops when they realized black bodies could stop Rebel bullets too. As Miller told his brother and sister in 1864, "There are some colored regiments going to the front and they make a very good appearance and the more nigers they get the better i will be suited for i would a little rather see a nigers head blowed of[f] than a white mans." Illinois recruit Benjamin Webb Baker told his mother that most of the boys in his regiment "don't like the idea of making soldiers of Negroes. But after all they will do to shoot at as well as anybody else." In the end other religious soldiers also concluded that if the use of black soldiers hastened the end of the war and relieved whites of some of their most odious wartime duties, then they too could share the terrible cost of freeing their people from slavery.[34]

No Compromise

By the latter half of 1862, some Northern Christians who believed slavery was the chief cause of the war were telling their loved ones they now agreed with the abolitionists, that the war should be vigorously prosecuted until slavery was utterly destroyed. Rapidly mounting casualties no doubt contributed to this increasing Northern resolve to extinguish the South's chattel slave system once and for all. As Pvt. Gasherie Decker explained to his sister Gertrude, the North had sacrificed too much in the war to consider compromising with the Southern slave empire now:

> *"Home,"* [and] *Peace,* are precious names to us but Compromise, [and] Armistice we detest, and despise. Death rather than an *ignoble* peace, where it will not be a pleasure to cherish the memory of fallen comrades and the cause for which they fell. We have suffered to much to feel like giving up now. But are more anxious than ever to push the thing through.[35]

For religious soldiers such as Pvt. Wilbur Fisk, who viewed the war as a struggle between good and evil, Northern compromise on the issue of slavery was unthinkable. Fisk confessed that while he and his comrades were "anxious to return to our peaceful avocations at home as soon as possible," it was "an insult to the dignity and patriotism of any soldier to ask him to fight for restoring slavery . . . to its former position of power and haughty defiance."[36] Later, in the spring of 1864, Fisk expressed his righteous indignation with those who timidly suggested that a compromise with slavery was the quickest path to peace:

> Compromise with Slavery, and restore the Union with Slavery in it still! As well might Jehovah compromise with Satan and give him back part of Heaven. . . . Never in a war did the rank and file feel a more resolute earnestness for a just cause, and a more invincible determination to succeed, than in this war; and what the rank and file are determined to do everybody knows will surely be done. We mean to be thorough about it too. We are not going to destroy the military power of the dragon Confederacy and not destroy its fangs also.[37]

Other religious soldiers shared Fisk's belief that the North's chief goal in the war should now be the destruction of slavery. In the spring of 1863, Pvt. James B. Lockney of Wisconsin complained to his brother about Americans' continued apathy for the cause of abolition and lamented, "Oh! hard as it may be, why are we not willing to prosecute and maintain a long and costly war so that our country may be purified of its *curse* and freed from its sins against high heaven which it has been wallowing in for the last 243 years."[38] Hoosier sergeant George T. Chapin also thought the North should keep fighting until the country's greatest national evil was finally rooted out:

> I hope the war will last until the *slave* shall be *free*. I am in for
> the war till liberty be established in every part of our country:
> till every man shall be free. We will never have *peace* till this be
> accomplished. We have had war on the subject of slavery ever
> since our existence as a nation and we are having blood shed
> by the ocean on its account and no other. Now let us make
> way with the *barbarous* corrupt and wicked institution and we
> shall be free indeed. . . . O that the end may be as sweet as the
> beginning has been bitter.[39]

A year and a half later, Chapin was still as committed as ever to the struggle against slavery. He told his brother that "the war had better last twenty years than that this institution should be perpetuated. I believe the Army feels that it/slavery is the source of all our woe and ought to be effectively crushed." Despite their terrible wartime suffering, religious soldiers now refused to countenance any potential peace that left the peculiar institution intact, convinced there could be no just and lasting peace as long as slavery survived in the South.[40]

When rumors of possible peace negotiations circulated his camp in the summer of 1863, John Blackwell told his wife he strongly opposed any peace treaty that tolerated the continued existence of Southern slavery. "If the southern states return as they now are I fear they will be allowed to return with the old slavery constitutions, and the battle will thus be over to fight again," he wrote. "God grant that we may be wise enough to put away the evil from us now and forever. Let us pray that God will not allow us to return to our old sins.[41] For Blackwell, and many other religious soldiers, emancipation had become so intimately connected with the cause of the Union that they no longer believed victory was possible without the complete destruction of slavery. While many of them had come to embrace new convictions about slavery and emancipation, other religious soldiers either lost sight of their traditional beliefs or felt increasingly trapped by them.

Chapter 9

Compromise and Conflict

Just as I am, though tossed about
With many a conflict, many a doubt,
With fears within and wars without,
O Lamb of God, I come! I come!

"Just as I Am, Without One Plea," *The Soldier's Prayer Book*

For I know that in me (that is, in my flesh,) dwelleth no good thing: for
to will is present with me; but *how* to perform that which is good I find
not. For the good that I would I do not: but the evil which I would not,
that I do.

Romans 7:18–19

AS NORTHERN CHRISTIANS enthusiastically marched off to war in the spring of 1861
and 1862, few imagined how severely their faith would be tested over the next four years.
Separated from their families and churches, religious soldiers struggled to resist the traditional temptations of army life in the demoralizing spiritual climate of their wartime
camps. Deprived of regular opportunities for worship and forced to live in an exclusively
male society that was at best apathetic if not openly hostile to organized religion, this
proved much more difficult than they first imagined. Richard Gould, one of seven pious
brothers from New York who volunteered to fight for the Union, drafted a letter to his
sister in which he explained the Christian soldier's moral predicament. Citing a line from

the Book of Common Prayer, Gould asked for his sister's prayers: "Hannah, this is a hard place for one to serve the Lord. I will try to serve him but I do a great many things that [I] ought not to do and leave undone things that I ought to do."[1] Robbed of their traditional spiritual supports and surrounded by unbelievers, many Christians found it difficult to avoid sins of commission and omission. Those who yielded to sin knew they could always obtain forgiveness from a Savior who had also experienced temptation. But some could not escape the terrible guilt they felt in having been proven unfaithful.

Disappointed with the obvious moral shortcomings of their comrades in the camps and their own spiritual inadequacies, religious soldiers were even more troubled by the terrible scenes of destruction that greeted them on the battlefield. Pvt. J. A. Dernten was obviously still processing his first awful encounter with the enemy when he tried to describe it to a girlfriend back home: "The sights and sounds of horror that crowded those days I hope may never come before your experiences." Although "some prophesied that if the two hostile armies should ever meet in battle array, they would drop their weapons and rush into each other's arms," Dernten sadly observed that his battlefields told "a terribly different story."[2] Caught up in the vicious guerrilla war that was ravaging Tennessee, Pvt. Gasherie Decker of the Third Wisconsin Artillery Battery was equally disturbed by the war's unprecedented violence and hatred: "You at home may read the papers till you are grey and never fully realise the horrors of this war. Neighbor against neighbor. Brother against Brother and Father against Son."[3]

Regardless of the justice of their cause, Christian combatants in both armies had to reconcile the terrible evils they witnessed on the war's battlefields, their family and comrades' grievous sacrifices, and the terrible suffering they inflicted on others with their faith in a good and just God. Surprisingly, most Northern Christians had little difficulty reconciling their wartime experiences with their faith. They rationalized the killing using traditional just war and holy war arguments, which maintained that violence sometimes had to be embraced as a last resort, or as a necessary evil to combat even greater injustices such as slavery and rebellion. There was always, however, a minority of religious soldiers who struggled to reconcile their religious values with their military duties. These soldiers generally concluded they might have to temporarily ignore or abandon some of their more problematic religious beliefs to wage a successful war against the South. But a few experienced serious spiritual conflict when they struggled to uphold all their morally troublesome values despite a growing conviction that their combat duties or some other sin was transgressing God's laws and thus potentially forfeiting their salvation. This chapter explores the rich diversity of Northern Christians' theological responses to the conflict and the degree to which they ultimately relied on their personal faith to successfully process the meaning of their wartime experiences.

The minority of Northern Christians who struggled to reconcile their wartime participation with their spiritual beliefs generally fell into two camps. The first and largest camp consisted of those who consciously or unconsciously compromised certain prewar religious beliefs that seemed to conflict with their military duties—such as the prohibitions against hating one's enemies, seeking vengeance, or murdering other human beings made in God's image. The second, far smaller camp of soldiers had experienced a wartime epiphany where they suddenly recognized their military conduct was somehow violating

God's commandments. Although they often experienced feelings of guilt about this conduct, they refused to abandon either their morally troublesome duties or the religious beliefs that condemned them. This frequently burdened the latter soldiers with various degrees of spiritual conflict and guilt for the duration of their wartime service.

Historical Context

Although religious soldiers may have experienced more spiritual compromises and conflicts than previously suspected, it is important to place these responses in proper historical context. First, only a small minority of religious soldiers had difficulty reconciling their faith with their military duties. So regardless of which camp the doubters fell into, they were the exception. Second, it should also be noted that in many cases these soldiers' spiritual doubts and compromises were probably rooted in, or exacerbated by, the earlier spiritual demoralization they had experienced in their wartime training camps. Third, although some soldiers may have adapted or compromised certain prewar beliefs, those who expressed such spiritual doubts rarely renounced their faith, or at least apparently retained it for the duration of the war.

In discussing the religious disillusionment of some Northern soldiers at the end of the Civil War in *Embattled Courage,* Gerald F. Linderman said that "the drift from religious faith should not be exaggerated. . . . There were few renunciations of belief in God, or even expressions mistrusting God's control of the evolution of the war."[4] Indeed, the research of numerous other distinguished Civil War historians, such as James M. McPherson, Reid Mitchell, Phillip Shaw Paludan, and, most recently, Steven E. Woodworth, suggests that if anything, Northern soldiers became more religious during the war.[5]

Religious soldiers who expressed doubts, modified beliefs, or experienced spiritual conflicts during the war also rarely abandoned their military duties. Few asked to be reassigned to rear area or noncombatant duties, and most continued fighting as long as they could, or at least until they had completed their term of duty. So if his faith sometimes caused the religious soldier to question the morality of his wartime duties, it also gave him the spiritual strength to complete his military mission.

Finally, while this chapter focuses on religious soldiers' compromises and conflicts, its important to recognize that other non-Christian Union soldiers likely experienced similar ethical dilemmas as they wrestled with the moral implications of performing some of their more odious duties. After all, Christians have never enjoyed a monopoly on matters of conscience. Thus the religious soldier's temptations and compromises represent—to some degree, at least—a microcosm of every good man's struggle to combat evil in a just manner.

The Worse Bore We Have

For many evangelical soldiers, this gradual process of spiritual demoralization began when they first assembled at local county fairgrounds or other outlying camps and joined an all-male military society. It was here that religious soldiers learned that the Union army did not always attach the same importance to religion as their communities had back home, and many previously sheltered young Christians were for the first time exposed to the ways of the world. In the Union army camps, religious soldiers were isolated from their former religious communities and deprived of many of the traditional religious resources that helped support their faith—a qualified and dedicated minister, weekly religious meetings, and the observance of a Sabbath day rest.

A number of religious soldiers blamed the rampant immorality they observed on the poor spiritual leadership of their regimental chaplains. While dozens of Union army chaplains were dedicated ministers of the gospel who worked tirelessly to meet their troops' spiritual and physical needs, most of the initial applicants turned out to be spiritually or professionally unqualified for their wartime ministries. This was mainly due to the unprecedented demand for chaplains in the many new Northern regiments, which rapidly exhausted the pool of qualified applicants. As Gardiner Shattuck explained in *A Shield and Hiding Place,* another contributing factor was the Union army's flawed process for selecting and confirming such officers. Just as popularity initially played a more important role than competency in the appointment of many regimental officers, at the beginning of the war chaplaincies were frequently "obtained by those more renowned for their congeniality with officers than for their pastoral or spiritual commitment."[6]

There was also a high rate of attrition in the Union army chaplaincy. The frequently less hardy men of the cloth proved highly susceptible to disease. Many returned home after they became seriously ill or discovered that their physical constitution was not up to the task of heavy marching and sleeping outdoors in inclement weather. Given the physical challenges and dangers, others soon had second thoughts about their new military ministries. These problems grew so acute that by late 1862 an increasing shortage of qualified chaplains made it impossible for some units to find a suitable replacement.[7] Of course, for some Union officers this was not a problem. Regimental commanders who were irreligious or disappointed with a previous chaplain's work often refused to appoint new ones.

In other cases, the units might have been better off without them. For far too often, the unit's original chaplain turned out to be immoral or incompetent. This was because few accomplished Northern ministers felt "called" to trade their comfortable, successful ministries in the North for the spartan and dangerous life of an underpaid chaplain. Veteran pastors probably also knew from experience how difficult it would be to minister to hardened men living outside the normal constraints of society. The end result was that the Union army chaplaincy was initially staffed with some of the North's least qualified ministers. This fact was well documented in the religious soldiers' correspondence, where they expressed strong—and usually extremely negative—opinions about their regimental pastors.[8]

Apparently, during the first half of the war, the charismatic and hard-working Union chaplain was more the exception than the rule. In February 1863, Sgt. George Chapin told his brother—who coincidentally also happened to be a preacher—that the Twenty-seventh Indiana Infantry Regiment had been poorly served by its government-appointed chaplain:

> Our chaplain has gone home on furlough tho' we do not miss
> him for he has been very little account to our regiment. I

believe it rightly considered the worst "bore" we have. If
it were not for [unintelligible] we might have a good upright
man to preach the Gospel at least once a week. But Thomas A
Witted has not preached over a dozen times to the 27th regiment and never held social religious meetings and what is far
more worse than this he has not walked circumspectly before
his men. His example is exceedingly inconsistent resembling
more that of a renegade than a Teacher of Christ. There has
been but little religious influence in our regiment at any time;
vice immorality always predomalyzing; our men are demoralized to a shocking extent. I wish it were otherwise.[9]

Lt. William Dalzell of the 142nd New York Volunteers complained that his regimental
chaplain seemed more interested in fraternizing with the officers than meeting the spiritual needs of his regiment:

Our chaplain has gone home for thirty days but I think it is a
small loss for I don't think a minister in the armey amounts to
much; I have heard him preach three times in three month[s]
standing under a large trees and I think that is about as often
as eny of them preaches and I don't think eny of them labors
where they are most needed. I think they are more apt to stay
with the sholder strap then they are to labor with the poor
soldier.[10]

Other religious soldiers were extremely disappointed when they discovered their spiritual shepherds were more interested in pursuing the pleasures of this world than ensuring the safe arrival of their flock in the next. In the fall of 1863, 1st Lt. John Blackwell
informed his wife of the "sad state" of religious affairs in his brigade: "I wrote you that
one of our chaplains has been sent home for drunkenness and now I have had the painful
duty of reporting another, the 116th chaplain, for lending his pants to a lewd woman
about camp to conceal her sex." One can only imagine how disheartening it must have
been for religious soldiers to suddenly discover that their principal spiritual shepherd, who
constantly assured them of the holiness of their cause and the salvation of every fallen
Christian soldier, was just as immoral as the next man.[11]

The reputation of the Northern chaplaincy, however, was partially redeemed by both
the dedicated chaplains who did perform their duties well and the more competent
chaplains who began filling the existing regimental vacancies in late 1862. By then the
worst of their kind had mostly returned home for health reasons, easier jobs, or because
their wartime ministries had foundered due to their professional or spiritual shortcomings. Most of the chaplains still serving in the ranks, meanwhile, had gradually earned
the respect of their units and commanders through their spiritual dedication, steadfast
courage under fire, and sacrificial service in meeting their regiments' personal mail, reading, medical, and supply needs. Three Union chaplains even received the Congressional
Medal of Honor for their heroic wartime service, either fighting at the front or caring for

wounded soldiers while under fire. So by the middle of 1863, the Northern chaplaincy had definitely improved. By then, however, many Northern believers and potential converts who might have benefited from their chaplains' ministries were dead, back home, or too emotionally traumatized by the fighting to seek out such spiritual guidance.

Northern troops were far more enthusiastic about the work of the U.S. Christian Commission, convinced that anyone who cared so much about their bodies must also be interested in saving their souls. Some religious soldiers contrasted the successful ministry of the commission with the paltry spiritual efforts of their chaplains. As Wilbur Fisk explained,

> I believe the soldiers like these Christian Commission delegates better than they do the regular army chaplains. I mean as a general thing. The chaplains they say, all they care for is to come out here and see the country, hold office, get a good swad of greenbacks each pay day, perhaps preach a tolerable good sermon on Sunday, if the weather is perfectly right, distribute the mail when it comes, and then when they get tired this, contrive some way to be out of health, resign, and go home. . . . Occasionally we have what Beecher would say was God's ideal of an army chaplain, but alas! they are scarce.[12]

We Have No Sabbaths

If the military chaplain was typically a poor substitute for the Christian soldier's more qualified and respected family pastor, army life in the Northern camps seemed even more inhospitable to their faith. Military duties frequently disrupted the religious soldiers' prewar habit of observing a Sabbath day rest. Like many other religious groups, evangelical Protestants practiced sabbatarianism, or the religious tradition of devoting one day a week to rest and worship. For Jews and Christians, this was required by the fourth commandment, which commanded believers to keep the Sabbath day holy by not performing any work from sunrise to sunset.

On a typical prewar Sabbath day, which Christians observed on Sundays, many Protestants would spend the morning and evening in religious worship, taking a midday break between the services to eat a light brunch (perhaps prepared the day before). After their meal, they would spend the afternoon discussing the morning's sermon, quietly reading the Scriptures, or corresponding with family and friends. There was to be no formal business conducted on Sundays, and many antebellum communities passed blue laws forbidding businesses to be open on the Sabbath.

Upon arriving at their training camps, many religious soldiers were shocked to discover the Union army did not attach the same importance to attending weekly religious services and observing the Sabbath as they did. Shortly after arriving at his camp near Mound City, Illinois, in September 1861, Pvt. Leander Knowles's captain informed him a regimental officer had been appointed to do the Sunday preaching and no one would be allowed to pass "through the guard to go to church in the town." Convinced he was being unjustly deprived of his freedom to worship, Knowles indignantly observed, "I had thought that we lived in a land of civil and religious liberty where *all* men were allowed to worship God according to the dictates of their *own* conscience but it seem that it is not so here." After his first few weeks as a soldier, Pvt. William McLean also realized he would have to modify some of his former religious practices. Writing from Cairo's Camp Defiance, McLean told his upstate friends that "there is not mutch chance to keep the Sunday here to tell the truth there is not mutch Sunday here and there is no chance to go to church."[13]

Although many units held worship services and observed the Sabbath when they could over the next few years, in some cases these religious practices were gradually discontinued. At the beginning of the war, a number of Union generals, including George B. McClellan, Ambrose Burnside, O. O. Howard, and William S. Rosecrans, strongly encouraged their troops to attend religious services. In September 1861, McClellan even issued a general order to the Army of the Potomac requiring it to henceforth observe a Sabbath day rest and hold regular religious services on that day whenever "military necessity did not absolutely prevent such worship." Unsympathetic regimental officers, however, quickly found a number of "military necessities" that justified the "temporary" suspension of such religious formalities. Other officers also opposed these religious observances because they interfered with Sunday morning training exercises, such as weekly inspection, drill, and parade.[14]

Sometimes the religious soldiers themselves did not seem interested in attending the army's religious services. Freed from what younger believers often considered their overly rigid religious society back home, soldiers sometimes skipped services when they did not feel well or had to contend with other pressing matters. In units where attendance at religious services was compulsory, others resented having to attend such services on Sunday afternoon after spending the morning in drill. Where religious attendance was optional, many soldiers succumbed to the temptation to skip the service and instead wile away their Sunday afternoons reading books, playing cards, or indulging in some other recreational diversion. Finally, even devout religious soldiers who attached great importance to regular weekly attendance at church were sometimes so disgusted with their chaplains' sermons and overall ministries that they sought out other means of obtaining religious instruction and enjoying regular fellowship with the body of Christ.

The religious soldiers who did appreciate these weekly religious exercises soon discovered that they were difficult to observe in wartime. Battles, forced marches, fortification work, and other important military duties frequently made it impossible for units to hold their regular religious meetings. During the active summer campaign season, units often temporarily suspended these religious meetings and Sabbath day observances. Soldiers who became accustomed to life without their weekly spiritual practices sometimes found it difficult to resume them when they returned to their winter camps. In other cases, units traumatized by prolonged fighting or excessive casualties—such as the midwestern regiments of the famous Iron Brigade—sometimes never replaced their initial chaplains after they died or went home and may have dispensed with regimental religious observances altogether.[15]

In discussing the difficulty of holding such religious meetings during the war, Gardiner Shattuck concluded:

The óbligation to hold worship services—the one duty actually specified for the chaplain—was sometimes difficult to
discharge. Whether a chaplain's unit was currently bivouacked
in camp or active in the field, difficulties frequently prevented
him from leading worship. If the army were stationary for a
time, poor weather, Sunday morning drills, or the entrance
of new recruits into camp could interfere with services. If the
regiment were on the march or about to engage in battle, on
the other hand, chaplains seldom even attempted to hold formal worship.[16]

In their letters, religious soldiers lamented this lack of regular worship and especially the
loss of their Sabbath day rest. A couple of months before the Battle of Gettysburg, Pvt.
Daniel Peck of the Ninth New York Cavalry told his sister that he had "not heard but two
sermons" since leaving home and confessed that he had never really appreciated what a
blessing church was until he had "been deprived of the privelege." Lt. William Dalzell
complained to his wife Lizzy that even in his winter camp in Virginia he and his men had
"as much work to do on the Sabeth as eny other day." Sometimes it was the nature of
those Sabbath day labors that troubled the consciences of religious soldiers. In September
1862, Sgt. Charles Norhood of the Third Wisconsin Cavalry found it ironic that he was
violating God's Sabbath day commandment to make bullets for the Union army, noting
they "were the first I ever help cast for the purpose of killing men with who are created
in the image of *God*." As the fighting continued, respect for the Sabbath also seemed to
diminish in the Union armies. In February 1864, this harsh reality prompted a somewhat
gloomy Iowa private to tell his friends, "We have no Sabbaths in the Army."[17]

Other soldiers believed the lack of such religious observances was having an adverse
impact on soldiers' faith. As John Blackwell and his regiment labored to complete a new
line of trenches outside Vicksburg on Sunday, June 14, 1863, Blackwell told his wife that
while he knew these Sabbath day labors were probably "necessary" he still wished they
could be "dispensed with" because he felt guilty about violating God's fourth commandment. Based on his other, similarly negative religious experiences in the army, Blackwell
concluded that war was "essentially demoralizing. . . . Its results are often good, always
so when the cause is just and right but the mode of carrying it on always involves the
disregard of many of God's laws."[18] Jacob Bartmess of the Thirty-ninth Indiana also
thought the Union army's complete disregard for the Sabbath was undermining his
countrymen's moral convictions:

'Tis sabbath, yes tis sabbath, but how little it is appreciated
as sabbath here. Indeed few know that it is the sabbath.
The regular duties change but little for sabbath. . . . Nearly
everyone is doing something diverse from the honor of the
Lord. . . . Alas! for the people of these united states! This war
is raging with a telling effect on their morals.[19]

The Wickedest Place I Ever Saw

At the same time they were deprived of some of their most important religious practices in the army, Christian soldiers also had to contend with the evils of Northern camp life. Having already lost many of their prewar spiritual supports, some religious soldiers were increasingly demoralized by the sins of their comrades. It was relatively easy for Northern Protestants to retain their innocence and purity back home, where the religious community carefully enforced public morality. But the real test had come when they marched off to war and were no longer subject to the local moral constraints of their churches, families, and local society. Since camp life represented many soldiers' first real experience living outside the strict moral confines of their religious communities, some men took advantage of their unprecedented freedom to indulge in sinful pleasures that were proscribed back home.

The most common transgressions that offended the religious sensibilities of Billy Yank were gambling, drinking, swearing, and visiting brothels. Many religious soldiers feared these sinful practices would corrupt other good soldiers and perhaps lead to even greater evils. Pvt. George W. Squier told his wife he would enjoy soldiering if the society was not "so awful. Gambling is the common practice of nearly all and swearing is the common dialect of the Soldier. There is but few men in our company . . . who do not habitually swear . . . one of my old favorites who formerly used no bad language is now as bad as his ass[o]ciates."[20] When his parents inquired about the nature of "Religion in the Camp," Pvt. James T. Miller told them his new home was "the roughest and most wickedest place I ever saw."[21] John F. L. Hartwell also thought his comrades' behavior was despicable: "Their only aim seems to be to drink, gamble, quarrel, desert, mingle their blood with the African race, [and] force defenseless Southern women to submit to indignities to shameful to tell."[22] Hartwell believed that even the best of men could be subtly seduced by these insidious evils, which often began innocently enough:

> In this regt. I know of many young men that left home
> determined to resist all temptations of a demoralizing
> influence but they have one by one like the autumn leaf
> fallen and into habits . . . not likely to honor them or help
> them in the future. Profanity, drunkardness, gambling and
> licentiousness are the worst evils. . . . Thousands of young men
> have come to love ardent spirits and to get beastly intoxicated
> on the same. . . . They say they never used it before coming in
> the army . . . but . . . they tell me it keeps them from taking
> cold during extreme heat or cold weather. . . . Some think they
> cannot be a soldier without using profanity at the beginning
> and end of each sentence they utter. . . . Gambling like
> swearing is carried on . . . by a large majority of the men, first
> they commence playing for pies, apples, cigars or any other
> small innocent stakes, by and by they are captivated by the play
> and venture large sums of money, the result is conclusive, many
> lose therby all or nearly all their hard earnings.[23]

Other religious soldiers thought the Northern camps—isolated as they were from the religious influences of Protestant society—naturally brought out the worst in the Union soldier. Perhaps Herman Melville and Nathaniel Hawthorne had been right about men needing to live within a society that restrained their inherently evil nature. After serving three months in the army, Henry Franklin Hole of the Seventeenth Illinois concluded that "there is no place I ever saw where the bad passions of men are drawn out like they are in camp life. Selfishness in all its beauty and in every shade is brought forth to public view." Pvt. Jasper Kidwell also found the soldier's life in the camps demoralizing: "There are a great many men who are very profane, and it seems to me that men give way to all their passions and are worse than they are at home."[24]

In a letter written to his cousin, Pvt. Ransom Bedell explained some of the reasons camp life had such a demoralizing effect "on the character and morals of the Soldiers":

> Camp demoralization amounts to this—Where hundreds of men are thrown together and exposed to privatation—and deprived of the restraining Influence of Society and Women— They at once follow the bent of their own depraved natures and cc cc For *instance* A. Co. is raised of patriotic though chicken hearted boys . . . a mixed Multitude with various tastes and habits and c— their liberty is at once limited by rigid Military rule—from plenteous tables—and to the hard fare of the camp—from warm sleeping rooms—to exposure through the long nights—of cold and heat mud rain dust sleet snow and frost in which hundreds die in hospitals—where tens die by the shock of Battle—and it is only the best of officers and the Best of Causes that can keep an army from utter demoralizaiton.[25]

Having already been deprived of their prewar religious freedoms and supports in the camps, harsh wartime conditions made it even more difficult for religious soldiers to resist the traditional temptations of army life.

As the provost officer for his Illinois unit, Charles Wills was in a particularly good place to monitor the ethical conduct of the Union troops occupying northern Mississippi, and in the winter of 1862 he told his sister he did not like what he saw:

> The army is becoming awfully depraved. How the civilized home folks will ever be able to live with them after the war, is, I think something of a question. If we don't degenerate into a nation of thieves, 'twill not be for lack of the example set by a fair sized portion of our army. Do you remember that I used to write that a man would no sooner lose his morality in the army than at home? I now respectfully beg to recall the remark, but I believe the sight of such devlish, pointless wickedness disgusts me, and that your brother's moral principles are strengthened by contact with these ungodly.[26]

Although Wills claimed he was personally unaffected, if not spiritually strengthened, by this flood of immorality, given the enormous wartime stresses and overall lack of spiritual accountability, other Christians undoubtedly yielded to temptations they might otherwise have resisted at home. Soldiers who succumbed to such evils knew they could always obtain forgiveness from a merciful heavenly Father who promised to wash away their sins and remove their transgressions "as far as the east is from the west." But many could not easily forget the evils they had committed or escape the terrible remorse they felt in having disappointed their Savior and grieved the Holy Spirit. In a highly emotional letter to a "Miss Mirriam" in May 1864, Sgt. Amos C. Weaver told his Indiana sweetheart, "I could scarcely refrain from crying when I read your letter I wished that I was as pure and upright in heart as you are. That I knew no more of sin than you do, that I knew not the wickedness of the world. Many are the temptations and inducements I have to contend against in the army." The Christian soldier who stumbled sometimes had a difficult time recovering his former sense of spiritual serenity and innocence.[27]

Things Which Make Any Feeling Man Shudder

While some soldiers' religious beliefs were severely tested or even undermined in the Northern camps, in most cases, it was the terrible wartime violence that ultimately posed the greatest challenge to their faith. When Northern Protestants emotionally responded to the first call for volunteers to put down the rebellion, few of these recruits had any idea what modern warfare was really like. The last major conflict that had significantly touched the lives of Northerners was not the Mexican War but the more distant War of 1812, and few living Americans had any recollection of that event. In 1861 most Americans still held a glorified image of war, largely drawn from Sir Walter Scott's chivalrous tales of medieval combat and patriotic American history. The first major battles cruelly dispelled these romantic notions of war.

Although religious soldiers often longed to "see the elephant," few were prepared for the sights, sounds, and smells that greeted them on their first battlefields.[28] After his baptism of fire at Shiloh, Pvt. Thomas F. Miller seemed as though he were still traumatized by the battle when he recounted the dreadful experience to an Illinois friend. After describing how the Rebel bullets had sung "mournful songs around my ears" and most of his friends had fallen "lifeless on the ground by my side," Miller somberly observed, "Since I have been in this place I have witnessed more hard seens and barbarity than I ever dreamed of."[29] For Pvt. George W. Squier, another religious soldier who fought at Shiloh, the real horrors began when night fell on the battlefield. As the sun began to set, ominous dark clouds appeared over the battlefield, and the resulting thunderstorms, which "finally put an end to the deadly stri[f]e," were almost as terrible as the battle itself:

> We lay on our armes withou[t] blankets or food while the rain
> poured down in torrents for nearly half the night. An awful
> night was that one. Could amid the roar of the thunder hear
> the groans of the wounded and dying. . . . Walking in the

dark one would perhaps stumble over some poor victim of the deadly bullet who lay cold and stiff in death, or some wounded and dying fellow who thus roused from his death stupor would call for help, perhaps for water. But why think of those scenes of terror, pain and death?[30]

Meanwhile, back East, even veterans such as Pvt. Abial H. Edwards thought the Antietam battlefield was "terrible beyond description. . . . The Battle raged all day the bursting of the shells the groans of the wounded and Dying made a scene that was awful beyond description. I hope I never shall see such another." Jacob Bartmess told his wife he did not believe he should even write about some of the horrors he had witnessed: "There are many things I can tell you when the happy day comes to come home, which I do not wish to write. I tell you Amanda there are many things that transpire here which utterly confound me. Things which will make any feeling man shudder."[31]

While some soldiers were later haunted by the wartime images that were burned indelibly into their minds, perhaps the most troubling aspect of this horrendous wartime carnage for religious soldiers was that it seemed to desensitize them to further violence and death. Infantrymen called this increasing desensitization "hardening" and thought it was a natural response to the unspeakable horrors of war. Veterans believed that this hardening process was the chief factor that distinguished the seasoned soldier from the raw recruit. It was popularly thought that those already adapted to the grim realities of war could better cope with various wartime stresses, such as unexpected enemy attacks, prolonged bombardments and periods of combat, and the sudden death or disfigurement of a friend. But hardening was more than just a growing familiarity with the sights and sounds of battle, it was a conscious or unconscious decision to embrace the unacceptable realities of war. As Gerald F. Linderman observed in *Embattled Courage,* "The infantryman occasionally drew a dry pleasure from a description of himself as 'a callous old soldier, who has seen too many horrors to mind either good or bad.'" It was this growing callousness, or moral apathy for the evils of war that religious soldiers found so disturbing.[32]

As they gradually lost their sense of moral outrage for the evils of war, some religious soldiers realized they too were becoming personally coarsened by the violence. This occurred when soldiers, no longer able to cope with the war's ever-increasing violence and human suffering, just emotionally shut down and withdrew into their own private shells. Perhaps this was a natural psychological response, or self-defense mechanism that helped soldiers preserve their sanity when their sensibilities were overwhelmed by the tragic destruction and injustice of war. In any case, like a drowning man instinctively struggling to save his life, many soldiers became increasingly oblivious to the plight of their neighbors.

In a war that constantly reminded men of the tenuous nature of their own lives, soldiers also began to emotionally distance themselves from their fallen comrades and other men they suspected would soon be dead. Most soldiers only discussed the death of their comrades in passing—rarely discussing the details of their friends' deaths or funerals. As Vermont war correspondent Wilbur Fisk sadly noted while observing the funeral of one of his comrades, perhaps this was because the soldier's death was "the saddest of all":

There are seldom any mourners here to follow him to his
grave, and no tears of sympathy and grief fall on his coffin as it
is lowered into the silent tomb. . . . As we fired the salute over
his grave, we felt life is held by a very frail tenure. Somewhere
among the wild hills of Vermont there are dear friends of this
man, whose hearts will be pierced with sorrow when they see
that name mentioned among the dead. And to know that he
died among strangers, with no friendly hand to minister to
his last wants, will be the keenest pang of all. But such events
occur every day till we begin to scarcely notice them.[33]

Like their Puritan ancestors, many nineteenth-century Americans feared death far less
than they feared dying alone. As Pvt. J. F. Hartwell explained to his wife,

If I was to die at home it would not have the dread to me as
the death that stares for me in the face but to see thousands
of men rotting unburied on the field of battle unburied and
unknown and if buried, thrown in a heap and covered with a
little earth to moulder them back to dust. If I could banish all
such thoughts and be sure if dying to be in the presence of my
beloved family . . I could go to battle with a brave heart . . .
but No alas my lot is now vest in a hand of strangers.[34]

For antebellum Protestants, dying on some distant battlefield, far from one's loved ones,
was one of the worst evils that could befall a man, and yet this was the likely fate of many
Civil War soldiers. Constantly reminded of this grim reality by their fellow soldiers'
deaths, religious soldiers increasingly steeled themselves against empathizing too closely
with their fallen comrades, because it was too easy and painful to imagine their own
broken bodies lying at the bottom of those graves.

As the fighting continued, religious soldiers sadly noted that they were becoming
increasingly indifferent to the plight of other human beings—both the living and the
dead. Writing his wife from an army camp in Columbus, Kentucky, Pvt. T. S. Seacord of
the Seventy-second Illinois Volunteers sadly noted that "life is as nothing here. Man dies
and is quickly forgotten." Pvt. John M. Barnard thought it was ironic that while Mother
Nature was busily ushering in another beautiful spring around his Murfreesboro camp, he
and his Southern counterparts were "arrayed in deadly Strife agan one another trying to
take life which is one of the Dearest Things on earth." After participating in Grant's failed
Yazoo River campaign, Daniel Webster told his fiancée that he was "completely disgusted
with war. Too much so to be a good soldier. Tis too brutalizing in its effect. During the
engagement I thought no more of riding over a dead man than if he had been a dog. But
this is always the case." Sergeant Weaver also confessed that "Death and Sickness and
Sorrow has become so common that I look upon it with uncommon indifference and [it]
has in a great measure ceased to effect me as it once did." This increasingly callous attitude
toward human life may have eventually eroded some religious soldiers' commitment to
the traditional scriptural principles governing warfare.[35]

Compromise

It was probably inevitable that some Northern Christians would compromise certain religious beliefs or experience spiritual conflicts during the war. After all, the Scriptures were filled with examples of God's chosen people doing the same thing. A religion that asked believers tainted with original sin to inhabit a fallen paradise brimming with temptations, evil, and other seductive sinners was just asking for trouble. Some of the promising new converts were bound to ignore the rules, mix things up, or get sidetracked from time to time. Indeed, it was precisely these real-world problems with Christianity that prompted the Apostle Paul to draft most of his New Testament Epistles. But even if we accept the inevitability of spiritual changes and conflicts during the war, including some limited declension, this still does not answer the question of why some soldiers embraced such compromises while others did not.

There are several possible explanations as to why some religious soldiers decided to disregard one or more of their faith's cardinal principles during the war. The simplest answer is that like many modern believers, Civil War soldiers simply pragmatically adapted their faith to the popular culture around them. Sensing that a few of their religious beliefs were no longer compatible with prevailing wartime attitudes, soldiers simply changed their beliefs to better suit the new realities. This could be done by simply ignoring the religious prohibition or altering their understanding of it. In other cases these modifications may have simply represented a temporary or permanent declension of religious belief, as a few men's childlike faith, previously sheltered by family and church, was finally tested and found wanting by the harsh realities of an often unforgiving world. Soldiers who were not well grounded in their faith may have also already been searching for reasons to discard certain childhood beliefs they had never fully understood or embraced anyway.

Perhaps it was the prior spiritual demoralization some soldiers experienced in their wartime camps and their gradual desensitization to the wartime violence that set the stage for their subsequent spiritual compromises. During one of the most difficult times of their lives these young Christians had been deprived of their traditional spiritual mentors and support mechanisms. And the spiritual substitutes the army provided, when they provided any at all, were often a poor excuse for the real thing. Removed from their former religious society, soldiers found themselves in a new military environment that frequently seemed to ignore or mock their spiritual values and sensibilities.

Then, as religious soldiers were still struggling to combat the unwholesome influences of their camps, they suddenly found themselves cast into their first battles, horrifically violent and chaotic affairs that permanently scarred their minds. With religious soldiers often deprived of their prewar spiritual support network, the war's violence and apparent injustice may have provoked moral questions and doubts some young believers could not possibly address on their own. Like other soldiers, in time the religious troops also became increasingly desensitized or hardened to the wartime violence and suffering. Combined with their earlier spiritual demoralization in the camps, this hardening probably made it more difficult for some soldiers to retain beliefs that hindered them in the performance of their duties or no longer seemed to make sense in the context of a bloody and seemingly endless civil war.

The first major compromises some religious soldiers made in the war were abandoning the prewar practices of attending various weekly religious meetings and observing a strict Sunday Sabbath. While the very nature of army life itself often made it difficult for soldiers to observe such prewar practices, most religious soldiers tried to create suitable substitutes for such meetings, and if they could not physically observe the Sabbath rest, they could consciously observe its spirit as best as they could under the circumstances. Compromisers, on the other hand, noted the loss of the Sabbath day rest in their letters but then never raised the issue again. Those who expressed little concern over the loss of their religious meetings and Sabbath often later compromised other major tenants of their faith as well. The loss of religious support mechanisms, such as competent chaplains, no doubt also contributed to this religious devolution, but the most decisive factor behind these new spiritual compromises may have been the war itself. As the war continued and casualties mounted, each side became increasingly frustrated with its opponent's stubborn refusal to abandon a costly and illegitimate cause. Increasingly embittered by their so-called Christian enemies' recalcitrance and the death of family members and friends, some Northern Protestants abandoned their religious framework for waging war so they could impose what they considered to be a more appropriate punishment on their Southern enemies. This spirit of frustration and bitterness set the stage for the religious soldiers most egregious wartime compromises: hating their Southern adversaries, seeking personal vengeance for their enemies' "crimes," and disregarding the moral distinction between killing and murder.

Hatred

Warfare was clearly sanctioned in the Old Testament and not specifically condemned by Christ in the gospels, but Christ defined the proper attitude of the Christian warrior, instructing believers to love their "enemies, bless them that curse you, do good to them that hate you, and pray for them which despitefully use you, and persecute you." Indeed, a constant refrain in Northern wartime sermons was that while war was a necessary evil in a wicked world, God still expected soldiers to retain their Christian identity and values in battle. Religious soldiers were not supposed to fight with a spirit of hatred. Since Christ had mercifully spared other sinners who deserved to die, they too were to spare the lives of enemy soldiers who surrendered and pray for their opponents' repentance—ideally— even as they fought and killed them on the battlefield.[36]

Although the angry passions and dreadful carnage unleashed during the Civil War seemed to contradict these noble religious sentiments, the average religious soldier did not passionately hate his sectional counterpart, plot personal vengeance against his foes, or boast about the number of "Rebels" he killed. Given the context of a bloody and protracted civil war, in the wake of battles Northern Protestants could be remarkably merciful to the wounded Southern soldiers and prisoners they had been trying to kill just a couple of hours earlier. The numerous friendly meetings of opposing pickets that took place during the war also testify to the fact that off the battlefield and away from their officers, Billy Yank and Johnny Reb genuinely enjoyed each other's company and rarely harbored any serious ill will toward their sectional counterparts. As Bruce Catton observed in *Recollections of the Civil War,* the war was fought between men "who when left alone, got along together beautifully." Most of the religious soldiers' anger and vituperation was directed at the Confederate leadership, not the Rebel rank and file.[37]

But as the violence continued to escalate and soldiers continued to lose friends and family members, some Northern religious soldiers lost whatever charitable feelings they had once felt for their Southern foe. Religious soldiers' wartime experiences in the South sometimes helped fuel this growing hatred. As they were increasingly exposed to Southern intransigence, on and off the battlefield—in the form of bullets, curses, glares, and other indignities—there was a gradual hardening of Northern hearts toward Southerners. As Pvt. Sylvester Bishop explained to his mother, "I have learned a great deal Since coming South I used to think all we had to do was to treat the Secesh well to gain them over to the Union. Experience has taught better, the milder you treat a Secesh the more bold and insolent he is. . . . I do not intend to molest their property myself . . . yet my sympathies are not so tender for Secesh who lose a little property as they were a few months ago."[38] Pvt. Michael Hayes Branniger also found it increasingly difficult to love his Southern neighbors as he became better acquainted with their sins:

> The people in the north know nothing of the wickedness of
> this rebellion They ought to come here and see and then pass
> there opinions Pen nor Tounge can not express the half that
> I have seen men that have been hunted for weeks by men and
> dogs and that dare not go near their homes for fear of being
> shot or hung and all just because they loved the old flag and
> would not fight against it. The longer I stay in the Army the
> more I hate the Rebs and there proceedings.[39]

Although the fierce judgment he later helped inflict on northern Virginia ultimately satiated Surgeon Daniel Holt's righteous anger, when he contemplated their moral crimes against his country at the beginning of the war, Holt confessed that it was difficult to forgive his Southern enemies and not harbor evil thoughts toward them:

> It is a hard thing, after all I said to the contrary, to keep down
> the old Adam which arises within me. The thought that all this
> has been brought upon us by brethren of the same faith and
> parentage as ourselves, and issue of blood and carnage which
> overspreads this land is being caused by those who should have
> had a common interest and cause to maintain—when I see all
> this, and feel the unjust cruelty which they have remorselessly
> continued to perpetrate upon us, I feel I cannot be too severe
> with them. While I know that it is improper for me to indulge
> in evil feelings and express so much wrath towards them, who
> are so closely connected to us be every tie of interest, the very
> knowledge of it intensifies the repugnance I feel towards them.
> They can plead no lack of information, and excuse themselves

by no acts of oppression which the North has inflicted upon them. . . . Indeed I have but little sympathy for them. This is perhaps wrong, but I cannot help having all the bitterness of my heart stirred up against them.[40]

Vengeance

As some Northerners came to hate Southerners for instigating a wicked war and killing their friends and relatives, their passionate hatred fueled an intense desire for revenge. The Scriptures repeatedly admonished believers that such vengeance belonged to the Lord. By taking such matters into their own hands, religious soldiers would not only sabotage God's more perfect judgment of their enemies but would subject themselves and their countrymen to a host of other evils. With the entire country now paying the price for the South's prewar sins, however, some Northern Christians were determined to make Southerners bear the brunt of the wartime judgment. For example, when Gen. William Tecumseh Sherman ordered Atlanta evacuated so the city could be more easily defended from Southern counterattacks, Pvt. John R. Siperly told his Delavan girlfriend that while he might once have felt sorry for the "thousands of families" who would have to "leave home and property" and be "exiled from all that is dear to them," he now believed the good citizens of Atlanta were merely reaping what they had sown:

> This to the superficial observer seems cruel and in fact it is hard, but look at the resting places of over half a million vic-tims—look at as many more hobling about cripled for life—and wasting away in hospitals—and then again—Oh god the thought is maddening—look at the 18 acre pen at Anderson ville . . . some 3500 with nothing on which to lie but the bare earth and no blankets . . . no one to see to or take care of them and dying there at the rate of nearly 200 per day . . . in short penned in like hogs with less priveleges, and treated ten times wose—I say look at and think of all this, consider the perpetra-tors of this hellish crime and then can you say it is unjust.[41]

Convinced the South alone was responsible for these wartime evils, for some religious soldiers vengeance became the order of the day. This was certainly the case in the merciless guerrilla war against Confederate partisans in Missouri and Tennessee. After Confeder-ate irregulars burned several local bridges near his Missouri Camp, Pvt. Edwin Sackett of the Fifty-second Illinois told his family that "they are a pack of cowards they are like a theif in the night if they are pursued by troops they cut and run to their homes if you go to their houses to question them and they are good union men. . . . I don't know any other way to subdue them only to shoot them down or hang them up."

For a few Christian soldiers, collective punishment was the preferred solution to the Confederate problem. Stationed a couple of hundred miles to the southeast in Nashville,

Captain Ayers told his wife that if he were in charge, "I would put the torch to every house in the state—the women may look out for themselves." Irish private David King Jr. of the Sixty-eighth Illinois was equally incensed with the cowards who used the cover of darkness to stab unsuspecting Union pickets and stage nighttime ambushes outside Cairo's Fort Defiance. "Just such *conduct* makes me feel like going through the war and shoot[ing] every rebbell in the field," he wrote. Although he thought the war was "horable," Pvt. John Banard wanted those "that brought it on" to suffer its evil consequences: "I do not want any compromise I want them Subdued or exterminated."[42]

Religious warriors battling Confederate guerrillas were not the only Protestant soldiers who usurped God's authority over the dispensation of vengeance. Just like Herman Melville's Captain Ahab, religious soldiers who lost family members or relatives in the war, or who heard about alleged Southern atrocities, sometimes embarked on their own personal quests for revenge. After one of his first battles in Virginia, Pvt. James T. Miller happily informed his brother he had been far cooler under enemy fire than expected. As the bullets whizzed by, "I could feel the wind of several of them as they passed my face and head and one of our boys was shot on my right that stood not more than a foot and a half from me he was shot through the face and the bullet that hit him must have passed within four i[n]ches of my nose." After this, Miller lost any prewar moral reservations he might have had about the killing and started shooting back: "The predominant fe[e]ling with me after the first fire or two was revenge se[e]ing comrades fall around me. I though more about revengeing them than I did of being hit myself."[43]

Pvt. John Lindley Harris of the Fourteenth Illinois Volunteers was equally determined to avenge his brother's death. As he commiserated with his heart-broken father:

> I can't think of it only with a shuder. I hope I may never be
> called upon to pass through an other such an ordeal while I
> live. It was a year ago today that your most noble son and my
> brother received his mortal wound, and may God Almighty,
> enable the rest of us to die as honorable a death, and be as well
> prepared to meet the savior as he was. I still hope to be able
> to avenge his death, by getting some of them to bite the dust
> before the war ends.[44]

Although his earlier letters seemed to suggest Pvt. John G. Jones was a devout, long-suffering Christian, one would have never suspected it after reading the following excerpt. In November 1863, Jones apparently embraced a different gospel when he learned that some of his comrades had allegedly been shot down in cold blood after surrendering to the enemy:

> We are inside the fortifications and ready to receive the rebels
> any time they feel the urge to try our strength. They will find
> things different this time. The rebs will have another reason
> to remember the 3rd. of November, what they did on that day
> will not be forgotten, they will be repaid. Many of our men
> had surrendered to them, only to be mowed down like grass.

It made our blood boil, and it will be a sorry day for the rebs
when we get at them.[45]

With a small number of religious soldiers beginning to nurse a spirit of terrible vengeance against their Southern enemies, it was not much of a leap for others to lose sight of the traditional Christian distinction between the justified killing and murder of their enemies in combat.

Killing with Malice

Nineteenth-century Protestants did not believe it was immoral to kill enemy soldiers, but they thought the attitudes and methods of those who did the killing could conceivably be sinful. Christians were not supposed to take pleasure in the physical act of killing other men made in God's image or celebrate the death of their enemies, for the Lord detested those who loved violence. In his righteous wrath God might destroy the wicked, but he took no "pleasure at all" in their death. So ideally, Christian soldiers were supposed to kill their enemies without malice on the battlefield and care for their wounded opponents after the battle.[46]

Perhaps twentieth-century Christian apologist C. S. Lewis summarized this traditional Protestant model of just warfare best when he explained that the greatest challenge for Christian warriors was not so much the physical act of killing, or even justifying such violence, but rather ensuring one always fought with the right attitudes:

> We may kill if necessary, but we must not hate and enjoy
> hating. We may punish if necessary, but we must not enjoy it.
> In other words, something inside us, the feeling of resentment,
> the feeling that wants to get one's own back, must simply be
> killed. . . . Even while we kill and punish we must try to feel
> about the enemy as we feel about ourselves—to wish he were
> not bad, to hope that he may, in this world or another, be
> cured: in fact to wish his good.[47]

Those who failed to check their darker passions in combat would likely be consumed by the terrible hatred and violence accompanying such warfare. According to Lewis, failing to love and forgive—even one's wartime enemies—would gradually cause the soldier to begin seeing everything, God, friends, family, and even themselves, "as bad, and [he would] not be able to stop doing it." He would in effect be "fixed for ever in a universe of pure hatred."[48] Given this Christian understanding of warfare, Protestant soldiers generally concluded it was morally justifiable to kill enemy soldiers threatening their families and God-ordained government as long as they fought with the right attitudes and were serving in official, government-sanctioned armies.

In addition to entertaining proper attitudes about the enemy, in the early stages of the war some religious soldiers seemed anxious to ensure their method of killing the enemy did not violate God's laws. The government had clearly authorized soldiers to serve as instruments of retributive justice, but the Scriptures enjoined them to exact such retribution in a just and carefully circumscribed manner. They were to punish evildoers, but in a manner that respected their special status as creatures made in God's image and avoided engendering a spirit of greater hatred and revenge in the hearts of enemy survivors. While it was their duty to defeat their enemies in battle, soldiers were only to employ the minimum amount of force needed to achieve that end.

So, even when armed with the government's authority to kill enemy soldiers, many religious soldiers still thought it was extremely important to ensure that they did not violate God's sixth commandment during the course of their duties. To resolve this problem, they carefully tried to distinguish between certain methods of killing that were morally justified and others that clearly were not. Since it was every soldier's duty to defeat the opposing army in battle, religious soldiers generally believed that shooting and killing enemy soldiers on the battlefield was morally justified but that other methods of killing enemy soldiers, such as sharpshooting, bushwhacking, and shooting pickets were nothing short of "murder." Most soldiers considered the latter methods immoral because they did not significantly influence the outcome of battles or give enemy soldiers a fair opportunity to defend themselves. And more important from a spiritual perspective, these unexpected acts of violence were evil because, unlike field battles, they did not allow enemy soldiers to make appropriate preparations for their deaths and could thus potentially condemn them to eternal hellfire.

Throughout the conflict many religious soldiers thought it was extremely important to observe this moral distinction between "justified killing" and "murder." Responding to the copperheads' argument in 1863 that the North should just admit that it did not have the proper authority to wage war against the South, Pvt. Wilbur Fisk claimed such an admission would be tantamount to a confession of murder: "Shall we confess to the rebels that we have been wrong and they have been right; that we have been murdering them, and they only killing us in self defense?"

A few Christian soldiers thought that the best way to preserve the distinction between justified wartime killing and "assassination" was to never make the killing personal by "deliberately aiming" at unsuspecting enemy soldiers or shooting at them when they were not on the battlefield.[49] In an early 1861 battle, "Uncle Levi" could not kill an enemy skirmisher he had deliberately targeted for destruction. His brother later recalled the incident:

> Your Uncle Levi had a rifle and took deliberate aim at one of
> the rebels at a distance so short that he could have sent him to
> eternity in a second, but says he could not fire on a man in that
> murderous fashion, and he dropped his gun, letting the rascal
> go. I think he did right. . . . In battle it would be different and
> I would be killing as many of them as possible.[50]

Even as late as 1865, Private Fisk felt morally compelled to justify a comrade's premeditated decision to "assassinate" a Confederate infantryman during a lull in the fighting around Petersburg:

> My nearest comrade, noticing one bold fellow walking
> leisurely along in open defiance of our bullets, drew up his
> faithful Springfield and taking deliberate aim—I fear with
> malice aforethought and intent to kill—fired. My friend is a
> good marksman, and as Secesh was not seen afterwards, the
> presumption is that he had an extra hole made in his body.
> Our vindictiveness had been aroused to an uncommon de-
> gree that morning, by the loss of one our number.[51]

Perhaps one of the reasons the phrase "deliberately aimed" held such a negative connotation in the minds of some religious soldiers was that thanks to recent technological
developments, they knew those who "aimed deliberately" would likely hit and kill their
human targets. Fifteen years earlier, U.S. armies had fought the Mexican War armed with
single-shot, smoothbore, muzzle-loading muskets with a maximum effective range of less
than one hundred yards. Soldiers armed with such weapons found it extremely difficult
to hit individual targets at longer ranges, and this dramatically influenced the way they
fought. Armed with similar smoothbore weapons at Waterloo, even at a range of fifty
yards, most of Wellington's musketeers had missed when they fired a volley at a column
of Napoleon's Imperial Guard. As John Keegan noted, this "reinforces suspicions that
many musketeers did not aim at all, or at least did not aim at a particular human target.
According to Keegan, this conclusion was borne out by the recollection of a Waterloo
officer that the word of command generally used was 'Level' rather than 'Aim.'"[52]

It was largely due to the inaccuracy of such smoothbore muskets that soldiers generally stood closely together in a firing line and pointed, rather than aimed, their muskets
at a common target before simultaneously unleashing a volley of bullets. As the cloud of
bullets spun off in various directions, at least a few of the rounds were bound to hit the
target. Collectively discharging weapons upon command in the general direction of the
enemy, and not knowing for sure whose shots were administering the fatal wounds, almost
certainly lessened the sense of personal moral responsibility each soldier felt in killing
the enemy.

Thanks to technological advances in the firearms industry between the Mexican and
Civil War, Northern religious soldiers could not enjoy that traditional sense of moral ambiguity. In the late 1840s, the introduction of a new, less-expensive bullet (the minié ball)
finally made it cost effective for firearm manufacturers to manufacture a new, dramatically
improved weapon. Rifling the barrel, or adding grooves that caused the expanding minié
ball to spin and better maintain its forward momentum, significantly increased the gun's
range and accuracy. This increased the effective range of the muzzle loader from between
fifty and one hundred yards to between three hundred and four hundred yards and
dramatically improved the weapon's accuracy. But as with most other new technologies,
there were moral consequences that accompanied the introduction and wide-scale use of
the rifled musket.

Armed with a Springfield rifle, a given soldier was now far more likely to hit what he
"deliberately aimed at." And since soldiers no longer had to stand closely together and fire
in unison to guarantee at least some of them hit the target, a soldier was far more likely

to know if it was his bullet that administered the fatal wound. Perhaps this explains why some religious soldiers felt so uncomfortable about "deliberately" targeting unsuspecting, individual enemy soldiers. It seemed more like murder than killing.

This also explains why soldiers on both sides loathed sharpshooters so much. Sharpshooters combined the improved killing power of the rifle with special long-range sights that enhanced the lethal nature of their weapons. Sharpshooters would move stealthily across the battlefield until they found some strategic vantage point, hidden from view, and then deliberately target and kill unsuspecting enemy officers, pickets, and skirmishers. Soldiers especially despised sharpshooters because they violated the unwritten moral code that it was immoral to target and deliberately kill unsuspecting soldiers and because their killing rarely had any effect on the outcome of battles. In short, they considered sharpshooters murderers.[53]

For the same reasons, John H. Pardington, a Michigan solider serving in the Iron Brigade, thought shooting at enemy pickets was akin to "murder." While enjoying the relative comforts of picket duty after fighting at Fredericksburg and Chancellorsville, Pardington told his wife, "All we have to do is whach the *Grey Backs* and they watch us. We are within rifle shot of them. But there in no fireing on Pickett now. . . . It aint no use for Picketts to fire on one another. It only seems like murder and it don't do any good to either side."[54]

While most religious soldiers believed they could faithfully adhere to the spirit of the sixth commandment if they only killed enemy soldiers on the battlefield, some soldiers— still troubled at the thought of taking another human life—concluded that while duty might require them to shoot "at" enemy soldiers on the battlefield, it did not oblige them to confirm they actually hit or harmed them. In *The Life of Billy Yank,* Bell Wiley observed that on the crowded, smoke-filled battlefields, Northerners "could rarely say with confidence after a fight that his bullets hit any foe" and the man who talked about how many enemies he had killed was the "exception." He then added that some soldiers, "fearful of conscience, preferred not to know the results of their fire." In *Civil War Soldiers,* Reid Mitchell identified two soldiers who seemed to struggle with the moral question of killing other men. Numa Barned "had shot at many Confederates but in battle his policy was 'as long as I can see the man in front of me I will shoot and never look at the consequences.'" Although he shot at his enemies, Barned confessed, "I don't know that I ever shot any one or don't want to know." Likewise, after fighting in a battle in which he had "shot at the Confederates as much as anyone else," an Illinois soldier named Henry C. Bear told his wife, "I hope I did not hit any person if they are Rebles."[55]

The question naturally arises as to how some religious soldiers "deliberately aiming" at the enemy could fail to notice whether they had hit anyone. The chaotic and extremely noisy and smoky atmosphere of the battlefield, and the numerous responsibilities that occupied a soldier's attention—such as trying to complete the arduous nine step process of reloading his muzzle-loading rifle while responding to orders under fire—may have made it difficult for soldiers to observe the effect of their fire. But as the enemy drew closer, and sometimes came within seventy-five yards of his firing position, it is hard to imagine how a soldier "deliberately aiming his rifle" at individual enemy soldiers could not witness any of the physical consequences of his shots over the course of a prolonged engagement. Perhaps the most logical answer is that at least a few religious soldiers, whose consciences were still troubled by this form of killing, were either living in a state of psychological denial concerning their handiwork or not "deliberately aiming" at anyone, but merely pointing their rifles in the general direction of the enemy and not observing the effects of their fire.[56]

In the first two years of the war, it was relatively easy for religious soldiers to observe a "Christian" code of warfare. As the fighting continued, however, and religious soldiers became increasingly coarsened by the prolonged violence, some found it increasingly difficult to maintain the traditional distinction between justifiable killing and murder.

By 1864 Richard Gould had grown accustomed to the Rebel sharpshooters who were constantly "pecking away" at him and did not seem very concerned about the fate of the Confederate defenders of a Petersburg fort that was about to be blown up:

> Some places the lines are but a few yards apart, and if a man
> from either side show his head he is prety sure to lose it. We
> are now undermining a large rebel fort in our front for the
> purpose of blowing it up. We will send a few Johnnies nearer
> Heaven than they would ever get. . . . We are getting just right
> now to fight. The men are hardened to it.[57]

The resulting explosion (which launched the disastrous Battle of the Crater) killed nearly three hundred unwary Confederates in a manner that gave them no chance to prepare for their deaths or defend themselves, but there is no evidence that Gould or any other religious soldier there that day ever regretted the circumstances surrounding their "murder."

Perhaps to ease their troubled consciences, religious soldiers obsessed with killing their sectional adversaries began describing Southerners as if they were somehow less civilized or human than Northerners. Rather than uphold the Noahidic covenant concerning man's unique moral status as a creature made in the image of God, a few religious soldiers dismissed their enemies' common humanity. This was not difficult for some Northerners, who had always viewed themselves as culturally superior to the poor Southern whites serving in the Confederate ranks. In any case, gradually transforming men into brute beasts made it much easier for Christians to disregard the scriptural warnings about murdering those who bore God's image. If religious soldiers were merely hunting primitive savages or animals, their methods and attitudes were of little consequence.[58]

After witnessing the fruits of Confederate guerrilla activity in eastern Tennessee, William Gould told his sister he had "seen enough of southern chiverly. They are the most Barbarious race of people in the civilized world. They are worse than the red man of the forest for . . . a great deal of these southerners that pretend to be your friend to your face . . . would kill you if they could get a chance."[59] Just as earlier U.S. administrations had labeled Native Americans "uncivilized savages" to rationalize robbing them of their lands, vindictive religious soldiers now stripped away Southerners' humanity to justify their destruction.

Soldiers who ignored the special moral status of their Southern enemies demonstrated their own inhumanity when they revealed they were not troubled at all by the killing but, rather, took pleasure in it. After all, most of them believed they were hunting animals, not men. Although he was very anxious before his first major battle, Pvt. William Onstot felt much better when he recalled he was fighting for a holy cause and "against a treasonable horde. . . . After this I was troubled no more with unpleasant feelings." As Onstot boasted to his sister, "I felt as cool as though I was *shooting chickens*." Pvt. George W. Squier told his wife Ellen that when he began to return the Rebels' fire at Shiloh he was "as cool and composed as if sitting down for a chat or shooting squirrels." A few months later, while defending Union supply trains from Confederate irregulars in Tennessee, Squier shared there was "something *rather* exciting in shooting, and particularly at one's fellow beings." Other religious soldiers began to take a perverse pleasure in the death throes of their enemies. After telling his brother that he thought his unit was justified in sacking a local Southern town, Arthur Lee Bailhache admitted that in the most recent battle, it was "a sad sight and yet a not unpleasant one to see those infernal rebels lying on the field—Kicking like a flock of dead partridges."[60]

Conflict

While a significant minority of religious soldiers compromised morally problematic or inconvenient beliefs during the war, a much smaller number of religious soldiers stubbornly clung to their beliefs throughout the conflict—even as they frequently failed to live up to them. Those who chose to retain their prewar religious principles, despite a growing conviction that some of their military duties were likely immoral, generally experienced spiritual conflicts.

These religious soldiers often began to express spiritual doubts about the morality of certain military duties, the escalating violence, or some other sin during the last two years of the war, when the fighting dramatically intensified and they were subjected to even greater wartime stresses. The prolonged fighting, widespread exhaustion, and unprecedented casualties associated with Sherman and Grant's final campaigns probably also contributed to some religious soldiers' subsequent spiritual crises. These conflicts posed a serious moral dilemma for the soldiers. Torn between their intense spiritual desire to please God and assure their place in heaven, and their equally strong commitment to their country and comrades, these soldiers probably experienced a certain degree of "cognitive dissonance."

This psychological disorder often occurs when individuals discern that they hold several conflicting or incongruous beliefs and attitudes, but for personal reasons refuse to relinquish any of them. Most people naturally seek consistency in their beliefs and behaviors. So when an individual's behavior or attitude contradicts one of his beliefs, he experiences dissonance, a profound sense of physical discomfort or moral tension. Because dissonance always makes the individual feel uncomfortable and stressed, the natural reaction is to try to restore consistency by reducing or removing the inconsistency. Since individuals usually find it more difficult to change their behaviors than their beliefs, the best way for them to restore consistency is by altering their beliefs about the deviant behavior. While individuals can also reduce dissonance by changing their perceptions about themselves, this is not encouraged as it can lead to highly destructive attacks on their self-concept.[61]

Protestant soldiers who experienced cognitive dissonance during the war, or a growing conviction their combat duties or some other personal sin was transgressing God's law, thus faced a terrible moral dilemma. They could absolve their dissonance or sense of guilt by either abandoning their deviant military behavior or changing their moral perception of it, but given their strong commitment to both their cause and comrades, as well as to their evangelical faith, either option was considered immoral.

This left Protestant soldiers with only one alternative for relieving their growing dissonance—changing their perceptions of themselves. As previously mentioned, this is always the least desirable solution for restoring moral consistency because it can cause the victim to question, or in some cases even attack, their self-concept. For deeply religious soldiers who already believed in the depravity of human nature and were struggling to live a Christian life in the army, this process of self evaluation was particularly harmful, as it usually only further reinforced their guilt in having failed to live up to God's laws. This intense moral scrutiny often burdened soldiers already suffering from the emotional consequences of cognitive dissonance with new doubts about themselves and their faith. In some of the more extreme cases of spiritual conflict, soldiers may have become depressed as they increasingly began to question some of their former religious certainties.[62]

By the summer of 1864, the war's enormous sacrifices had robbed Pvt. Abial Edwards of much of his earlier enthusiasm for a "just and holy" cause. Having once expressed no doubts about the eventual triumph of the Union armies, now Abial doubted whether even the fall of Atlanta and Mobile would significantly improve the North's military situation:

> Oh Anna, I shall be so glad when this war is over. I see the
> dredful effects of it more and more each day would that we
> could settle it this summer but thank God old Maine has
> not yet seen its effects I lost a Dear Cousin last week before
> Petersburg How sad so many falling so little gained. Would
> that my mind was comprehensive enough to see the good. But
> still I think that [even] if Mobil is captured and Atlanta that
> little good will accrue from it.[63]

Although it is difficult to diagnose a soldier's psychological state on the basis of a few letters, in some cases soldiers struggling to reconcile their faith with their duties sounded as though they were manifesting classic symptoms of depression: a loss of interest in the events of everyday life, feelings of general fatigue and malaise, recurrent thoughts about death, and inappropriate guilt.[64]

For example, while traveling aboard the steamboat *Empress* in January 1863, Pvt. Daniel Webster thought many of his comrades no longer seemed interested in the war or the ultimate fate of their cause:

> We do not see that enthusiasm among our soldiers that we did
> one year ago. All appear to merely exist and act as if they go
> into battle because they were obliged to, and not because they
> felt any interest in it or cared whether our cause succeeded

> or not. I tell you what, it is a very hard matter for a man to
> keep up good courage and spirits with such a manifest feeling
> existing around him.[65]

In an army largely composed of citizen-soldiers, such apathy could be both highly con-
tagious and deleterious to the soldiers' morale, and even the most ardent patriots' health
suffered when they kept fighting despite their troubled consciences. In January 1864,
Sgt. Amos C. Weaver confessed that the emotional and physical demands of the war were
literally ruining him and his comrades:

> We are all deeply interested in our country's cause, though we
> have sickened and desired to turn away from the sad battlefield
> scene though we deeply abhor the ferocious atrocities perpetuated
> during this cruel war and [are] mourning over many dear friends
> who have fallen in defense of our countrys interest, yet we are
> not disposed to relinquish our intended design, to crush rebel-
> ion, and restore our Government, to this end we are toiling
> and striving enduring hardships and privations that neither pen
> nor tongue can describe. all this proves to be deleterious to our
> health and is frightfully shortening our lives and hurrying us
> off to the Tomb many of us will be if we are so fortunate as to
> escape the battlefield will be disqualified and so indisposed that
> home comforts will never restore us to our former condition.[66]

Although the hardships Weaver described were primarily physical in nature, given our
increasing understanding of the relationship between stress and human illness, one can
only imagine how much additional nervous tension was created by these soldiers' spiritual
conflicts and what the long-term impact of all this was on the soldiers' health.

In their physically exhausted and depressed states, some religious soldiers already
seemed unhealthily obsessed with the subject of death. In an 1864 letter to his sister,
Richard Gould initially sought to shield his sister from the terrible realities of his military
predicament. But even his hopeful expressions that God might still grant the North
"complete success" and bring soldiers like her brother safely back "to our homes and
friends" were punctuated with more ominous messages indicating things were worst than
he let on: "Our Div lost about 1800 men last wensday in about two hours"; "The rebs
are making a desprate stand"; and "Things look rather hard at present." Finally, Gould
dropped his pretense and shared the reality of his wartime situation:

> You that are at home know nothing of the hardships that a
> soldier has to endure. When we was at home, when we got
> tired we could rest. Now we have got to go till our Gen. Says
> rest. A fellow gets so tired that he is almost inclined to think
> that death would be a relief. Some times I have almost been
> like that myself, but then I have got into it and I will make
> the best of it. Expect the worst and hope for the best.[67]

While awaiting the next major attack on Vicksburg in early 1863, a disillusioned Wisconsin private named Robert Steele seemed increasingly concerned that God might not permit him to survive it: "I am sick of this cursed war and it is enough to make any one sick that has a heart to see the way thing[s] are carried on. I hope through the mercy of God to see the end and be permitted to return to our home in safety."[68]

Other religious soldiers thoughts also turned more and more to the subject of death. When he learned his favorite aunt back home had passed away, Pvt. John G. Jones became almost obsessed with what he believed was his own imminent death and repeatedly inserted the text of Matthew 24:44, a verse about Christ's second coming, into his loved ones' letters. After surviving Sherman's first disastrous attack on Vicksburg, Jones quoted the passage in a letter to his parents: "You probably know better than we do how many were lost. I know that a very large number had to face the last judgment and eternity. We are daily warned 'Therefore be ye also ready: for in such an hour as ye think not the Son of man cometh.'" Three weeks later, Jones cited the ominous passage again as he penned a letter near one of his regiment's improvised graveyards. After recording the verse, Jones gloomily noted: "We are being daily forewarned by seeing others from our regiment being buried." One wonders whether Jones was prepared for his own final judgment when he was killed a year later in a battle near Jackson, Louisiana.[69]

The principal cause of these soldiers' depression was not so much the fear they might be killed in the next battle, but that their God might not forgive them for having violated his commandments. Over the course of the four-year conflict, some had come to realize that the Scriptures were a double-edged sword. The same Bible that soldiers used to justify their holy crusade against the South also appeared to condemn the wartime violence.

The Scriptures warned God would demand a special accounting for "whoso sheddeth man's blood . . . for in the image of God made he man." Other passages, such as Christ's admonition to Peter to put back his sword "for all they that take the sword shall perish with the sword," seemed to condemn the violence of war.[70] Evildoers pursued warfare, bloodshed, and ruin.[71] But numerous Old Testament and New Testament passages urged believers to "eschew evil" and "seek peace."[72] Indeed, the apostle Paul could not have been clearer on this point:

> Recompense to no man evil for evil. Provide things honest
> in the sight of all men. If it be possible, as much as lieth in
> you, live peaceably with all men. Dearly beloved, avenge not
> yourselves, but *rather* give place unto wrath: for it is written,
> Vengeance *is* mine; I will repay, saith the Lord. Therefore if
> thine enemy hunger, feed him; if he thirst, give him drink.
> Be not overcome of evil, but overcome evil with good.[73]

Such passages undoubtedly played an important role in the early church's strict commitment to Pacifism in the first centuries of Christianity. After all, in his sermon on the Mount Christ had blessed the peacemakers, not the warriors, and the prophetic books of both the Old and New Testaments spoke of a time when the spirit of Christ would inspire men to "beat their swords into plowshares and their spears into pruning hooks."[74]

Religious soldiers who were convicted of this truth but kept fighting anyway frequently began to question whether a good God would ever forgive them for consciously doing that which they knew was evil. Gerald Linderman and James M. McPherson have both touched on this theme in their works. In *Embattled Courage,* Linderman noted that by 1865 even the renowned Christian veteran Col. Joshua Chamberlain had begun to entertain doubts about whether Union "soldiers were doing the work God intended them to do. . . . The carnage perplexed him and he was no longer sure that by killing rebels he and his men continued to execute God's will."[75] After a particularly savage battle along Quaker Road, in the final stages of the fighting outside Petersburg, Chamberlain stared at the shattered soldiers littering the battlefield and observed:

> We had with us, to keep and care for, more than five hundred
> bruised bodies of men,—men made in the image of God, mar-
> red by the hand of God, and must we say in the name of God?
> And where is the reckoning for such things? And who is an-
> swerable? One might almost shrink from the sound of his own
> voice, which had launched into the palpitating air words of
> order—do we call it?—fraught with such ruin. Was it God's
> command we heard, or His forgiveness we must forever
> implore?[76]

In the afterword to *Religion and the American Civil War,* James M. McPherson also shared some examples of soldiers who seemed to have unresolved spiritual conflicts about their duties:

> How could a true Christian take up arms to kill his fellow
> man? "I think it is a hard job to learn to fight, and to be a
> Christian at the same time," wrote an Illinois recruit in 1861.
> Even after two years of combat experience, the lieutenant
> colonel of the 57th Indiana continued to agonize about the
> question: "How can a soldier be a Christian? Read all of
> Christ's teachings, and then tell me whether *one engaged
> in maiming and butchering men*—men made in the express
> image of God himself—*can be saved* under the Gospel." He
> had still not resolved the question when he was killed at
> Resaca in May 1864.[77]

Common religious soldiers convicted by their consciences also feared the eternal consequences of violating God's laws. By embracing the gospel of war instead of the gospel of Christ, or committing some other sin, had they somehow forfeited their place in heaven? Lt. John Blackwell obviously had serious doubts. After surviving another "close call" in battle in the fall of 1862, Blackwell confided his deepest fears with his wife:

> I am not happy. You know how often I fell doubts of my safety,
> how dark my soul is and how sin mars all my happiness. . . .
> Business drives me all day long but at quiet hours, in the still-

ness of the night conscience wakes and stings me. Dearest I'm
afraid that just so near as that bullet was to my heart just so
near I was to eternal ruin and yet so near hell once, has made
so little impression on me that I fear I am no nearer heaven
now but rather further off. But drops of grief can not repay the
debt I owe. And besides I make you sad. Keep these things as
our secrets. God knows them.[78]

Increasingly troubled with his own spiritual doubts, Pvt. Hamlin Coe of the Nineteenth
Michigan Volunteers also apparently lost his former certainty concerning salvation. As
he recalled a furious midsummer's battle in Georgia, Coe recalled:

Many a poor fellow fell, and we gained nothing but a little
ground. . . . The sun set clear and bright, too lovely for the
scenes about us, but such are the horrors of war. Will God
forgive men for such work is a question I often ask myself, but
I receive a silent reply and utter my own prayers for the safety
of my poor soul and my country.[79]

Although Coe never received the heavenly reassurance he so earnestly sought, like
Lincoln, he obviously retained his faith in a sovereign God whose ways might often prove
inscrutable but nonetheless faithfully heard and answered his people's prayers.

Although only a minority of religious soldiers failed to reconcile their faith with
their military service, the preceding survey illustrates the diversity of their theological
responses to the dilemma. When they perceived there was a conflict between their faith
and military duties, most concluded that one's duty to country came first and adapted
their faith accordingly. These spiritual compromises could be conscious or unconscious,
principled or pragmatic, but once implemented, they were rarely retreated from. The
gradual realization of an incompatibility between faith and duty, however, did not always
result in a compromise of religious principle—at least in the heart of the believer. A
handful of believers refused to abandon either their beliefs or a growing conviction that
their military duties were immoral and might rob them of their temporal and eternal
salvation.

So what, if any, impact did these soldiers' spiritual compromises and conflicts have
on the war or their fighting abilities? Before considering the subject, it is important to
remember that only a minority of religious soldiers entertained such doubts or compromises; the vast majority did not see any incongruity in serving in both the Union army
and the army of the Lord. So it is doubtful whether the internal religious struggles of
a few religious soldiers had a significant impact on the war. As for their impact on the
common religious soldiers' military performance, the soldiers who compromised certain
prewar beliefs rarely expressed any further spiritual doubts about their wartime activities
and generally seemed to perform their military duties as well as the next man. Can the
same be said of the soldiers who experienced a spiritual crisis of sorts when they continued
to fight despite a growing personal conviction that their wartime service was an affront
to God?

These soldiers experienced varying degrees of cognitive dissonance, and at times some of them seemed deeply disturbed by their seemingly irreconcilable spiritual conflicts. The question naturally arises: Did some soldiers' acute episodes of cognitive dissonance impede the performance of their military duties or place them at greater risk on the battlefield? Although such a link seems plausible, the limited sample of evidence gathered by this study precludes any conclusive answer to this question. Although three of the soldiers experiencing such conflict in this study were subsequently killed in battle, the rest survived and returned home with distinguished wartime records.

Perhaps the best conclusion we can draw about the religious soldiers' faith is that it cut both ways. It imposed a terrible emotional burden on soldiers by convicting them of their wartime sins, but also reminded them that they were only sojourners on this planet and that a far better heavenly home awaited those who embraced causes higher than themselves. This hope, however, could not spare soldiers from either the dangers of the battlefield or the heartache of a wounded conscience.[80]

Soldiers who experienced spiritual crises as they sincerely, if unsuccessfully, struggled to fulfill their duty to both God and country undoubtedly suffered more psychologically than those who compromised their beliefs. Although the former faithfully executed their duties to the end, their seemingly irreconcilable moral dilemmas burdened them with tremendous guilt that caused many to become depressed or experience serious doubts about their faith. Fortunately, these feelings apparently waned as the Union armies' prospects brightened. With the exception of Joshua Chamberlain, the afflicted soldiers made no further mention of them as the Confederacy entered its final death throes in the spring of 1865. It would be interesting to know whether the faith of these conscience-stricken soldiers, after they had steadfastly performed their duties to the end, was ultimately strengthened by their fiery wartime trial, exonerated, or lost. Soldiers who compromised their beliefs experienced little if any such dissonance during the war. The latter's spiritual compromises certainly proved expedient at the time, but at what long-term cost? For as Christian soldiers knew, perhaps better than anyone else, there was nothing worse than a guilty conscience.

Chapter 10

Soldiers of Christ

But volunteers like ours were held by a consciousness not only rooted in instinctive love and habitual reverence but also involving spiritual and moral considerations of the highest order. The motive under which they first sprung to the front was an impulse of sentiment,—the honor of the old flag and love of Country. All that the former stood for, and all that the latter held undetermined, they did not stop to question. . . . There was, indeed, an instinctive apprehension of what was involved in this; but only slowly as the struggle thickened, and they found their antagonists claiming to rest their cause on principles similar to their own, they were led to think more deeply, to analyze their concrete ideals, to question, to debate, to test loyalty by thoughts of right and reason.

> Joshua Lawrence Chamberlain, *The Passing of the Armies*

From strength to strength go on,
wrestle and fight and pray,
tread all the powers of darkness down
and win the well-fought day.
Still let the Spirit cry
in all his soldiers, "Come!"
till Christ the Lord, descends from high
and takes the conquerors home.

> Charles Wesley, "Soldiers of Christ, Arise," 12th Stanza

> Thou therefore endure hardness, as a good soldier of Jesus Christ. No
> man that warreth entangleth himself with the affairs of *this* life; that he
> may please him who hath chosen him to be a soldier.

2 Timothy 2:3–4

THIS BRIEF REVIEW of Northern religious soldiers' spiritual justifications for fighting in the "Army of the Lord" demonstrates that Billy Yank took his faith far more seriously than previously imagined. Popular stereotypes about the irreligious nature of Northern soldiers are deeply rooted. They probably have their origins in the work of postwar Southern apologists such as William W. Bennett and J. William Jones, whose one-sided histories of the late-war revivals in the Southern armies played an important role in creating the Lost Cause legend of the Christian Southern soldier. Essentially, this was the story of how a few faithful Southern soldiers heroically fought against impossible odds to save their homes and families from hordes of godless Northern invaders. Although twentieth-century historians eventually rejected most of this Lost Cause apologia, for some reason the myth of the irreligious Yankee has stubbornly persisted until recent times. But as Steven Woodworth, Reid Mitchell, and others have increasingly emphasized, Northern soldiers could be and often were just as religious as their Southern counterparts.[1]

Many Union soldiers were intensively religious. Religion was the prism through which they viewed and interpreted all their wartime experiences. As the historian Edward L. Ayers noted, "Faith, theology, and church constituted the very language of self-understanding, defined the limits of sympathy and imagination, [and] provided the terms of vengeance and solace."[2] In an age Mark Noll and others have characterized as "the golden age of Protestantism," most antebellum Americans had been raised in a society steeped in evangelical values and traditions. With their own identity and worldview so firmly rooted in a commonsense reading of the Scriptures, antebellum believers naturally turned to religion when confronted with life's inevitable trials and tragedies. So in the tsunami of death, suffering, and chaos produced by a protracted civil war, the common soldiers' faith became a source of immeasurable strength. The common soldier's faith provided him with the spiritual justifications for the wartime violence and suffering. And perhaps more important, it gave him the hope that his wartime sacrifices, and those of his comrades, were not in vain and would someday be rewarded.

One of the problems with the postwar literature about religious soldiers, which is often still unintentionally perpetuated in today's limited literature on the subject, is that many of these works often define the soldiers' faith too simplistically. Christian soldiers are erroneously portrayed as otherworldly saints whose naïve faith never wavered in the face of constant wartime temptations, dangers, hardships, and military reverses. This study, and particularly the examples of soldiers who compromised their faith and suffered crises during the war, belies this one-dimensional stereotype by demonstrating that even devout soldiers sometimes stumbled or expressed spiritual doubts when confronted with the hardships and moral dilemmas of a protracted civil war.

The common soldiers' faith was actually far more realistic and comprehensive than previously imagined; realistic in that it was practical faith that seriously addressed believers' everyday problems living in a fallen world, and comprehensive because it both tolerated and could meet the needs of a wide range of believers at their different spiritual levels—from the steadfast certitude of the seasoned saint to the spiritual ebbs and flows of a new believer. So, if their faith's realism anticipated human frailties and failures, its comprehensive nature had already provided believers with the means for overcoming such problems—or at least successfully coping with them. In times of crisis the Scriptures assured religious soldiers that a merciful heavenly Father would grant his children the strength to endure their temporary trials. They could also take comfort in the promise that Christ would eventually deliver them from such evil, either in this life or the next. That so many of them ultimately weathered the wartime spiritual crisis is a testimony to the authenticity and flexibility of their faith.

In the end, the vast majority of Northern Protestants who enlisted in Lincoln's crusade to save the Union apparently had little difficulty finding religious rationales, and in some cases, multiple rationalizations, to justify their decision to embrace the evils of war. Many Northern Christians offered simple variations of the traditional holy war or just war doctrines to justify their wartime participation, but others offered surprisingly sophisticated theological arguments: The war was God's judgment on a wicked nation or section, a severe testing of God's people to sift out the faithful from the chaff, or a providential means of sanctifying the Republic. Although the soldiers addressing this issue had virtually the same evangelical beliefs, they often arrived at completely different conclusions or interpretations, depending on which Scriptures they emphasized or whether they leaned more toward Arminianism or Calvinism. These conclusions demonstrate the rich theological diversity of nineteenth-century evangelical Protestantism and prove that even a literal, commonsense reading of the Scriptures often resulted in a fascinating diversity of theological interpretations.

In addition to helping soldiers justify their military service, these religious rationales also served as larger spiritual models that helped Protestant soldiers successfully interpret their subsequent wartime experiences and retain their faith in final Union victory. For example, soldiers who thought an immanent God was leading them in a holy war against the Confederacy were convinced that certain key Union victories at decisive moments of the war—such as the fall of Atlanta and rout of Jubal Early's army on the eve of the 1864 presidential election—were clear evidence that an inscrutable God was ultimately superintending events in their favor. Billy Yanks who believed the protracted civil war was a national judgment on the United States, meanwhile, were encouraged by the thought that as soon as the nation sincerely repented and atoned for its sins, a merciful God would lift the dreadful wartime judgment. Even those who could not discern why a good God would permit such a traumatic national tragedy to take place could ultimately take comfort in the belief that an inscrutable God must providentially be using the conflict to advance some higher purpose which could only be effected through these means.

Religious soldiers actually employed both religious and secular arguments to justify their wartime participation, and the latter arguments often mirrored those advanced by their secular comrades. Three nonreligious rationales both groups cited were duty to one's country and family, the just war doctrine, and, to a lesser extent, the abolition of slavery. Although these justifications were not always overtly religious, the Christian soldiers who employed them thought they were perfectly compatible with their Reformed Protestant worldview. Not surprisingly, the more pious Billy Yanks also invoked uniquely religious justifications for waging war on their Southern neighbors: the North was engaged in a holy crusade against the South, and the war was a divine test of the religious soldier's faithfulness or the severe chastening of an almost-chosen people.

The soldier's faith provided him with justifications for embracing the wartime violence and helped sustain his commitment to the cause for which it was being employed. But his beliefs could also serve as a moral restraint, checking the worst excesses of his wartime behavior. For example, when meting out their retribution on the South, even the religious soldiers who embraced the harsh biblical model of Israel's collective punishment against the land of the Canaanites generally reserved their harshest judgment for the spiritual leaders of the Confederacy and the enemy guerrillas most guilty of violating the just war code. Perhaps this was because the Christian soldier's worldview also informed him that he would someday be judged by the same measure he used to judge others.

Protestant soldiers' beliefs and attitudes generally seem to confirm Lewis O. Saum's thesis that the religious values of common nineteenth-century Americans more closely resembled those of their more Calvinistic Puritan ancestors than their modern American descendants. Most Christian soldiers believed they were morally accountable to a sovereign creator God whose omnipotence and omniscience ensured the proper unfolding of justice, in either this life or the next. Above all, they retained faith in an immanent God who was still there, providentially superintending the destinies of men and nations, hearing their prayers, and protecting them in battle. Soldiers' letters generally included far more references to the divine judge of the Old Testament than to the compassionate Savior of the gospels.

Northern Protestant soldiers also had a much more pessimistic outlook on life than their more progressive leaders: it taught them to expect the worst and then rejoice when events turned out better than expected. Hence the common religious soldier probably empathized more with Hawthorne and Melville's pessimistic view of human nature and fatalistic approach to the future than Emerson's optimistic vision of man's virtues and unlimited potential for future progress. Finally, most soldiers shared their Puritan ancestors' belief that the Scriptures represented the "living word of God" and constantly turned to them for spiritual comfort, advice, and assurance about the ultimate meaning of life and death.

So did the religious soldier's faith ultimately make him a better soldier? In *For Cause and Comrades,* James McPherson thought so. He claimed religion made Civil War soldiers brave—by dispelling their natural fear of death—and helped them fulfill their terms of service by improving their capacity to withstand combat stress. The author's research seems to confirm these conclusions. Regardless of whether they subscribed to an Arminian or Calvinistic concept of salvation, religious soldiers generally placed their wartime fate in God's hands, did their duty, and hoped for the best. Some were not certain whether God would shield them on the battlefield. But they all knew life on earth was at best fleeting and that an infinitely more satisfying eternal existence awaited those who faithfully fulfilled their obligations to God and country. The soldier's faith also helped sustain his morale by convincing him that his cause was just, comforting him when he felt traumatized by the wartime violence, and assuring him that the faithful warrior who fell in the War for the Union would surely be rewarded a place in heaven.[3]

Examining Northern Protestants' theological motives for fighting improves our understanding of how men use religion to justify and sustain their military service. For example, one important religious motive Christian soldiers cited for fighting was that they felt it was their duty to defend their family and country. Such loyalties had originated in earlier religious societies, where young men were taught to respect and uphold their family clans, religious traditions, and larger tribe. These religious and political allegiances had then later been transferred to more advanced city-states, kingdoms, and empires. Although the early church had completely rejected this blending of church and state loyalties, in mid-nineteenth-century America, a popular revivalist faith and nascent nationalism had combined to create an aggressive new civil religion. Grateful for their national government's disestablishment of the colonial churches, the country's new evangelical churches rewarded their host by encouraging their congregations to extend their traditionally local religious loyalties to the nation as well. This increasing church-state cooperation— something the Puritan and Congregational churches had been striving to recreate since the colonial period—was vigorously promoted by both sections' churches and governments throughout the 1850s. So when the war finally came, both governments had little difficulty securing the support of their section's largest evangelical churches. Given their society's traditional commitments to religion, family, and liberty, and leaders' exhortations to defend the nation that upheld these sacred institutions and freedoms, it often proved extraordinarily difficult for men of conscience to resist the Union's call to arms.

After Northern Christians heeded their society's call to defend America's evangelical republican institutions, they immediately began to construct, with the clergy's enthusiastic assistance, additional religious rationales to justify the profound costs associated with the war—most of which would be borne by the common soldiers and their families. These religious justifications, all carefully tied to the soldier's worldview, helped soldiers cope with the war's consequences: their families' personal sacrifices and deprivations, the enormous carnage and destruction, the loss of friends and comrades, disillusioning military reverses, and other senseless tragedies. By reminding Northern religious soldiers of the "higher purposes" for which they were fighting and assuring them that God was on *their side,* these spiritual rationales helped strengthen soldiers' confidence in the righteousness of their cause and the inevitability of final Union victory.

Since most Northern churches simply endorsed their side's cause and helped mobilize the Union armies, it would seem that just like the Southern churches, they may have sometimes neglected their prophetic and evangelical ministries in Northern society. But could Lincoln have won the war and destroyed slavery without the Northern churches' sanctification of the Union war effort and general support for most of Lincoln's war policies? If Northern victory was inevitable, yes, but many historians suspect it was not—that there were several pivotal moments during the war when the South could possibly have achieved the military stalemate that would have secured its independence. If so, then these Northern Reformed churches' role in the war was probably akin to that of the abolitionists. They may have helped provoke and sustain a civil war that killed more than

620,000 Americans, but their uncompromising commitment to the Northern cause also helped win it. Indeed, the Northern clergy deserve much of the credit for defeating the Confederacy and ending slavery. Most churches did an exemplary job encouraging their finest sons to march off to war in 1861. They augmented the administration's unofficial propaganda machine, assisted with the mobilization of Union troops, and helped sustain Northern morale during some of the darkest days of the war. Finally, when the Union cause seemed to be foundering in 1862, they joined the abolitionists in vigorously pressing Lincoln to embrace emancipation and later became some of the new freedmen's strongest advocates.

In the end, however, it was the common Christian soldiers who bore the brunt of the wartime punishment. Like sacrificial lambs, they willingly laid down their lives for the sins of their country and churches. But then who was better suited to make such a sacrifice than the sincere believer, who had already been called upon to lay his life down for Christ and for whom death had lost its sting?

Epilogue

Tocqueville's ecclesiastical politicians simply decided that institutional maintenance had to take precedence over prophetic moral leadership. Intoxicated by their success among unchurched masses in post Revolutionary America, the clergy found the cost of defying popular feeling toward blacks and their enslavement too high a price to pay.

C. C. Goen, *Broken Nation, Broken Churches*

But Jesus perceived their wickedness, and said, Why tempt ye me, *ye* hypocrites? Shew me the tribute money. And they brought unto him a penny. And he saith unto them, Whose *is* this image and superscription? They say unto him, Caesar's. Then saith he unto them, Render therefore unto Caesar the things which are Caesar's; and unto God the things that are God's.

Matthew 22:18–21

AS THIS STUDY demonstrates, the American Civil War makes a fascinating case study for those interested in further exploring the relationship between religion and violence. Before the nation was divided by the sectional conflict over slavery, its churches were. More than any other American institution, it was the churches and clergymen who helped transform a political firestorm over the expansion of slavery into a sectional holy war. And when the war finally came, both sides' largest churches helped spiritually sanctify their respective causes and demonize the enemy. Without this decisive religious support, neither side could have enlisted so many citizen-soldiers or sustained their war efforts as long as they did. So if God had indeed ordained this war, America's largest churches had helped advance his purposes.

Clearly ecclesiastical leaders and organizations can play a vital role in spiritually justifying and supporting such violence or morally condemning and rejecting it. For example, the events leading up to the Civil War offer two important lessons. First, that the absence or breakdown of mediating religious institutions or hierarchies in a country can lead to serious conflict between competing religious groups. Mark Noll has discussed the importance of such mediating bodies in diverse religious societies and how the absence of such institutions in the mid-nineteenth-century United States helped precipitate the Civil War. According to Noll, in a rapidly evolving society that embraced a literal, commonsense reading of the Scriptures, it was vitally important to have mediating theological institutions that could help build broad theological consensus across different religious communities concerning the ways the Scriptures should be read and interpreted. This was because when there were no longer any "national" American churches whose legitimacy was recognized by the wider society, rival regional churches were more likely to develop different theological interpretations, which exponentially increased the likelihood of future sectional conflict.[1]

The second lesson is that the American experience from the Revolution to the Civil War seems to confirm the value of disestablishing state churches and strictly separating religious and political institutions. Religious individuals and ideas will always be involved in politics, but politicians and clergymen need to direct their attentions to their own distinct ministries. In the history of the early Republic, disestablishment benefited both the government and the church enormously. Freeing America's republican government and church from the corrupting influence of politicized religion helped set the stage for the phenomenal expansion of the nation's new evangelical churches. Maintaining strict separation between the church and state makes it less likely that the more dominant institution will illegitimately intrude in matters not under its jurisdiction and thus helps ensure that both institutions will focus on their own unique and vital ministries. The early history of the United States also demonstrates the dangers of ignoring such ecclesiastical-political distinctions. As will be discussed shortly, when the nation's largest antebellum churches lost sight of their primary spiritual role and embraced a political role they were never intended to play, they failed in both respects.[2]

Given the fact that most of the religious soldiers identified in this study had little difficulty reconciling the war with their religious beliefs and many used their churches' teachings to justify and sustain their military activities, the question naturally arises as to whether there was a casual relationship between these soldiers' revivalist faith and the resulting war. The remainder of this chapter will offer some tentative conclusions regarding this complex question of causality.

While the religious soldiers identified in this study only represented a minority of the soldiers who served in the Union armies, they accurately reflect their Protestant society's attitudes toward war. We already know about evangelical Protestants' role in the events leading up to the war and in the subsequent fighting, but this study suggests evangelical revivalism and a biblicist approach to the Scriptures played key roles in the initial mobilization of troops and the common soldiers' subsequent justification of their military duties. Did evangelical fervor help ignite the fires of the Civil War? If so, what does this tell us about the relationship between religious revivalism, or what modern Americans pejoratively refer to as "religious fundamentalism," and the violence of war?

Revivalist religious impulses undoubtedly played a decisive role in the early-nineteenth-century reform movements such as abolitionism and thus either directly or indirectly contributed to the sectional breakdown. The antebellum period was marked by a series of almost continuous religious revivals that began with the Great Awakening in the 1820s and culminated in the "Businessman's Revival" of 1858. One of the consequences of this extensive revivalism was that it heightened many Americans' consciousness of good and evil in Northern society. It was this popular quest for moral righteousness, in both the individual's life and his larger society, that birthed many of the early nineteenth century's most successful reform movements, from the crusades against liquor and prostitution to the increasingly radical abolition movement—where New England preachers dominated the early abolitionist societies' membership rolls. Many of these movements undoubtedly improved the moral character of the United States by energetically attacking nineteenth-century institutions and attitudes that exploited or ignored the weakest and most vulnerable segments of the population. But the same religious currents that awakened Northern Christians to corporate evils such as slavery also reminded them that such national sins had to be publicly confessed and mercilessly rooted out lest God punish the entire country for tolerating the evil. It was this conviction, and the actions it inspired, that inadvertently helped stoke the flames of sectional discord and set the country on the path to war.

Mid-nineteenth-century Northern Protestantism still contained many vestiges of the old Puritan worldview that emphasized the communal consequences of individual sin. Just like their Puritan ancestors, most antebellum Protestants believed sins within the church needed to be immediately addressed. Otherwise the bad example of the few would corrupt the rest of the body and subject the larger community to God's judgment. Believers were thus constantly encouraged to scrutinize their lives, and those of their family and neighbors, for any trace of sin that might jeopardize their faith or retard the spiritual progress of their wider community. The Scriptures clearly delineated the course of action to be followed when such sins were discovered. Believers were to confess their sins, publicly turn away from them, and restore their proper relationship to God and their neighbors. Designed to humble the prideful sinner, this process of atonement and restoration was an anathema to the stubborn sinner, who did not feel convicted of the error of his ways. Some would rather die in their sins than submit to such a humiliating regime, or the God behind it.

Perhaps this explains why so many believers focused their energies on identifying and rooting out the "specks" of sin in their neighbors' lives. It was too painful to remove the planks from their own. A combination of motives, however, probably inspired would-be Yankee saints to obsess over the sins of their Southern neighbors: they had a genuine heart for saving the spiritually "lost," wished to avoid confronting their own personal sins, genuinely feared that evils practiced elsewhere might someday encroach their communities, or they sincerely thought their toleration of such sin would usher in national judgment. More than anything else, however, it was the extremist rhetoric and tactics of the religious abolitionists that gradually alienated the sections and transformed what had been a heated political dispute into an intense moral drama where there could no longer be any sectional political compromises over slavery—only a succession of crises that finally culminated in civil war.

Once hostilities officially commenced, the uncompromising Reformed Protestant worldview made it relatively easy for Northern clergymen to convince their followers that Southern Christians who refused to repent of their sins of slavery and rebellion were "wicked" backsliders or "heathen" who deserved to be punished. Given evangelicals' belief in a literal, commonsense interpretation of the Bible, evangelical clergy were also able to build a firm and independently verifiable moral case for waging a holy war against the South. Scriptural precedents, such as Joshua's invasion of the Promised Land to punish the wicked Canaanites, seemed to justify religious soldiers' invasion of the South and wartime role as instruments of God's judgment. Having received their spiritual leaders' assurances that they had the proper moral grounds and biblical authority to wage war against the South, most young religious soldiers had little trouble justifying the wartime killing. Few apparently shared the more mature and forgiving faith expressed in Lincoln's second inaugural address, which recognized God would someday judge believers with the same measure they used to judge others and that his judgments and purposes did not always mirror theirs.

The ideas and behavior inspired by the Second Great Awakening were important factors in the events leading up to the Civil War, and there are numerous other historical examples that seem to support a possible connection between religious revivalism and war. In *Christians in the American Revolution,* Mark Noll observed that in the wake of the First Great Awakening, Americans increasingly began to view their political disagreements in black-and-white religious terms and portray them as life-and-death struggles with eternal consequences. When colonial political contests between the Crown and colonial assemblies were transformed into epic contests between good and evil, and compromise was demonized as a sinful betrayal of principle, the American Revolution became virtually inevitable. As Noll concluded, perhaps this explains why two of America's most deadly wars were fought only a few decades after its greatest religious awakenings.[3] Nor has this cycle of religious enthusiasm and war been restricted to the United States. Countless other examples come to mind: the major religious revivals that swept eleventh-century Europe on the eve of the Crusades, the wars of religion sparked by the Protestant Reformation that culminated in the horrific Thirty Years' War, the great Arab conquest unleashed by Muhammad's revelations, the Sufi brotherhood's role in the phenomenal expansion of the Ottoman Empire, and the Wahhabi conquest of Arabia.

In light of all this damning evidence, are we to conclude that nineteenth-century evangelical Protestants' religious enthusiasm and "commonsense" approach to scriptural exegesis played a more important role in causing the American Civil War than scholars have heretofore recognized—and that similar revivalist movements are probably responsible for many other wars throughout world history? Revivalism and fundamentalist believers do, after all, make convenient scapegoats in today's more secular, post-Judeo-Christian societies. This answer, however, probably oversimplifies the problem because it makes at least two assumptions about revivalism that are not true: first, that such religious movements are inherently political in nature, and second, that the state and church exercise little or no control over them. The popular enthusiasm engendered by revivalism can undoubtedly be harnessed with political vengeance—witness, for example, the role of Jerry Falwell's Moral Majority and Pat Robertson's Christian Coalition in the conservative revolution of the 1980s—but such need not be the case, as the fundamentalist retreat from politics after the Scopes trial and modern mainline Protestant churches' reluctance to enter political battles over abortion demonstrate.

Although revivalist movements have historically influenced governments and been exploited by them for political purposes, they have traditionally been ignited by local religious leaders at the popular grass-roots level—not carefully orchestrated government programs or policies—and have usually been focused on God's rights to the believer's time, talents, and worship, not the citizen's rights to legal, political, and economic equality. According to the revivalists, man's best hope for salvation lies not in the ballot box but in a return to a more commonsense reading of the Scriptures, genuine imitation of the life of Christ, and complete rejection of manmade religious idols and traditions. Given these religious movements' grass-roots spiritual origins, spontaneity, fierce independence, resiliency, and widespread pervasiveness, perhaps they should be viewed more as naturally occurring phenomena, such as fire and water—which can be harnessed and channeled for good or evil—rather than as manmade political movements. After all, the same revivalist impulses that governments have historically manipulated to mobilize their people for war can also inspire individuals to repent of their sins, lead new social reform movements, construct new schools and hospitals in underdeveloped countries, or contribute their time and money to humanitarian causes. So if fundamentalist revivalism has historically been used to sanctify the use of violence, perhaps the real problem is not so much revivalism itself as the church and state's propensity to use this powerful religious tool to advance their own institutional goals at the expense of true religion. The temptation to intermingle the affairs of church and state probably stems from the traditional, and fairly universal, competition between these two important institutions.

An important chapter in the history of almost every modern Western nation has been the historic struggle between church and the state as both seek to secure the institutional power and influence they need to fulfill their respective societal functions. Although the church often plays an important role in the formative years of many nations, over time sovereign states generally begin to encroach upon the traditional jurisdiction of the church as they advance their own political and economic interests. This expansion of power and authority nearly always comes at the expense of the church, which increasingly loses more and more of its former power and influence in society. The clergy fiercely resist their growing marginalization, but barring some unexpected national crisis that weakens the central government, the church nearly always loses this contest and is either suppressed or increasingly subordinated to the state. For example, in the United States, from 1776 on, the powers of the highly influential Congregational and Anglican churches were gradually curbed by new state and federal constitutions that banned compulsory religious attendance, taxes, and religious tests for office. By the turn of the century both churches had been officially disestablished and no longer enjoyed their former political influence.

Most governments try to promote religious movements that advance their interests and suppress those that conflict with their secular agenda. In the case of the antebellum

United States, the disestablishment of the old colonial churches advanced the governments' interests in numerous ways: They ended the New England churches' irritating political interference in national politics, promoted the revolutionary principle of freedom of conscience, and set precedents discouraging the formation of any future government church. By facilitating the growth of more democratic and popular evangelical sects in the West, disestablishment accomplished the government's goal of uniting the country's disparate and highly diverse frontier communities under a common American umbrella of Protestant evangelical culture and republican political institutions. Grateful for the tremendous expansion their churches experienced under the government's new disestablishment policy, the country's evangelical churches taught western settlers to cherish and defend the republic that guaranteed their Christian freedoms. Antebellum Southern states, on the other hand, initially had to suppress the "political" preaching of their new Methodist and Baptist sects because it was directed against slavery and the smoking, drinking, and gambling habits of the planter elite. After these churches were properly integrated into Southern society, however, and Southern evangelicals learned that Yankee abolitionism—not Southern slavery—was the real enemy, the Southern governments strongly encouraged such "political" expression. These Northern and Southern ecclesiastical examples from the antebellum era all demonstrate that the modern state can, to a certain degree, restrict, redirect, or promote religious expression and revivalism in ways that help advance its political agenda.

Unless their country is badly divided along religious lines, nations also generally find it useful to promote religious expression and revivalism during times of crisis or war, when believers and even fence-sitters are often predisposed to turn to God. There are many examples of nations—even completely secular ones—invoking and promoting national "holy wars" against their enemies. Although its use of revivalism for martial purposes may have been more obvious during the American Revolution and Civil War, the United States also turned to religion in a very public way during the First and Second World Wars. During such times of crisis, there has usually been a discernible relaxation of the normally strict wall of separation between church and state, as government officials attend public religious services together and invoke traditional religious themes to justify their cause and demonize the enemy. The state also uses religious revivalism to sustain the morale of its troops and, increasingly in modern democracies, the popular support of its civilian population back home. Indeed, it is often in the state's interest to seek out religious recruits and provide them with an effective chaplaincy, for the devout religious warrior who believes God is on his side is less likely to question the morality of his cause, entertain doubts about the certainty of final victory, or be afraid of losing his life in battle. In short, he makes the ideal state soldier. So during times of war and national crisis, the state often pragmatically loosens its control over the church and promotes a more public expression of faith to justify its cause and inspire greater sacrifices on the part of its people.

Although when most people hear the term "holy war" they usually immediately think of the historic religious wars waged by the older monotheistic faiths of Judaism, Christianity, and Islam, it should be remembered that the totalitarian states of the twentieth century, driven by their more secular, nationalist worldviews caused far more suffering and death than their monotheistic predecessors. The Christian crusader and Muslim holy warrior may have killed their thousands in the name of God or Allah, but armed with the more sophisticated tools of the modern industrial state, the Soviet NKVD and the Nazi SS exterminated millions in the name of their new "religious" orders. So it would seem that secular nationalist or internationalist ideologies can be just as effective as the older monotheistic faiths when it comes to inspiring followers, commanding their unconditional obedience and encouraging them to fight and die for causes higher than themselves. While such regimes have historically used religion to advance their own secular agendas—even going so far as to create their own "national churches" to bolster their spiritual legitimacy in the eyes of the people—ultimately states cannot effectively promote or channel genuine religious enthusiasm without the active cooperation of popularly recognized religious authorities. Indeed, historically, revivalist movements have only fueled aggression in countries where popular religious leaders deliberately politicized their faiths to promote holy wars against their state's enemies.

This appears to have been what happened between 1840 and 1860, when the churches of the North and South became unprecedentedly politicized as they sought to expand their popular influence in the United States. For example, until they embraced the economic and social values of the cotton kingdom, the Southern churches never really enjoyed much public or political influence in the South. In the colonial period, the Anglican churches in the South never achieved the kind of political influence their established counterparts enjoyed in the North. Later, the more popular Baptist and Methodist evangelical sects sought to energize the Southern masses, but their ministries never prospered until they abandoned their principled stands against the planters' excessive materialism and abuse of their slaves. Desperate to expand their struggling ministries in the South, Southern evangelicals ultimately compromised their antislavery convictions and embraced the values of the Southern elite. On probation, and still regarded with suspicion by the ruling planter class, Southern evangelicals were encouraged to focus exclusively on "spiritual" issues such as individual salvation and steer clear of societal or "political" problems such as slavery.

Strident Northern abolitionist attacks on the South's peculiar institution in the 1830s, however, finally rescued the Southern churches from their political exile. As the abolitionist campaign grew increasingly militant, the planter elite dropped their previous opposition to "political preaching" and began encouraging Southern evangelicals to publicly defend their section's labor system. The churches happily complied, and for the next three decades, grateful Southern clergymen demonstrated their newfound loyalty to the cotton kingdom by waging a rhetorical holy war in defense of slavery.

If moral compromise with slavery and integration into the cotton kingdom were the keys to Southern evangelicals obtaining a more public role in their society, Northern evangelicals could thank their government's disestablishment policy for providing them with new national constituencies. Thanks to the disastrous witchcraft episode in Salem and popular new ideas flowing out of the Enlightenment, the established churches of New England lost most of the political influence they enjoyed in the colonial era. Given the post–Revolutionary War generation's growing disenchantment with the undemocratic theology and hierarchical organization of New England's established churches, some Americans suspected the new republic's disestablishment policy would finally mark the end of the Northern clergy's political influence. But instead of killing off the last vestiges of ecclesiastical influence in the North, disestablishment turned out to be the Northern clergy's savior.

Finally freed from the persecution of the established colonial churches, the more popular, evangelical wings of the Baptist, Methodist, and Presbyterian churches enjoyed unprecedented growth in the decades between the Revolution and the Civil War. Evangelical churches spread like wildfire along the ever-receding western frontier as millions of new believers were ushered into these more democratic churches. But new temptations accompanied all this worldly success. As evangelical revivalism extended its influence throughout Northern society, this popular influence soon translated into political influence. The evangelicals' rapidly expanding ministries, aggressive networking with other denominations, and creation of a benevolent empire of dozens of interdenominational religious aid societies gave them nationwide political constituencies and greater influence over the nation's political life. As the country became increasingly divided over the slavery question, Northern evangelicals seized their opportunity to become more involved in national politics. Many increasingly supported their government's evolving position on slavery from the pulpit.

The Northern churches, however, had to pay a high price for their newfound popularity and political power. Just like their counterparts in the South, Northern evangelicals soon discovered that if they wished to preserve their successful new ministries and obtain further political influence, they would have to sacrifice their prophetic role of critiquing American society. In short, the Northern churches would have to forget about their earlier moral reservations concerning slavery and leave this "political" problem in the hands of the federal government. Until passage of Stephen Douglas's Kansas-Nebraska Act in 1854, this usually meant condemning abolitionist extremism and supporting the government's policy of appeasing the Southern slave power for the sake of national political unity and continued prosperity. If some Northern churches, like the New School Presbyterians, were reluctant to compromise their strong antislavery stands, the dramatic sectional divisions of the Methodist and Baptist churches in the mid-1840s were a clear warning of the consequences that awaited churches that did not embrace the government's official position on slavery. Churches that charted their own moral course on the slavery question risked losing their large congregations and political influence and further dividing their churches and country. In the end most Northern churches decided the costs of publicly opposing slavery were simply too high. Thus by the late 1840s, many clergymen had sacrificed their religious responsibility to identify and battle national sin for the secondary goals of preserving their large congregations and growing political influence in the Union. Stepping into the moral vacuum left by the their government's and churches' failure to confront the evils of slavery, for a time Northern abolitionists carried on the fight alone, often with utter disregard for the laws and authority of their compromised institutions.[4]

Northern churches finally awakened to the dangers of the Southern "slave power conspiracy" after passage of the Kansas-Nebraska Act. They then partially redeemed themselves by vehemently condemning the act and enthusiastically participating in the grass-roots organization of the new Republican Party. But even this eleventh-hour spiritual epiphany concerning slavery was somewhat suspect as it neatly coincided with Northern Whigs' and Democrats' political reappraisal of the slavery question, leaving one to question whether this was a genuine change of heart or simply a shrewd political reassessment of the North's shifting attitudes toward slavery. In any event, after the attack on Fort Sumter, most Northern clergymen enthusiastically enlisted their churches in the Northern war effort, and many became unapologetic propagandists for the Lincoln administration, fully persuaded that God was on their side.[5]

As many of the Northern clergy allowed their churches to become increasingly politicized, however, their political activities began to undermine their ministries' effectiveness and integrity. Every sermon preached in support of the war or some new administration policy was precious time lost for preaching the gospel and building up the saints. Churches that made a regular practice of keeping their congregations informed about wartime events may have also inadvertently left their congregation's with the impression that temporal political or military events were somehow just as important as the eternal fruits of repentance and sanctification. Perhaps most troubling of all, though, was the popular idea conveyed by the churches that the causes of the Union and Christ were the same, and its implicit corollary, that Lincoln's Republican administration was the true Christian government. These high-minded but spiritually presumptuous sentiments could often prove confusing, if not downright disillusioning, to new believers and would-be converts. After all, if an immanent God was truly leading the Northern armies into battle, then why was the South winning so many decisive victories in the East and the North suffering such heavy casualties? And if Lincoln's Republican government was the true Christian republic, why was his administration plagued with so much rebellion, warfare, political dissension, and scandal? Could the clergy possibly be wrong about God's purposes in the war and the moral character of their government? And if so, how could religious soldiers trust their pastors' counsel concerning other, even weightier spiritual matters?

As Harry Stout recently noted in *Upon the Altar of the Nation,* with the possible exception of the abolitionist crusade, "for all intents and purposes, most Northern Protestant pulpits and publications espoused Republican views" during the Civil War.[6] Frequently following the lead of the Lincoln government, the North's largest Reformed Protestant churches dutifully supported many of the administration's wartime policies from the pulpit. In return for the churches' wartime support and tactful silence concerning the administration's malfeasance, numerous violations of civil liberties, and other constitutionally questionable acts, a grateful administration temporarily lowered the high wall separating church and state during the war. The Lincoln administration also symbolically honored Northern churches' political influence by declaring four official days of fasting and prayer, making the religious celebration of Thanksgiving a national holiday, inscribing "In God We Trust" on the nation's coins, and lending token support to a national Protestant campaign to amend the preamble of the U.S. Constitution so that the American people would acknowledge "Almighty God as the source of all authority." Shortly before his death, Lincoln also implicitly acknowledged the Protestant clergy's vital wartime cooperation by inviting one of the North's most preeminent wartime preachers, Henry Ward Beecher, to deliver the main address at the official Fort Sumter flag-raising ceremony in April 1865.

Most of the Northern clergy seemed content with these token government acts reaffirming the importance of the country's historic Christian faith, and the ecclesiastical alliance with the state ultimately survived Lincoln's assassination. As for the president himself, the Northern clergy remained faithful to their wartime ally even beyond the grave. Despite having entertained earlier doubts about his salvation, they decided to honor his memory by transforming the former skeptic into a religious martyr. Indeed, given most of their churches' strong, historical commitment to his administration's policies, regardless of the hypocrisy, perhaps the Northern clergy felt duty-bound to recast their wartime ally as a Christian after his assassination. With their enthusiastic support, Lincoln's future sainthood in America's civil religion was guaranteed.

In the decades following the war, however, the church would have reason to regret its inappropriate political affair with the state. During Reconstruction, Northern churches generally supported the agenda of the Republican Party. Most Northern clergymen supported the party's harsh postwar policies in the South, ignored the widespread scandals and corruption of the Grant administration, and then—perhaps at the point of their spiritual nadir—shamefully supported the Compromise of 1877, abandoning blacks to their fate in the postwar South. When the Republican administrations and churches of the Gilded Age often later turned a blind eye to the robber barons' corruption of the country's political and economic institutions and exploitation of the American worker, it seemed as though only Northern journalists and Democrats were serving as the conscience of the nation. The illegitimate church-state alliance may have proven militarily expedient for the Lincoln administration and useful for advancing the Republicans' postwar political agenda, but its long-term spiritual costs were inestimable. In the end, many Northern churches' attempt to serve two masters, or effectively promote both a political and religious agenda, had undermined their own spiritual mission to save the lost and seek social justice for the poor and dispossessed.

The end of the Civil War arguably marked the high tide of Protestant evangelical political power in the United States, but the churches paid a high price for their political influence. To obtain this political power in the decades leading up to the war, many evangelical churches had abandoned their traditional role as the moral conscience of the nation and increasingly subordinated religion to politics. Once embarked upon, this divergent political path soon opened them up to further compromises. To avoid the temporal consequences of confronting the sin of slavery, these Northern evangelicals soon discovered they would not only have to ignore their Southern neighbors' sins but tacitly approve of and abet them by vehemently denouncing abolitionism, defending slave owners' rights, and urging their congregations to comply with the new Fugitive Slave Act. Southern churches, meanwhile, seemed more interested in waging a rhetorical war in defense of slavery than spreading the gospel to its poorest citizens and slaves. A growing prewar belief that some slave owners were not treating their slaves properly—even by local slave code standards—would not even be addressed by the Confederate clergy until military reverses convinced them of the need to repent of this secret sin. One can only speculate as to what might have happened if all the major national churches had joined the abolitionists in taking a unified stand against chattel slavery in the 1830s, but the nation's clergy had chosen a different path for the nation, a spiraling, downward trail of sectional scheming and conflict that would ultimately lead to war.

So was the common soldiers' revivalist faith responsible for the tragic violence unleashed by the American Civil War? This is the principal and perhaps most problematic question raised by this study. Although it would probably take a great deal of additional research to make a hard-and-fast conclusion regarding the matter, many of the themes we have already treated in this book suggest that it was the moral failure of the nation's largest Reformed Protestant churches, or at least many of their clergymen, not the common soldier's revivalist faith that set the stage for a bloody Civil War.[7] As evangelical churches became increasingly obsessed with expanding and preserving their growing institutional power in the early nineteenth century, many clergymen had allowed their ministries to become too politicized—with disastrous consequences. The nation's churches had then erred grievously when most initially chose to downplay or ignore the nation's festering sore of slavery. By the time some churches finally felt compelled to address this rapidly metastasizing cancer in the mid-1840s, it was too late. Chattel slavery was too deeply rooted in Southern society and the entire country was profiting from it. The resulting national church divisions set important precedents for the political divisions that followed in 1860–61.

A number of other historians have also discussed the clergy's role in the events leading up to the war. After carefully examining antebellum and wartime sermons from both sections, David Chesebrough concluded that the evangelical clergy were convinced that God was on their side, that he had "ordained" a war between the sections, and that he would spiritually sanctify the resulting violence. It was thus the clergy, more than anyone else, who helped transform a political conflict over slavery into a holy war.[8]

Other scholars have emphasized the growing politicization of the churches as an important factor contributing to the sectional breakdown. Sydney E. Ahlstrom described how the United States' antebellum preachers increasingly poisoned sectional relations from their pulpits. James Wood Jr., Richard Beringer, Herman Hattaway, and Archer Jones thought the churches' unprecedented politicization in the last two decades before the war probably had something to do with a civil war fought primarily "between the churches of the North and those of the South." C. C. Goen argued that the Northern clergy's obsession with institutional maintenance, both religious and political, broke the nation's churches and helped set the stage for the subsequent breakdown of the U.S. government. George Fredrickson has also recently emphasized the Northern clergy's increasing politicization and "quasi-theocratic ambitions" in the Civil War era. It does seem ironic that when the nation's clergy finally did energetically confront the slavery issue in the late 1850s, they were mainly exercising a political role in their societies by embracing and promoting their respective government's political stands on slavery. This eleventh-hour intervention, however, probably only exacerbated matters, as churches on both sides proceeded to demonize the opposing section and transform a political contest over slavery into an epic struggle between good and evil. By increasingly associating the political goals of their sectional rival with those of the devil, the clergy made a civil war over slavery virtually inevitable.[9]

So it was the increasing politicization of the North's antebellum churches rather than the soldiers' revivalist faith that helped provoke the conflict. But it is difficult to imagine how the North could have fought and won the war without the support of these more politicized churches. With the advent of war, many clergymen completely subordinated their ministries to each section's war effort. Churches served as major recruiting centers for both sides' armies, collected and delivered tons of food and clothing for the troops, helped provide medical care for the wounded, and became unofficial propaganda arms of their governments. With many churches hopelessly politicized, the clergy became even more convinced of the righteousness of their cause after Lincoln issued his Emancipation Proclamation in 1863. With decisive victory finally in sight, the Reformed Protestant churches refused to abide any dissent. "Disloyal" Democratic preachers who failed to support, or publicly opposed, the Republican politicization of the North's largest Reformed Protestant churches were officially censored, withdrawn from duty, or ultimately expelled by church governing bodies to ensure their denominations remained fully committed to the war effort. The country would later pay a steep price for this politicization of religion, however, when a compromised Northern church frequently failed to hold its Republican and big business allies accountable for their corruption and a compromised Southern church opened up its doors to the Klan. In the end, by demonstrating they were often more intent on advancing sectional political agendas than fulfilling their prophetic and evangelical roles in society, some clergymen had betrayed their primary religious mission and revealed they were more interested in securing the favor of this world than the kingdom of heaven.

Appendix

Prayers of the Christian Soldier

The following printed prayers were found enclosed in a letter that Pvt. John G. Jones of the Twenty-third Wisconsin Volunteers sent to his parents on May 29, 1863.

1. On the Eve of Battle

I would humbly and confidently commit myself to thy holy keeping in the prospect of coming battle. May thoughts suitable to so solemn an occasion take possession of my mind, and in the fear of the Lord may I go forward. Believing that the cause in which I am engaged is just and righteous, and in defense of the government which thou has graciously given to my country. I would desire to feel the courage and determination of a loyal soldier, and to perform my duty faithfully. Thou are my almighty shield, and canst ward off danger in the midst of the conflict. If it be thy holy will, may my life be preserved while I remain steadfast to my post, and let all cowardly fear be banished from my heart. May I feel safe under the providence, and may I trust thee for life or for death. Grant that my soul may be redeemed by the blood of Christ, and should it be thy purpose that I should fall, may the sting of death which is sin, be taken away. May the shield of thy protection be placed before my comrades, and may they all cast themselves upon thy mercy. O Lord, grant that victory may rest on our banners, and discomfit our enemies who are in rebellion against lawful authority. May God pardon their sins and save their souls, and may they return to their allegiance. To thee, O Lord, I now commit my soul and body, and may I not forget thee amidst the roar of battle. This I earnestly seek for Christ's sake; and to the Father, Son and Holy Ghost shall be all the praise. Amen.

2. A Prayer When Sick and Wounded

O most righteous God, thou hast seen fit to lay me aside from active duty, and to appoint for me pain and suffering. May I patiently submit to thy holy will and be kept from murmuring and repining. Thou canst heal the maladies of the body, and make the remedies employed efficacious. If it be to thy glory may I be restored to health, and may I yet live to serve my God and my country. Grant too, that I may be prepared for all that may happen, so that whether I live, I may live to the Lord, or whether I die, I may die to the Lord, and living or dying still be his. This I ask for the Savior's sake. Amen.

Notes

Introduction

1. Will to Kitty Crandall, Nov. 3, 1864, Crandall Family Correspondence, Wisconsin Historical Society, Madison (hereafter cited as Crandall Family Correspondence). Rather than overwhelm readers with repeated uses of "[*sic*]," I have tried to replicate as accurately as possible the exact spelling, spacing, and punctuation of these soldiers' letters, except for when this seriously impeded the readability or meaning of the excerpt. For example, in a few cases, I silently corrected run-on sentences. Also, words that were underlined in the originals have been italicized here.

2. Newman Hall, *Come to Jesus: No. 110,* Evangelical Tract Society, Petersburg, Va., 1863[?], Call No. 4683, Rare Book Collection, University of North Carolina, Chapel Hill, Documenting the American South, http://docsouth.unc.edu/imls/hallnewm/hallnewm.html/, 5–6 (accessed Feb. 20, 2008).

3. In this book I have generally used the phrase "Northern church" to represent the greater body of Protestant believers or all the major Reformed Protestant churches in the North. The focus of this study, however, is generally on the dominant nineteenth-century evangelical branches of the Northern Baptist, Methodist, Presbyterian, and Congregational churches.

4. 1 Pet. 4:17 (KJV). All subsequent Bible citations are to the King James Version.

5. James McPherson, "Afterword," in *Religion and the American Civil War,* ed. Randall M. Miller, Harry S. Stout, and Charles Reagan Wilson (New York: Oxford Univ. Press, 1998), 411.

6. Earl J. Hess, *The Union Soldier in Battle: Enduring the Ordeal of Combat* (Lawrence: Univ. Press of Kansas, 1997).

7. Steven E. Woodworth, *While God Is Marching On: The Religious World of Civil War Soldiers* (Lawrence: Univ. Press of Kansas, 2001).

8. The sample base of religious soldiers was compiled from the following primary sources. I examined over 330 collections from the Wisconsin Historical Society, Indiana Historical Society, Emory University's Robert W. Woodruff Library, Abraham Lincoln Presidential Library, and the Sheboygan County Historical Society. Other letters were drawn from published accounts of religious soldiers' letters. Over the course of this research I ultimately identified more than one hundred religious soldiers.

9. Generally, soldiers were only deemed religious if I discovered at least two or more references to religion in their correspondence or diaries, There were, however, a few cases where I found an excellent religious excerpt but could not apply my normal formula due to the incomplete nature of the collection. Since there is always a degree of subjectivity involved in making such determinations, it is possible that I may have erred in concluding that a given soldier was "religious," but throughout the process I sought to be as objective as possible. In the vast majority of the cases, a careful reading of the correspondence will reveal two or more excerpts where the soldier is clearly employing religious themes, imagery, or rhetoric to define, interpret, or justify some wartime experience and thus qualifies as a believer for the purposes of this study.

10. Other scholars also have favored this more comprehensive approach when writing social histories about the Civil War. See Randal C. Jimerson, *The Private Civil War: Popular Thought During the Sectional Conflict* (Baton Rouge: Louisiana State Univ. Press, 1988), 6.

11. Timothy L. Smith, *Revivalism and Social Reform: American Protestantism on the Eve of the Civil War* (New York: Harper & Row, 1957), 17. The 15 percent statistic does not take into account regular churchgoers, the converts from the subsequent 1857–58 "Business Man's Revival" or the United States' three million Roman Catholics. Some readers might initially question this membership statistic as far too conservative, especially given the fact that in today's far more secular age, almost 90 percent of the population claims to be believe in God and more than half claim to belong to some kind of organized church. After all, most scholars consider the nineteenth century "the golden age" of American Protestantism. It must be remembered however that nineteenth-century Americans were far more serious about their religious commitments than modern Americans. In some of the more traditional early-nineteenth-century churches (Congregational), individuals could only become members after "proving" in front of a body of elders or local ministers that they had experienced "saving grace." Needless to say, in some churches, the application process was so rigorous and intimidating that it discouraged all but the most religious and articulate from applying. Finally, just like today, many antebellum Americans who were sincere Christians did not join a church because they could not accept certain church doctrines, were disillusioned by the hypocrisy in the church, or did not believe they were good enough to join one.

12. Gardiner Shattuck Jr., *A Shield and Hiding Place: The Religious Life of the Civil War Armies* (Macon, Ga.: Mercer Univ. Press, 1987), 92. While an exact number is impossible to pin down, the 10–15 percent figure would be a very conservative estimate. For example, if one begins with the 15 percent national membership statistic in 1855 and applies it to a Northern population of 20 million, it yields roughly 3 million potential members. One must then subtract the women (who usually outnumbered the men three to one in the nation's churches), which leaves roughly 750,000 male members.

If one further excludes men who were too old, unhealthy, or otherwise employed, or conservatively subtracts well over half the remaining men, the final figure is roughly 200,000–300,000 men, which would constitute 10–15 percent of the up to 2 million soldiers who eventually served in the Northern armies.

13. The 30 percent figure has been used by Ahlstrom, Smith, and others.

14. Reid Mitchell, "Christian Soldiers? Perfecting the Confederacy," in *Religion and the American Civil War*, ed. Randall M. Miller, Harry S. Stout, and Charles Reagan Wilson (New York: Oxford Univ. Press, 1998), 302–5. If anything, the number of Christian soldiers in the Northern armies actually increased during the war. Here, as Reid Mitchell has noted, it should be remembered that this estimate of 20–25 percent does not include the 100,000 to 200,000 Union soldiers—5–10 percent of those enlisted—who converted during the wartime revivals, the 145,000 Roman Catholic Irish Christians whose faith was generally disregarded as illegitimate by antebellum Protestants, or the 200,000 mainly Christian black soldiers who joined the Union armies.

15. After much soul-searching I finally decided to use the King James Version of the Bible for passages the soldiers cited or alluded to in their letters. For the benefit of my readers, at one point I replaced the more archaic text with a much more readable and easily understood New International Version when it did not compromise the original meaning of the passages. But given my central purpose of trying to accurately recreate the religious soldiers' worldview and theological interpretations, I ultimately decided to provide readers with the same translation the soldiers would have used.

16. Mark A. Noll, "The Bible and Slavery," in *Religion and the American Civil War*, ed. Randall M. Miller, Harry S. Stout, and Charles Reagan Wilson (New York: Oxford Univ. Press, 1998), 46–47.

17. Richard J. Carwardine and Lewis O. Saum also use biblical verses directly in their text. See Carwardine's *Evangelicals and Politics in Antebellum America* (New Haven, Conn.: Yale Univ. Press, 1993) and Saum's *The Popular Mood of Pre–Civil War America* (Westport, Conn.: Greenwood Press, 1980). Nineteenth-century Americans could hardly avoid the literal biblical hermeneutic that dominated their society. Biblical texts and principles were incorporated into childhood textbooks like the McGuffey Readers, inscribed on their public buildings, and routinely discussed at Sabbath day social functions. In the 1840s a coalition of Catholics and Democrats only narrowly defeated a Protestant campaign to make the King James Bible a reading textbook in America's public schools. The idea for including biblical passages at the beginning of each chapter was inspired by their usage in W. E. B. Du Bois's classic book *John Brown: By W. E. Burghardt Du Bois* (Philadelphia: George W. Jacobs, 1909).

1. The Role of Religion in the American Civil War

1. Thomas F. Miller to Ben Newton, May 2, 1862, Thomas F. Miller Papers, Abraham Lincoln Presidential Library, Springfield, Ill. (hereafter cited as Thomas F. Miller Papers); Matt. 26:52.

2. Thomas F. Miller to Ben Newton, May 2, 1862, Thomas F. Miller Papers. Springfield. Statistics on Civil War casualties are derived from James M. McPherson,

Battle Cry of Freedom: The Civil War Era (New York: Oxford Univ. Press, 1988), 854; and other sources.

3. See Randall M. Miller, Harry S. Stout, and Charles Reagan Wilson, eds., *Religion and the American Civil War* (New York: Oxford Univ. Press, 1998). Shortly after I completed my first draft for this book, the prolific Civil War historian Steven E. Woodworth published a comprehensive, first-rate volume on the religious life of the Civil War armies, *While God Is Marching On,* which helped fill a huge gap in the religious historiography of the war. A new generation of Civil War scholars are also heeding the call to take a closer look at the various roles religion played in influencing and sustaining the common soldier on the battlefield. See Jason Phillips, "Religious Belief and Troop Motivation: 'For the Smile of My Blessed Savior,'" in *Virginia's Civil War,* ed. Peter Wallenstein and Bertram Wyatt-Brown (Charlottesville: Univ. Press of Virginia, 2005), 101–13; and Kent T. Dollar, "Strangers in a Strange Land: Christian Soldiers in the Early Months of the War," in *The View from the Ground: Experiences of Civil War Soldiers,* ed. Aaron Sheehan-Dean (Lexington: Univ. Press of Kentucky, 2006), 145–69.

4. Edward L. Ayers, review of *Religion and the American Civil War, Journal of Southern Religion,* 1998–99, http://jsur.as.wvu.edu/ayers.htm/ (accessed Jan. 12, 2008).

5. McPherson, "Afterword," 412. As a note of caution, the subsequent survey does not even pretend to cover these topics in all the rich detail and complexity they deserve. Those interested in gaining a deeper understanding of them should consult the cited works.

6. John Locke, *The Second Treatise on Government,* ed. Thomas Peardon (New York: Liberal Arts Press, 1956), 14, chap. 3, sec. 21.

7. Quoted in Harry S. Stout and Christopher Grasso, "Civil War, Religion, and Communications," in Miller, Stout and Wilson, *Religion and the American Civil War,* 322.

8. Abraham Lincoln, "Meditation on the Divine Will," Sept. 2, 1862, in *The Collected Works of Abraham Lincoln,* vol. 5, ed. Roy P. Basler (New Brunswick, N.J.: Rutgers Univ. Press, 1953), 403–4. Note: The emphasis appears in the original text. Although after his death Lincoln's secretaries Nicolay and Hay maintained that Lincoln wrote his "Meditation" on September 30, 1862, most modern historians and the editors of this work believe Lincoln penned it on September 2, 1862, after the disastrous Union defeat at the Second Battle of Bull Run.

9. Stout and Grasso, "Civil War, Religion, and Communications," 321–23.

10. George M. Fredrickson, "The Coming of the Lord: The Northern Protestant Clergy and the Civil War Crisis," in Miller, Stout, and Wilson, *Religion and the American Civil War,* 122; Abraham Lincoln, "Proclamation of Thanksgiving," Oct. 3, 1863, in *Collected Works,* vol. 6, ed. Basler, 497.

11. This more successful government support of religion in the Northern armies may have been a legacy of the Puritan communal tradition in which church and state often worked closely together to help govern their communities. Chapter 2 will examine this issue in greater detail. Shattuck, *Shield and Hiding Place,* 9, 52–63, 104–5.

12. Ibid., 47, 63–68.

13. Over the course of my research, I discovered that during the first half of the war, more often than not, religious soldiers were frequently disappointed with the

work of their chaplains. I did not, however, come across *any* letters disparaging the work of the U.S. Christian Commission delegates.

14. Wilbur Fisk, *Anti-Rebel: The Civil War Letters of Wilbur Fisk,* ed. Emil Rosenblatt (Croton-on-Hudson, N.Y.: Emil Rosenblatt, 1983), 213.

15. Shattuck, *Shield and Hiding Place,* 31–32.

16. Ibid., 88–89.

17. Ibid., 76–77, 104–5. Lest anyone draw too close a relationship between Southern martial ability and religious faith, it should be remembered that the less successful Southern generals (Braxton Bragg, Joseph E. Johnston, and John Bell Hood) also converted to Christianity during the wartime revivals.

18. David Herbert Donald, *Lincoln* (New York: Simon and Schuster, 1995), 337, 514–15, 566–68. Historians have had a difficult time pinning down Lincoln's wartime religious beliefs. Modern historians such as Steven B. Oates, Allen C. Guelzo, and David Donald emphasize Lincoln's fundamental fatalism or doctrine of necessity (which conveniently combined Lincoln's parents' hard-shell Baptist belief in the Calvinistic doctrine of predestination with his own education in the ideas and Deistic religious notions of the Enlightenment), but beyond that they don't tell us much about the evolution of his religious beliefs. While Guelzo seems skeptical that Lincoln was moving toward a more orthodox Christian worldview, other historians, such as Mark A. Noll, have concluded that Lincoln's ultimate religious standing remains something of a mystery. Earlier minister-turned-historians were absolutely convinced Lincoln was a Christian president, and his earliest biographer, Josiah Holland, corroborated this surprising revelation. Lincoln's law partner William Henry Herndon, however, immediately tried to refute this allegation with his own set of interviews. John Nicolay, Lincoln's loyal chief of staff, was absolutely convinced that Lincoln's religious beliefs did not change from the time he left Springfield to the day of his death but candidly confessed he did not know what they were to begin with. Nicolay's comment helps illustrate the central problem of this historical debate, which is that by the time he became president, Lincoln was no longer openly sharing his own private religious views—even with his own family. This was somewhat understandable given his troubled childhood and history of being publicly attacked for his unconventional religious views. During the Civil War his Confederate adversaries' habit of ostentatiously displaying their Christian commitments may have further strengthened Lincoln's resolve to keep his own evolving beliefs private. Lincoln's lifelong friend Joshua Speed—a skeptic himself—later insisted that Lincoln's faith was "growing" during his presidency. Lincoln privately shared that his religious beliefs underwent a "process of crystallization" after the death of his son Willie. Lincoln's subsequent wartime speeches, letters, and comments also seem to suggest he may have been gravitating toward a more orthodox Christian faith. But since he kept his evolving religious views largely to himself, it is impossible to determine whether he privately, and apparently secretly, embraced Christianity just before his premature death. His final religious state must therefore remain an enigma.

19. Donald, *Lincoln,* 568; Lincoln, "Meditation on the Divine Will," 5:403–4.

20. Lincoln, "Meditation on the Divine Will," 5:403–4; Ronald C. White Jr., "Lincoln's Sermon on the Mount: The Second Inaugural," in Miller, Stout, and Wilson, *Religion and the American Civil War,* 222. White's article and subsequent

book on the speech explores some of the deeper religious themes and symbols that pervade Lincoln's second inaugural speech and concludes that the address was in part Lincoln's answer to the question of how a good God could allow his servants to endure such terrible suffering. Lincoln's conclusion seemed to be that the war was God's judgment against an "almost chosen nation" that stubbornly refused to repent of its national sin of slavery. And that the war had been prolonged either because of the magnitude of the crime or because, even in the midst of the wartime judgment, many Americans still clung to their original sin and opposed emancipation. By fulfilling their divine duties to *submit* to God's judgments, *acknowledge* the righteousness of his judgments, and *practice* Christ's Golden Rule, Americans could end their nation's wartime judgment and "establish a just, and a lasting peace, among ourselves, and with all nations."

21. James M. McPherson, *For Cause and Comrades: Why Men Fought in the Civil War* (New York: Oxford Univ. Press, 1997), 63–64; McPherson, "Afterword," 409–10; James I. Robertson Jr., *Soldiers Blue and Gray* (Columbia: Univ. of South Carolina Press, 1988), 170. Other scholars who have noted the extensive religiosity of the Northern armies and Northern society during the war include Drew Faust, Reid Mitchell, Gardiner Shattuck, and Philip Shaw Paludan.

22. Phillip Shaw Paludan, "Religion and the American Civil War," in Miller, Stout, and Wilson, *Religion and the American Civil War,* 24–25; Shattuck, *Shield and Hiding Place,* 23.

23. McPherson, *For Cause and Comrades,* 62–75.

24. Shattuck, *Shield and Hiding Place,* 30–33, 80, 86. According to Shattuck, some of the popular stereotypes concerning Christian soldiers were that they were more disciplined, less fearful, more accepting of hardships, and did not "break" as easily on the battlefield.

25. Saum, *Popular Mood,* 72. Nearly all the wartime revivals took place in the winter, late fall, or early spring, following precisely the same seasonal pattern as the antebellum revivals. Shattuck, *Shield and Hiding Place,* 89.

26. Smith, *Revivalism and Social Reform,* 63–64, 76; Shattuck, *Shield and Hiding Place,* 83–84.

27. Woodworth, *While God Is Marching On,* 253.

28. Ibid., 220, 253–54.

29. Mitchell, "Christian Soldiers?" 303, 297–308; Shattuck, *Shield and Hiding Place,* 92–96; William W. Bennett, *A Narrative of the Great Revival Which Prevailed in the Southern Armies During the Late Civil War Between the States of the Federal Union* (1876; reprint, Harrisonburg, Va., 1989); J. William Jones, D.D., *Christ in the Camp: or, Religion in the Confederate Army* (1904; reprint, Harrisonburg, Va., 1986). For an opposing view, see Shattuck, *Shield and Hiding Place,* 104–5. According to Reid and Shattuck, roughly one hundred thousand of the one million Confederate soldiers converted, and between one hundred thousand and two hundred thousand Federal soldiers were "saved" in an army that eventually included two million soldiers. I included the higher Union figure because the more conservative estimates have traditionally excluded African American and Roman Catholic "conversions."

30. See, for example, Sydney E. Ahlstrom, *A Religious History of the American People* (New Haven, Conn.: Yale Univ. Press, 1972), 670–73; and James Silver,

Confederate Morale and Church Propaganda (Tuscaloosa: Univ. of Alabama Press, 1957), 101.

31. David B. Chesebrough, *"God Ordained This War": Sermons on the Sectional Crisis* (Columbia: Univ. of South Carolina Press, 1991), 9; Shattuck, *Shield and Hiding Place*, 79, 83.

32. Shattuck, *Shield and Hiding Place*, 81–82. Some of the other factors historians cite when discussing the reasons for the Union victory at Missionary Ridge include the Cumberland soldiers' desire to prove themselves after being assigned a secondary role in the battle, the rivalry that existed between the western soldiers and Hooker's newly arrived eastern soldiers, the confusion caused by Bragg's order to have his men fall back from their first line of entrenchments after firing one volley, the vulnerability of the Cumberland soldiers at the base of the ridge, poorly sited Confederate fortifications, and the low morale of Bragg's army. The number of theories scholars have advanced over the years to try to explain this incredible Northern victory against an "impregnable" Confederate position, however, further corroborates the truly extraordinary nature of this victory.

33. Ahlstrom, *Religious History of the American People*, 676; Shattuck, *Shield and Hiding Place*, 89.

34. Paludan, "Religion and the American Civil War," 24; Phillip Shaw Paludan, *A People's Contest: The Union and Civil War, 1861–1865* (Lawrence: Univ. Press of Kansas, 1988), 349; Shattuck, *Shield and Hiding Place*, 89.

2. Covenant and Revival

1. Mitchell, "Christian Soldiers?" 302; Paludan, "Religion and the American Civil War," 24.

2. C. C. Goen, *Broken Churches, Broken Nation: Denominational Schisms and the Coming of the American Civil War* (Macon, Ga.: Mercer Univ. Press, 1985), 41; Randall M. Miller, Harry S. Stout, and Charles Reagan Wilson, introduction to Miller, Stout, and Wilson, *Religion and the American Civil War*, 6.

3. Samuel S. Hill Jr., *The South and the North in American Religion* (Athens: Univ. of Georgia Press, 1980), 10.

4. Perry Miller, *Errand into the Wilderness* (Cambridge: Harvard Univ. Press, 1956), 47–72. According to Miller, the New England Puritans derived their concept of covenant theology from Dr. William Ames, but it also could be largely deduced from a literal, commonsense reading of Old Testament passages concerning the covenants between God and the early Jewish patriarchs.

5. Ibid., 1–6, 47–66.

6. Paul Johnson, *A History of the American People* (New York: HarperCollins, 1997), 39, 51–52.

7. Cotton Mather, *The Wonders of the Invisible World: Being an Account of the Tryals of Several Witches, Lately Executed in New-England: and of Several Remarkable Curiosities Therein Occurring. Together with, I. Observations Upon the Nature, the Number, and the Operations of the Devils. II. A Short Narrative of a Late Outrage Committed by a Knot of Witches in Swede-land, Very Much Resembling, and so Far*

Explaining, That Under Which New-England has laboured. III. Some Councels directing a Due Improvement of the Terrible Things Lately Done by the Unusual and Amazing Range of Evil Spirits in New-England. IV. A Brief Discourse Upon Those Temptations Which are the More Ordinary Devices of Satan (Boston: John Dunton, 1693; Ann Arbor , Mich.: University Microfilms, n.d.).

8. Miller, *Errand into the Wilderness*, 2–15, 143–47.

9. Hill, *South and the North in American Religion*, 73–74.

10. Perry Miller, *The Life of the Mind in America: From the Revolution to the Civil War* (New York: Harcourt, Brace and World, 1965), 4–7; Jerald C. Brauer, *Protestan tism in America: A Narrative* (Philadelphia: Westminster Press, 1965), 103; Nathan O. Hatch, *The Democratization of American Christianity* (New Haven, Conn.: Yale Univ. Press, 1989), 59–60.

11. Hatch, *Democratization of American Christianity*, 62; Alexis de Tocqueville, *Democracy in America*, trans. Henry Reeve (New York: Colonial Press, 1900), 308; Schaff quoted in Smith, *Revivalism and Social Reform*, 18.

12. Figures based on a compilation of facts and statistics from Goen, *Broken Churches, Broken Nation*, 25, 43, 50, 59–62; Smith, *Revivalism and Social Reform*, 17, 21–23, 53–54; and Robert Baird, *Religion in America: The Origin, Progress, Relation to the State, and Present Condition of the Evangelical Churches in the United States* (New York: Harper & Brothers, 1844), 264–66. It should be noted that the 5 percent increase in national Protestant church membership between 1800 and 1855 does not reflect the increasing presence of the Catholic Church in America. The Roman Catholic Church in America had grown from a few thousand members at the close of the Revolution to a church of at least one and a half million by 1855. See Smith, *Revivalism and Social Reform*, 17; and Braüer, *Protestantism in America*, 129.

13. Smith, *Revivalism and Social Reform*, 8, 20–21; Ahlstrom, *Religious History of the American People*, 324–25, 436–39; Brauer, *Protestantism in America*, 56–57; Baird, *Religion in America*, 245–46. With the possible exception of Arminianism and perfectionism, the Methodist confession of faith was very similar to that of other Reformed Protestant churches.

14. Mark A. Noll, *America's God: From Jonathan Edwards to Abraham Lincoln* (New York, 2005), 168–69.

15. Brauer, *Protestantism in America*, 75–76, 100–101, 182–83; Mark A. Noll, *A History of Christianity in the United States and Canada* (Grand Rapids, Mich.: Eerdman's, 1992),171–74; Goen, *Broken Churches, Broken Nation*, 78–90; Smith, *Revivalism and Social Reform*, 20.

16. Smith, *Revivalism and Social Reform*, 15, 17; Goen, *Broken Churches, Broken Nation*, 55.

17. Quoted in Goen, *Broken Churches, Broken Nation*, 55.

18. Smith, *Revivalism and Social Reform*, 17; Baird, *Religion in America*, 205; quoted in Goen, *Broken Churches, Broken Nation*, 55.

19. Quoted in Brauer, *Protestantism in America*, 142–43, 145. Although a Union of Congregationalists and Presbyterians took the lead in forming the first of these voluntary religious societies, other denominations, such as the Baptists and Methodists, soon had their own rival organizations. In many cases the societies were interdenominational.

20. Noll, *History of Christianity*, 227; Smith, *Revivalism and Social Reform*, 36. To note one remarkable example of the evangelicals' success in developing a popular publication industry, almost one million copies of the religious tract *Quench Not the Spirit* (n.p., n.d.) had been distributed by 1850.

21. Smith, *Revivalism and Social Reform*, 36.

22. Baird, *Religion in America*, 150–51; Smith, *Revivalism and Social Reform*, 40–41.

23. Noll, *History of Christianity*, 241–43.

24. Charles Forrester Dunham, *The Attitude of the Northern Clergy Toward the South, 1860–1865* (Philadelphia: Porcupine Press, 1974), 5; Smith, *Revivalism and Social Reform*, 37.

25. Goen, *Broken Churches, Broken Nation*, 55.

26. See Richard E. Beringer, Herman Hattaway, Archer Jones, and William N. Still Jr., eds., *The Elements of Confederate Defeat: Nationalism, War Aims and Religion* (Athens: Univ. of Georgia Press, 1988), 32.

27. Ibid., 3–4.

28. Baird, *Religion in America*, 219, 265; Noll, "Bible and Slavery," 47–48; Goen, *Broken Churches, Broken Nation*, 13; Smith, *Revivalism and Social Reform*, 28–29.

29. Smith, *Revivalism and Social Reform*, 32–33.

30. Baird, *Religion in America*, 266–67.

31. Donald G. Mathews, "Christianizing the South—Sketching a Synthesis," in *New Directions in American Religious History*, ed. Harry S. Stout and D. G. Hart (New York: Oxford Univ. Press, 1997), 86.

32. Goen, *Broken Churches, Broken Nation*, 18–19; Smith, *Revivalism and Social Reform*, 33, 28, 80.

33. Chesebrough, *"God Ordained This War,"* 5; Ahlstrom, *Religious History of the American People*, 79.

34. Chesebrough,*"God Ordained This War,"* 5; White, "Lincoln's Sermon on the Mount," 219. The concept of an immanent God both perplexed and comforted Lincoln. He readily admitted he could not understand the ways of a God who could allow the wartime carnage to continue, but recognizing his own finite understanding, he refused to abandon his faith in God's immanence or goodness. In his biography of the president, David Herbert Donald argued that Lincoln's understanding of God's immanence and "divine purposes" comforted the president by allowing him to shift the burden of responsibility for the wartime suffering to a higher power. See Donald, *Lincoln*, 514–15.

35. Mark A. Noll, *Christians in the American Revolution* (Washington, D.C.: Christian College Consortium, 1977), 163–69; Noll, *History of Christianity*, 317; Ahlstrom, *Religious History of the American People*, 81; quoted in Paludan, "Religion and the American Civil War," 22.

36. Baird, *Religion in America*, 291; quoted in Smith, *Revivalism and Social Reform*, 28, 32; Noll, "Bible and Slavery," 47–48. An excellent example of these new liberal Christian pioneers was the brilliant Congregational clergyman and theologian Horace Bushnell.

37. Baird, *Religion in America*, 268.

38. Smith, *Revivalism and Social Reform*, 7–8, 45, 135–36, 236; Chesebrough, *"God Ordained This War,"* 25; Baird, *Religion in America*, 268.

3. Forward into the Red Sea of War

1. Fredrickson, "Coming of the Lord," 118. Regardless of whether patriotic preachers such as Beecher harbored "quasi-theocratic ambitions," Fredrickson has persuasively argued that by linking themselves so intimately to the government, they may have compromised their spiritual mission in Northern society.

2. Dunham, *Attitude of the Northern Clergy.*

3. Chesebrough, *"God Ordained This War,"* 84.

4. Harry S. Stout, *Upon the Altar of the Nation: A Moral History of the Civil War* (New York: Viking, 2006), 283.

5. Byron C. Andreasen, "Proscribed Preachers, New Churches: Civil Wars in Illinois Protestant Churches during the Civil War," *Civil War History* 44 (1998), Questia. com, http://www.questia.com/read/5001377854/ (accessed Feb. 11, 2008).

6. Henry Ward Beecher, "The Battle Set in Array," Apr. 14, 1861, in *Freedom and War: Discourses on Topics Suggested by the Times,* by Henry Ward Beecher (1863; reprint, Freeport, N.Y.: Books for Librairies Press, 1971) (hereafter cited as *Freedom and War*), 89–90.

7. Ibid.

8. Kenneth M. Stampp, *And the War Came: The North and the Secession Crisis 1860–1861* (Baton Rouge: Louisiana State Univ. Press, 1950), 294; Bell Irvin Wiley, *The Life of Billy Yank: The Common Soldier of the Union* (Garden City, N.Y.: Doubleday, 1971), 18.

9. Wiley, *Life of Billy Yank,* 21.

10. William C. Robinson to Charlie, Apr. 28, 1861, William C. Robinson Papers, Abraham Lincoln Presidential Library, Springfield, Ill. (hereafter cited as Robinson Papers).

11. Ibid.

12. Wiley, *Life of Billy Yank,* 18.

13. Jeanie Attie, *Patriotic Toil: Northern Women and the American Civil War* (Ithaca, N.Y.: Cornell Univ. Press, 1998), 22–23; Agatha Young, *The Women and the Crisis: Women of the North in the Civil War* (New York: McDowell, Obolensky, 1959), 43–44; quoted in Attie, *Patriotic Toil,* 27.

14. Attie, *Patriotic Toil,* 26–27; Young, *Women and the Crisis,* 43, 45.

15. Mary Elizabeth Massey, *Bonnet Brigades* (New York: Knopf, 1966), 30–31; Wiley, *Life of Billy Yank,* 18, 21. In the course of reviewing letters at the Indiana Historical Society, I came across at least two other letters that confirmed the story about Indiana girls ignoring men who did not enlist.

16. Wiley, *Life of Billy Yank,* 18; Attie, *Patriotic Toil,* 24; Young, *Women and the Crisis,* 45; Massey, *Bonnet Brigades,* 30.

17. Lutie Bennett to Uncle Ned, Aug. 8, 1862, Edward H. Ingraham Papers, Abraham Lincoln Presidential Library, Springfield, Ill. (hereafter cited as Ingraham Papers).

18. John Jones to parents, Oct. 12, 1862, John G. Jones Letters, Wisconsin Historical Society, Madison (hereafter cited as John G. Jones Letters); Benjamin W. "Webb" Baker to Grandfather, in Benjamin W. Webb Baker, *Testament: A Soldier's Story of the Civil War,* ed. Benson Bobrick (hereafter cited as *Testament*) (New York: Simon and Schuster, 2003), 194.

19. Abraham Boynton to friends, Apr. 29, 1861, Abraham Boynton Letters, Wisconsin Historical Society, Madison (hereafter cited as Boynton Letters).

20. John MacLachlan to Susan (wife), Apr. 17, 1864, John MacLachlan Letters, Wisconsin Historical Society, Madison.

21. Heb. 12:14; Matt. 19:19.

22. McPherson, "Afterword," 410; Exod. 20:13.

23. Beecher, "Battle Set in Array," 84–99.

24. Ibid.

25. A few of the numerous examples of these apparent "contradictions" include Abraham lying about his wife Sarah's marital status, Jacob coveting his brother Esau's birthright, and David and his men eating the holy showbread during their flight from King Saul. Rahab, the Jericho prostitute who saved the lives of two Hebrew spies by lying, also was honored as a hero of the faith in Hebrews 11:31.

26. Beecher, "Battle Set in Array," 94–95.

27. Charles Mumford to wife, Mar. 15, 1863, Charles Norwood Mumford Letters, Wisconsin Historical Society, Madison (hereafter cited as Mumford Letters).

28. Ibid.

29. Alexander Miller Ayers to wife, Jan. 1, 1863, Alexander Miller Ayers Papers, Manuscript, Archives, and Rare Book Library, Robert W. Woodruff Library, Emory University (hereafter cited as Ayers Papers).

30. Matt. 2:52; Luke 3:14; Rev. 19:15.

31. Deut. 7:1–2; Acts 13:22.

32. Ps. 144:1; Eccles. 3:8.

4. For Family and Country

1. Fisk, *Anti-Rebel,* 150.

2. Benjamin W. "Webb" Baker to Grandfather, in *Testament,* 194.

3. Gerald F. Linderman, *Embattled Courage: The Experience of Combat in the American Civil War* (New York: Free Press, 1987), 11–16.

4. "Webb" Baker to Grandfather, in *Testament,* 198; Luther H. Cowan to wife, Feb. 1, 1862, Luther H. Cowan Letters, Wisconsin Historical Society, Madison (hereafter cited as Cowan Letters); Luther H. Cowan to wife, Feb. 4, 1862, Cowan Letters.

5. Dwight Fraser to Sister Lizzie, May 3, 1864, Dwight and Joshua Fraser Letters, Indiana Historical Society, Indianapolis (hereafter cited as Fraser Letters).

6. James F. Drish to wife, Mar. 29, 1862, James F. Drish Papers, Abraham Lincoln Presidential Library, Springfield, Ill.

7. Francis Harvey Bruce to mother, Feb. 25, 1865, Bruce Family Papers, Abraham Lincoln Presidential Library, Springfield, Ill. (hereafter cited as Bruce Family Papers).

8. Henry Ward Beecher, "The National Flag," in *Freedom and War,* 129.

9. Beecher, "Battle Set in Array," 95; S. P. Leeds and S. D. Phelps quoted in Chesebrough, *"God Ordained This War,"* 86–87.

10. Robert Crandall to sister Kittie, Oct. 21, 1862, Crandall Family Correspondence; T. S. Seacord to wife, Oct. 5, 1862, Thomas S. Seacord Papers, Abraham Lincoln Presidential Library, Springfield, Ill. (hereafter cited as Seacord Papers).

11. 1 Tim. 2:2; Gen. 1:28; Gen. 9:1; Eph. 5:22–33; Eph. 6:4; 1 Tim. 5:8; John 15:13.

12. John Lindley Harris to Susan, Dec. 18, 1863, John Lindley Harris Papers, Abraham Lincoln Presidential Library, Springfield, Ill. (hereafter cited as Harris Papers); William C. Robinson to Charlie, May 29, 1861, Robinson Papers.

13. Isaac Tucker to Kitty Crandall, Jan. 30, 1862, Crandall Family Correspondence.

14. Dunham, *Attitude of the Northern Clergy,* 142–43; quoted in Chesebrough, *"God Ordained This War,"* 84, 85, 88, 341; Beecher, "Modes and Duties of Emancipation," in *Freedom and War,* 176; Shattuck, *Shield and Hiding Place,* 60. According to Shattuck, one of the most popular wartime sermons preached by Union army chaplains concerned soldiers' patriotic duty to fight for their country.

15. Philip Welshimer to wife Julia, June 6, 1861, Philip Welshimer Papers, Abraham Lincoln Presidential Library, Springfield, Ill. (hereafter cited as Welshimer Papers).

16. Joseph J. Dimock Sr. to sister Sallie, June 30, 1861, Dimock Family Papers, Manuscript, Archives, and Rare Book Library, Robert W. Woodruff Library, Emory University (hereafter cited as Dimock Family Papers).

17. Daniel Webster to Gertrude, Feb. 16, 1862, Daniel Webster Letters, Wisconsin Historical Society, Madison (hereafter cited as Webster Letters).

18. Andrew McGarrah to wife, Oct. 1, 1862, Andrew J. McGarrah Letters, Indiana Historical Society, Indianapolis (hereafter cited as McGarrah Letters); Amos W. Hostetter to brothers and sisters, Mar. 9, 1864, Amos W. Hostetter Papers, Abraham Lincoln Presidential Library, Springfield, Ill. (hereafter cited as Hostetter Papers)

19. Harley Wayne to wife Ellen, Dec. 29, 1861, Harley Wayne Papers, Abraham Lincoln Presidential Library, Springfield, Ill. (hereafter cited as Wayne Papers).

20. David Rose Simpson to wife, May 6, 1863, David Rose Simpson Papers, Abraham Lincoln Presidential Library, Springfield, Ill.

21. Peter Welsh, *Irish Green and Union Blue: The Civil War Letters of Peter Welsh, Color Sergeant, 28th Regiment, Massachusetts Volunteers,* ed. Frederick L. Kohl, Richard Cossé, and Margaret Cossé (New York: Fordham Univ. Press, 1986), 64–67; Alexander Miller Ayers to wife, Feb. 5, 1863, Ayers Papers.

22. David E. Beem to Hala, Sept. 9, 1861, David E. Beem Papers, Indiana Historical Society, Indianapolis (hereafter cited as Beem Papers).

23. Noll, *Christians in the American Revolution,* 39, 45–47, 62–77; Miller, *Errand into the Wilderness,* 1–5; 143–47.

24. Goen, *Broken Churches, Broken Nation,* 24.

25. Miller, *Life of the Mind in America,* 5–7, 11, 69.

26. Tocqueville, *Democracy in America,* 310.

27. Ibid., 311.

28. Henry Ward Beecher, "Energy of Administration Demanded," in *Freedom and War,* 158; McPherson, "Afterword," 410.

29. Mitchell, "Christian Soldiers?" 302.

30. John Lindley Harris to Miss Susan, Apr. 3, 1863, Harris Papers; Sylvester C. Bishop to mother, Dec. 25, 1861, Sylvester Bishop Letters, Indiana Historical Society, Indianapolis (hereafter cited as Bishop Letters).

31. William L. Dillon to Mr. Livis Dillon, Feb. 21, 1862, William L. Isaiah T. and William L. Dillon Papers, Abraham Lincoln Presidential Library, Springfield, Ill.

32. William H. Tebbetts to sister, Mar. 2, 1862, William H. Tebbetts Papers, Abraham Lincoln Presidential Library, Springfield, Ill.

33. Quoted in McPherson, *Battle Cry of Freedom,* 309; Reid Hiriam to friends, Sept. 15, 1862, Reid Hiriam Letters, Indiana Historical Society, Indianapolis (hereafter cited as Hiriam Letters).

34. Amos C. Weaver to Miss Mirriam, June 20, 1864, Amos C. Weaver Letters, Indiana Historical Society, Indianapolis (hereafter cited as Weaver Letters); James McIlrath to wife, Jan. 31, 1862, James McIlrath Papers, Abraham Lincoln Library, Springfield, Ill.; Daniel Webster to fiancée Gertrude, Nov. 28, 1861, Webster Letters; George Russell to Elizabeth, May 31, 1861, Russell Family Papers, Abraham Lincoln Presidential Library, Springfield, Ill. (hereafter cited as Russell Family Papers).

35. Andrew J. McGarrah to brother B. F. Dock, Oct. 20, 1863, McGarrah Letters.

36. Gen. 9:5–6; Rom. 13:4. Martin Luther and John Calvin both cited Romans 13:4 when they argued that governments—and in certain cases, lower magistrates—had the right to wage just wars, and that Christians also had a duty to "bear the sword" in defense of their governments. It was somewhat ironic that a once pacifist church later developed moral criteria for waging "just" wars against fellow Christians. In any case, this apparent moral contradiction produced some of the Civil War's most memorable episodes, such as the moment at Fredericksburg when, peering down at the vast human slaughter, the South's premier Christian spokesman Robert E. Lee noted that it was a good thing that war was so terrible or good Christian gentlemen like himself might learn to love it.

37. James Drake, "Restraining Atrocity: The Conduct of King Philip's War," *New England Quarterly* 70, no. 1 (1997): 36–37, 44–45. In this article, Drake explains why the Puritans believed their conduct during the Pequot War, and especially their devastating attack on the Pequots' Mystic Village, were completely justified according to the "law of nations." The Pequots had fortified their village and refused to surrender.

38. Fred W. Anderson, "The Hinge of the Revolution; George Washington Confronts a People's Army, July 3, 1775," *Massachusetts Historical Review,* 1999, http://www.historycooperative.org/journals/mhr/1/anderson.html (accessed June 23, 2007); Russell F. Weigley, *The American Way of War: A History of United States Strategy and Policy* Reprint (Bloomington: Indiana Univ. Press, 1973), 13; Robert Trout, "Life, Liberty, and the Pursuit of Happiness: How the Natural Law of G. W. Leibniz Inspired America's Founding Fathers," *Fidelio Magazine* 6, no. 1 (Spring 1997), http://www.schillerinstitute.org/fid_97-01/971_vattel-2.html (accessed June 23,

2007); Scott R. Morris, "The Laws of War: Rules by Warriors for Warriors," *Army Lawyer,* Dec. 1997, 6–7.

39. Steven Ambrose, *Duty, Honor, Country: A History of West Point* (Baltimore: John Hopkins Univ. Press, 1966), 63; R. Ernest DuPuy, *Men of West Point: The First 150 Years of the United States Military Academy* (New York: Sloane, 1951), 118.

40. Patrick Finnegan, "The Study of Law as a Foundation of Leadership and Command: The History of Law Instruction at the United States Military Academy at West Point," *Military Law Review* 181 (2004): 112–13. In addition to their extensive outside reading, students had to attend four hours of instruction in this subject each week; Alan Aimone (reference librarian at the United States Military Academy, West Point), e-mail to author, June 14, 2007.

41. Stout, *Upon the Altar,* 457, 460, xvi.

42. Stout's only reference to Vattel is his inclusion of some excerpts from a speech by Ohio Peace Democrat Samuel S. Cox in which the congressman employed the "spirit" of Vattel's "classic just-war treatise" to chastise the Lincoln administration's decision to wage a harsher war targeting Confederate property and the institution of slavery. To rebut such charges, however, Republican supporters need only point out the precise letter of Vattel's guidelines, which clearly authorized the use of these harsher measures when "punishing" an enemy.

43. See David Rolfs, "The Civilized and the Savage: The Ethical Conduct of the U.S. Army During the Second Seminole War," *Selected Annual Proceedings of the Florida Conference of History* 6 and 7 (Dec. 1999): 151–62; and Drake, "Restraining Atrocity."

44. Emmerich Vattel, "Of the Rights of Nations in War,—And First, of What We Have a Right to Do, and What We Are Allowed to Do to the Enemy," bk. 3, chap. 8, sec. 147 of *The Laws of Nations Or the Principles of Natural Law in Four Books* (1758), by Emmerich Vattel, trans. Joseph Chitty, 1797, Lonang Library ed., http://www.lonang.com/exlibris/vattel/vatt-000.htm (accessed June 20, 2007); "Lieber Code" of 1863, General Orders No. 100, "Section III.—Deserters—Prisoners of War—Hostages—Booty on the Battlefield," Article 50, U.S. Regulars Civil War Archives, http://www.usregulars.com/Lieber.html (accessed June 25, 2007).

45. Although the Union later attempted to make a legal distinction between Confederate irregular forces and guerrillas, during the war some of the Confederate irregular forces in the West, like Quantrill's outfit, were operating more along guerrilla lines and hence did not deserve the right to be treated as irregulars in name or practice. Robert E. Lee and Davis ultimately concurred, and the Confederacy later repealed the Partisan Ranger Act.

46. Vattel, *Laws of Nations,* bk. 3, chap. 9, "Of the Right of War, With Regard to Things Belonging to the Enemy," sec. 167.

47. Ibid., bk. 3, chap. 9, sec. 172, "General Rules of Moderation respecting the evil which may be done to an enemy"; sec. 160, "Principles of the right over things belonging to the enemy"; and sec. 169, "Bombarding Towns."

48. Ibid., bk. 3, chap. 8, sec. 138, "The right to weaken an enemy by every justifiable method"; and chap. 9, sec. 173, "Rule of the voluntary law of nations on the same subject."

49. Stout, *Upon the Altar,* 193, xvii.

50. Letter excerpts from the Project Gutenberg e-book of William Tecumseh Sherman, *The Memoirs of General W. T. Sherman, Complete,* 364, http://www.gutenberg.org/catalog/world/readfile?pageno=1andfk_files=71106 (accessed June 18, 2007).

51. Ibid., 364–65.

52. Vattel, *Laws of Nations,* bk. 3, chap. 8, sec. 147.

53. Stout, *Upon the Altar,* 457.

54. An important exception would be the secondary theaters such as the Trans-Mississippi, Kansas, Tennessee, and western Virginia, where persistent guerrilla warfare and numerous wartime atrocities prompted many Northern soldiers to condemn their treacherous Southern enemies. The most common Northern *jus in bello* complaints were that the Confederacy was employing illegal irregular and guerrilla warfare tactics in Union-occupied regions of the Confederacy, sacking and burning Northern cities, executing captured black soldiers fighting for the Union, and deliberately mistreating and starving Union prisoners of war.

55. Beecher, "Modes and Duties of Emancipation," 182.

56. William H. Onstot to Sister Lizzie, Aug. 18, 1861, William H. Onstot Papers, Abraham Lincoln Presidential Library, Springfield, Ill. (hereafter cited as Onstot Papers).

57. Abraham Boynton to "Friends," Apr. 29, 1861, Boynton Letters.

58. Jasper N. Kidwell to Niniveh, July 20, 1865, Jasper N. Kidwell Letters, Indiana Historical Society, Indianapolis (hereafter cited as Kidwell Letters).

59. Rom. 13:1–2.

60. Horace Bushnell, "Popular Government by Divine Right," in Chesebrough, *"God Ordained This War,"* 117–18; Chesebrough, *"God Ordained This War,"* 85.

61. Rom. 13:4; Saum, *Popular Mood,* 21.

62. Michael Hayes Branniger Cunningham to wife, Dec. 12, 1863, Michael Hayes Branniger Cunningham Letters, Wisconsin Historical Society, Madison (hereafter cited as Cunningham Letters).

63. Joseph Manson to friends, Feb. 3, 1864, Joseph Manson Correspondence, Manuscript, Archives, and Rare Book Library, Robert W. Woodruff Library, Emory University (hereafter cited as Manson Correspondence).

64. Donald, *Lincoln,* 269; "Declaration of Independence" and "Northwest Ordinance," in *Sources of Our Liberties: Documentary Origins of Individual Liberties in the United States Constitution and Bill of Rights,* ed. Richard L. Perry and John C. Cooper (Buffalo, N.Y.: William S. Hein, 1991), 321, 397.

65. Henry Ward Beecher, "The Southern Babylon," in *Freedom and War,* 432; Beecher, "National Flag," 114

66. Beecher, "Battle Set in Array," 109.

67. Quoted in Chesebrough, *"God Ordained This War,"* 84–85.

68. Harley Wayne to wife, Jan. 17, 1861, Wayne Papers; Andrew J. McGarrah to brother James, Oct. 6, 1863, McGarrah Letters; Benjamin "Webb" Baker to mother, in *Testament,* 198.

69. Michael Hayes Branniger Cunningham to wife, Jan. 12, 1863, Cunningham Letters.

70. James B. Lockney to mother, Feb. 12, 1863, James Browne Lockney Papers, Wisconsin Historical Society, Madison (hereafter cited as Lockney Papers).

71. John R. Siperly to Jenny Safford, 1863 [?], Jennie Safford Smith Correspondence, Manuscript, Archives, and Rare Book Library, Robert W. Woodruff Library, Emory University (hereafter cited as Smith Correspondence).

72. Beecher, "Energy of Administration Demanded," 157, 159.

73. Beecher, "Modes and Duties of Emancipation," 180–81.

74. Ransom Bedell to cousin, 1861, Ransom Bedell Papers, Abraham Lincoln Presidential Library, Springfield, Ill. (hereafter cited as Bedell Papers).

75. Michael Hays Branniger Cunningham to wife, May 10, 1864, Cunningham Letters.

5. The Great Northern Crusade

1. Henry Franklin Hole to friends, Aug. 25, 1861, Henry Franklin Hole Papers, Abraham Lincoln Presidential Library, Springfield, Ill. (hereafter cited as Hole Papers).

2. Henry Ward Beecher, "Against a Compromise of Principle," Nov. 29, 1860, in *Freedom and War,* 41; Henry Ward Beecher, "The Success of American Democracy," Apr. 13, 1862, in *Freedom and War,* 263–64.

3. James D. Liggett, "Our National Reverses," quoted in Chesebrough, "*God Ordained This War,*" 98.

4. Stanley Lathrop to parents, July 7, 1865, 91S, Stanley E. Lathrop Papers, Wisconsin Historical Society, Madison.

5. Benjamin W. "Webb" Baker to Cousin Amos, in *Testament,* 207.

6. William C. Robinson to Charlie, May 29, 1861, Robinson Papers; John Lindley Harris to Susan, Dec. 18, 1863, Harris Papers.

7. Stanley Lathrop to father, Mar. 16, 1865, Lathrop Papers.

8. Henry Ward Beecher, "The Camp, Its Dangers and Duties," May 1861, in *Freedom and War,* 152.

9. Ransom Bedell to cousin, [1861], no location given, Bedell Papers; Henry Matrau, *Letters Home: Henry Matrau of the Iron Brigade,* ed. Marcia Reid-Green (Lincoln: Univ. of Nebraska Press, 1993), 75; Amos W. Hostetter to brothers and sisters, Apr. 4, 1864, Hostetter Papers.

10. James H. Leonard to Mary, Aug. 15, 1861, James H. Leonard Letters, Wisconsin Historical Society, Madison (hereafter cited as Leonard Letters).

11. Fisk, *Anti-Rebel,* 299.

12. David E. Beem to wife, Oct. 19, 1862, Beem Papers; Michael Hayes Branniger Cunningham to wife, Oct. 12, 1864, Cunningham Papers.

13. James A. Connolly, *Three Years in the Army of the Cumberland: The Letters and Diary of Major James A. Connolly,* ed. Paul M. Angle (Bloomington: Indiana Univ. Press, 1959), 282.

14. Fisk, *Anti-Rebel,* 298.

15. Matt. 26:52, Rev. 13:10; Benjamin W. "Webb" Baker to Grandfather, in *Testament,* 194.

16. Quoted in Woodworth, *While God Is Marching On,* 49.

17. 2 Tim. 3:11–12; 2 Cor. 4:8–18; Rom. 10:12–13.

18. Saum, *Popular Mood,* 80.

19. Quoted in Woodworth, *While God Is Marching On,* 48.

20. Saum, *Popular Mood,* 103.

21. Quoted in Woodworth, *While God Is Marching On,* 48–49.

22. Benjamin Harris, *The New England Primer,* quoted in *The Giant Book of American Quotations,* ed. Gorton Carruth and Eugene Ehrlich (New York: Gramercy, 1988), 168.

23. Ibid.

24. Quoted in McPherson, *For Cause and Comrades,* 68–69.

25. William C. Robinson to friend Charlie, Apr. 28, 1861, Robinson Papers.

26. Quoted in Shattuck, *Shield and Hiding Place,* 60.

27. James Henry Gooding, *On the Altar of Freedom: A Black Soldier's Civil War Letters From the Front / James Henry Gooding,* ed. Virginia Matzke Adams (Amherst: Univ. of Massachusetts Press, 1991), 22.

28. William Wiley, *The Civil War Diary of a Common Soldier: William Wiley of the 77th Illinois Regiment,* ed. Terrence J. Winschel (Baton Rouge: Louisianan State Univ. Press, 2001), 9.

29. Wilson Garrett Piston and Richard W. Hatcher III, *Wilson's Creek: The Second Battle of the Civil War and the Men Who Fought It* (Chapel Hill: Univ. of North Carolina Press, 2000), 237.

30. Quoted in Woodworth, *While God Is Marching On,* 105.

31. Ibid.

32. Seymour Dexter, *Seymour Dexter, Union Army: Journal and letters of Civil War Service in Company K, 23rd New York Volunteer Regiment of Elmira,* ed. Carl A. Morrell, (Jefferson, N.C.: McFarland, 1996), 108.

33. George H. Allen, *Forty-six Months with the Fourth R.I. Volunteers, in the War of 1861–1865* (Providence, R.I.: J. A. and R. A. Reid, 1887), 109, 148.

34. Franklin Aretas Haskell, *Haskell of Gettysburg: His Life and Civil War Papers,* ed. Frank L. Byrne and Andrew Thomas Weaver (Kent, Ohio: Kent State Univ. Press, 1989), 246.

35. William H. Onstot to sister Lizzie, Nov. 16, 1861, Onstot Papers.

36. Robert Steele to parents, Dec. 18, 1862, Robert Steele Papers, Wisconsin Historical Society, Madison (hereafter cited as Steele Papers).

37. Andrew J. McGarrah to cousin, Apr. 9, 1863, McGarrah Letters.

38. Welsh, *Irish Green and Union Blue,* 74.

39. Quoted in Woodworth, *While God Is Marching On,* 48.

40. William Gould, *Dear Sister: The Civil War Letters of the Brothers Gould,* ed. Robert F. Harris and John Niflot (Westport, Conn.: Praeger, 1998), 75.

41. Henry B. Hibben to sister, Oct. 30, 1861, Kidwell Letters.

42. Sylvester C. Bishop to mother, Sept. 20, 1862, Bishop Letters.

43. Quoted in Chesebrough, *"God Ordained This War,"* 19.

44. Charles Sumner, "On the Crime Against Kansas," May 1856, http://www.iath.virginia.edu/seminar/unit4/sumner.html (accessed July 6, 2006).

45. Quoted in Chesebrough, *"God Ordained This War,"* 24.

46. Andrew J. McGarrah, personal essay or speech, May 29, 1863, McGarrah Letters. It is unclear whether this is an essay or speech, but it was found enclosed in one of the letters and appears to have been written by McGarrah.

47. In the 1624 Virginia census, Africans were still listed as servants. Although colonial records indicate that some Virginians were beginning to buy and sell African "slaves" by the 1640s, the laws institutionalizing slavery in Virginia did not come until the 1660s.

48. In drafting the Kentucky and Virginia Resolutions, Thomas Jefferson and James Madison, the author of the Declaration of Independence and principal architect of the Constitution and Bill of Rights, had unintentionally offered a legal rationale and precedent for asserting states' rights. In the *South Carolina Exposition and Protest* Calhoun explained exactly how a state could legally go about "nullifying" an unconstitutional federal law: Because the states had created the compact of the Union by calling for special state conventions to ratify the Constitution, states could use the same legal process to nullify an unconstitutional federal act or, if necessary, secede from the Union.

49. Ironically, up to the eve of the war, religious abolitionists were also expressing interest in seceding from the Union because of the federal government's compromises with slavery in the Constitution. See Chesebrough, *"God Ordained This War,"* 59.

50. New England Puritans also began importing African slaves for use as household servants as early as the 1630s, and a decade later New England merchants became actively involved in the slave trade between Africa and the English Caribbean Islands. Although New England had far fewer slaves, and their "household servant" version of slavery was far milder than Southern chattel slavery, it was the economic center of the slave trade until well after the Revolution, when most Northern states passed gradual emancipation laws.

51. Fisk, *Anti-Rebel*, 206–7.

52. Lev. 18:25.

53. Feb. 16, 1862, Mar. 1865, William P. Moore Diary, Wisconsin Historical Society, Madison.

54. Lev. 26:25; Num. 14:12; Deut. 32:24–26; 1 Kings 8:37–40; 2 Chron. 7:12–22, 20:9; Jer. 24:10; Jer. 29:17; Ezek. 5:12–27.

55. Quoted in Jimerson, *Private Civil War*, 159.

56. As chapter 9 will discuss in greater detail, this powerful ecclesiastical critique of the South's culture and faith may have unintentionally contributed to some religious soldiers' failure to respect their Confederate enemies' special moral status as creatures made in the image of God.

57. Beecher, "Success of American Democracy," 263, 265; quoted in Chesebrough, *"God Ordained This War,"* 57.

58. Ibid., 58.

59. Wiley, *Life of Billy Yank*, 96–97.

60. Gould, *Dear Sister*, 81–82.

61. Quoted in William C. Harris, ed., *In the Country of the Enemy: The Civil War Reports of a Massachusetts Corporal*, New Perspectives on the History of the South series (Gainesville: Univ. Press of Florida, 1999), 5.

62. Daniel M. Holt, *A Surgeon's Civil War: The Letters and Diary of Daniel M. Holt, M.D.*, ed. James M. Greiner, Janet L. Coryell, and James R. Smither (Kent, Ohio: Kent State Univ. Press, 2000), NetLibrary e-Book, http://www.netlibrary.com/ Reader/ (accessed June 29, 2007), 263.

63. Ibid., 224.

64. Ibid., 163–64.

65. Charles W. Wills, *Army Life of an Illinois Soldier: Including a Day-by-day Record of Sherman's March to the Sea: Letters and Diary of Charles W. Wills,* ed. Mary E. Kellogg (Carbondale: Southern Illinois Univ. Press, 1996), NetLibrary e-book, http://www.netlibrary.com/Reader/ (accessed June 29, 2007), 255, 121.

66. Quoted in Chesebrough, *"God Ordained This War,"* 20.

67. Ibid.

68. Ibid., 59.

69. Henry Ward Beecher, "Our Good Progress and Prospects," Nov. 27 1862, in *Freedom and War,* 379.

70. William Fifer to wife, Feb. 1865, Bentley Historical Library, Univ. of Michigan, http://bentley.umich.edu/research/guides/civilwar/civilwar_search.php?id=129/ (accessed June 6, 2007); Benjamin Webb Baker to Cousin Amos, Mar. 17, 1862, Benjamin Webb Baker, *Testament: A Soldier's History of the Civil War,* ed. Benson Bobrick (New York: Simon and Schuster, 2003), 207; Fisk, *Anti-Rebel,* 206–7; quoted in Woodworth, *While God Is Marching On,* 104–5.

71. Wills, *Army Life of an Illinois Soldier,* 316; Edward Ingraham to Alice, n.d., Ingraham Papers.

72. Elisha Hunt Rhodes, *All for the Union: The Civil War Diary and Letters of Elisha Hunt Rhodes,* ed. Robert Hunt Rhodes (New York: Orion Books, 1985), 153, 189.

73. Gould, *Dear Sister,* 81.

74. Ibid., 86.

75. Haines, *In the Country of the Enemy,* 149; Holt, *Surgeon's Civil War,* 263–66.

76. Wills, *Army Life of an Illinois Soldier,* 104.

77. Elisha Hunt Rhodes, *All for the Union: The Civil War Diary and Letters of Elisha Hunt Rhodes,* ed. Robert Hunt Rhodes and Geoffrey C. Ward; Lewis Chase to mother, Mar. 8, 1865, Lewis Chase Papers, Wisconsin Historical Society, Madison; Deforest quoted in Woodworth, *While God Is Marching On,* 261.

78. Fisk, *Anti-Rebel,* 32; Alexander Miller Ayers to wife, Dec. 25, 1862, Ayers Papers; Wilbur Fisk, *Hard Marching Every Day: The Civil War Letters of Private Wilbur Fisk, 1861–1865,* ed. Emil Rosenblatt and Ruth Rosenblatt (Lawrence: Univ. Press of Kansas, 1992), 65–66.

79. Matt. 7:1–5. Although the context of this passage suggests Christ is specifically rebuking hypocritical judgments here, given the Northern people's own endemic racism and historic participation in the evolution of chattel slavery, it would seem that Christ's admonition could be directed to these soldiers as well. As commander in chief, Lincoln pretty much said the same thing in his second inaugural address: "It may seem strange that any men should dare to ask a just God's assistance in wringing their bread from the sweat of other men's faces; but let us judge not that we be not judged."

80. 2 Pet. 2:20–21.

81. Ransom Bedell to cousin, [1861], no location given, Bedell Papers.

82. John Lindley Harris to Miss Susan, Sept. 21, 1863, Harris Papers.

83. Philip Welshimer to wife, July 16, 1863, Welshimer Papers; Joseph Whitney, *Kiss Clara for Me: The Story of Joseph Whitney and his Family, Early Days in the Midwest, and Soldiering in the American Civil War,* ed. Robert J. Snetsinger (State

College, Pa.: Carnation Press, 1969), 47. Although Welshimer and Whitney's chaplain may have only been employing figurative language here, given nineteenth-century Reformed Protestants' literal, commonsense hermeneutics, and belief in both the existence and immanent nature of such beings, it is also possible that they were not.

84. Wills, *Army Life of an Illinois Soldier,* 62; Bell Irvin Wiley, quoted in Wiley, *Life of Billy Yank,* 103; John Lindley Harris to father, Aug. 22, 1862, Harris Papers.

6. God's Will

1. Charles Wickesberg to parents, Oct. 3, 1862, Alfred Wickesberg Collection, Sheboygan County Historical Research Center, Sheboygan Falls, Wisc. (hereafter cited as Wickesberg Collection).

2. Charles Wickesberg to parents, Jan. 17, 1864, Wickesberg Collection.

3. Noll, *History of Christianity,* 241–43.

4. Gen. 1:1; 1 Chron. 29:12; Isa. 44:24–26; Pss. 100:19, 119:91; John 1:3.

5. In the course of my research, the theological constructs of immanence and transcendence never surfaced in any of the primary material. Interestingly, Webster's 1828 dictionary, which incorporates so much Protestant religious language and imagery and so often included Protestant theological definitions in many of its selections, did not provide any theological meaning to these two words. Webster defined the word "immanent" as "inherent; intrinsic; internal," and the word "transcendent" as "1. To rise above; to surmount; as lights in the heavens transcending the region of the clouds. 2. To pass over; to go beyond. 3. To surpass; to outgo; to excel; to exceed." *Noah Webster's 1828 Dictionary of the American Language,* Electronic Reprint, CTI Technologies, CD ed., 2000, s.v. "immanent" and "transcendent." See also Exod. 3:14; John 8:58; and *Matthew Henry's Commentary on the Whole Bible: Complete and Unabridged in One Volume* (Peabody, Mass.: Hendrickson, 1991), 100.

6. *Noah Webster's 1828 Dictionary of the American Language,* CD ed., s.v "omniscient"; Job 42:2; Jer. 32:17; Matt. 19:26; Mark 10:27; Job 28:20–24; Jer. 1:5; John 2:24, 16:30, 21:17; Rom. 8:28.

7. *Noah Webster's 1828 Dictionary of the American Language,* CD ed., s.v. "providential"; Saum, *Popular Mood,* 3.

8. *Noah Webster's 1828 Dictionary of the American Language,* CD ed., s.v. "providential," and "providence."

9. *Noah Webster's 1828 Dictionary of the American Language,* CD ed., s.v. "will" (n. and v.t.). Perhaps included to defend the biblical doctrines of God's perfect justice and man's free will, buried deep within Webster's definition of "will" is the qualification that "great disputes have existed respecting the freedom of the will. Will is often quite a different thing from desire." In other words, according to Webster, God does not want evil to exist, but it happens to be a necessary corollary of human freedom. Some modern theologians have introduced concepts such as God's "perfect" and "permissive" will to clarify such distinctions.

10. Chesebrough, *"God Ordained This War,"* 6.

11. Beecher, "Battle Set in Array," 94.

12. Quoted in Chesebrough, *"God Ordained This War,"* 6.

13. Prophets were essentially the Hebraic equivalent of an ancient oracle or seer. They served as God's divine spokespersons, communicating His thoughts and will to people for the purposes of instruction, warning, correction, and encouragement.

14. Ps. 91:1–7.

15. Various biblical passages testified that God would guard the course of the just and preserve the lives of the faithful: Jer. 39:17–18; Prov. 2:8; Pss. 1:6, 31:23, 97:10.

16. Saum, *Popular Mood,* 13–15, 65; Heb. 11:4–38.

17. Phil. 2:12–13; James 2:17–26.

18. John T. McMahon, *John T. McMahon's Diary of the 136th New York, 1861–1864,* ed. John Michael Priest (Shippensburg, Pa.: White Mane, 1993), 66.

19. Quoted in Woodworth, *While God Is Marching On,* 265.

20. David Beem to fiancée Hala, Oct. 6, 1861, Beem Papers.

21. Joseph Judson Dimock Sr. to father, June 30, 1861, Dimock Family Papers.

22. Caleb Beal Clark to mother and father, n.d., Caleb B., Joseph J., and William Clark Letters, Wisconsin Historical Society, Madison.

23. Private Abraham Boynton to friends, May 3, 1863, Boynton Letters.

24. Matt. 10:29–31; Ps. 23; Luke 15:3–31; John 10:11–14; Ps. 147:7–9; Gen. 1:31; Num. 14:8; 1 Sam. 17:34–37; 2 Sam. 22:43–44; Pss. 18:18–20, 50, 34, 41:11, 56:13, 86:12–17, 104:21, 116.

25. Felix Brannigan to sister, July 26, 1862, quoted in McPherson, *For Cause and Comrades,* 66; Ransom Bedell to Cousin Theoda, June 12, 1862, Bedell Papers. To remind Union soldiers that a higher being was providentially watching over them and protecting them, one of the publishers of government stationary for the soldiers had this allusion to Matt. 10:29 printed as a letterhead.

26. John A. Blackwell to wife, June 15, 1863, John A. Blackwell Letters, Indiana Historical Society, Indianapolis (hereafter cited as Blackwell Letters).

27. Gould, *Dear Sister,* 33.

28. 2 Kings 6:15–17; Matt. 18:10.

29. William G. Baugh to mother, June 15, 1864, William G. Baugh Letters, Manuscript, Archives, and Rare Book Library, Robert M. Woodruff Library, Emory University (hereafter cited as Baugh Letters); William G. Baugh to mother, June 30, 1864, Baugh Letters.

30. Charles N. Mumford to wife, Aug. 30, 1864, Mumford Letters.

31. *Noah Webster's 1828 Dictionary of the American Language,* CD ed., s.v. "inscrutable."

32. Saum, *Popular Mood,* xxiii.

33. Deut. 5:22–23; Job 38:1; Isa. 29:6; Ps. 111:10; Prov. 1:7; Prov. 2:5; Ps. 2:11; Isa. 33:6; Job 4:14; Amos 9:8; Phil. 2:12; Pss. 34:16, 76:11–13; Deut. 6:13–15; Rom. 11:33–34; 1 Cor. 1:20–25, 3:19; Eccles. 11:5; 1 Cor. 2:6–9.

34. A. H. Edwards to Anna, in A. H. Edwards, *"Dear Friend Anna": The Civil War Letters of a Common Soldier From Maine,* ed. Beverly Hayes Kallgren and James L. Crouthamel (Orono: Univ. of Maine Press, 1992), 70.

35. Wesley Gould to brother-in-law Marvin Thomas, in Gould, *Dear Sister,* 17.

36. Lincoln, "Meditation on the Divine Will," 5:403–4.

37. Abraham Lincoln, "Letter to Thurlow Weed," Mar. 15, 1865, in ibid. 8:356.

38. Andrew J. McGarrah to parents, Feb. 22, 1864, McGarrah Letters.

39. Exod. 20:12; Deut. 5:16: Mark 10:19; Eph. 6:2 ; 1 Tim. 5:8.

40. James 4:13–16.

41. Welsh, *Irish Green and Union Blue*, 42.

42. Amos C. Weaver to mother, May 8, 1862, Weaver Letters.

43. Quoted in Woodworth, *While God Is Marching On*, 49.

44. Daniel Webster to fiancée Gertrude, Nov. 28, 1861, Webster Letters.

45. Luke 8:13; 1 Thess. 3:2–3; 2 Thess. 1:4; 1 Pet. 1:6; 2 Pet. 2:9; 1 Pet. 5:9–10; James 1:2–3; Mal. 3:17–18.

46. B. P. Bruce to mother, June 28, 1863, Bruce Family Papers.

47. Joseph Manson to wife, Oct. 29, 1865, Manson Correspondence.

48. Jacob W. Bartmess to wife, Sept. 6, 1864, Jacob W. Bartmess Letters, Indiana Historical Society, Indianapolis (hereafter cited as Bartmess Letters).

49. Amaziah Hadden to wife, June 12, 1862, Amaziah Hadden Papers, Abraham Lincoln Presidential Library, Springfield, Ill. (hereafter cited as Hadden Papers).

50. John G. Jones to parents, Jan. 2, 1863, John G. Jones Letters.

51. Adam Muenzenberger to wife Barbara, Dec. 16, 1862, Adam Muenzenberger Letters, Wisconsin Historical Society, Madison.

52. Robert Steele to wife, Feb. 14, 1863, Steele Papers.

53. Fisk, *Anti-Rebel*, 323–24.

54. John Blackwell to wife, July 1, 1863, Blackwell Letters.

55. *Noah Webster's 1828 Dictionary of the American Language*, CD ed., s.v. "submission."

56. Rom. 9:18–21.

57. Saum, *Popular Mood*, 13–14.

58. Noah Webster defined the word "murmur" as "2. To grumble; to complain; to utter complaints in a low, half articulated voice; to utter sullen discontent; with at, before the thing which is the cause of discontent; as, murmur not at sickness; or with at or against, before the active agent which produces the evil," and he illustrated its meaning with two biblical examples: "The Jews murmured at him. John 6" and "The people murmured against Moses. Ex.13." *Noah Webster's 1828 Dictionary of the American Language*, CD ed., s.v. "murmur"; 1 Cor. 10:10.

59. T. S. Seacord to wife, Sept. 6, 1862, Seacord Papers.

60. Amaziah Hadden to wife, June 12, 1862, Hadden Papers.

61. Dwight Fraser to Sister Lizzie, May 3, 1864, Fraser Letters.

62. Reid Hiriam, Mar. 20, 1863, Hiriam Letters.

63. Pss. 33:10, 19:9; 1 Cor. 10:10.

64. T. S. Seacord to wife, Nov. 3, 1862, Seacord Papers.

65. Abraham Boynton to friends, Mar. 25, 1864, Boynton Letters.

66. Robert Steele to wife, Dec. 22, 1862, Steele Papers.

67. William Edmund Brush to father, Mar. 30, 1862, Brush Family Papers, Abraham Lincoln Presidential Library, Springfield, Ill.

7. A Divine Judgment

1. Quoted in Woodworth, *While God Is Marching On,* 261, 103.

2. Harry Stout, *The New England Soul: Preaching and Religious Culture in Colonial New England* (New York: Oxford Univ. Press, 1986), 77–82; Miller, *Errand into the Wilderness,* 7.

3. Sacvan Bercovitch, *The American Jeremiad* (Madison: Univ. of Wisconsin Press, 1978), 8, 17–18, 117–32.

4. Miller, *Errand into the Wilderness,* 2–15.

5. Stout, *Upon the Altar,* 38.

6. John Brown, "John Brown's Last Speech to the Court, November 2, 1859," in *For the Record: A Documentary History of America,* 2 vols., ed. David E. Shi and Holly A. Mayer (New York: W. W. Norton, 1999), 1:574.

7. Quoted in Fredrickson, "Coming of the Lord," 118; quoted in Chesebrough, *"God Ordained This War,"* 85, 120.

8. Quoted in Fredrickson, "Coming of the Lord," 119.

9. Henry Ward Beecher, "Our Blameworthiness," Jan. 4 1861, in *Freedom and War,* 63–64, 70.

10. James H. Moorehead, *American Apocalypse: Yankee Protestants and the Civil War* (New Haven, Conn.: Yale Univ. Press, 1978), 52.

11. In *Civil War Soldiers,* Reid Mitchell also concluded that some Union soldiers viewed themselves as "righteous tools of God's judgment." Reid Mitchell, *Civil War Soldiers* (New York: Viking, 1988).

12. Beecher, "Battle Set in Array," 107; Exod. 21:19–22:1. The word "vengeance" appears thirty-nine times in the King James Bible but is nearly always used in the context of God's future judgment of sinners. The word "revenge" only appears five times. The word "punishment," meanwhile, appears twenty-three times. While there is no reference to the word "retribution," the word "recompense" is cited twenty-five times and is almost always used in the context of legal amends for various human sins.

13. Dietrich Smith to friend, May 19, 1861, Dietrich C. Smith Letters, Abraham Lincoln Presidential Library, Springfield, Ill. (hereafter cited as Dietrich C. Smith Letters); James H. Leonard to Mary, June 15, 1862, Leonard Letters; Alexander Miller Ayers to wife, Nov. 9, 1862, Ayers Papers.

14. Haskell, *Haskell of Gettysburg,* 55.

15. Peter Weyhrich to Friend Dietrich, Apr. 19, 1863, Dietrich C. Smith Letters.

16. Wills, *Army Life of an Illinois Soldier,* 320.

17. Quoted in Woodworth, *While God Is Marching On,* 251.

18. Ibid.

19. Ibid.

20. Quoted in Paludan, *People's Contest,* 301, 351; McPherson, *Battle Cry of Freedom,* 810, 826.

21. William G. Baugh to parents, Mar. 27, 1865, Baugh Letters.

22. Francis Russell to mother, Sept. 5, 1862, Russell Family Papers.

23. Wills, *Army Life of an Illinois Soldier,* 316; Haines, *In the Country of the Enemy,* 149.

24. Holt, *Surgeon's Civil War,* 138, 382.

25. Michael H. B. Cunningham to wife, Oct. 3, 1863, Cunningham Letters.

26. Shattuck, *Shield and Hiding Place,* 18.

27. Quoted in Woodworth, *While God Is Marching On,* 263.

28. Fisk, *Anti-Rebel,* 66–67.

29. Horace Bushnell, *The Vicarious Sacrifice, Grounded in Principles of Universal Obligation* (New York: Charles Scribner, 1866); Paludan, "Religion and the American Civil War," 28.

30. Paludan, "Religion and the American Civil War," 28; Ahlstrom, *Religious History of the American People,* 686.

31. Harriet Beecher Stowe, "Reply to an Affectionate and Christian Address of Many Thousands of Women of Great Britain and Ireland to Their Sisters the Women of the United States of America," *Atlantic Monthly,* Nov. 27, 1862.

32. John A. Blackwell to wife, May, [1863], Blackwell Letters.

33. John Blackwell to wife, July 17, 1863, Blackwell Letters.

34. Jacob W. Bartmess to wife Amanda, June 7, 1863, Bartmess Letters.

35. Matt. 5:7, 7:2; James 2:13.

36. Harlan to Kitty Crandall, July 21, 1864, Crandall Family Correspondence.

37. See, for example, the stories of the Israelites being defeated in their retributive war against the tribe of Benjamin and the disastrous defeat of the Hebrews when they first sought to storm the Promised Land without God's blessing: Judg. 20; Num. 14:39–45.

38. Bushnell, "Popular Government by Divine Right," 121; quoted in Chesebrough, *"God Ordained This War,"* 90.

39. Peter Weyhrich to Friend Dietrich, Dec. 1, 1862, Dietrich C. Smith Letters.

40. Quoted in Reid Mitchell, *The Vacant Chair: The Northern Soldier Leaves Home* (New York: Oxford Univ. Press, 1993), 119.

41. Quoted in Woodworth, *While God Is Marching On,* 103.

42. 2 Chron. 7:13–14.

43. Richard Brown to John A. Blackwell, Apr. 30, 1863, Blackwell Letters.

44. Donald, *Lincoln,* 337, 514; Ronald C. White Jr., *Lincoln's Greatest Speech: The Second Inaugural* (New York: Simon and Schuster, 2002), 108–12, 128–49. White's book seems to have made important new contributions to our understanding of Lincoln's carefully guarded but evolving faith.

45. Basler, *Collected Works* 4:482.

46. Ibid. 6:156.

47. Allen C. Guelzo, *Abraham Lincoln: Redeemer President* (Grand Rapids, Mich.: Eerdman's, 1999), 446.

48. Donald, *Lincoln,* 514.

49. White, *Lincoln's Greatest Speech,* 138–49, 154–55. Based on the recent work of David Herbert Donald, Mark Noll, Allen C. Guelzo, Ronald C. White, and Steven Woodworth, no one knows for certain where that spiritual journey ended. The evidence is unclear as to whether Lincoln remained what Guelzo calls a "Calvinized deist" or experienced an extremely private and profoundly personal conversion to Christ late in his presidency. Even if Lincoln did secretly embrace a more orthodox Christianity, given his refusal to officially join a church and frequent visits to the

theater, many of his religious contemporaries would probably still have technically labeled him a "non-Christian."

50. Quoted in ibid., 184.

51. Stout, *Upon the Altar*, 425; Noll, *America's God*, 426.

52. Quoted in White, *Lincoln's Greatest Speech*, 184.

53. Fisk, *Anti-Rebel*, 323–39.

8. Embracing Emancipation

1. These religious abolitionists only represented a small minority of the larger abolitionist movement, which despite its increasing popularity during the war never represented more than a small percentage of the Northern population.

2. Francis Russell to G. J. Russell, July 13, 1861, Russell Family Papers.

3. Quoted in Woodworth, *While God Is Marching On*, 113–14.

4. Francis Russell to Brother Spence, Oct. 20, 1862, Russell Family Papers.

5. Francis Russell to Brother Spence, May 27, 1862, Russell Family Papers.

6. The phrase "winepress of His wrath" is a direct allusion to Revelation 14:19–20: "The angel swung his sickle on the earth, gathered its grapes and threw them into the great winepress of God's wrath. They were trampled in the winepress outside the city, and blood flowed out of the press." Juliet Ward Howe was obviously alluding to this apocalyptic biblical language when she added the words "he is trampling out the vintage where the grapes of wrath are stored" to the text of "Battle Hymn of the Republic"; Ransom Bedell to Cousin, n.d., no location given, Bedell Papers.

7. Quoted in Woodworth, *While God Is Marching On*, 113.

8. Joseph Dimock to Sister Jennie, May 11, 1861, Dimock Family Papers.

9. The North's largest ethnic and religious minorities, such as the Irish and Catholics, were particularly opposed to the abolition of slavery as free blacks would likely pose a direct threat to their economic interests in Northern cities. See Iver Bernstein, *The New York City Draft Riots: Their Significance in American Society and Politics in the Age of the Civil War* (New York: Oxford Univ. Press, 1990).

10. Wiley, *Life of Billy Yank*, 40; McPherson, *For Cause and Comrades*, 117–18. Based on my own research, I suspect Wiley's figure of roughly 10 percent of Northern enlisted men expressing interest in emancipation is probably a more accurate reflection of enlisted soldiers' initial opinions about slavery and McPherson's higher figure reflects soldiers' increasing support for confiscation and emancipation measures in the second year of the war, after McClellan's defeat on the peninsula and the disaster at Second Bull Run forced the North to embrace more drastic war measures. Since McPherson noted that his sample overrepresented officers and enlisted men from Northern Republican regions such as Michigan, Iowa, and Massachusetts and underrepresented soldiers from Democratic regions such as New York and the border states, his 30 percent figure may still be too high for the pre–Emancipation Proclamation period.

11. Henry Ward Beecher, "The Beginning of Freedom," Mar. 9 1862, in *Freedom and War*, 238.

12. Fredrickson, "Coming of the Lord," 114–15.

13. Beecher, "Modes and Duties of Emancipation," 177–78.

14. James D. Liggett, "Our National Reverses," Sept. 7, 1862, in Chesebrough, *"God Ordained This War,"* 94–97.

15. Ibid., 98.

16. Ibid., 100.

17. Ibid., 100–102.

18. Ibid., 102–3.

19. Ransom Bedell to cousin, [1861], no location given, Bedell Papers; John F. L. Hartwell, *To My Beloved Wife and Boy at Home: The Letters and Diaries of Orderly Sergeant John F. L. Hartwell,* ed. Ann Hartwell Britton and Thomas J. Reed (Madison, N.J.: Fairleigh Dickinson Univ. Press 1997), 26; James B. Lockney to mother and friends, Apr. 9, 1863, Lockney Papers.

20. James T. Miller, *Bound to Be a Soldier: The Letters of Private James T. Miller,* ed. Jerediah Morris and Galen R. Wilson (Knoxville, Tenn., 2001), 52; Amos W. Hostetter to brother and sister, Jan. 29, 1863, Hostetter Papers.

21. George T. Chapin to Rev. John Chapin, Jan. 12, 1864, George T. Chapin Papers, Indiana Historical Society, Indianapolis (hereafter cited as Chapin Papers).

22. McPherson, *For Cause and Comrades,* 123–24. Based on his research, McPherson concluded that Union officers and soldiers who were prewar professionals overwhelmingly supported emancipation (four to one), whereas former blue-collar workers were less enthusiastic (two to one) in their support. Soldiers from Democratic strongholds in the Northeast, and from the Midwest and border states, frequently opposed Lincoln's Emancipation Proclamation.

23. Wills, *Army Life of an Illinois Soldier,* 127.

24. Haines, *In the Country of the Enemy,* 9, 77, 80, 147.

25. Holt, *Surgeon's Civil War,* 163–64.

26. Alexander Miller Ayers to wife, Jan. 25, 1863, Ayers Papers.

27. Fisk, *Anti-Rebel,* 207.

28. Miller, *Bound to Be a Soldier,* 109–10.

29. Jefferson Newman to Caroline Newman Kirkpatrick, May 20, 1863, Samuel Cotter Kirkpatrick Letters, Wisconsin Historical Society, Madison.

30. Amos Hostetter to brother and sister, Jan. 29, 1863, Hostetter Papers.

31. Richard Brown to John A. Blackwell, Apr. 30, 1863, Blackwell Letters.

32. Black soldiers may have worn the same uniform and been subjected to the same dangers as their white comrades, but they did not originally receive the same wages. Although Republicans initially tried to pass legislation granting them equal pay, Northern Democrats strongly opposed the measure, and in the end blacks were paid a few dollars less each month until 1864. See McPherson, *Battle Cry of Freedom,* 788–89.

33. Fisk, *Anti-Rebel,* 230.

34. Fisk, *Anti-Rebel,* 230; Miller, *Bound to Be a Soldier,* 135; Baker, *Testament,* 227.

35. Gasherie Decker to Gertrude, Apr. 4, 1863, Gasherie Decker Diaries and Letters, Wisconsin Historical Society, Madison (hereafter cited as Decker Diaries and Letters).

36. Fisk, *Anti-Rebel,* 34.

37. Ibid., 206–7.

38. James B. Lockney, Apr. 10, 1863, Lockney Papers.

39. George T. Chapin to Wife Ella, Oct. 14, 1862, Chapin Papers.

40. George T. Chapin to brother Rev. John Chapin, Jan. 12, 1864, Chapin Papers.

41. John Blackwell to wife, July 17, 1863, Blackwell Letters.

9. Compromise and Conflict

1. Gould, *Dear Sister,* 64.

2. J. A. Dernten to Kittie Crandall, Oct. 29, 1862, Crandall Family Correspondence.

3. Gasherie Decker to Sister Gertrude, Aug. 22, 1863, Decker Diaries and Letters.

4. Linderman, *Embattled Courage,* 255. *Embattled Courage* presents one of the best histories of Civil War combat, but even with his qualification, Linderman probably still overstated his case regarding the religious disillusionment of the Northern armies. Other scholars' work, such as James M. McPherson's *For Cause and Comrades,* and especially Gardiner Shattuck's and Steven Woodworth's more extensive studies of religion in the Union armies, do not support Linderman's claim that the Northern armies became increasingly disillusioned with religion at the end of the war. Perhaps it would be more accurate to state that while there was less time and energy devoted to religious activities during the continuous fighting that occurred in the last year of the war, and more spiritual breakdowns as a result of that terrible stress, this probably had more to do with Grant's aggressive campaigning strategy, than a general disillusionment with Christianity in the Northern camps. After all, when the fighting finally ended, the religious revivals returned—something which should not have happened if the eastern troops had truly abandoned their faith. According to Shattuck, there were widespread revivals when the Northern armies assembled for the last time in Washington, D.C., for a "Grand Review" and final mustering-out ceremonies. Membership statistics for the major Northern denominations during this period also seem to belie any widespread disillusionment with religion in the North. Despite the wartime death of over three hundred thousand Northern men, membership in the North's churches actually significantly increased between 1860 and 1866. See McPherson, *For Cause and Comrades;* Shattuck, *Shield and Hiding Place;* and Smith, *Revivalism and Social Reform,* 20–21.

5. See *For Cause and Comrades,* 62–76; Mitchell, "Christian Soldiers?"; and Paludan, "Religion and the American Civil War," 24–25.

6. Shattuck, *Shield and Hiding Place,* 53, 63. While dated, Shattuck's book ambitiously—and in my opinion, successfully—examines the religious life of both armies and contains an excellent summary of the work and contributions of the Confederate and Union army chaplaincies. The best modern treatment of the Civil War armies' religious life, however, is Steven E. Woodworth's *While God Is Marching On.*

7. Ibid.

8. Ibid., 53.

9. George T. Chapin to brother, Feb. 17, 1863, Chapin Papers.

10. William Dalzell to wife Lizzy, Jan. 8, 1863, William Dalzell Letters, Manuscript, Archives, and Rare Book Library, Robert M. Woodruff Library, Emory University (hereafter cited as Dalzell Letters).

11. John Blackwell to wife, Oct. 24, 1863, Blackwell Letters. Union army chaplains initially were given a rather vague role in the Union army. They received the salary of a cavalry captain (seventeen hundred dollars a year), wore no regular uniform, and were not given an official military rank. At the same time, except for being told to hold religious services "whenever possible" and to promote and report on "the social happiness and morale improvement" of the troops, their duties were never clearly spelled out. Until the spring of 1863, most were not even sure of their combatant status.

12. Fisk, *Anti-Rebel*, 213.

13. Leander Knowles to sister, Sept. 8, 1861, Leander Knowles Papers, Abraham Lincoln Presidential Library, Springfield, Ill.; William A. McLean to friends, May 12, 1861, William A. McLean Papers, Abraham Lincoln Presidential Library, Springfield, Ill.

14. Wiley, *Life of Billy Yank*, 268–69; Shattuck, *Shield and Hiding Place*, 52, 60, 76.

15. Shattuck, *Shield and Hiding Place*, 63; Alan T. Nolan, *The Iron Brigade: A Military History* (Bloomington: Indiana Univ. Press, 1994), 203. After the chaplain of the Second Wisconsin Regiment was discharged in May 1862, the subsequent commanders of the Second Wisconsin did not make any attempts to replace him and the Sixth Wisconsin had no chaplain from November 1861 to 1864.

16. Shattuck, *Shield and Hiding Place*, 60.

17. Daniel Peck to Rachel, Apr. 19, 1863, Daniel Peck Collection, Robert M. Woodruff Memorial Library, Emory University; William Dalzell to Lizzy, Jan. 8, 1863, Dalzell Letters; Charles Norwood to wife, Sept. 16, 1862, Mumford Letters; Joseph Manson to friends, Feb. 17, 1864, Manson Correspondence.

18. John A. Blackwell to wife, June 14, 1863, Blackwell Letters.

19. Jacob W. Bartmess to Amanda, Jan. 3, 1863, Bartmess Letters.

20. George W. Squier, *This Wilderness of War: The Civil War Letters of George W. Squier, Hoosier Volunteer,* ed. Julie A. Doyle, John David Smith, and Richard M. McMurry (Knoxville: Univ. of Tennessee Press, 1998), 29.

21. Miller, *Bound to Be a Soldier*, 7.

22. Hartwell, *To My Beloved Wife and Boy at Home*, 217.

23. Ibid., 336–37.

24. Henry Franklin Hole to Minerva, Aug. 19, 1861, Hole Papers; Jasper Kidwell to sister, Oct. 30, 1861, Kidwell Letters; Herman Melville, *Moby Dick* (New York: Modern Library, 1926); Nathaniel Hawthorne, *The Scarlet Letter* (New York: Harper, 1950).

25. Ransom Bedell to cousin, Mar. 31, 1862, Bedell Papers.

26. Wills, *Army Life of an Illinois Soldier*, 136.

27. Ps. 103:12; Eph. 4:30; Amos C. Weaver to Mirriam, May 13, 1864, Weaver Letters.

28. "Seeing the elephant" was a common expression soldiers used to describe their baptism of fire.

29. Thomas F. Miller to Ben Newton, May 2, 1862, Thomas F. Miller Papers.

30. Squier, *This Wilderness of War,* 19.

31. Edwards, *"Dear Friend Anna,"* 33; Jacob W. Bartmess to Amanda, Oct. 25, 1863, Bartmess Letters.

32. Linderman, *Embattled Courage,* 241.

33. Fisk, *Anti-Rebel,* 183.

34. Hartwell, *To My Beloved Wife and Boy at Home,* 26.

35. Private T. S. Seacord to wife, Oct. 5, 1862, Seacord Papers; John M. Barnard to wife, Feb. 12, 1863, John M. Barnard Letters, Indiana Historical Society, Indianapolis (hereafter cited as Barnard Letters); Daniel Webster to Gertrude, Jan. 3, 1863, Webster Letters; Amos C. Weaver to Miss Mirriam, June 20, 1864, Weaver Letters.

36. Matt. 5:39–44, 18:22; Luke 6:27.

37. Bruce Catton, *Reflections on the Civil War* (Garden City, N.Y.: Doubleday, 1981), 46. After the war, the South's most famous Christian general, Robert E. Lee, claimed he had never harbored any bitter or vindictive feelings toward his Northern enemies and that during the war he had prayed every day for "those people" who were waging war against his beloved Virginia.

38. Sylvester C. Bishop to mother, July 21, 1862, Bishop Letters.

39. Michael Hayes Branniger to wife, May 10, 1864, Cunningham Letters.

40. Holt, *Surgeon's Civil War,* 22.

41. John R. Siperly to Jennie, Sept. 21, 1864, Smith Correspondence.

42. Edwin C. Sackett, Dec. 27, 1861, Edwin C. and John H. Sackett Papers, Abraham Lincoln Presidential Library, Springfield, Ill.; Alexander Miller Ayers to wife, Nov. 11, 1862, Ayers Papers; David King Jr. to sister, July 1, 1861, King Family Papers, Abraham Lincoln Presidential Library, Springfield, Ill.; John M. Barnard to wife, Mar. 19, 1863, Barnard Letters.

43. Miller, *Bound to Be a Soldier,* 52

44. John Lindley Harris to father, Apr. 6, 1863, Harris Papers.

45. Private John G. Jones to parents, Nov. 21, 1863, John G. Jones Letters.

46. Ezek. 18:23, 32; Ezek. 33:11; Ps. 11:5; Isa. 59:6–7.

47. C. S. Lewis, *Mere Christianity,* a revised and amplified edition, with a new introduction, of the three books *Broadcast Talks, Christian Behavior,* and *Beyond Personality* (San Francisco: HarperCollins, 2001), 119–20.

48. Ibid., 118.

49. Fisk, *Anti-Rebel,* 67.

50. Quoted in McPherson, *For Cause and Comrades,* 74.

51. Fisk, *Anti-Rebel,* 22.

52. John Keegan, *The Face of Battle: A Study of Agincourt, Waterloo and the Somme* (London: Penguin, 1976), 172.

53. Linderman, *Embattled Courage,* 72, 147–49.

54. John H. Pardington, *Dear Sarah: Letters Home from a Soldier of the Iron Brigade,* ed. Coralou Peel Lassen (Bloomington: Indiana Univ. Press, 1999), 119.

55. Wiley, *Life of Billy Yank,* 83; quoted in Mitchell, *Civil War Soldiers,* 79–80.

56. Although many battles were fought at longer ranges, there are numerous accounts of opposing lines of infantry coming within seventy-five yards of each other

to trade volleys. For a couple examples, see Stephen W. Sears, *Landscape Turned Red: The Battle of Antietam* (Boston: Houghton Mifflin, 1983), 202; and Nolan, *Iron Brigade*, 90, 95.

57. Gould, *Dear Sister*, 74, 130.

58. Although some religious soldiers dehumanized their Southern enemies quite early in the war, and more embraced this attitude as the fighting continued, the vast majority did not seem to hate their Southern enemies. Actually, as the war continued and they discovered their common predicament and trials, most soldiers developed an increasing respect for their counterparts on the other side. As a result of the wartime revivals, both armies also genuinely became more religious and determined to see their cause through until victory or death.

59. Gould, *Dear Sister*, 81.

60. William H. Onstot, Nov. 16, 1861, Onstot Papers; Squier, *This Wilderness of War*, 11, 24; Arthur Lee Bailhache to brother, Oct. 22, 1861, Bailhache-Brayman Papers, Abraham Lincoln Presidential Library, Springfield, Ill.

61. *Webster's Ninth New Collegiate Dictionary* (Springfield, Mass.: Mirriam-Webster, 1987), 257; Jeff Stone, "Behavioral Discrepancies and the Role of Construal Processes in Cognitive Dissonance," in *Cognitive Social Psychology: The Princeton Symposium on the Legacy and Future of Social Cognition*, ed. Gordon B. Moskowitz (Mahwah, N.J.: Lawrence Erlbaum Associates, 2001), 41–44, 46–49, 51–52, 57.

62. Herbert C. Kelman and Reuben M. Baron, "Inconsistency as a Psychological Signal," in *Theories of Cognitive Consistency: A Source Book*, ed. Robert P. Abelson, Elliot Aronson, William J. McGuire, Theodore M. Newcomb, Milton J. Rosenberg, and Percy H. Tannenbaum (Chicago: Rand McNally, 1968), 332–34; Eva M. Pomerantz, Jill L. Saxon, and Gwen A. Kenney, "Self-Evaluation: The Development of Sex Differences," in *Cognitive Social Psychology: The Princeton Symposium on the Legacy and Future of Social Cognition*, ed. Gordon B. Moskowitz (Mahwah, N.J.: Lawrence Erlbaum Associates, 2001), 63.

63. A. H. Edwards to Anna, in Edwards, *"Dear Friend Anna,"* 14, 96.

64. David E. Larson, ed., *Mayo Clinic: Family Health Book* (New York: William Morrow, 1990), 1018.

65. Daniel Webster to Gertrude, Jan. 6, 1863, Webster Letters.

66. Amos C. Weaver, Jan. 22 1864, Weaver Letters.

67. Richard Gould to sister, in Gould, *Dear Sister*, 127.

68. Robert Steele to wife, Jan. 31 1863, Steele Papers.

69. Matt. 24:44; Private John G. Jones to parents, Jan. 5, 1863, and Jan. 24, 1863, John G. Jones Letters.

70. Gen. 9:5–6; Matt. 26:52.

71. Isa. 59:1–8; Rom. 3:15–17; Ps. 120:6–7.

72. Isa. 32:17–18; Ps. 34:12–14; Mark 9:50; Heb. 12:14; 1 Pet. 3:11.

73. Rom. 12:17–21.

74. Mic. 4:1–3; Isa. 2:4–5.

75. Linderman, *Embattled Courage*, 256.

76. Joshua Chamberlain, *The Passing of the Armies: An Account of the Final Campaigns of the Army of the Potomac, Based upon Personal Reminiscences of the Fifth Army* (Lincoln: Univ. of Nebraska Press, 1998), 55.

77. McPherson, "Afterword," 410.

78. John Blackwell to wife, Oct. 11 1862, Blackwell Letters. One of Blackwell's last sentences, "But drops of grief can not repay the debt I owe," might well be alluding to the final verse of "At the Cross" by Isaac Watts, the prolific nonconformist English hymn writer. The first lines of the last verse read, "But drops of grief can ne'er repay; / The debt of love I owe."

79. Quoted in Linderman, *Embattled Courage,* 256–57.

80. McPherson, *For Cause and Comrades,* 68.

10. Soldiers of Christ

1. See Mitchell, "Christian Soldiers?"; Phillip Shaw Paludan, *A People's Contest: The Union and the Civil War, 1861–1865* (New York: Harper and Row, 1988); and Woodworth, *While God Is Marching On.*

2. Ayers, review of *Religion and the American Civil War.*

3. McPherson, *For Cause and Comrades,* 68–69, 76.

Epilogue

1. Noll, "Bible and Slavery," 43–73.

2. In suggesting that the proper spheres of church and state be strictly separated, I do not by any means advocate having the church embrace the South's prewar "spirituality of the church" doctrine. Complete segregation or isolation, like that modeled by the early-twentieth-century American fundamentalist movement, represents the other extreme that should be avoided. The church has a clear moral duty to address all the major social and ethical problems of its day and should encourage believers to actively confront the greatest evils of their age. But the clergy and churches should not lead the political struggle themselves or align their churches with a particular political party. Political battles should be fought by the laity, outside the formal jurisdiction of the church. The church should simply concentrate on fulfilling its own difficult goals of boldly and creatively proclaiming the Good News of the Gospel, ministering to the body, and serving as the moral conscience of the nation.

3. Noll, *Christians in the American Revolution,* 48.

4. The best modern examination of the churches' contribution to the sectional breakdown remains C. C. Goen's groundbreaking book *Broken Churches, Broken Nations,* which argued that the United States' broken Protestant churches presaged a broken nation.

5. The Northern churches probably did not consciously "manipulate" religious belief to promote a holy war against the Confederacy. Usually those who exploit religious feeling for the purpose of advancing political goals do so with the best of intentions, convinced that they are motivated by the sincerest of religious convictions and are advancing the highest of religious causes. But as history so often proven, the path to hell is paved with good intentions. Those who blend the separate spheres of religion and politics rarely consider the potential long-term consequences of their actions. In

times of crisis, such as war or direct assault, some states and churches do consciously manipulate religious feeling to defend their institutions, but in this case their behavior can be likened to that of a drowning swimmer who, in his desperate struggle to stay afloat, instinctively employs every means at his disposal—legitimate or not—to survive.

6. Stout, *Upon the Altar,* 283.

7. My speculative conclusion here does, however, draw on similar conclusions re garding the clergy's role in the causes and subsequent moral failures of the Civil War reached in the well-researched histories of C. C. Goen, Harry Stout, and David Chesebrough. See Goen's *Broken Churches, Broken Nation;* Stout's *Upon the Altar;* and Chesebrough's *"God Ordained This War."*

8. Chesebrough, *"God Ordained This War,"* 1–9.

9. Ahlstrom, *Religious History of the American People,* 672; Beringer et al., *Elements of Confederate Defeat,* 32–33; C. C. Goen, *Broken Churches, Broken Nation,* 148–49; Fredrickson, "Coming of the Lord," 118.

Bibliography

MANUSCRIPTS

Manuscript, Archives, and Rare Book Library, Robert W. Woodruff Library, Emory University

Armstrong, Henry. Located in Jennie Safford Smith Correspondence.
Ayers, Alexander Miller. Papers.
Barlow, William W. Located in Jennie Safford Smith Correspondence.
Baugh, William G. Letters.
Brigham, Alfred Milo. Letters.
Brown, Lucius Franklin. Papers.
Cox, Charles Harding. Papers.
Cox, Harvey Warren. Papers.
Craig, Samuel. Letters.
Dalzell, William. Letters.
Darling, Charles B. Correspondence.
Dimock, Joseph J. Dimock Family Papers.
Elwood, John W. Papers.
Fish, Edwin R. Papers.
Gates, Luther L. Letters.
Ghirdner, Ephraim L. Papers.
Hamilton, David. Letters.
Harmon, Arthur A. Letters.
Manson, Charles A. Papers.
Manson, Joseph. Correspondence.

Nailer, George W. Papers.
Newton, Nathan G. Letters.
Oswald, Peter. Letters.
Parkinson, William M. Letters.
Peck, Daniel. Collection. Cataloged under Microfilm Miscellany.
Siperly, John R. Located in Jennie Safford Smith Correspondence.
Slack, Albert L. Correspondence.
Taylor, Thomas Thomson. Papers.
Wesson, Hale. Correspondence.
Wightman, Edward King. Correspondence.

Abraham Lincoln Presidential Library, Springfield, Illinois

Adams, Franklin. Newton Bateman Papers.
Anderson, Edward. John and Charles Black Papers.
Andrews, Austin S. Andrews Family Papers.
Austin, William H. John Sargent Papers.
Bailhache, Arthur Lee. Bailhache-Brayman Papers.
Bedell, Ransom. Papers.
Black, John Charles. Papers.
Black, William P. John Charles Black Papers.
Blair, Jonathan. Papers.
Blake, Austin. Philip Welshimer Papers.
Brayman, Mason. Bailhache-Brayman Papers.
Bruce, B. P. Bruce Family Papers.
Bruce, Francis Harvey. Bruce Family Papers.
Brush, William Edmond. Brush Family Papers.
Buchan, James E. Papers.
Burden, John. Daniel Ferguson and Family Papers.
Call, Thomas. William S. Macomber Papers.
Clark, George R. Daniel Ferguson and Family Papers.
Cleveland, Lewis P. James P. Snell Papers.
Cochran, William F. Papers.
Cox, Joseph R. Papers.
Cromwell, John Nelson. Papers.
Crum, William H. Crum Family Papers.
Derrick, William H. Thomas S. Seacord Papers.
Dewolf, David. Papers.
Dillon, William L. Isaiah T. and William L. Dillon Papers.
Dinsmore, John C. Papers.
Dodds, James W. John Lindley Harris Papers.
Drish, James F. Papers.
Ege, James H. Edwin W. and Ira A. Payne Papers.
Fielding, Edward E. John Charles Black Papers.

Fifer, George H. Joseph Wilson Fifer Papers.
Fithian, William K. John Charles Black Papers.
Floyd, Charles H. Papers.
Forest, Joseph. Papers.
Fox, James Garner. Papers.
Frazee, Thomas J. Papers.
Frost, Luther. Luther and Orville Frost Papers.
Frost, Orville. Luther and Orville Frost Papers.
Gilbert, Edwin. Papers.
Glenn, John F. Papers.
Hadden, Amaziah. Papers.
Harding, Jacob Oscar. Papers.
Harris, John Lindley. Papers.
Hatch, Alexander S. Hatch and Fessenden Families Papers.
Henderson, Thomas W. Daniel Ferguson and Family Papers.
Herdman, John H. Papers.
Hole, Henry Franklin. Papers.
Hostetter, Amos W. Papers.
Ingraham, Duncan G. Edward H. Ingraham Papers.
Ingraham, Edward H. Papers.
Kennedy, William J. Papers.
Kennedy, William W. John Schuler Wilcox Papers.
King, Charles Speer. King Family Papers.
King, David, Jr. King Family Papers.
King, Henry. Zebulon Parker Papers.
King, James S. King Family Papers.
Kircher, Henry. Engelmann-Kirscher Family Papers.
Knowles, Leander. Papers.
Kyger, Tilmon D. Papers.
Leand, Sherman. Wallace-Dickey Papers.
Lippincott, Charles E. Newton-Bateman Papers.
Lyon, Joseph H. Lease Family Papers.
Markle, Richard. Papers.
Marsh, William H. Papers.
Miller, Thomas F. Papers.
Miner, James. Papers.
McClanahan, John W. Brush Family Papers.
McIlrath, James. Papers.
McLean, William A. Papers.
McMackin, Warren Emmitt. McMackin and Family Papers.
Meinhard, Frederick. Papers.
Merriam, Jonathan. Papers.
Miller, Thomas F. Papers.

Needham, Lyman H. Papers.

Onstot, William H. Papers.

Orme, William Ward. Papers.

Overmire, Jacob J. James W. Anthony and Charles E. Smith Papers.

Paisley, Joel B. Papers.

Payne, Edwin W. Edwin W. and Ira A. Payne Papers.

Payne, Ira A. Edwin W. and Ira A. Payne Papers.

Payne, Lucien A. Edwin W. and Ira A. Payne Papers.

Phillips, Daniel J. M. John Messinger Papers.

Poak, David W. Papers.

Post, William H. Post Family Papers.

Rand, William Lucius. Rand Family Papers.

Ransom, Frederick Eugene. Douglas Hapeman Papers.

Reese, George W. Papers.

Robinson, William C. Papers.

Ross, Leonard Fulton. Papers.

Russell, Francis J. Russell Family Papers.

Russell, George W. Russell Family Papers.

Sackett, Edwin C. Edwin C. and John H. Sackett Papers.

Sackett, John H. Edwin C. and John H. Sackett Papers.

Seacord, Thomas S. Papers.

Simpson, David Rose. Papers.

Smith, Dietrich C. Letters.

Snell, Henry A. James P. Snell Papers.

Snell, James H. James P. Snell Papers.

Starring, Frederick A. Bailhache-Brayman Papers.

Steffins, August. Geza Mihalozty Papers.

Stewart, Levi. Papers.

Suiter, James P. Papers.

Swales, James M. Papers.

Teal, Thomas. Papers.

Tebbetts, William H. Papers.

Treadway, David P. Papers.

Van Deusen, Ira. Papers.

Vieria, Augustine. Papers.

Walker, Samuel S. Papers.

Wayne, Harley. Papers.

Welshimer, Philip. Papers.

Weyhrich, Peter. Dietrich C. Smith Papers.

Wilcox, Edward S. John Schuler Wilcox Papers.

Wilcox, William H. John Schuler Wilcox Papers.

Woolard, James B. Papers.

Indiana Historical Society, Indianapolis

Barnard, John M. Letters.
Bartmess, Jacob W. Letters.
Beem, David E. Papers.
Bishop, Sylvester. Letters.
Blackwell, John A. Letters.
Botkins, Thomas W. Letters.
Bower, William A. and Edmond T. Papers.
Brenton, William. Papers.
Brown, Richard. John A. Blackwell Letters.
Chapin, George T. Papers.
Connelly, Jesse B. Letters.
Corwin, Cornelius. Diary.
Craig, Isaac Newton. Papers.
Dunn, Helim Hatch. Papers.
Dunn, William. Letters.
Eldridge, Franklin. Letters.
Forder Family. Letters.
Fraser, Dwight and Joshua. Letters.
Gallager, Hugh D. Papers.
Hall, Perry. Letters.
Hamrick, Simpson S. Papers.
Harris, James Henry. Letters.
Harrison, Thomas J. Letters.
Haskell, Oliver C. Diary.
Hiriam, Reid. Letters.
Johnson, Andrew and Nathaniel. Letters.
Ketcham, William A. Papers.
Kidwell, Jasper N. Letters.
King, Jeptha. Letters.
Little, James M. Letters.
Madden, Cornelius J. Letters.
McCutchan, Charles A. Papers.
McGarrah, Andrew J. Letters.
Merrill, Samuel H. Letters.
Morse, Justus. Letters.
Neely, Joseph W. Diary.
Owen, Bennett. Reid Hiriam Letters.
Prickett, Thomas. Letters.
Runske Family. Letters.
Shanklin, George and Robert P. Letters.
Spencer, William. Letters.
Strong, Henry R. Letters.

Thomas, James S. Letters.
Tribbet, Robert. Letters.
Van Dyke, Augustus. Letters.
Warren, Jeremiah. Letters.
Weaver, Amos C. Letters.
Wheeler, George M. Letters.
Wilkens, John Adam. Letters.

Wisconsin Historical Society, Madison

Baker, William Henry. Diaries.
Barney, John J. Papers.
Baxter, John B. G. Papers.
Beecham, Henry W. Letters.
Beecham, Robert K. Letters.
Beers, Elon G. Diary.
Bennett, Van S. Diary.
Bly, Adelbert M. Correspondence.
Boynton, Abraham. Letters.
Brothers, David J. Diary.
Brown, William. Letters.
Carter, George B. Letters.
Carter, Richard E. Correspondence.
Chaplain, Jones. Jenkin Lloyd Diaries.
Chase, Lewis. Papers.
Childs, Albert M. Letters.
Church, William Henry. Papers.
Clark, Caleb B., Joseph J., and William. Letters.
Clemons, Henry. Letters.
Comstock, Eugene E. Diary and Letters.
Cooley, George. Diary.
Coon, David. Letters.
Covill, Wilson S. Letters.
Cowan, Luther H. Letters and Diary.
Crandall, Robert B. Crandall Family Correspondence.
Crowe, Richard Robert. Letters.
Culbertson, Henry Miller. Letters.
Culver, Newton H. Papers.
Cunningham, Michael Hayes Branniger. Letters.
Currier, Horace. Papers.
Cushing, William Barker. Letters.
Decker, Gasherie. Diaries and Letters.
Demarest, Burnett. Papers.
Dickinson, Charles H. Diary.

Dillon, Henry. Letters.

Drake, Henry T. Letters.

Dwight, Edward C. Papers.

Fitch, Michael Hendrick. Diary.

Flint, Horace R. Letters.

Fowler, James B. Diary.

Ghormley, James. Diary.

Goodhue, William F. Papers.

Hansen, Hans. Letters.

Hanson, William. Letters.

Hatchard, Thomas. Diary.

Hauxhurst, Sidney. Letters.

Hillier, Joseph W. Diary.

Hinkley, Julian Wisner. Papers.

Howard, Franklin B. Letters.

Hulbert, David S. Letters.

James, David Goodrich. Correspondence.

Jameson, Orin M. Diary.

Johnson, John A. Letters.

Jones, Jenkin Lloyd. Diary.

Jones, John G. Letters.

Jones, Newton. Letters.

Keene, Henry S. Diary.

Kennedy, John W. Letters.

Kirkpatrick, Samuel C. Letters.

Knight, John Henry. Letters.

Knilans, William A. Diaries.

Kurz, Ferdinand. Reminiscence.

Larke, Alured. Letters.

Larsen, Peter. Papers.

Lathrop, Stanley E. Papers.

Leigvam, Ole Kittelson. Diaries.

Leonard, James H. Letters.

Lindsey, Charles H. Diary.

Lockney, James Browne. Papers.

MacLachlan, John. Letters.

Mather, Jessie. Letters.

McCann, John W. Letters.

McLachlan, John. Letters.

McMillan, George B. Papers.

Meffert, William C. Diaries.

Merville, Hiram P. Letters.

Moore, William P. Diary.

Muenzenberger, Adam. Letters.

Mumford, Charles Norwood. Letters.

Nickel, Levi H. Diary.

Noble, William. Diary.

Norton, De Have. Letters.

Olson, Rollin. Letters.

Palmetier, Charles. Letters.

Perry, Matthew R. Letters.

Perry, James M. Diaries and Papers.

Persons, Horace T. Diaries.

Phillips, William L. Letters.

Proudfit, James Kerr. Correspondence.

Quiner, Emilie. Diary.

Richards, Robert. Letters.

Roberts, Israel, William, and Jesse M. Letters.

Roberts, John H. Letters.

Root, George W. Letters.

Salisbury, James K. Diary.

Saunders, Joseph H. Letters.

Simpson, John Hemphill. Diary.

Smith, Byron J. Letters.

Spaulding, George T. Papers.

Spencer, Charles H. Papers.

Steele, Robert. Papers.

Sterling, Levi. Journal.

Strong, Henry P. Letters.

Swain, Samuel Glyde. Papers.

Trabner, Henry J. Letters.

Trott, Lucille J. Harrison Family Papers.

Twining, Henry Harrison. Letters.

Tyler, James Monroe. Diaries.

Waldo, Charles D. Diary.

Warner, Robert T. Letters.

Waugh, Albert F. Letters.

Webster, Daniel. Letters.

Wheeler, Cornelius. Letters.

Wittenberger, Frank. Diary.

Wood, Warden A. Letters.

Woodman, Edwin Ellis. Diary.

Young, Henry F. Papers.

MISCELLANEOUS SOLDIERS

Sheboygan County Historical Research Center, Sheboygan Falls, Wisc.

Wickesberg, Charles. Alfred Wickesberg Collection.

Bentley Historical Library, University of Michigan, Ann Arbor

Fifer, William. Michigan in the Civil War Collection. http://bentley.umich.edu/ research/guides/civilwar/civilwar_search.php?nameid=335/ (accessed June 6, 2007).

PUBLISHED PRIMARY SOURCES

Allen, George H. *Forty-six Months with the Fourth R.I. Volunteers, in the War of 1861– 1865.* Providence, R.I.: J. A. and R. A. Reid, 1887.

Baker, Benjamin W. Webb. *Testament: A Soldier's Story of the Civil War.* Edited by Benson Bobrick. New York: Simon and Schuster, 2003.

Beecher, Henry Ward. "Against a Compromise of Principle." Nov. 29, 1860. In Beecher, *Freedom and War,* 28–56.

———. "The Battle Set in Array." Apr. 14, 1861. In Beecher, *Freedom and War,* 84–110.

———. "The Beginning of Freedom." Mar. 9, 1862. In Beecher, *Freedom and War,* 223–47.

———. "The Camp, Its Dangers and Duties." N.d. In Beecher, *Freedom and War,* 130–52.

———. "Energy of Administration Demanded." N.d. In Beecher, *Freedom and War,* 153–73.

———. *Freedom and War: Discourses on Topics Suggested by the Times.* 1863. Reprint, Freeport, N.Y.: Books for Libraries Press, 1971.

———. "Modes and Duties of Emancipation." N.d.. In Beecher, *Freedom and War,* 174–99.

———. "The National Flag." N.d. In Beecher, *Freedom and War,* 111–29.

———. "The Nation's Duty to Slavery." Oct. 30, 1859. In Beecher, *Freedom and War,* 1–27.

———. "Our Blameworthiness." Jan. 4, 1861. In Beecher, *Freedom and War,* 57–83.

———. "The Southern Babylon." N.d. In Beecher, *Freedom and War,* 420–45.

———. "The Success of American Democracy." Apr. 13, 1862. In Beecher, *Freedom and War,* 248–69.

Bernstein, Iver. *The New York City Draft Riots: Their Significance in American Society and Politics in the Age of the Civil War.* New York: Oxford Univ. Press, 1990.

Brett, David. *"My Dear Wife": The Civil War Letters of David Brett, 9th Massachusetts Battery, Union Cannoneer.* Edited by Frank Putnam Deane II. St. Louis: Warren H. Green, 1964.

Brown, John. "John Brown's Last Speech to the Court, November 2, 1859." In *For the Record: A Documentary History of America,* vol. 1, edited by David E. Shi and Holly A. Mayer, 574. New York: W. W. Norton, 1999.

Bushnell, Horace. *Horace Bushnell: Selected Writings on Language, Religion, and American Culture.* Edited by David L. Smith. Chico, Calif.: Scholars Press, 1984.

———. *Horace Bushnell: Sermons.* Edited by Cherry Conrad. New York: Paulist Press, 1985.

———. "Popular Government by Divine Right." Nov. 24, 1864. In Chesebrough, *"God Ordained This War,"* 103–22.

———. *The Vicarious Sacrifice, Grounded in Principles of Universal Obligation.* New York: Charles Scribner, 1866.

Chamberlain, Joshua. *The Passing of the Armies: An Account of the Final Campaigns of the Army of the Potomac, Based upon Personal Reminiscences of the Fifth Army.* Lincoln: Univ. of Nebraska Press, 1998.

Chesebrough, David B. *"God Ordained This War": Sermons on the Sectional Crisis.* Columbia: Univ. of South Carolina Press, 1991.

Connolly, James A. *Three Years in the Army of the Cumberland: The Letters and Diary of Major James A. Connolly.* Edited by Paul M. Angle. Bloomington: Indiana Univ. Press, 1959.

Cram, George F. *Soldiering with Sherman: Civil War Letters of George F. Cram.* Edited by Jennifer Cain Bohrnstedt. DeKalb: Northern Illinois Univ. Press, 2000.

Dexter, Seymour. *Seymour Dexter, Union Army: Journal and Letters of Civil War Service in Company K, 23rd New York Volunteer Regiment of Elmira.* Edited by Carl A. Morrell. Jefferson, N.C.: McFarland, 1996.

Edwards, A. H. *"Dear Friend Anna": The Civil War Letters of a Common Soldier from Maine.* Edited by Beverly Hayes Kallgren and James L. Crouthamel. Orono: Univ. of Maine Press, 1992.

Fisk, Wilbur. *Anti-Rebel: The Civil War Letters of Wilbur Fisk.* Edited by Emil Rosenblat. Croton-on-Hudson, N.Y.: Emil Rosenblatt, 1983.

———. *Hard Fighting Every Day: The Civil War Letters of Private Wilbur Fisk, 1861–1865.* Edited by Emil Rosenblat and Ruth Rosenblat. Lawrence: Univ. Press of Kansas, 1992.

Fitzhugh, George. *Sociology for the South: Or, The Failure of Free Society.* Richmond, Va.: A. Morris, 1854.

Gooding, James Henry. *On the Altar of Freedom: A Black Soldier's Civil War Letters from the Front / James Henry Gooding.* Edited by Matzke Adams. Amherst: Univ. of Massachusetts Press, 1991.

Gould, William, Wesley Gould, and Richard Gould. *Dear Sister: The Civil War Letters of the Brothers Gould.* Edited by Robert F. Harris and John Niflot. Westport, Conn.: Praeger, 1998.

Haines, Zenas T. *In the Country of the Enemy: The Civil War Reports of a Massachusetts Corporal.* Edited by William C. Harris. New Perspectives on the History of the South series. Gainesville: Univ. Press of Florida, 1999.

Hall, Newman *Come to Jesus: No. 110.* Evangelical Tract Society, Petersburg, Va., 1863[?]. Call No. 4683, Rare Book Collection, University of North Carolina, Chapel Hill. Documenting the American South. http://docsouth.unc.edu/imls/ hallnewm/hallnewm.html/ (accessed Feb. 20, 2008).

Hartwell, John F. L. *To My Beloved Wife and Boy at Home: The Letters and Diaries of Orderly Sergeant John F. L. Hartwell.* Edited by Ann Hartwell Britton and Thomas J. Reed. Madison, N.J.: Fairleigh Dickinson Univ. Press, 1997.

Haskell, Franklin Aretas. *Haskell of Gettysburg: His Life and Civil War Papers.* Edited by Frank L. Byrne and Andrew Thomas Weaver. Kent, Ohio: Kent State Univ. Press, 1989.

Hodge, Charles. *Essays and Reviews.* Edited by Bruce Kuklick. New York: Garland, 1987.

Holt, Daniel M. *A Surgeon's Civil War: The Letters and Diary of Daniel M. Holt, M.D.* Edited by James M. Greiner, Janet L. Coryell, and James R. Smither. Kent, Ohio: Kent State Univ. Press, 2000. NetLibrary e-book. http://www.netlibrary.com/ Reader/ (accessed June 29, 2007).

Kallgren, Beverly Hayes, and James L. Crouthamel, eds. *"Dear Friend Anna": The Civil War Letters of a Common Soldier from Maine.* Orono: Univ. of Maine Press, 1992.

Lieber, Francis. "Lieber Code" of 1863. General Orders No. 100. "Section III.— Deserters—Prisoners of War—Hostages—Booty on the Battlefield." Article 50. U.S. Regulars Civil War Archives. http://www.usregulars.com/Lieber.html/ (accessed June 25, 2007).

Liggett, James D. "Our National Reverses." Sept. 7, 1862. In Chesebrough, *"God Ordained This War,"* 94–103.

Lincoln, Abraham. "Letter to Thurlow Weed." In *The Collected Works of Abraham Lincoln,* vol. 8, edited by Roy P. Basler. New Brunswick, N.J.: Rutgers Univ. Press, 1953.

———. "Meditation on the Divine Will." In *The Collected Works of Abraham Lincoln,* vol. 5, edited by Roy P. Basler. New Brunswick, N.J.: Rutgers Univ. Press, 1953.

Locke, John. *The Second Treatise of Government.* Edited by Thomas Peardon. New York: Liberal Arts Press, 1956.

Mather, Cotton. *The Wonders of the Invisible World: Being an Account of the Tryals of Several Vvitches, Lately Executed in New-England: and of Several Remarkable Curiosities Therein Occurring. Together with, I. Observations Upon the Nature, the Number, and the Operations of the Devils. II. A Short Narrative of a Late Outrage Committed by a Knot of Witches in Swede-land, Very Much Resembling, and so Far Explaining, That Under Which New-England has laboured. III. Some Councels directing a Due Improvement of the Terrible Things Lately Done by the Unusual and Amazing Range of Evil Spirits in New-England. IV. A Brief Discourse Upon Those Temptations Which are the More Ordinary Devices of Satan.* Boston, John Dunton, 1693; Ann Arbor: Univ. Microfilms, n.d..

Matrau, Henry. *Letters Home: Henry Matrau of the Iron Brigade.* Edited by Marcia Reid-Green. Lincoln: Univ. of Nebraska Press, 1993.

McMahon, John T. *John T. McMahon's Diary of the 136th New York, 1861–1864.* Edited by John Michael Priest. Shippensburg, Pa.: White Mane, 1993.

Miller, James T. *Bound to Be a Soldier: The Letters of Private James T. Miller, 111th Pennsylvania Infantry, 1861–1864.* Edited by Jedediah Mannis and Galen R. Wilson. Knoxville: Univ. of Tennessee Press, 2001.

Pardington, John H. *Dear Sarah: Letters Home from a Soldier of the Iron Brigade.* Edited by Coralou Peel Lassen. Bloomington: Indiana Univ. Press, 1999.

Rhodes, Elisha Hunt. *All for the Union: The Civil War Letters of Elisha Hunt Rhodes.* Edited by Robert Hunt Rhodes and Geoffrey C. Ward. New York: Orion Books, 1985.

Sherman, Francis T. *Quest for a Star: The Civil War Letters and Diaries of Colonel Francis T. Sherman of the 88th Illinois.* Edited by Knight C. Aldrich. Knoxville: Univ. of Knoxville Press, 1999.

Sherman, William Tecumseh. *The Memoirs of General W. T. Sherman Complete.* Project Gutenberg e-book. http://www.gutenberg.org/catalog/world/readfile?pageno=1andfk_files=71106/ (accessed June 18, 2007).

Shi, David E., and Holly A. Mayer. *For the Record: A Documentary History of America.* 2 vols. New York: W. W. Norton, 1999.

Squier, George W. *This Wilderness of War: The Civil War Letters of George W. Squier, Hoosier Volunteer.* Edited by Julie A. Doyle, John David Smith, and Richard M. McMurry. Knoxville: Univ. of Tennessee Press, 1998.

Stowe, Harriet Beecher Stowe. "Reply to An Affectionate and Christian Address of Many Thousands of Women of Great Britain and Ireland to Their Sisters the Women of the United States of America." *Atlantic Monthly,* Nov. 27, 1862.

Sullivan, James P. *An Irishman in the Iron Brigade: The Civil War Memoirs of James P. Sullivan, Sergt., Company K, 6th Wisconsin Volunteers.* Edited by William Beaudot and Lance Herdegen. New York: Fordham Univ. Press, 1993.

Sumner, Charles. "On the Crimes Against Kansas, May 1856." http://www.iath.virginia.edu/seminar/unit4/sumner.html (accessed July 6, 2006).

Taylor, Joseph K. *"The Civil War Letters of Joseph K. Taylor of the Thirty-Seventh Massachusetts Volunteer Infantry.* Edited by Kevin C. Murphy. Lewiston, N.Y.: Edwin Mellen Press, 1998.

Vattel, Emmerich. *The Law of Nations; Or the Principles of Natural Law in Four Books (1758).* Translated by Joseph Chitty, Esq., 1797. Lonang Library ed. http://www.lonang.com/exlibris/vattel/vatt-000.htm/ (accessed June 20, 2007).

Weld, Theodore D. *American Slavery as It Is.* New York: American Anti-Slavery Society, 1839.

Welsh, Peter. *Irish Green and Union Blue: The Civil War Letters of Peter Welsh, Color Sergeant 28th Regiment Massachusetts Volunteers.* Edited by Frederick L. Kohl, Richard Cossé, and Margaret Cossé. New York: Fordham Univ. Press, 1986.

Whitney, Joseph. *Kiss Clara for Me: The Story of Joseph Whitney and His Family, Early Days in the Midwest, and Soldiering in the American Civil War.* Edited by Robert J. Snetsinger. State College, Pa: Carnation Press, 1969.

Wiley, William. *The Civil War Diary of a Common Soldier: William Wiley of the 77th Illinois Regiment.* Edited by Terrence J. Winschel. Baton Rouge: Louisiana State Univ. Press, 2001.

Wills, Charles W. *Army Life of an Illinois Soldier: Including a Day-by-day Record of Sherman's March to the Sea: Letters and Diary of Charles W. Wills.* Edited by Mary E. Kellogg. Carbondale: Southern Illinois Univ. Press, 1996. NetLibrary e-book. http://www.netlibrary.com/Reader/ (accessed June 29, 2007).

SECONDARY SOURCES

Abelson, Robert P., Elliot Aronson, William J. McGuire, Theodore M. Newcomb, Milton J. Rosenberg, and Percy H. Tannenbaum, eds. *Theories of Cognitive Consistency: A Sourcebook.* Chicago: Rand McNally, 1968.

Ahlstrom, Sydney E. *A Religious History of the American People.* New Haven, Conn.: Yale Univ. Press, 1972.

Ambrose, Steven. *Duty, Honor, Country: A History of West Point.* Baltimore: Johns Hopkins Univ. Press, 1966.

Anderson, Fred W. "The Hinge of the Revolution; George Washington Confronts a People's Army, July 3, 1775." *Massachusetts Historical Review,* 1999. http://www.historycooperative.org/journals/mhr/1/anderson.html/ (accessed June 23, 2007).

Andreasen, Byron C. "Proscribed Preachers, New Churches; Civil Wars in Illinois Protestant Churches during the Civil War." *Civil War History* 44 (1998). Questia.com. http://www.questia.com/read/5001377854/ (accessed Feb. 11, 2008).

Attie, Jeanie. *Patriotic Toil: Northern Women and the Civil War.* Ithaca, N.Y.: Cornell Univ. Press, 1998.

Ayers, Edward L. Review of *Religion and the American Civil War. Journal of Southern Religion,* 1998–99. http://jsr.fsu.edu/ayers.htm/ (accessed Jan. 12, 2008).

Baird, Robert. *Religion in America: The Origin, Progress, Relation to the State, and Present Condition of the Evangelical Churches in the United States.* New York: Harper & Brothers, 1844.

Barton, Michael. *Goodmen: The Character of Civil War Soldiers.* University Park: Pennsylvania State Univ. Press, 1981.

Basler, Roy P., ed. *The Collected Works of Abraham Lincoln.* 9 vols. New Brunswick, N.J.: Rutgers Univ. Press, 1953–55.

Beard, Charles A., and Mary R. Beard. *The Rise of American Civilization.* New York: Macmillan, 1927–42.

Beauvois, J. L., and Roule Joule. *A Radical Dissonance Theory.* London: Taylor & Francis, 1996.

Benedict, Michael Les. *The Impeachment and Trial of Andrew Johnson.* New York: W. W. Norton, 1973.

Bennet, William W. *A Narrative of the Great Revival Which Prevailed in the Southern Armies During the Late Civil War.* 1876. Reprint, Harrisonburg, Va.: Sprinkle, 1989

Bercovitch, Sacvan. *The American Jeremiad.* Madison: Univ. of Wisconsin Press, 1978.

Berends, Kurt O. "Wholesome Reading Purifies and Elevates the Man: The Religious Military Press in the Confederacy." In Miller, Stout, and Wilson, *Religion and the American Civil War,* 131–66.

Beringer, Richard E., Herman Hattaway, Archer Jones, and William N. Still Jr. *The Elements of Confederate Defeat: Nationalism, War Aims, and Religion.* Athens: Univ. of Georgia Press, 1988.

Berkin, Carol. *First Generations: Women in Colonial America.* New York: Hill and Wang, 1996.

Bernstein, Iver. *The New York City Draft Riots: Their Significance in American Society and Politics in the Age of the Civil War.* New York: Oxford Univ. Press, 1990.

Billings, John Davis. *Hardtack and Coffee; or, The Unwritten Story of Army Life, including Chapters on Enlisting, Life in Tents and Log Huts, Jonahs and Beats, Offences and Punishments, Raw Recruits, Foraging, Corps and Corps Badges, the Wagon Trains, the Army Mule, the Engineering Corps, the Signal Corps, etc.* Boston: G. M. Smith, 1887.

Bishop, Isabella L. *The Aspects of Religion in The United States of America.* Reprint, New York: Arno Press, 1972.

Boles, John B. *The Irony of Southern Religion.* New York: Peter Lang, 1994.

Bowman, John S., ed. *Almanac of America's Wars.* Hong Kong: Mallard Press, 1990.

Bradford, Ned, ed. *Battles and Leaders of the Civil War.* New York: Fairfax Press, 1956.

Brauer, Jerald C. *Protestantism in America.* Philadelphia: Westminster Press, 1965.

Carter, Dan T. *When the War Was Over: The Failure of Self-Reconstruction in the South, 1865–1867.* Baton Rouge: Louisiana State Univ. Press, 1985.

Carwardine, Richard J. *Evangelicals and Politics in Antebellum America.* New Haven, Conn.: Yale Univ. Press, 1993.

Catton, Bruce. *The Army of the Potomac: A Stillness at Appomattox.* Garden City, N.Y.: Doubleday, 1953.

————. *The Army of the Potomac: Glory Road*. Garden City, N.Y.: Doubleday, 1952.

————. *The Army of the Potomac: Mr. Lincoln's Army*. Garden City, N.Y.: Doubleday, 1962.

————. *The Coming Fury*. Garden City, N.Y.: Doubleday, 1961.

————. *Never Call Retreat*. Garden City, N.Y.: Doubleday, 1965.

————. *Reflections on the Civil War*. Garden City, N.Y.: Doubleday, 1981.

————. *Terrible Swift Sword*. Garden City, N.Y.: Doubleday, 1963.

Channing, Edward. *A History of the United States*. 6 vols. New York: Macmillan, 1905–25.

Channing, Steven A. *Crisis of Fear: Secession in South Carolina*. New York: Simon and Schuster, 1970.

Coldwell, Stephen. *The Position of Christianity in the United States*. Philadelphia: Lippincott, Grambo, 1854.

Craven, Avery O. *Civil War in the Making, 1815—1860*. Baton Rouge: Louisiana State Univ. Press, 1959.

————. *The Coming of the Civil War*. Chicago: Univ. of Chicago Press, 1957.

Dollar, Kent T. "Strangers in a Strange Land: Christian Soldiers in the Early Months of the War." In *View from the Ground: Experiences of Civil War Soldiers*, edited by Aaron Sheehan-Dean, 145–70. Lexington: Univ. of Kentucky Press, 2006.

Donald, David Herbert. *Lincoln*. New York: Simon and Schuster, 1995.

Drake, James. "Restraining Atrocity: The Conduct of King Philip's War." *New England Quarterly* 70, no. 1 (1997): 35–36.

Du Bois, W. E. B. *John Brown: By W. E. Burghardt Du Bois*. Edited by Ellis Paxson Oberholtzer. Philadelphia: George W. Jacobs, 1909.

Dunham, Chester Forrester. *The Attitude of the Northern Clergy Toward the South, 1860–1865*. Philadelphia: Porcupine Press, 1974.

Dupuy, R. Ernest. *Men of West Point: The First 150 Years of the United States Military Academy*. New York: Sloane, 1951.

Fehrenbacher, Don E. *Prelude to Greatness: Lincoln in the 1850's*. New York: McGraw-Hill, 1964.

Ferling, John. *A Wilderness of Miseries*. Westport, Conn.: Greenwood Press, 1980.

Festinger, Leon. *Conflict, Decision, and Dissonance*. Stanford, Calif.: Stanford Univ. Press, 1964.

Finnegan, Patrick. "The Study of Law as a Foundation of Leadership and Command: The History of Law Instruction at the United States Military Academy at West Point." *Military Law Review* 181 (2004): 112–37.

Foner, Eric. *Free Soil, Free Labor, Free Men: The Ideology of the Republican Party Before the Civil War*. New York: Oxford Univ. Press, 1970.

Frank, Joseph A. and George A. Reaves. *Seeing the Elephant: Raw Recruits at the Battle of Shiloh.* New York: Greenwood Press, 1989.

Frederickson, George M. "The Coming of the Lord: The Northern Protestant Clergy and the Civil War Crisis." In Miller, Stout, and Wilson, *Religion and the American Civil War,* 110–30.

Frey, Sylvia R., and Betty Wood. *Come Shouting to Zion: African American Protestantism in the American South and British Caribbean to 1830.* Chapel Hill: Univ. of North Carolina Press, 1998.

Gaff, Alan D. *If This Is War: A History of the Campaign of Bull's Run by the Wisconsin Regiment Thereafter Known as the Ragged Ass Second.* Dayton, Ohio: Morningside House, 1991.

Gallay, Alan. *The Formation of a Planter Elite: Jonathan Bryan and the Southern Colonial Frontier.* Athens: Univ. of Georgia Press, 1989.

Genovese, Eugene D. *The Political Economy of Slavery: Studies in the Economy and Society of the Slave South.* New York: Pantheon Books, 1965.

Gillette, William. *Retreat from Reconstruction, 1869–1879.* Baton Rouge: Louisiana State Univ. Press, 1979.

Goen, C. C. *Broken Churches, Broken Nation.* Macon, Ga.: Mercer Univ. Press, 1985.

Guelzo, Allen C. *Abraham Lincoln: Redeemer President.* Grand Rapids, Mich.: Eerdman's, 1999.

Hall, Thomas C. *The Religious Background of American Culture.* Boston: Little, Brown, 1930.

Haller, William. *The Rise of Puritanism: Or, the Way to the New Jerusalem as Set Forth in Pulpit and Press from Thomas Cartwright to John Lilburn and John Milton, 1570–1643.* New York: Harper & Row, 1957.

Handy, Robert T. *A Christian America: Protestant Hopes and Historical Realities.* New York: Oxford Univ. Press, 1971.

Harvey, Paul. "Yankee Faith and Southern Redemption: White Southern Baptist Ministers, 1850–1890." In Miller, Stout, and Wilson, *Religion and the American Civil War,* 167–86.

Hatch, Nathan O. *The Democratization of American Christianity.* New Haven, Conn.: Yale Univ. Press, 1989.

Hawthorne, Nathaniel. *The Scarlet Letter.* New York: Harper, 1950.

Herring, William W., ed. *The Statutes at Large of Virginia.* 13 vols. New York: N.p., 1819–23.

Hess, Earl J. *Liberty, Virtue, and Progress: Northerners and Their War for the Union.* New York: New York Univ. Press, 1988.

———. *The Union Soldier in Battle: Enduring the Ordeal of Combat.* Lawrence: Univ. Press of Kansas, 1997.

Hewitt, Glenn A. *Regeneration and Morality: A Study of Charles Finney, Charles Hodge, John W. Nevin, and Horace Bushnell.* Brooklyn, N.Y.: Carlson, 1991.

Heyrman, Christine Leigh. *Southern Cross: The Beginnings of the Bible Belt.* Chapel Hill: Univ. of North Carolina Press, 1997.

Hill, Samuel S., Jr. "Religion and the Results of the Civil War." In Miller, Stout, and Wilson, *Religion and the American Civil War,* 360–82.

———. *The South and the North in American Religion.* Athens: Univ. of Georgia Press, 1980.

———. *Southern Churches in Crisis.* New York: Holt, Rinehart and Winston, 1967.

Hill, Samuel S., Jr., Edgar T. Thompson, Anne Firor Scott, Charles Hudson, and Edwin S. Gaustad, eds. *Religion and the Solid South.* Nashville: Abingdon Press, 1972.

Holt, Michael F. *The Political Crisis of the 1850s.* New York: Wiley, 1978.

Hudson, Winthrop S. *Religion in America.* New York: Charles Scribner's Sons, 1981.

Jennings, Francis. *The Invasion of America: Indians, Colonialism, and the Cant of Conquest.* Chapel Hill: Institute of Early American History and Culture by the Univ. of North Carolina Press, 1975.

Jimerson, Randal C. *The Private Civil War: Popular Thought During the Sectional Conflict.* Baton Rouge: Louisiana State Univ. Press, 1988.

Johnson, Paul. *A History of the American People.* New York: HarperCollins, 1997.

Jones, D. D., and J. William. *Christ in the Camp: or, Religion in the Confederate Army.* 1904. Reprint, Harrisonburg, Va.: Sprinkle, 1986.

Jones, James Pickett. *Yankee Blitzkrieg: Wilson's Raid Through Alabama and Georgia.* Athens: Univ. of Georgia Press, 1976.

Jordan, Winthrop D. *White Over Black: American Attitudes Toward the Negro, 1550–1812.* Kingsport, Tenn.: Kingsport Press, 1968.

Keegan, John. *The Face of Battle: A Study of Agincourt, Waterloo and the Somme.* London: Penguin, 1976.

Lewis, C. S. *Mere Christianity.* A revised and amplified edition, with a new introduction, of the three books *Broadcast Talks, Christian Behavior,* and *Beyond Personality.* San Francisco: HarperCollins, 2001.

Linderman, Gerald F. *Embattled Courage: The Experience of Combat in the American Civil War.* New York: Free Press, 1987.

Litwack, Leon F. *Been in the Storm So Long: The Aftermath of Slavery.* New York: Vintage Books, 1979.

Massey, Mary Elizabeth. *Bonnet Brigades.* New York: Knopf, 1966.

Matthews, Donald G. "Christianizing the South—Sketching a Synthesis." In Stout and Hart, *New Directions in American Religious History,* 84–115.

Melville, Herman. *Moby Dick*. New York: Modern Library, 1926.

McDonough, James Lee, and James Pickett Jones. *"War So Terrible": Sherman and Atlanta*. New York: Norton, 1987.

McFeely, William S. *Yankee Stepfather: General O. O. Howard and the Freedmen*. New York: W. W. Norton, 1994.

McPherson, James M. "Afterword." In Miller, Stout, and Wilson, *Religion and the American Civil War*, 408–12.

———. *Battle Cry of Freedom: The Civil War Era*. New York: Oxford Univ. Press, 1988.

———. *For Cause and Comrades: Why Men Fought in the Civil War*. New York: Oxford Univ. Press, 1997.

Miller, Perry. *Errand into the Wilderness*. Cambridge: Harvard Univ. Press, 1956.

———. *The Life of the Mind in America: From the Revolution to the Civil War*. New York: Harcourt, Brace and World, 1965.

Miller, Randall M. "Catholic Religion, Irish Ethnicity, and the Civil War." In Miller, Stout, and Wilson, *Religion and the American Civil War*, 261–96.

Miller, Randall M., Harry S. Stout, and Charles Reagan Wilson, eds. *Religion and the American Civil War*. New York: Oxford University Press, 1998.

Mitchell, Reid. "Christian Soldiers? Perfecting the Confederacy." In Miller, Stout, and Wilson, *Religion and the American Civil War*, 297–309.

———. *Civil War Soldiers*. New York: Viking, 1988.

———. *The Vacant Chair: The Northern Soldier Leaves Home*. New York: Oxford Univ. Press, 1993.

Moorehead, James H. *American Apocalypse: Yankee Protestants and the Civil War*. New Haven, Conn.: Yale Univ. Press, 1978.

Morris, Scott R. "The Laws of War: Rules by Warriors for Warriors." *Army Lawyer*, Dec. 1997, 4–13.

Moskowitz, Gordon B., ed. *Cognitive Social Psychology: The Princeton Symposium on the Legacy and Future of Social Cognition*. Malwah, N.J.: Lawrence Erlbaum Associates, 2001.

Nevins, Allan. *Ordeal of the Union*. New York: Charles Scribner's Sons, 1947.

Nolan, Alan T. *The Iron Brigade: A Military History*. Bloomington: Indiana Univ. Press, 1961.

Noll, Mark A. *America's God: From Jonathan Edwards to Abraham Lincoln*. New York: Oxford Univ. Press, 2005.

———. "The Bible and Slavery." In Miller, Stout, and Wilson, *Religion and the American Civil War*, 43–73.

———. *Christians in the American Revolution*. Washington D.C.: Christian College Consortium, 1977.

———. *A History of Christianity in the United States and Canada*. Grand Rapids, Mich.: William B. Eerdmans, 1992.

Norton, Mary Beth. *Liberty's Daughters: The Revolutionary Experience of American Women, 1750–1800*. Ithaca, N.Y.: Cornell Univ. Press, 1980.

Oates, Stephen B. *To Purge This Land with Blood*. Amherst: Univ. of Massachusetts Press, 1984.

Olmstead, Clifton E. *History of Religion in the United States*. Englewood Cliffs, N.J.: Prentice-Hall, 1960.

———. *Religion in America: Past and Present*. Englewood Cliffs, N.J.: Prentice-Hall, 1961.

Otis, George H. *The Second Wisconsin Infantry*. Edited by Alan D. Gaff. Dayton, Ohio: Morningside Bookshop Press, 1984.

Paludan, Phillip Shaw. *A People's Contest: The Union and Civil War, 1861–1865*. Lawrence: Univ. Press of Kansas, 1988.

———. "Religion and the American Civil War." In Miller, Stout, and Wilson, *Religion and the American Civil War*, 21–40.

Perry, Richard L., and John C. Cooper., eds. *Sources of Our Liberties: Documentary Origins of Individual Liberties in the United States Constitution and Bill of Rights*. Buffalo, N.Y.: William S. Hein, 1991.

Phillips, Jason. "Religious Belief and Troop Motivation: 'For the Smile of My Blessed Savior.'" In *Virginia's Civil War*, edited by Peter Wallenstein and Bertram Wyatt-Brown, 101–13. Charlottesville: Univ. of Virginia Press, 2005.

Piston, Wilson Garret, and Richard W. Hatcher III. *Wilson's Creek: The Second Battle of the Civil War and the Men Who Fought It*. Chapel Hill: Univ. of North Carolina Press, 2000.

Potter, David M. *The Impending Crisis, 1848–1861*. Edited by Don E. Fehrenbacher. New York: Harper & Row, 1976.

———. *The South and the Sectional Conflict*. Baton Rouge: Louisiana State Univ. Press, 1968.

Randall, James G. *The Civil War and Reconstruction*. Boston: Heath, 1937.

Rhodes, James Ford. *The History of the United States from the Compromise of 1850 to the Restoration of Home Rule at the South*. 7 vols. New York: N.p., 1892–1906.

Robertson, James I. *Soldiers Blue and Gray*. Columbia: Univ. of South Carolina Press, 1988.

———. *Stonewall Jackson: The Man, the Soldier, the Legend*. New York: Macmillan, 1997.

Rolfs, David. "The Civilized and the Savage: The Ethical Conduct of the U.S. Army During the Second Seminole War." In *Selected Annual Proceedings of the Florida Conference of Historians* 7 (Dec. 1999), 151–62.

Sanborn, Franklin B., ed. *John Brown: Liberator of Kansas and Martyr of Virginia.* Cedar Rapids, Iowa: Torch Press, 1910.

Saum, Lewis O. *The Popular Mood of Pre-Civil War America.* Westport, Conn.: Greenwood Press, 1980.

Schlesinger, Arthur Meier. *The Vital Center: The Politics of Freedom.* Boston: Houghton Mifflin, 1949.

Sears, Stephen W. *Landscape Turned Red: The Battle of Antietam.* Boston: Houghton Mifflin, 1983.

Shaara, Michael. *The Killer Angels.* New York: Valentine Books, 1974.

Shattuck, Gardiner H. *A Shield and Hiding Place: The Religious Life of the Civil War Armies.* Macon, Ga.: Mercer Univ. Press, 1987.

Sheehan-Dean, Aaron., ed. *The View from the Ground: Experiences of Civil War Soldiers.* Lexington: Univ. Press of Kentucky, 2006.

Smith, Timothy L. *Revivalism and Social Reform: American Protestantism on the Eve of the Civil War.* New York: Harper & Row, 1957.

Stampp, Kenneth M. *America in 1857: A Nation on the Brink.* New York: Oxford Univ. Press, 1990.

————. *And the War Came: The North and the Secession Crisis, 1860—1861.* Baton Rouge: Louisiana State Univ. Press, 1950.

————. *The Era of Reconstruction, 1865–1877.* New York: Vintage Books, 1965.

————, ed. *The Causes of the Civil War.* Englewood Cliffs, N.J.: Prentice-Hall, 1974.

Stern, Fritz, ed. *The Varieties of History: From Voltaire to the Present.* Cleveland: World Publishing, 1956.

Stout, Harry S. *The New England Soul: Preaching and Religious Culture in Colonial New England.* New York: Oxford Univ. Press, 1986.

————. *Upon the Altar of the Nation: A Moral History of the Civil War.* New York: Viking, 2006.

Stout, Harry S., and Christopher Grasso. "Civil War, Religion, and Communications: The Case of Richmond." In Miller, Stout, and Wilson, *Religion and the American Civil War,* 313–59.

Stout, Harry S., and Darryl G. Hart, eds. *New Directions in American Religious History.* New York: Oxford Univ. Press, 1997.

Stowell, Daniel W. "Stonewall Jackson and the Providence of God." In Miller, Stout, and Wilson, *Religion and the American Civil War,* 187–207.

Sweet, William W. *Religion in the Development of American Culture.* Gloucester, Mass.: Charles Scribner's Sons, 1952.

Tanner, Robert G. *Stonewall in the Valley: Thomas J. "Stonewall" Jackson's Shenandoah Valley Campaign, Spring 1862.* Mechanicsburg, Pa.: Stackpole, 1996.

Tocqueville, Alexis de. *Democracy in America*. Translated by Henry Reeve. New York: Colonial Press, 1900.

Trout, Robert. "Life, Liberty, and the Pursuit of Happiness: How the Natural Law of G. W. Leibnitz Inspired America's Founding Fathers." *Fidelio Magazine* 6, no. 1 (Spring 1997). http://www.schillerinstitute.org/fid_97–01/971_vattel-2.html/ (accessed June 23, 2007).

Vaughn, Alden T. *New England Frontier: Puritans and Indians, 1620–1675*. 3rd ed. Norman: Univ. of Oklahoma Press, 1995.

Ward, Geoffrey C., Ric Burns, and Ken Burns. *The Civil War: An Illustrated History*. New York: Knopf, 1990.

Wiley, Bell Irvin. *The Life of Billy Yank: The Common Soldier of the Union*. Garden City, N.Y.: Doubleday, 1971.

Wilson, Charles Reagan. "Religion and the American Civil War in Comparative Perspective." In Miller, Stout, and Wilson, *Religion and the American Civil War*, 385–407.

Wheeler, Richard. *Witness to Gettysburg: Inside the Battle that Changed the Course of the Civil War*. New York: Penguin Books, 1987.

White, Ronald C., Jr. *Lincoln's Greatest Speech: The Second Inaugural*. New York: Simon and Schuster, 2003.

———. "Lincoln's Sermon on the Mount: The Second Inaugural." In Miller, Stout, and Wilson, *Religion and the American Civil War*, 208–25.

Woodworth, Steven E. *While God Is Marching On: The Religious World of Civil War Soldiers*. Lawrence: Univ. Press of Kansas, 2001.

Wyatt-Brown, Bertram. *The Shaping of Southern Culture: Honor, Grace, and War, 1760s–1890s*. Chapel Hill: Univ. of North Carolina Press, 2001.

Young, Agatha. *The Women and the Crisis: Women of the North in the Civil War*. New York: McDowell, Obolensky, 1959.

Index

No Peace for the Wicked was designed and typeset on a
Macintosh computer system using CS3 InDesign software.
The body text is set in 9/12.5 ITC Galliard, as is the display
type. One exception is the chapter number which is set in
Bodoni Antiqua. This book was designed and typeset by
Barbara Karwhite and manufactured by Thomson-Shore, Inc.

DATE DUE
